What Works for Africa's Poorest

Praise for this book

'After 50 years of "development", the number of Africans living in dire poverty remains tragically and disgracefully high. This book brings together important new insights on the understanding that outsiders themselves must achieve before they can begin to think about reaching the poorest and changing their reality.'

Ian Smillie, author of Freedom from Want *and* Diamonds

'If responding to extreme poverty was easy or obvious, the world would surely have figured it out by now. But it's neither easy nor obvious, so we need the types of context-specific insights exemplified by these excellent chapters, which are grounded in an informed dialogue between careful research, hard-won experience and ethical advocacy.'

Michael Woolcock, World Bank and Harvard University

What Works for Africa's Poorest

Programmes and policies
for the extreme poor

Edited by
David Lawson, Lawrence Ado-Kofie
and David Hulme

**Practical
ACTION
PUBLISHING**

Practical Action Publishing Ltd
27a Albert Street, Rugby, CV21 2SG, Warwickshire, UK
www.practicalactionpublishing.org

A catalogue record for this book is available from the British Library.

A catalogue record for this book has been requested from the Library of Congress

ISBN 9781853398438 Hardback
ISBN 9781853398445 Paperback
ISBN 9781780448435 Library Ebook
ISBN 9781780448442 Ebook

Citation: Lawson, D., Ado-Kofie, L., and Hulme, D.(eds) (2017) *What Works for Africa's Poorest : Programmes and policies for the extreme poor*, Rugby, UK: Practical Action Publishing, <http://dx.doi.org/10.3362/9781780448435>

Since 1974, Practical Action Publishing has published and disseminated books and information in support of international development work throughout the world. Practical Action Publishing is a trading name of Practical Action Publishing Ltd (Company Reg. No. 1159018), the wholly owned publishing company of Practical Action. Practical Action Publishing trades only in support of its parent charity objectives and any profits are covenanted back to Practical Action (Charity Reg. No. 247257, Group VAT Registration No. 880 9924 76).

Cover photo: Sorting site near Dandora dump, Nairobi, Kenya, where shredded waste plastic is cleaned and foreign materials like small metal pieces are removed with magnets.
Copyright: Sven Torfinn/Panos
Cover design: Mercer Design
Typeset by vPrompt eServices, India

Contents

http://dx.doi.org/10.3362/9781780448435.000

Figures, Tables, and Boxes

Figures

Tables

Boxes

Preface

This book has arisen out of an earlier collaboration between David Lawson and David Hulme when working with the Chronic Poverty Research Centre (CPRC) and Brooks World Poverty Institute (BWPI) at the Institute for Development Policy and Management (IDPM), University of Manchester. From that collaboration we produced *What Works for the Poorest?* (Practical Action, 2010) with our colleagues Imran Matin and Karen Moore. That book looked at programmes to assist the poorest from across the world, but with a particular focus on South Asia.

Having spent considerable parts of the last 25 years living, working, and researching in some of the poorest communities across 15 sub-Saharan African countries, David Lawson was keen to highlight examples of programmes in Africa that have sought to improve the life prospects of extreme poor people and developed the idea of producing another 'what works for the poorest' collection focused on sub-Saharan Africa. David Hulme, with over 40 years of development experience, and Lawrence Ado-Kofie were recruited to collaborate on this project, and a meeting in London on 13 January 2014 provided an opportunity for the authors to review each other's chapters and take the publication forward. Many thanks to Rory Brooks at MML Capital for making available MML's boardroom and generously hosting that meeting.

Our book cannot claim to be comprehensive, but it does seek to raise awareness of the hundreds of millions of people still trapped in extreme poverty in Africa and to strengthen understanding of the forms of practical action that can support their own efforts to improve their lives. It is also unique, as with the prior volume of *What Works for the Poorest?*, in that we bring together academics, policy practitioners, and policymakers to hear their voices of what works for the poorest.

A large number of people and organizations have made the London workshop and book possible. Particular thanks to Rory Stanton at the Global Development Institute (GDI), who pulled the final manuscript together and did a thorough edit that greatly improved the text. Special thanks to Denise Redston and Julia Brunt at GDI for logistical support. Many others also provided support: to all of them our sincere thanks. We also acknowledge the financial assistance of GDI.

Last but not least, our gratitude to the many poor and very poor people in Africa who, over the years, have helped the authors and editors of this collection to understand the nature of extreme poverty and the indomitable spirit of the world's poorest to improve their lives, create better prospects for their children, and achieve social justice.

David Lawson, Manchester, June 2016
David Hulme, Manchester, June 2016
Lawrence Ado-Kofie, Manchester, June 2016

Foreword

When I was growing up in Uganda, the cleverest girl I knew was called Agnes. Agnes was always top of the class despite the times she missed school because she had to care for a sick family member, collect water, or harvest crops. But Agnes never made it through secondary school. She was poor, she was a girl, and she was a refugee from Rwanda. As good as my school system was for me, it couldn't break down those three barriers for her and I am saddened when I think of where Agnes probably is now: still very poor, still working very hard to look after her family.

It is surprising how rare and even radical it is – even in development circles – to ask what really works for the poorest such as Agnes. Working to reach the poorest involves considering multiple layers of exclusion and deprivation as well as trade-offs between competing groups. It is a complex area.

But of course there is no justification for leaving anyone behind, or for believing that the poor will catch up in time. Poverty figures from the World Bank indicate that significant numbers of people are likely to remain in chronic poverty after 2030, and also that widening inequality is making efforts to overcome poverty more difficult.

In macro-economic debates the case for focusing on the bottom as well as the top (the notion of inclusive growth) is increasingly compelling, too. IMF studies point to extreme inequality harming the durability and sustainability of overall economic growth whilst the World Economic Forum consistently raises widening inequality amongst its top global risks. Even the world's elite are recognizing that if it doesn't work for the poorest, in the long run, we all lose out.

Such shifts in thinking are welcome, providing as they do a more favourable climate for pursuing programme and policy work focused on the poorest, but they do not in themselves answer the question of how to really do it. For that, we have to move away from economic theory and into the field; and to examine policies and programmes and how they work with specific groups of poor people in a specific context. We also have to be honest. Many agencies such as Oxfam have large areas of programming focused on the poor – for instance around cash transfers and social protection – and yet we would be wise to remain humble in our claims that we always reach the poorest of the poor.

What Works for Africa's Poorest is therefore a timely study into why policies and programmes work – and why they don't. With a strong approach to evidence and research, and clear analysis but a determination to avoid generalized policy conclusions, this volume should be invaluable to practitioners, NGO staff, policymakers, and donor agencies.

Winnie Byanyima is Executive Director of Oxfam International. She has previously served in the Ugandan Parliament, the African Union Commission, and as Director of Gender and Development at the United Nations Development Program. She co-founded the Global Gender and Climate Alliance and chaired a UN task force on gender aspects of the Millennium Development Goals, and on climate change.

Acknowledgements

Many people have helped us to achieve the publication of this book. Our greatest thanks has to go to the many African people, many of them living in poverty, who have patiently answered our questions over the years as we have talked to them in an effort to better understand the challenges they face and their strategies to improve their lives and the prospects of their children.

Especial thanks are due to Rory Stanton who took over the editing of the volume when it was a set of computer files and who diligently progressed it to a completed manuscript and publication – many, many thanks Rory.

Our thanks also to Julia Brunt and Denise Redston at the Global Development Institute, University of Manchester, for administrative support in the early stage of this initiative, and in organising the workshop. Thanks also to Rory Brooks and MML Capital who hosted our authors' workshop in London and who (through the Brooks World Poverty Institute) sponsored and encouraged us to undertake much of the research on which this book is based. A grant from the Department for International Development (DFID) for the Chronic Poverty Research Centre (CPRC) at the University of Manchester several years ago created the academic opportunity for us to conduct research on the poorest people in Africa.

David Lawson
Lawrence Ado-kofie
David Hulme

PART A

Who are sub-Saharan Africa's extreme poor and how to target them

CHAPTER 1
What works for Africa's poorest?

David Hulme and David Lawson

This chapter presents both the context from which this volume evolved as well as the situational backdrop for the chapters that follow. In so doing, it asks who are the very poorest in sub-Saharan Africa (SSA), how do they survive, and establishes the precariousness of their situation in relation to the steadily, if slowly, improving development picture experienced by many more of the world's poorest. Rather than focus on macro-level conceptualisations of 'being poor' this volume is partially structured around a micro and meso-level lifecycle analysis of extreme poverty that focuses on evidence showing people can be extremely poor at different points in their life. The volume, thus, hopes to: (i) raise awareness of the problems faced by the very poorest people in SSA; (ii) encourage policy-makers and development practitioners to identify projects, programmes, and policies that can assist the very poorest, in the next few years; and (iii) provide practical examples of 'what works for SSA's poorest'.

Keywords: Sub-Saharan Africa; extreme poverty; micro and meso analysis; targeting; survival; lifecycle

Introduction

Over the past 20 years, the world has experienced an unparalleled period of economic growth and dramatic reductions in income/consumption (and multi-dimensional) poverty. This is a cause for optimism, but at the same time, we must note that the benefits of this contemporary growth have been very unevenly spread. The world's richest 62 people now own assets that have the same value as those held by the poorest 3.6 billion; the bottom half of humanity (Oxfam, 2016).

At the global level, the benefits have been concentrated within China, India, and Southeast Asia, while other regions – sub-Saharan Africa (SSA), much of South Asia, the Andean region, the states of the former Soviet Union, and the Pacific – have improved at much slower rates, and in some countries (including Egypt, Iraq, Somalia, Syria, and Zimbabwe) life has got harder. SSA countries, long seen as being locked in poverty traps (Collier, 2007) that kept the well-being levels of the majority of their population very low (a more accurate concept might be ill-being), have recently escaped this 'Afro-pessimism' image. Across the continent, economic growth rates have improved and human development indicators have risen. In 2015 Ethiopia, for example, was the world's

http://dx.doi.org/10.3362/9781780448435.001

fastest growing economy (World Economic Forum, 2016), with Côte d'Ivoire predicted to be the world's second fastest in 2016.[1] Additionally, since 1990, infant mortality for SSA children under the age of five years has been reduced by 43 per cent, and the number of maternal deaths has also declined by 47 per cent (Save the Children, 2013; see Ado-Kofie and Lawson (2016) for further discussion).

However, things vary greatly from country to country and at the sub-national level. A common pattern is that many urban areas have seen dramatic improvements in their average levels of income and in human development indicators. By contrast, rural areas, and particularly remote rural areas and conflict zones, have seen little or no benefits. It is evident that the types of broadly based growth that generated the relatively egalitarian East Asian Miracle of the mid- and late-twentieth century – growth with mass poverty reduction – are different from contemporary growth processes in Africa. SSA's dependence on hydrocarbons and minerals for its recent growth, combined with the region starting from a much higher level of socio-economic inequality, have meant that Africa's growth has been concentrated in fewer hands than in East Asia. As Kofi Annan, former Secretary-General of the United Nations, put it: 'Africa is a rich continent with a lot of poor people' (BBC World, 27 July 2015).

This extreme and chronic poverty has spatial and social relational dimensions. Spatially, it is often concentrated in particular areas, for example, mountainous regions, arid/semi-arid lands and landlocked regions across Africa, and informal 'settlements' in the major cities. Socially, it is concentrated within specific groups, such as indigenous or 'tribal' groups (in Botswana, DRC, and elsewhere), ethnic and religious minorities, internally displaced people, and refugees. At the micro level – the household, village, or community – particularly vulnerable individuals, including older people, widows, orphans, and disabled people, are likely to find that they can barely maintain their lives and that they have minimal or no prospects for improvement. At the extreme, the poorest simply disappear, dying unregistered but easily preventable deaths.

This volume arises out of the concerns of a group of development practitioners, policymakers, and researchers about the poorest. It builds on our earlier work (Lawson et al., 2010), and seeks to provide ideas and guidance about how the poorest might be assisted in their personal efforts to sustain themselves and improve their prospects. There have been significant breakthroughs in assisting the poor – from jobs in garment and shoe factories, to cash transfers, to microfinance – but there is also a growing recognition that these have rarely reached the poorest. At the global level, the new UN Sustainable Development Goals promise that 'no one will be left behind' – a grand aspiration, but at the same time, an acknowledgement that hundreds of millions have been left behind during an exceptional period of prosperity in the developing world. The book's orientation is explicitly practical and policy-focused. It does not seek to propound general theories about causes of extreme poverty or universal generalizations about how to tackle it. The focus is on the micro- and meso-level projects, programmes, and policies that seek to improve the condition of Africa's poorest people in the short and medium terms.

We realize that this leaves us open to criticisms. Neo-classical macro-economists can argue that we have neglected the analysis of international trade, economic liberalization, and macro-economic policies. From the opposite end of the ideological spectrum, radical political economists can argue that we fail to examine the social relations engendered by contemporary global capitalism, ranging from worker exploitation to violent conflicts. We acknowledge such lacunae in this volume and refer the reader to other sources (Collier, 2007; CPRC, 2008; Greig et al., 2007; Hulme, 2015) that address such 'macro' issues. In our defence, we argue that there has been a relative neglect in the literature on how to assist the poorest in operational terms. This volume seeks to partially fill this gap, complementing and extending upon the previous volume of *What Works for the Poorest* (2010), and to provide practitioners and policymakers with ideas and experiences that may provide insights and guidance.

In this volume we seek to:

1. Raise awareness of the problems faced by the poorest people in SSA.
2. Encourage policymakers and development practitioners to identify projects, programmes, and policies that will assist the poorest in the next few years. The poorest cannot afford to wait for growth to trickle down or good governance to emerge: they may die or have their capabilities (e.g. physical and mental health, cognitive abilities, reproductive capacity) disabled or destroyed while 'waiting'.
3. Provide a number of practical examples from 12 countries and four regions across SSA, and draw some policy conclusions for practitioners and policymakers of 'what works for the poorest'. These may serve as 'models' for action, but our preference is for them to inspire new experiments based on a mix of inspiration and the nitty-gritty routines of planning, implementing, monitoring, learning, and strengthening projects and programmes in the field. Ultimately, we have to build networks of institutions that can support the efforts of Africa's poor people.

We are fully aware that writing and editing papers about assisting the poorest is the easiest part of such efforts. Planning, managing, and implementing these initiatives on a day-to-day basis, and running the public agencies and NGOs that take the lead in such work, are the critical ingredients, of which the world needs more.

Who are the poorest?

Defining and/or identifying 'the poorest' is challenging in terms of both concepts and methods. There are five main ways in which extreme poverty can be conceptualized. The most common are income- or consumption-based poverty lines based on an assessment of the amount of money needed to acquire food that meets the minimum calorific needs of a human being; these are used by most economists and policymakers. This is commonly estimated to be around 2,100 to 2,500 calories per day for an adult, but there are many assumptions and technical issues behind such estimations. In many developing countries the extreme poverty line is defined as a percentage of the overall poverty line.

Since 1990, a global 'extreme poverty' line has been identified: the widely used US$1/day measure (which became the $1.25/day measure in 2008 and the $1.90/day measure in 2015). This was computed by World Bank economists for the *World Development Report 1990*, which argued that in 1985, anyone with consumption valued at less than $1/day (in purchasing power parity (PPP) terms) was extremely poor.[2] The most recent detailed application of this yardstick to the global population estimates that, in 2010, 1.2 billion people were extremely poor, and that 410 million (an increase from 205 million in 1981) of these were sub-Saharan Africans (World Bank, 2013). As a result, and despite a percentage decline in extreme poverty in SSA (from 57 per cent in 1990 to 43 per cent in 2012; Beegle et al., 2016), the extreme poor in SSA now represent a third of the world's extreme poor (11 per cent in 1981) (World Bank, 2013).

However, there are big questions about the arbitrariness of the $1.90/day line and about the quality of data available. A particular disadvantage of this concept is that it cannot be used in the field to practically identify the poorest people, as collecting accurate data on the income of very poor people is costly, time-consuming, and beyond the capacity (and the cost structures) of most service delivery agencies. Large numbers of development specialists (managers, policymakers, researchers) believe that assessing poverty purely in terms of income and consumption is logically flawed, and prefer the concept of 'human development'. This developed out of the work of Paul Streeten, Mahbub ul Haq, and Amartya Sen and has been popularized by the United Nations *Human Development Reports*. Human development views poverty and extreme poverty as multi-dimensional deprivation: lack of food and income, illiteracy, inadequate access to health services and potable water, and other factors.

For almost 20 years such analysts used the UNDP's Human Development Index (HDI), but this was of no use in examining the poverty headcount number, as it is an aggregate national measure. This shortcoming has been tackled by Sabina Alkire and colleagues at the Oxford Poverty and Human Development Initiative through the computation of a global Multi-dimensional Poverty Index (MPI).[3] The MPI assesses levels of severe deprivation in health, education, and living standards at the individual level. It has ten weighted indicators: nutrition; child mortality; years of schooling; school attendance; access to cooking fuel; sanitation; potable water; electricity; quality of flooring; and household ownership of basic assets. If someone is deprived in more than one-third of these ten basic needs indicators, they are identified as 'MPI poor'.

If they experience extreme deprivation in these indicators (for example, they have experienced the deaths of two of their children), then they are 'MPI destitute'. The global MPI measure has made great progress since its 2010 launch, and by 2014 it was covering 108 countries and 78 per cent of the world's population.[4] According to the MPI around 460 million people in SSA are multi-dimensionally deprived and the vast majority of them, more than 85 per cent, live in rural areas.

So what difference would the use of the MPI – with its advantages of more closely mirroring the reported experiences of poor people, and its not needing PPP adjustments – make, when compared to using the $1.25/day measure?[5] In terms of static comparisons, MPI poverty headcounts are significantly higher than $1.25/day counts in some countries, such as Côte d'Ivoire, Ethiopia, Senegal, and Uganda. Very worryingly, for Ethiopia the MPI headcount is 86 per cent against a $1.25/day headcount of 32 per cent; that is, tens of millions of 'additional' poor people. By contrast, in countries such as Nigeria and Zambia the MPI headcounts are much lower. For Nigeria, an MPI headcount of 42 per cent contrasts with a $1.25/day poverty headcount of 68 per cent; from an MPI perspective, poverty in Nigeria appears less serious than from an income perspective.[6] The MPI and income poverty perspectives would also suggest different dynamics of poverty reduction in different countries. The MPI indicates that poverty reduction has been faster in Rwanda and Ghana than does the income poverty measure. But for Ethiopia, poverty reduction appears to have been significantly slower than the $1.25/day measure suggests. But, just like the $1.25/day measure, the MPI has experienced great criticism. This includes the many assumptions that lie behind the lists, the choice of cut-off points for deprivation, and the number of deprivations needed to be classed as multi-dimensionally poor or destitute.

A third possible means of identifying the poorest is the duration of poverty. The Chronic Poverty Research Centre (CPRC) has been spearheading such an approach (CPRC, 2004, 2008; Hulme and Shepherd, 2003) that has used the $1/day measure to estimate that over 400 million people are chronically poor: they had been in extreme poverty for five years or more. CPRC has encouraged the use of human development measures, but these have only been taken up to a very limited degree (Gunter and Klasen, 2009). Interestingly, Gunter and Klasen's (2008) work suggests that the correlation between chronic poverty in the income and non-income dimensions is very low, and non-income poverty is certainly more stable over time than income poverty. Calvo and Dercon (2009) have argued that analytically and practically the challenge is to identify who is likely to remain poor in the future. These are the people whom the policy must try to prioritize.

A particularly important component of CPRC's work has focused on the intergenerational transmission of poverty. Arguably, those households in which the poverty of the parents is likely to be transferred to children – through the blocking of their capabilities by poor nutrition, ill health, lack of education, and other factors – can be regarded as among the poorest.

The fourth means of identifying the poorest is more intuitive, and is an approach used by organizations and practitioners at the field level. It is to identify an indicator that can be easily assessed and is believed to reveal that an individual or a household is experiencing extreme poverty. The most common such indicator is access to food: 'have you gone without food this year?' or 'how many meals a day do you eat?' Kabeer (2010) found that the simple question, 'what category best describes the food situation in your household over the last year: chronic food shortage, occasional food shortage, 'break-even' food supply, or food surplus?' could identify the consumption poor with great accuracy. Combinations of indicators can be used, as shown by Sen and Begum (2010). Data on housing quality, land holding, and occupation can be used to rapidly and accurately identify the poorest people in Bangladesh.

The fifth approach is participatory. This includes a variety of different methods ranging from the widely used Participatory Rural Appraisal techniques described by Robert Chambers (1994) to the more Freirian and dialogical methods proposed by Xavier Godinot (2000). This approach has received much attention in recent years with Narayan et al.'s (2000) *Voices of the Poor* and Krishna's (2009) 'Stages of Progress' methodology. The BRAC Targeting the Ultra-Poor Programme analyzed by Hulme and Moore (2010) and its many 'replicas' use the classic PRA technique of wealth ranking to initially identify the poorest people in rural Bangladesh before proceeding to use more 'objective' methods.

The volume is partially structured around a lifecycle analysis in recognition of the evidence that people can be extremely poor at different stages in their life, that extreme poverty early on in the lifecycle raises the probability of experiencing poverty at later stages and/or for a whole lifetime, and that strategies to tackle extreme poverty should incorporate a lifecycle analysis to be effective. Evidence continues to reveal the ways in which 'the first 1,000 days' of a child's life – from inception to the age of two – profoundly affect lifetime capabilities and achievements. The extreme poverty of many people commences *in utero*, when a mother (often experiencing poverty) is unable to gain access to an adequate diet and basic medical care. Inadequate access to nutrients, including micro-nutrients such as iodides, can limit the physical and cognitive ability of people in later life, and may predispose them to higher levels of health problems as adults. Mothers who do not receive basic maternal health screening – in some countries defined as four check-ups during pregnancy – are more likely to deliver babies with medical problems that could have been avoided, miss an opportunity for learning about caring for infants, and face higher levels of personal health risk during their pregnancy (especially preeclampsia).

Childbirth should be in an environment that is clean and overseen by a trained birth attendant – ideally with access to medical services, should they be needed (but, this may be more than the health services of many poor countries can afford at present). The first two years of life are profoundly important, as these can set limits on the capabilities of the child for the rest of the lifecycle. While the rich world may know 'breast is best', this is not known by some poor people who may have been 'educated' that milk powder is better, and/or it may not be feasible if household income is dependent on the mother working 12–14-hour shifts in a factory without childcare facilities. In such instances breastfeeding is simply not possible. So, infant nutrition is crucially important, but also 'decent work' that permits mothers to care for their children whilst being employed. As the child moves to supplementary feeding, access to good-quality food prepared in hygienic surroundings with clean water becomes essential. The food, the 'kitchen', and the water do not need to be high cost, they just need to be uncontaminated and prepared by someone with a basic understanding of hygiene. Easy to prescribe, but difficult to achieve if you live in a remote arid area (where there is a lack of vegetables and potable water) or a dense urban slum (with a 'kitchen' or a cooking pot beside an open drain with flowing sewage and flies). During the infancy stage, health appointments to receive vaccinations and simple checks on physical and cognitive ability (especially checking growth and weight) provide immunity from common diseases, and can identify children who need feeding assistance and/or more specialist, but low-cost, medical treatment.

As the baby moves to toddler stage and above, nutrition, basic health care, and being in a safe environment become priorities, as they are through to adulthood. Gaining access to primary education is essential for girls and boys, and those who may be seen as 'disabled'. Not getting a basic education is in many contexts a sentence to a lifetime of being economically disadvantaged and socially and politically disempowered. As the lifecycle progresses, the continuing contribution of good nutrition and education must be recognized, but only recently have the needs of 'youth' been recognized. The transition from child to adult is far from 'easy' in most societies, and there are particular vulnerabilities (CPRC, 2008). In particular, girls from poor households face risks of sexual exploitation and abuse and even trafficking. Girls and boys in urban contexts may be exposed to addictive drugs and substance abuse, and those who do not get access to jobs may experience feelings of worthlessness and associated mental ill-being (depression or worse). Gaining market-relevant skills and access to employment is therefore crucial during the transition to adulthood.

Throughout the adult working phase, generating a livelihood that meets minimum personal and family needs becomes essential, along with access to basic services. For many decades it was thought that state-provided social protection (ensuring that people could meet at least their basic needs) for the poorest in Africa was infeasible and 'too expensive'. The recent 'quiet revolution' across the world in rolling out social protection (child support grants, old age pensions, cash for public works programmes, and others) has challenged this (see Hanlon et al., 2010; and McCord in this volume) and there is increasing evidence that well-designed programmes can support poor and very poor households, and significantly increase the likelihood of adults being able to live valued lives while improving the prospects of their children (through better nutrition, education, and access

---

Box 1.1 Njuma, the gleaner

Njuma lives in a relatively remote village on the slopes of Mount Elgon in Uganda. She is a childless widow who is almost 70 years old. Her house is a small mud hut with a dilapidated grass roof. Since her husband died around seven or eight years ago, she has lived alone and been largely dependent on gifts of food from relatives and neighbours. They do not wish to see her suffer from hunger, but they are also poor and vulnerable, and do not see it as their role to provide beyond her basic need for food. If she gets sick she just has to wait until she gets better, as she has no access to health services. She gets no support from the government or NGOs.

Despite feeling tired and often low-spirited, and having no formal access to land or productive assets, she seeks opportunities to be economically active. Her main work is gleaning coffee from the bushes of neighbours when they have finished picking. It takes a lot of work to harvest one or two kilograms of beans from bushes that have been picked already, are poorly maintained, and are on steep slopes. We estimate that she earns the equivalent of US$0.02–0.04 for each hour that she works. The government's economic surveys and the census would class her as poor and not working. An alternative view is that she is employed in some of the lowest paid work in the world. Gleaning is the only way she can get the money to replace her one worn dress or pay someone to patch the holes in her roof before the wet season starts. We also suspect it is of psychological importance to Njuma; she may be dependent, but she has plans of her own.

Source: Hulme in CPRC (2004:3).

---

to health services). These programmes are still only being introduced in most of SSA (South Africa is the exception, with almost universal coverage in some programmes). North of the Limpopo, the sub-continent's largest programme is Ethiopia's Productive Safety Nets Programme (PSNP) covering 11 per cent of households. Like many of SSA's social protection programmes it is based on providing work and income for those who are productive but cannot find gainful employment, rather than the principles of needs and rights.

Many elderly people are extremely poor, often after a life of poverty and/ or the dissolution of their household. This is particularly the case for widows and abandoned women. Such elders are often classed as 'not working', but, as the case of Njuma in Box 1.1 demonstrates, many continue to seek gainful employment. Although the focus of the volume is predominantly on the earlier phases of life, an increasing number of programmes have shown that old age pensions are feasible and effective in low- and middle-income SSA countries, and we refer the reader to the growing literature on these programmes, which are increasingly becoming national policies.

How do the poorest survive?

For those of us wealthy enough to have access to the media (television coverage, social media, and newspapers), the popular image of the poorest in Africa is of children and desperate mothers on the edge of survival in the context of a natural disaster, 'famine', or violent conflict. Such images do indeed capture one aspect of extreme poverty, but it goes beyond gut-wrenching photographs that produce outbursts of charitable donations, responses by aid agencies, and publicity-seeking promises. Providing famine relief, emergency assistance, tents, and potable water is very difficult, but it also may be one of the easiest aspects of assisting the poorest because of the positive responses of politicians in the face of such desperate scenes.

For the vast majority of the extreme poor, deprivation is not a sudden, intense experience. Rather, it is an enduring, day-to-day experience overshadowed by vulnerability, destitution, physical pain, and easily preventable death (for oneself or one's children and close relatives) in the very near future. It is grinding poverty, manually labouring for eight to 16 hours a day to provide for the minimum food requirements of one's family, waiting for weeks for sick children to get better (or die) because basic health services are not accessible, watching other children go to school while you cannot attend because your parents cannot buy a uniform, being beaten or worse most days by your employer – these are the characteristics of poverty that is extreme and endures. Such 'quiet violence' (Hartmann and Boyce, 1984) rarely attracts the media or politicians.

For most of the world's poorest people, survival is not based on assistance from donors, NGOs, or government programmes. Instead, they survive primarily from their own efforts – casual labouring, gleaning, recycling waste, begging, using common property resources – and the support that is offered by relatives and neighbours. Njuma, an elderly, childless widow in Uganda, provides an example. She survives from gifts of food from her neighbours and gleaning post-harvest coffee beans for $0.02 to $0.04 an hour (Box 1.1). For most of the poorest, the poverty-reduction initiatives of NGOs, governments, and donors are too distant to be relevant. Only a very limited set of public actions, such as immunization and emergency relief, are likely to reach the poorest with any regularity.

An overview of this book

This book has four main sections. This first section looks at answering the question of *'who' are SSA's extreme poor*, and explores 'how' they might be identified and targeted. We open with these issues because we believe that anti-poverty policies often have a tendency to treat the poor as though they are a homogeneous group who can be assisted by the same types of programme. We seek to encourage researchers and practitioners to disaggregate the poor and, in particular, pose the questions 'who are the poorest?' and 'how might they be targeted?' Following this, chapters by Atlaf and Pouw, and Schubert build on several chapters from the previous volume *What Works for the Poorest?* (2010) (including Sen and Begum for Bangladesh (2010), and Alviar et al. (2010) for Kenya) that provide alternative strategies for identifying the poorest in communities.

Altaf and Pouw use the Participatory Assessment of Development (PADev) methodology to examine the participation of very poor people in development programmes in Benin. This methodology permits communities to analyze their historical experience and the outcomes of development interventions. It reveals that very poor people are not being reached, even by well-intentioned programmes. Both processes of exclusion practised by development agencies and non-poor villagers, and processes of self-exclusion (i.e. the very poor choosing not to engage with development interventions), explain the failure of programmes to reach the poorest. In the conclusion, the book proposes 'active targeting' approaches to ensure that the very poor benefit from development programmes, with a particular focus on how to avoid the cognitive and psychological barriers that exclude the poorest. Programmes that show respect for and recognize the dignity of the poorest are more likely to achieve their goals. In Chapter 3, Schubert reviews the lessons learnt about targeting the poorest in the first three years of the Zimbabwe Harmonised Social Cash Transfer Programme (HSCT). This programme prioritizes providing transfers to the poorest and, in particular, targets very poor and vulnerable households that do not have any able-bodied members, i.e. who cannot participate in 'cash for work' schemes. These are usually comprised of the elderly, chronically ill or disabled, widows and orphans, and vulnerable children. Their examination provides many lessons generated by evaluations of HSCT including detailed changes to targeting mechanisms (and the querying of proxy means testing approaches), the need to ensure that there is a transparent grievances process so that non-targeted households can challenge decisions and the fairness of decisions can be demonstrated, and the development of a community feedback mechanism, that is, a low-cost device to ensure that informal community assessments of the HSCT inform programme managers.

The second section of the book focuses on *Africa's children and youth* programmes that seek to ensure the survival and advancement of disadvantaged children. The section starts with a chapter by Ado-Kofie and Lawson, who provide an overview of different dimensions of extreme poverty in SSA, with a particular focus on young children. If you are born in SSA, then the probability that you will die before your fifth birthday is almost 17 times greater every year than if you are born in a developed country; and 397,000 babies born in SSA die each year on their first day of life. The chapter provides a statistical background of early childhood mortality, and complements this with an analysis of maternal mortality. For the period 1990–2015, child and maternal mortality trends reveal that those countries with lower poverty levels appear to have made the most progress; however, child well-being and maternal health have widened over the last two decades, where 12 of the 13 countries in the world that have made no progress in achieving under-five mortality target reduction are from SSA. The case study of Uzazi Bora, DR Congo Care, highlights that good governance is one aspect of achieving the maternal health targets, by identifying barriers related to the use of services and increasing dialogue between the community, service providers, and authorities as part of the strategy.

This policy component is, to some extent, further highlighted by a case study from Rwanda in Chapter 5 by Roelen, Karki Chettri, and Delap, focusing on child well-being and care that emphasizes the need for far greater integration of social protection and child care. BRAC's Empowerment and Livelihoods for Adolescent Girls Programme in Uganda and Tanzania forms the basis of Chapter 6 by Banks, who emphasizes that youth empowerment programmes that combine life skills and livelihoods training, and generate strong peer support networks, can go beyond improved employment outcomes to also improve social conditions and health outcomes for participants and the broader community.

The third section of the book, *getting Africa to 'work'*, moves to the next stage of the lifecycle by focusing on employment programmes. Adopting an agricultural focus, Dimova and Gang, in Chapter 7, find that greater access to credit, fertilizer, and seed coupons for Malawian women is a key policy intervention for enabling women to enter commercialized/more profitable agriculture, and once entered, this increases the chances of a household exiting extreme poverty. Chapter 8, by Sulaiman, focusing on South Sudan, found the food for training impact on household labour supply resulted in lower levels of child labour and higher school enrolment for girls, but significantly lower household incomes. McCord, in Chapter 9, then provides an overview of the lessons from public works programmes in addressing poverty in Ethiopia, Rwanda, and South Africa, highlighting the need for political commitment and secure financing, but recognizing that graduation from such programmes is perhaps unlikely. Graduation from social protection programmes remains the focus of the following two chapters by Mishra and Mtambie (Chapter 10) who focus on Tanzania's Social Action Fund, and Devereux (Chapter 11) for Burundi, Ethiopia, and Rwanda. Several factors are identified that enable or constrain sustainable graduation: programme (design and implemen-tation); community; market; and environment, and the need to adapt programmes. Devereux also questions the assumption of a smooth linear 'graduation pathway' for the graduation potential of labour-constrained households.

The concluding section of the book looks at *implementation and policy thoughts* for poverty reduction programmes for Africa's poorest. Linking to the previous chapters, it focuses on social protection. Holmes (Chapter 12), with respect to the case of Nigeria, highlights that political commitment and fiscal sustainability, and an ability to design social protection programmes appropri-ately, are key. A clear message from the social protection/graduation chapters is that graduation programmes can also risk diverting the focus of social protection away from managing risk and vulnerability towards achieving poverty reduction targets. Chapter 13, by Pellerano and Barca, and Chapter 14 by Ayala consider implementation of social welfare programmes and more specifically cash transfer programmes, and highlight the need to consider supply constraints, and the lessons that can be learnt from Latin America when implementing in SSA. The penultimate chapter of the book provides a focus on a key policy area that is commonly under-researched, that of access to justice for Africa's poorest. Using the case study of Uganda, Dubin and Lawson highlight that justice programmes need to cut across government and civil society agencies to ensure coordinated and multifaceted approaches to access to justice provision for Africa's extreme poor. The final chapter of the book by Hulme, Lawson, and Ado-Kofie brings together the lessons learnt from the book, providing a policy focus and conclusions for research and practitioners.

Notes

1. This assumes an accounting period of July to June for Ethiopia.
2. For detailed discussions of the strengths and weaknesses of this measure see Ravallion (2002), Deaton (2001), and Reddy and Pogge (2002).
3. For a full explanation of the MPI, MPI Reports, and the dataset, go to www.ophi.org.uk/multidimensional-poverty-index
4. The year of assessment for a country depends on data availability, so the data do not refer to a specific year.
5. Extracted from Global Multidimensional Poverty Index 2014 Briefing Paper (2014), 8.
6. But, note that recent and future PPP adjustments to the Nigeria income poverty headcount are likely to reduce this number.

References

Ado-Kofie, L. and Lawson, D. (2016) 'Africa's extreme poor: Surviving early childhood', in D. Lawson, L. Ado-Kofie, and D. Hulme (eds), *What Works for Africa's Poorest: Poverty Reduction Strategies for Extremely Poor People*. Practical Action Publishing, Rugby.

Alviar, C., Ayala, F. and Handa, S. (2010) 'Testing combined targeting systems for cash transfer programs: The case of the CT-OVC programme in Kenya', in D. Lawson, D. Hulme, I. Matin, and K. Moore (eds), *What Works for the Poorest? Poverty Reduction Programmes for the World's Extreme Poor*. Practical Action Publishing, Rugby.

Beegle, K., Christiaensen, L., Dabelen, A. and Gaddis, I. (2016) *Poverty in a Rising Africa*. World Bank, Washington DC.

Calvo C. and Dercon, S. (2009) 'Chronic poverty and all that: The measurement of poverty over time', in T. Addison, D. Hulme, and R. Kanbur (eds), *Poverty Dynamics: Inter-disciplinary Perspectives*. Oxford University Press, Oxford.

Chambers, R. (1994) 'The origins and practice of participatory rural appraisal', *World Development* 22(7): 953–70 <http://dx.doi.org/10.1016/0305-750X(94)90141-4>.

Collier, P. (2007) *The Bottom Billion*. Oxford University Press, Oxford.

CPRC (2004) *The Chronic Poverty Report 2004–05*. Chronic Poverty Research Centre, Manchester. Available at www.chronicpoverty.org/uploads/publication_files/CPR1_ReportFull.pdf

CPRC (2008) *The Chronic Poverty Report 2008–09*. Manchester, UK: Chronic Poverty Research Centre. Available at www.chronicpoverty.org/publications/details/the-chronic-poverty-report-2008-09

Deaton, A. (2001) 'Counting the world's poor: Problems and possible solutions', *World Bank Research Observer* 16(2): 125–47 <http://dx.doi.org/10.1093/wbro/16.2.125>.

Godinot, X. (2000) *Participation Works: Involving People in Poverty in Policy Making*. ATD Fourth World, London.

Greig, A., Hulme, D. and Turner, M. (2007) *Challenging Global Inequality*. Palgrave, London.

Gunter, I. and Klasen, S. (2009) 'Measuring chronic non-income poverty', in T. Addison, D. Hulme, and R. Kanbur (eds), *Poverty Dynamics: Interdisciplinary Perspectives*. Oxford University Press, Oxford.

Hanlon, J., Hulme, D. and Barrientos A. (2010) *Just Give Money to the Poor: The Development Revolution from the Global South*. Kumarian Press, West Hartford, CT.

Hartmann, B. and Boyce, J.K. (1984) A *Quiet Violence*. University Press Limited, Dhaka.

Hulme, D. (2015) *Global Poverty: Global Governance and Poor People in the Post-2015 Era*. Routledge, London.

Hulme D. and Moore, K. (2010) 'Assessing the poorest in Bangladesh: Learning from BRAC's 'Targeting the Ultra Poor' programme', in D. Lawson, D. Hulme, I. Matin, and K. Moore (eds), *What Works for the Poorest? Poverty Reduction Programmes for the World's Extreme Poor*. Practical Action Publishing, Rugby.

Hulme, D. and Shepherd, A. (2003) 'Conceptualising chronic poverty', *World Development* 31(3): 403–24 <http://dx.doi.org/10.1016/S0305-750X(02)00222-X>.

Kabeer, N. (2010) 'Alternative accounts of chronic disadvantage: Income deficits versus food security', in D. Lawson, D. Hulme, I. Matin, and K. Moore (eds), *What Works for the Poorest? Poverty Reduction Programmes for the World's Extreme Poor*. Practical Action Publishing, Rugby.

Krishna, A. (2009) 'Subjective assessments, participatory methods and poverty dynamics: The stages of progress method', in T. Addison, D. Hulme, and R. Kanbur (eds), *Poverty Dynamics: Inter-disciplinary Perspectives*. Oxford University Press, Oxford.

Lawson, D., Hulme, D., Matin, I. and Moore, K. (eds) (2010) *What Works for the Poorest? Poverty Reduction Programmes for the World's Extreme Poor*. Practical Action Publishing, Rugby.

Narayan, D., Patel, R., Schafft, K., Rademacher, A. and Koch-Schulte, S. (2000) *Can Anyone Hear Us? Voices of the Poor*. Oxford University Press for the World Bank, New York, NY. <http://dx.doi.org/10.1596/0-1952-1601-6>.

Oxfam (2016) 'An economy for the 1%: How privilege and power in the economy drive extreme inequality and how this can be stopped', *Oxfam Briefing Paper* 210. Oxfam, Oxford.

Ravallion, M. (2002) 'Comment on 'Counting the world's poor' by Angus Deaton', *World Bank Research Observer* 16(2): 149–56 <http://dx.doi.org/10.1093/wbro/16.2.149>.

Reddy, S. and Pogge, T.W. (2002) 'How *not* to count the poor', *Mimeo*. Barnard College, New York, NY.

Save the Children (2013) *Surviving the First Day: State of the World's Mothers 2013*. Save the Children International, London.

Sen, B. and Begum S. (2010) 'Identifying and targeting the extreme poor; A methodology for rural Bangladesh', in D. Lawson, D. Hulme, I. Matin, and K. Moore (eds), *What Works for the Poorest? Poverty Reduction Programmes for the World's Extreme Poor*. Practical Action Publishing, Rugby.

World Bank (2013) *The State of the Poor: Where are the Poor and Where are They Poorest? PREM, Draft Background Note*. World Bank, Washington DC.

World Economic Forum (2016) '10 things the IMF wants you to know about Africa's economy' [online]. Geneva, World Economic Forum. Available at: www.weforum.org/agenda/2016/04/10-things-the-imf-wants-you-to-know-about-africas-economy [accessed 21 May 2016].

About the authors

David Hulme is Professor of Development Studies and Founder–Director of the Chronic Poverty Research Centre and the Brooks World Poverty Institute, University of Manchester. He is now Executive Director of the recently established Global Development Institute at Manchester.

David Lawson is a Senior Lecturer in Development Economics and Public Policy at the Global Development Institute, University of Manchester. He has worked extensively on SSA and specializes in poverty dynamics in African countries.

CHAPTER 2

Defining, targeting, and reaching the very poor in Benin

Anika Altaf and Nicky Pouw

How can the very poor be reached by development initiatives? This case study in Nikki, Benin shows that reaching the very poor is a difficult and time-consuming task, but certainly not impossible. By taking a comprehensive approach to poverty and well-being, specifically unravelling the interconnections between material, relational, and psychological aspects of poverty, this chapter sheds light on the two-way process of exclusion. On the one hand, the government, NGOs, and the community exclude the very poor, and on the other hand, the poor exclude themselves. This case study further shows that any approach seeking to reach the very poor should be rooted in local understandings of poverty, and draw in the help of others to build long-term trust.

Keywords: targeting, very poor, psychological, well-being, exclusion

Introduction

The global debate around the new Millennium Development Goals has signalled the need to 'leave no one behind' (UNA-UK, 2012; United Nations, 2012; United Nations, 2013). Reaching out to the very poor and structurally marginalized has proven to be difficult, however (Hulme and Moore, 2008; Lawson et al., 2011). The very poor are not only difficult to reach via development interventions, but also in evaluating the impact of development on different categories of poor beneficiaries. In 2012 a comprehensive four-year study of a new methodology for monitoring and evaluation, called PADev (Participatory Assessment of Development), was completed that included detailed field-testing in rural areas of Ghana and Burkina Faso (Dietz, 2012; Dietz et al., 2012; Dietz and the PADev Team, 2013).

PADev is a bottom-up, participatory, and holistic approach to development evaluation that enables communities to assess the (historical) process and outcomes of development interventions in their region, and to do so with the involvement of a multitude of stakeholders and categories of beneficiaries (Pouw et al., 2016). A major finding of this study was that many development interventions (by government, the private sector, NGOs, and religious organizations) often failed to have a positive impact on the very poor, and that this impact even lessened over time (Pouw and Janvier, 2014). In a spin-off study

http://dx.doi.org/10.3362/9781780448435.002

of the PADev study in 2010, Kazimierczuk (2010) found that the poorest were unable to evaluate development interventions in their region (rural Ghana), since these interventions did not reach them directly. The very poor appear to be socially and statistically invisible, and extremely difficult to target and include throughout project intervention (ibid.). Social and psychological factors seem to play a role in co-determining the complex processes of in/exclusion of the very poor in development interventions. Yet, the inclusion of the very poor in development can be argued to be a pre-condition for transformative local change and inclusive growth in Africa (ACET, 2014; Pouw et al., 2016; UNCTAD, 2014).

This raises the question of how to target the very poor, and under what conditions can they be effectively reached? This chapter therefore addresses these questions, and is based on a recent field-study on the effectiveness of including the very poor in a series of development interventions by a local development agency in the commune of Nikki, in the Borgou department of Benin.[1] This agency is supported by the Dutch development organization 'Woord & Daad', which has an established reputation for its commitment to reaching out to the poorest of the poor (Woord & Daad, 2013: p. 10). This study has been carried out from a dynamic process perspective of poverty (Krishna, 2004; Krishna, 2010; Narayan et al., 2000a and 2000b); that is, it has been influenced and shaped by (non-material) social and political forces (Ferguson, 1990; Harriss-White, 2006; Sen, 1999), and is deeply affecting social and psychological dimensions of well-being (McGregor, 2004). The three dimensions of human well-being recognized by McGregor (2004) and Gough and McGregor (2007) have been used to collect primary data, and to structure the chapter's data analysis.

The chapter begins with a description of the field-research location and local culture. Theoretical points of departure and research methodology are then explained, as well as the selection of respondents. This is followed by a description of poverty, in terms of its local understandings as a process, along with a discussion of people's movements into poverty based on life histories. This section further analyses the material, social–relational, and psychological/mental dimensions of being very poor, and how factors within each of these domains interact with (failed) development interventions. An examination of the inclusiveness and exclusiveness of development initiatives in the research area is then presented. Finally, the chapter's conclusion indicates potential further research, and some initial recommendations are presented.

Field-research location and local culture

Compared to other sub-Saharan African countries, Benin is one of the poorest, despite recent improvements with respect to the Human Development Index (HDI). In 2013 Benin's HDI was measured at 0.476, positioning it at 165 out of 187 countries, thus classifying it as a low human development country (UNDP, 2014).

Benin is divided into 12 departments, which are further subdivided into 77 communes. These communes are again divided into cities (districts) or villages. Nikki is a commune situated in the Borgou department (see Figure 2.1 below), and has approximately 137,721 inhabitants while covering approximately 3,170 square kilometres.[2] In 2007 Borgou along with Alibori were considered the poorest departments of Benin (International Monetary Fund, 2011). However, in 2009 Borgou exhibited improvement, and was no longer regarded as one of Benin's poorest departments (ibid.).

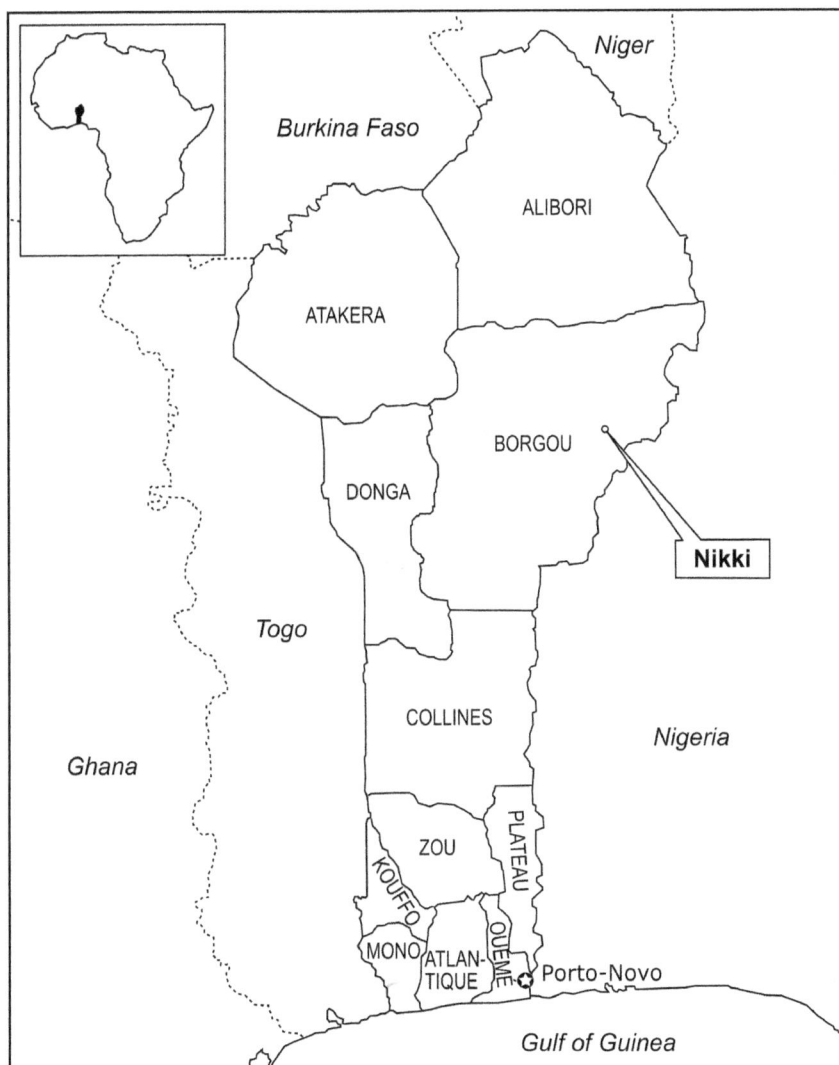

Figure 2.1 Map of Benin

Table 2.1 Incidence of different forms of poverty based on department

Department	2007		2009	
	Income poverty	Non-income poverty	Income poverty	Non-income poverty
Alibori	0.43	0.46	0.35	0.33
Atacora	0.33	0.65	0.36	0.69
Atlantique	0.36	0.31	0.37	0.24
Borgou	**0.39**	**0.46**	**0.28**	**0.32**
Collines	0.31	0.29	0.44	0.17
Couffo	0.35	0.49	0.46	0.42
Donga	0.34	0.39	0.31	0.21
Littoral	0.26	0.17	0.23	0.13
Mono	0.27	0.49	0.46	0.45
Ouémé	0.25	0.28	0.24	0.19
Plateau	0.35	0.44	0.33	0.28
Zou	0.32	0.43	0.41	0.32
National	0.32	0.40	0.35	0.31

Source: International Monetary Fund (2011)

Unlike other parts of Benin, the majority of Nikki's population is comprised of Muslims, followed by Christians and Animists. However, it is important to note that, while most of those who adhere to either Islam or Christianity are also Animists, this has been, along with socio-historical issues surrounding ethnic diversity, a source of tension between these groups. Among the many ethnicities present in Nikki are the minority Dendi, Otamari, Yoruba, Fon, Adja, Yom, and Lokpa. The Batonou or Bariba, the Fulani, and Gando, however, are the dominant ethnic groups in this area, with the Bariba officially the largest ethnic group in Nikki (45.4 per cent), followed by the Fulani and Gando together (40.4 per cent).[3]

The tension between these groups originates from a period in history that saw the Gando exploited as slaves by the Bariba. This latter ethnic grouping forms part of the kingdom of Borgou, situated in the northeast of Benin as well as into the northwest of Nigeria. The Gando, in turn, are considered the discarded children of the Bariba. Among Bariba beliefs it is held that, if the mother died giving birth, the child was either killed by smashing it against a Baobab, or abandoned. These orphans or foundlings were often taken in by the Fulani, who used them as slaves. The Gando have therefore adopted the culture and language of the Fulani, and oppose the Bariba who, consequently, feel superior to the Gando. Ultimately, the Gando are seen as former slaves, while the Bariba believe they are descendants of the Borgou kingdom.

Furthermore, there is tension surrounding the question of which ethnicity is poorer. A Bariba will claim that the Bariba are the poorest, as the

Gando and Fulani have access to larger pieces of land. Non-Bariba believe the Gando people are poorer, since they live in the bush on the outskirts of the commune, and lack access to education, health care, and clean drinking water. A final, but noteworthy, characteristic of this area is the discernible presence of fetishism, or so-called 'black magic'. How this affects society as a whole, and relationships between poor and non-poor in particular, will be elaborated below.

Theoretical and methodological approach

The research methodology underpinning this chapter is based on three core theoretical premises or frameworks that are summarized here.

One of the starting points in this research is the social–relational approach that pays attention to the fact that poverty is embedded in a social–cultural and political context (du Toit and Hickey, 2013; Ferguson, 1990; Harriss-White, 2006; Mosley, 2012; Mosse, 2010; Sen, 1999). This emphasizes that poverty itself, and how it is constructed, can only be understood when placed into its institutional context. Thus, cultural, social, political, and economic institutions and relationships (re)produce poverty and inequality. This social–relational perspective of poverty is also embraced by our second framework, one that is focused on the dynamics of poverty. Poverty is not a static characteristic, but a dynamic process influenced by multiple factors and life events (e.g. Baulch and Hoddinott, 2000; Krishna, 2010; Narayan et al., 2000a and 2000b). These factors, causing movement downward or upward, *differ* from each other, which sets the approach apart from, in particular, the income-based approach to poverty. The third framework our research draws upon is the human well-being approach (e.g. see also Alkire, 2002; Collard, 2003; Dasgupta, 1993; Doyal and Gough, 1991; Gasper, 2004; Kabeer, 1996; McGregor, 2004), which builds on the previous two approaches, but draws attention to the psychological/cognitive aspect of well-being, and not just the material and social–relational. Consequently, as McGregor (2004) argues, priorities of the poor can be better understood if objective and subjective evaluations of their own well-being are accommodated.

Drawing on these three perspectives, we adopted a bottom-up, participatory, and all-inclusive approach to poverty assessment. Initially, it was thought the PADev approach would be most appropriate to implement the field-research methodology (Pouw et al., 2016). However, given that collective workshops form an instrumental part of the PADev approach, this methodology, while useful in the case of community officials, proved impracticable in the case of the very poor. The very poor did not show up, were very often reluctant to speak, or were difficult to talk to, and were even difficult to locate in the first instance. This is why the life histories method was eventually adopted as a way to converse with the very poor people on an individual basis.

Being mindful of potentially sensitive issues, this method was conducted in a secure and private environment, while taking time enough to gain trust to enable discussion around key psychological/cognitive issues.[4]

To conduct this life histories approach, it was necessary to consult many different groups. As Woord & Daad had been working for over 12 years in the area implementing a range of projects (e.g. on education, food security, agribusiness, and microcredit), they were initially consulted, in their capacity as a local counterpart NGO, in the sample selection stage of the research. Three villages were purposefully selected on the basis of the variety of different NGO projects up and running in each. The aim was to see if, for example, economic initiatives were better able to reach the poorest than educational initiatives or vice versa.

Prior to establishing which villages and their circumstances would be studied, however, a PADev workshop was conducted with relevant community officials (government officers, teachers, NGO employees, etc.) in Nikki city. This was to establish the wealth categories in the Nikki commune as a whole, and also to learn if there were any already-existing approaches specifically targeting the very poor.

The first village selected was Tepa, which comprises approximately 500 inhabitants, and is located roughly eight kilometres north of Nikki city. Tepa is a mixed village in terms of ethnicity, although the majority are Fulani and Gando. The second village was Ouenou, approximately eight kilometres east–southeast of Nikki city. Ouenou has 1,430 inhabitants according to the 2001 census conducted by the municipality of Nikki.[5] It is predominantly a Bariba village, with some Fulani and Gando living in the bush on the outskirts of the community. The third village selected was Tontarou, found approximately ten kilometres south–southeast of Nikki city. Tontarou consists of 2,549 inhabitants that, like Ouenou, are mostly Bariba living in the core village, with Fulani and Gando dwelling in the periphery.[6]

In collaboration with NGO staff in Nikki, those community members that could be classified locally as poor, average, and rich were invited from the three selected villages to participate in six PADev workshops.[7] In total, there were 40 participants across all workshops. Problems initially occurred in identifying the very poorest primarily due to a prevailing culture of shame regarding speaking about poverty amongst the Bariba. This factor made it hard to speak about being poor, let alone being very poor. However, after numerous visits to the respective villages, building trust, and locating candidates willing to help ease the search for the very poor, ten life histories were eventually conducted, seven of which were male and three female. These life histories were cross-checked with information provided by community members on the very poor via interviews and informal conversations. Additionally, several interviews were also conducted with NGOs, religious organizations, and government bodies to discover what initiatives for the very poor were implemented, and what target approaches were used.

What does it mean to be very poor in rural Nikki, Benin?

In order to find the very poor, it was crucial to discover who they were, and how they were defined locally. Inhabitants of different wealth groups from the three villages were therefore asked to define the very rich, rich, average, poor, and very poor in their society.[8] Table 2.2 presents the descriptions that were composed by the workshop participants.

Generally, the very poor were depicted negatively by the workshop participants, e.g. they are 'not considered' and people 'pity' them and 'laugh at them'. They are 'suffering' and their 'absence goes unnoticed'.

Table 2.2 The very poor in rural Nikki

Very Poor:	*In the local language:* **Bariba**: Saaroo, Nyaro **Fulani**: Talkadjo
Who:	The very poor can be recognized at first sight (OW). They are those who are always suffering. They are always praying for their lives to change (DM). And they are praying for someone to help them. They have nothing (YM, DW). They are beggars and bless those who give something to them. People pity them and people laugh at them (YM, YW). They are not considered in the society (OM). It is not their fault; it is destiny (OW). But some do not have the will to work, which is why they are needy. They do not want to make an effort, but they are born like that, it is destiny. Everything they have is given by others (OM). They have no job, but they can help people with the transportation of their goods (YW). Others will do other chores for people to earn money (OW). The absence of a very poor person will go unnoticed (YM).
Characteristics:	
Education:	The very poor cannot send their children to school (DM). Only if they are assisted by relatives or through projects will their children be able to go to school. They go to public schools (OW).
Farm/land/harvest:	They often do not go to their farmlands (OM). They can farm, but if they do not want to farm, they are lazy (YM). They have access to farmland, but the production is not sufficient (OW); it is their destiny (DW).
Food:	Food is a major problem. The very poor are always thinking how they will manage to get food (DM). They need help from others to get food for themselves and their families (OW). They have to beg for food (YW, OM) and go from place to place to get it (YM). If the community will not provide them with food, they cannot eat (OM). If they receive food, they will usually get the leftovers or spoilt (rotten) food (DM). The children will get whatever is left by their parents (OW). They are recognized through their red hair and big bellies, which is a sign of malnutrition (OM). Some will work for a rich person in order to get food (DM, YM). Others will have to steal food (YM).

(Continued)

Table 2.2 Continued

Housing:	Their houses and roofs are covered with straw (OW, OM). But even the straw is sometimes insufficient. Sometimes, they may have a roof of old tin, which was given to them (DM). They cannot build their house on their own; they need help. If the roof has to be repaired, they need help. If no one will help, they cannot repair or replace it (DW). They do not clean their houses and everything is dirty. They can sleep on an old torn mattress (DM). Others stay with their family (YM) or may be given a small house to stay in (YM). But the very poor usually do not stay at one place for a very long time (YM); they may live with someone for one month and go to someone else the next month (OM). The very poor live within the community (OW, YW). Some live around the village (YW).
Livestock:	They do not have animals; if someone has animals they do not belong to the very poor (DW).
Social (support):	Some of them have a wife and children and some do not (DM, YW, OW). It is difficult for their wives to eat and dress themselves. When they are sick, it not easy to have access to a hospital (YW). Even when they give birth, they need assistance to get medical care and clothes for their baby (OW). But even if the very poor men have a wife, they can be divorced, because they cannot take care of their wives (YM). Sometimes, they cannot control their wives, since they are the ones who bring the food for the family. The very poor women have more success in marriage; once they are married, they are safe and taken care of. Sometimes, it will be both the husband and the wife who are very poor but sometimes, it is only one of them (OW).
Other:	The very poor are given old clothes by the community. They cannot buy it themselves (DM, OM, OW). They only have one cloth (OW) and they also cannot buy shoes. They look like a mad man (OM). They have no bike (DM). Their wives, when they cook to sell, nobody will buy it because they are so dirty (OW).

Source: Anika Altaf, definitions provided by workshop participants
Note: OM: old men; OW: old women; YM: young men; YW: young women; DM: NGO men beneficiaries: DW: NGO women beneficiaries

The multi-dimensions of being very poor and interactions with development

This section examines what the very poor think are the main causes of their poverty, the dynamics of their poverty, what difficulties they face, their social relations, and lastly the cognitive aspect of their poverty. We will pay marginal attention to the material aspects of poverty, given these are thoroughly studied by others, and so the focus here is on the social–relational and psychological/cognitive dimensions of poverty.

Falling into and out of poverty

The most important reason offered for falling into extreme poverty is the loss of a partner, either through death or abandonment. According to the interviewees, quality of life deteriorates dramatically very soon after the loss of a partner. As one 75-year-old interviewee, whose husband died 15 years previously, explained:

> ... my husband passed away. He was thinking too much about his sickness and he passed away. During that period I was also thinking too much, I was looking at him and worrying. Life became hard after that. I did not have the strength anymore to take care of myself.

Often, the loss of a partner goes hand in hand with losing their entire, or a substantial part of their, means of income, while another major reason for falling into poverty is personal illness or, for example, a child in need of treatment. There is a range of factors that can make illness a cause of extreme poverty.

Illness does not just take a toll on economic activities; it can also impact people socially. For this 40-year-old woman, her disease means being evicted by her husband, resulting in her isolation and falling into extreme poverty:

> [B]ecause of my sickness he wants me to leave now ... I am poor because I am ill.

Sometimes, required treatment can cause people to lose everything they have saved or built, such as in the case of this male interviewee:

> One of the children of my wife's first husband fell ill and I had to sell everything for the treatment of this child. The father of this child did not take care of him. I even had to take a loan. To repay that, I had to sell a lot of my soya production.

Drunkenness is also mentioned as a cause of falling into poverty. This impacts individuals directly, whereby the person affected by alcohol use may be evicted or abandoned. Alternatively, the family as a whole may fall into poverty, and suffer additionally, due to behaviour associated with drunkenness. A further reason mentioned for falling into poverty is family size. For example, this 43-year-old man experienced difficulties after having four twins.

> [W]e had another twin. I wondered if life would not become difficult, since I had a fourth twin and I wondered if I would be able to feed them. And it turned out to be difficult. It was difficult to give the children money for koko (i.e. porridge) and even to clothe them.

Perhaps the most remarkable reason mentioned is fetishism. Interviewees mentioned that bad spirits and black magic severely affected people (not exclusively very poor people). Moreover, community members with evil intentions sometimes went to fetishists in order to harm others through black magic, as one 40-year-old interviewee stated:

> I remember that my husband wanted to spend most of his time with me and he even travelled with me, without the second wife. She got jealous

and annoyed, she put something in my food and I ate it. Since I ate that food, I became sick (possibly epilepsy). I went to see a visionary (charlatan) and she told me that it was the second wife who did this to me.

Sometimes, falling into poverty is caused by a combination of different factors, such as illness and the loss of a partner or loved one. The factors leading to poverty described above should not be held solely responsible for causing poverty. At times, it can be as simple as 'just being in the wrong place at the wrong time'.

The use of life histories makes it very clear that, in many cases, wealth status rarely remains static, as one 39-year-old male interviewee describes:

> When I was a young boy, my father had cattle and I used to take the cattle in the bush, like the Fulani people do. I used to climb in the tree to look around and often I could not find food the entire day ... When I came back home, my mother would give me food ... then I went to meet my friends, play football and we used to chat. But I was not happy though; I saw others going to school, while I had to stay at home and take care of the cattle and farm. It made me angry ... I saw a lady in my village and I came back to my parents to tell them I wanted to marry her ... When we got married, my wife was making koko and we earned together. After about three months she was pregnant with our firstborn. I was happy, because I got married to have children. I was very happy then; even when my child was bugging my wife, I would take care of the child, so she could work.

Happy, sad, easy, and difficult periods alternate in the lives of the interviewees. The question remains, however, can those very poor interviewees climb out of poverty again? Those who have children hope that their situation may improve through them, and, in some cases, this is a realistic aspiration. For example, the 43-year-old man who has four twins, and so struggled, stated:

> Since five years, this (struggling) has changed though, because the children are growing up and they can help me, so I can focus on the tool making. It is true that things changed, but for example our house still has sand inside. Food is better now, but money is still a problem.

Others who are less fortunate, and do not have relatives close by, may not see better times soon unless they are aided. Some are too old and incapable of taking care of themselves any more, and instead would have to rely on social protection measures that are currently not in place. Therefore, it seems less likely that they will not be able to climb out of their poverty circumstances soon.

Social relations and networks

Difficulties, thus, come in different forms, but what is striking here is that a component of mental stress can be found in almost every difficulty, if not all, and yet little attention is paid to this in current literature. In such difficult circumstances, social relations, and networks, play a vital role.

Social relations and networks are essential for the survival of the very poor. All the interviewees had received some form of help from one of their relatives, neighbours, friends, or community members. It became clear that those who had good relations with their family were more likely to recover from shocks and stressful events. Aid from family also allowed people not only to cope with shocks, but to also improve their current status to some small extent, as a 43-year-old male interviewee explains:

> When the villagers wanted to change the roof of the school, I went to ask the chief if I could have some of the tin for my roof. I got some tin, and I borrowed CFA10,000 [US$17] from my brother-in-law, and my brother in Nigeria who died, I borrowed some money from him as well. That is how I managed to get a tin roof.

However, those assisted by family in this way were in the minority. Likewise, just as family, especially immediate family, can elevate people in this way, it can also push them (further) into poverty, as one 75-year-old interviewee outlines:

> My daughters do not come to visit me; if they came, how could I be in need of food? According to my girls, it is my son who should be taking care of me, not them, so they do not come. Since my boys had died, I remained unhappy, until today. If my boys were still alive, I would not suffer like I am suffering. They would help me. But the youth of today, they do not want to do anything. The boy (son) that I am staying with now does not help me.

Neighbours and friends also played a large role supporting the very poor, for example, through food assistance, lending money, providing land to farm, or in some cases a roof over their heads, as illustrated by one 40-year-old female interviewee:

> When we came here, someone gave us land. Someone gave us the house, since it was empty. Someone had built the house, but they left and so we moved in. However, we are not living there now, since the rain has destroyed it. Our neighbour told us to come and live with him, since no one was staying in the room we are staying in.

Besides support from family and friends, occasional aid from community members is also important in meeting such basic needs as food, clothes, medicines, and so forth. However, some exceptions aside, the problem persists that aid is not provided structurally. That is to say, a community member may provide aid one day, but not the next. An immediate crisis may prompt community members to provide some assistance, but this is not a type of support that can help move a person or family out of extreme poverty.

Accessing development projects in such cases entails being part of a network, and having strong social relations. The very poor are thus excluded, as they lack both.

Clearly, aid is ordinarily delivered in the material sphere, and not in a cognitive one. Perhaps sometimes it is more important to secure love and respect from others, thus giving the recipient a feeling of being human, and of being a valued person. The next subsection will elaborate on this.

Self-image and self-esteem

Self-perception plays an important role for people when considering who they think they can be, or what they can do. Self-image and self-esteem are part of the cognitive aspect of poverty that is still not adequately addressed. One of the immediate and noteworthy findings from this research is that half of the interviewees thought of themselves as being a 'bad or not good' person, despite each having different reasons to conclude this. A 40-year-old woman blames her illness:

> I cannot do anything. Because I am sick no one wants to be near to me [or] come close to me; it makes me feel that I am a bad person. Other people think my life is over. I cannot do anything good for anyone.

For this 75-year-old woman, it is her lack of material wealth that has diminished her self-esteem:

> I would say I am not a good person, because I have nothing now. In the past, I was a good person, because I did not lack anything.

Almost all had experienced insults from family members and their wider community. Usually, the smaller their network, the fewer people there were to protect them from insults or offer respect, and so they were more likely to suffer low self-esteem. As a consequence, they were discouraged from taking any initiatives to improve their situation, including deliberately excluding themselves from attending village meetings regarding new development projects.

None of the development organizations active in this area had considered these factors in their approach to targeting and reaching the very poor, or when ensuring the very poor felt confident and secure enough to remain in a project. To some extent, this further emphasizes the diminished hopes and dreams of the very poor. One 48-year-old male participant made the following entreaty:

> Then I wanted children, I wanted to be a big man who could build nice houses, not like in the village, but with cement and people could rent them. Now I am asking God to give people enough, so they can help me. I am asking God to give me my daily food.

Clearly, this interviewee's dream has drastically changed over time. Moreover, he holds no hope that his situation may change, and he cannot contemplate his ever becoming that big man he envisaged for himself. Losing hope for the life they once aspired to was a condition that all interviewees shared. A 60-year-old man placed his hope and solace for a better life in the afterlife.

> I know my life is different from other people, but I trust in God. In this life, I have nothing, but I have hope that when I will die, I will have a good life with God.

Not believing you deserve better, or that you will ever be able to turn a corner, can also demotivate a person, preventing them from improving their situation, making them passive, and potentially trapping them in a vicious cycle.

Fatalism and fetishism

Most of the very poor interviewed were quite fatalistic. This meant that they believed that their lives, to a great extent, are predetermined and therefore unalterable, for example, as the following interviewees (a 40-year-old female, and a 48-year-old male) argue respectively:

> People say, look at this sick person. When I hear it, I am sad, but I reply to myself, it is only God who does things [or] They will say, look at this poor man, even in my own house, they will say he has nothing ... I will say, it is only God who does things, only He knows why ...

Accordingly, there is a sense of passivity in people's responses to hardship. There is also a great presence of fetishism in the society, as described by a number of older women participants:

> In 2008, there was a conflict amongst some people in one of the villages. There were some people who were each individually involved in sorcery. They killed other villagers through their magic. They would use plants or organs of dead people that they would dig from the graves to perform spells.

This one example of many demonstrates that, not only is distrust generated amongst communities, but also certain problems, which are often remediable through conventional medicines in fact persist due to certain beliefs, as a 40-year-old female participant explains:

> I still have this disease. I had it since I was a little girl. My parents suffered a lot because of it, but when they wanted to go to the hospital people said, this disease is not for the hospital, it should be treated traditionally (herbs and fetishists). I was born in the farm and people say maybe I met bad spirits there.

Not believing one is capable of changing one's situation and following traditions does not boost self-esteem. Rather, it contributes to a process of self-exclusion.

Targeting and reaching the very poor

In studying the targeting methods of the NGO collaborating in this research, it became clear they possess a thorough knowledge of the different wealth categories within their areas of focus. They do not, however, actively target the very poor. By employing an 'open access for everyone' method, they fail to attract the poorest, in that the very poor are both reluctant to join village meetings, and are also not invited to join. While it may appear considerate to open a project up for everyone and be inclusive, this does not necessarily work in practice. Furthermore, the very poor are also excluded from such economic initiatives as the NGO's microcredit scheme. This is due to microcredit initiatives being organized in groups to which the very poor do not have access. It can be said the very poor are isolated in their communities, as the targeting methods used have not been adapted to the circumstances of the very poor, and so fail to reach them. According to the very poor and the wider community, other NGOs working in the area have not had much success either.

According to the community, the only projects or initiatives that manage to reach the very poor are those public ones that benefit all, including the very poor, such as streetlights. Most initiatives fail to reach the very poor, and are seen to predominantly reach the rich and the non-poor. Elite corruption is mentioned by older male participants as an important reason for this:

> For example, a HIV initiative that was to be carried out in the area, but the poor people who wished to benefit from it, did not belong to the same political party as the mayor and were excluded from the project. We heard that the money was transferred to rich people who were supposed to carry out HIV-related activities, but they kept the money for private purposes.

However, the very poor also exclude themselves. By way of example, the interviewees spoke of a shea butter processing initiative, whereby community members worked with machines to do the processing. One very poor person had entered the initiative, but withdrew quickly. According to their co-workers, this person was afraid to be held responsible if something went wrong (i.e. if something went missing, or a machine broke down). Seemingly, the very poor have the impression that others will assume they would steal, or would blame them for damaged equipment. A lack of self-esteem, combined with mistreatment by members of their community, may play a role here.

Not reaching the very poor is, thus, a two-way process. On the one hand, the very poor are excluded by organizations and members in the community due to social stigmatization. On the other hand, the very poor exclude themselves due to lack of trust, self-confidence, shame, and a dearth of social relations.

Conclusions and recommendations

This research demonstrates how, despite the best of intentions, the very poor in the villages studied are seldom ever reached by those particular development interventions that were looked at. The few occasions the very poor were reached it was typically via public initiatives that benefited the village as a whole, such as street lighting or provision of a free water pump.

The primary reason for failing to reach the very poor is due to a two-way process of exclusion and the deep, psychological dimensions of poverty, the role of which cannot be underestimated. On the one hand, development organizations and the community exclude the very poor both consciously and unconsciously: unconsciously, through the use of inappropriate targeting methods, and consciously through elite capture of development initiatives. On the other hand, the very poor exclude themselves from taking part in any (development) initiatives. Shame, fear, passivism, fatalism, remaining loyal to old traditions (fetishism), lack of self-esteem and trust, and a lack of social networks hinder these groups from entering development initiatives or, when they do, from staying on board. Employing expertise on social–relational aspects, mental health, and disability is critically important to tackle these issues. Moreover, a circle-of-family/friends approach can be taken to build a relationship of mutual trust and confidence. It also creates an early, indirect, channel of access to the very poor, which can grow into direct contact and a long-standing relationship at later stages.

The very poor need to be actively targeted, and included in development initiatives given open-access methods have failed to include them in the areas studied. Moreover, the very poor should be targeted directly, and not through local leaders. Targeting the very poor is a complex and time-consuming process where organizations and donors should be prepared to invest in long-term trajectories, rather than aim for short-term gains. Indeed, a 'tandem approach' may satisfy both the need for quick gains, and also those benefits that can accrue from long-term trajectories. Projects for the poor can be deemed 'profitable and successful', whereas projects for the very poor might (initially) be seen as 'non-profitable' and long term.

What also became evident is that the cognitive/psychological component of poverty is crucial in understanding how poverty is (re)constructed. Friendship, respect, and feeling human are essential in nurturing one's self-esteem. Without such, it is difficult to convince a person that they can, in fact, change their own situation, and deserve it. Development initiatives that include the very poor may not prove very successful without prior consideration of their psycho-logical and social capabilities. Even if consideration is given to how groups are targeted, it remains important to pay due attention to these aspects in order to counteract any potential abandonment of the initiative at an early stage.

Reaching the very poor and marginalized is thus a great challenge, and may require a different approach in different contexts. However, what we have sketched above are some general principles that can be adopted in various contexts and situations. Targeting and reaching the very poor is both an ambitious and time-consuming process, and one that needs the appropriate recognition and incentive. Rather than downgrading investments in the poorest of the poor to a 'non-profitable' undertaking, more credit should be paid to those organizations and groups that do manage to effectively reach and engage with the very poor, and make a difference.

Notes

1. The name of the local agency is not stated here for reason of confidentiality. The outcomes of this study are being used at the moment, together with the study findings from Ethiopia and Bangladesh, to distil lessons learnt, and translate findings into concrete measures for improving the organization and its outreach.
2. This is an estimation of the municipality of Nikki. The last census was conducted in 2001.
3. Percentages provided by the statistical department of Nikki municipality.
4. The participants were asked to describe their lives from their childhood until the time of the workshop. There was an emphasis on emotions, and how they felt at certain events in their lives, to capture the cognitive component. Moreover, certain items such as hopes and dreams, support systems, and solutions were discussed. The participants were also asked to describe a 'normal' day for them in the rainy and dry seasons.
5. These numbers were provided by the mayor's office in Nikki.
6. These numbers were provided by the mayor's office in Nikki.
7. The different workshops consisted of old men (above 40), young men, old women, young women, NGO men beneficiaries, and NGO women beneficiaries. Several PADev exercises were conducted during these workshops; amongst them were the events, changes, wealth group categorization, project recall, and best/worst projects exercises.
8. The majority of the workshop participants belonged to the average and poor wealth groupings, as defined locally. There were some rich, none very rich, and very few very poor who were specifically asked to be invited.

References

ACET (2014) *2014 African Transformation Report: Growth With Depth*. African Centre for Economic Transformation, Accra.

Alkire, S. (2002) *Valuing Freedoms: Sen's Capability Approach and Poverty Reduction*. Oxford University Press, Oxford.

Baulch, B. and Hoddinott, J. (2000) *Economic Mobility and Poverty Dynamics in Developing Countries*. Frank Cass Publishers, London.

Collard, D. (2003) 'Research on well-being: Some advice from Jeremy Bentham', *WeD Working Paper No. 2*. Wellbeing in Developing Countries ESRC Research Group, Bath <http://dx.doi.org/10.1177/0048393106289795>.

Dasgupta, P. (1993) *An Inquiry into Well-Being and Destitution*. Clarendon Press, Oxford.

Dietz, T. (2012) 'Participatory assessment of development in Africa', in N.R.M. Pouw and I.S.A. Baud (eds), *Local Governance and Poverty in Developing Nations*, pp. 215–39. Routledge, New York, NY.

Dietz, T., Bymolt, R., Bélemvire, A., van der Geest, K., de Groot, D., Millar, D., Obeng, F., Pouw, N., Rijneveld, W. and Zaal, F. (2012) *PADev Guidebook*. KIT Publishers & ASC Leiden, Amsterdam/Leiden.

Dietz, T. and the PADev Team (2013) *The PADev Story: End of the Project Report.* ASC Leiden, Leiden.

Doyal, L. and Gough, I. (1991) *A Theory of Human Need.* Palgrave Macmillan, London. <http://dx.doi.org/10.1016/0016-3287(92)90123-w>.

du Toit, A. and Hickey, S. (2013) 'Adverse incorporation, social exclusion, and chronic poverty', in A. Shepherd and J. Brunt (eds), *Chronic Poverty: Concepts, Causes and Policy, pp. 134–59.* Palgrave Macmillan, Basingstoke. <http://dx.doi.org/10.1057/9781137316707.0012>.

Ferguson, J. (1990) *The Anti-Politics Machine: 'Development', Depoliticization and Bureaucratic Power in Lesotho.* Cambridge University Press, Cambridge.

Gasper, D. (2004) 'Human well-being: Concepts and conceptualizations', *UNU/WIDER Discussion Paper No. 2004/006.* United Nations University-World Institute for Development Economics Research, Helsinki.

Gough, I. and McGregor, J.A. (2007) *Wellbeing in Developing Countries. From Theory to Research.* Cambridge University Press, Cambridge. <http://dx.doi.org/10.1017/CBO9780511488986>.

Harriss-White, B. (2006) 'Poverty and capitalism', *Economic and Political Weekly* 41(13): 1–7.

Hulme, D. and Moore, K. (2008) 'Assisting the poorest in Bangladesh: Learning from BRAC's targeting the ultra-Poor project in Bangladesh', in A. Barrientos and D. Hulme (eds), *Social Protection for the Poor and Poorest: Concepts, Policies and Politics*, pp. 194–210. Palgrave Macmillan, London. <http://dx.doi.org/10.1057/9780230583092>.

International Monetary Fund (2011) *Benin: Poverty Reduction Strategy Paper*, Washington: International Monetary Fund Publication Services <http://dx.doi.org/10.5089/9781463922573.002>.

Kabeer, N. (1996) 'Agency, well-being and inequality: Reflections on the gender dimensions of poverty', *IDS Bulletin* 27(1): 11–22 <http://dx.doi.org/10.1111/j.1759-5436.1996.mp27001002.x>.

Kazimierczuk, A. (2010) '*Gbangbu follow-up workshop report: Inclusion of the poor', PADev Working Paper W.2010.2.* The Amsterdam Institute for Social Science Research, Amsterdam.

Krishna, A. (2004) 'Escaping poverty and becoming poor: Who gains, who loses, and why?', *World Development* 32(1): 121–36 <http://dx.doi.org/10.1016/j.worlddev.2003.08.002>.

Krishna, A. (2010) *One Way Illness: How People Become Poor and How They Escape Poverty.* Oxford University Press, New York, NY. <http://dx.doi.org/10.1093/acprof:osobl/9780199584512.001.0001>.

Lawson, D., Hulme, D., Matin, I. and Moore, K. (eds) (2011) *What Works for the Poorest? Poverty Reduction Programmes for the World's Extreme Poor.* Practical Action Publishing, Rugby. <http://dx.doi.org/10.3362/9781780440439>.

McGregor, J.A. (2004) 'Researching well-being: Communicating between the needs of policy makers and the needs of people', *Global Social Policy* 4(3): 337–58 <http://dx.doi.org/10.1177/1468018104047491>.

Mosley, P. (2012) *The Politics of Poverty Reduction.* Oxford University Press, Oxford.

Mosse, D. (2010) 'A relational approach to durable poverty, inequality and power', *Journal of Development Studies* 46(7): 1156–78 <http://dx.doi.org/10.1080/00220388.2010.487095>.

Narayan, D., Patel, R., Schafft, K., Rademacher, A. and Koch-Schulte, S. (2000a) *Can Anyone Hear Us? Voices of the Poor*. Oxford University Press for the World Bank, New York, NY. <http://dx.doi.org/10.1596/0-1952-1601-6>.

Narayan, D., Chambers, R., Shah, M.K. and Petesch, P. (2000b) *Crying Out for Change: Voices of the Poor*. Oxford University Press for the World Bank, New York, NY. <http://dx.doi.org/10.1596/0-1952-1602-4>.

Pouw, N.R.M. and Janvier, K. (2014) 'Missing the very poor with development interventions: Results from the PADev methodology in Burkina Faso', *ASC Infosheet No. 19*. African Studies Centre, Leiden.

Pouw, N., Dietz, T., Bélemvire, A., de Groot, D., Millar, D., Obeng, F., Rijneveld, W., Van der Geest, K., Vlaminck, Z. and Zaal, F. (2016) 'Participatory assessment of development interventions: Lessons learned from a new evaluation methodology in Ghana and Burkina Faso', *American Journal of Evaluation*, 12 April 2016: 1–13. <http://dx.doi.org/10.1177/1098214016641210>.

Sen, A. (1999) *Development as Freedom*. Oxford University Press, Oxford.

UNA-UK (2012) *Global Development Goals. Leaving No One Behind*. World Bank, Washington, DC.

UNCTAD (2014) *Economic Development in Africa Report 2014. Catalyzing Investment for Transformative Growth in Africa*. United Nations, Geneva. <http://dx.doi.org/10.18356/21a553ce-en>.

UNDP (2014) *Human Development Report 2014: Sustaining Human Progress: Reducing Vulnerabilities and Building Resilience*. UNDP, New York, NY. <http://dx.doi.org/10.18356/34bf7a52-en>.

United Nations (2012) *Post-2015 UN Development Framework*, UN Conference. United Nations, New York, NY.

United Nations (2013) *The Role of Philanthropic Organizations in the Post-2015 Setting*, UN Workshop. United Nations, New York, NY.

Woord & Daad (2013) *People: Annual Report 2013*. Woord & Daad, Gorinchem.

About the authors

Anika Altaf is a PhD fellow at the Governance and Inclusive Development programme at the Amsterdam Institute of Social Science Research at the University of Amsterdam, and the African Studies Centre of the University of Leiden. She is currently completing her PhD research on targeting the ultra-poor in poverty-alleviation initiatives. Field research was carried out in Bangladesh, Benin, and Ethiopia.

Nicky Pouw is a development economist and assistant professor at the Governance and Inclusive Development programme at the Amsterdam Institute of Social Science Research at the University of Amsterdam. She is project leader of two NWO–WOTRO research projects: 'Women Food-Entrepreneurship in Kenya and Burkina Faso', and 'Breaking the Vicious Circle between Poverty and Ill-Health in Ghana and Kenya'. Her research interests include the poorest of the poor, inclusive development, gender and economic growth, and the economics of well-being.

CHAPTER 3

Towards inclusive targeting: The Zimbabwe Harmonized Social Cash Transfer (HSCT) programme

Bernd Schubert

How can a low-income country like Zimbabwe focus social transfers on its poorest, most vulnerable and most excluded citizens? In operational terms the Zimbabwe Harmonized Social Cash Transfer Programme (HSCT) defines extreme poverty as living below the food poverty line. It defines households as socially and economically vulnerable, when they have no or insufficient work capacity or manpower. HSCT classifies these households as labour constrained. Households that live in extreme poverty and are at the same time labour constrained are excluded from meeting their most basic needs in terms nutrition, basic health care, education and shelter and from earning a livelihood through productive work. This category of households forms the target group of HSCT.

The HSCT targeting and verification mechanism resulting from the three year learning process is designed to avoid elite capture while at the same time making full use of the community's local information and willingness to participate. Targeting is done by a census approach implemented by the Department of Social Services (DSS) in cooperation with the national statistics office. The census identifies the demographic structure and the poverty status of all households in the programme area using a Proxy Means Test (PMT). The poverty scores of the PMT are aligned to the poverty indicators used in the Zimbabwe national household survey.

Keywords: systemic social protection, life-cycle approach, labour-constrained, social cash transfers, targeting mechanisms, verification systems

Introduction

This chapter describes the first three years of a learning process aimed at achieving a sustainable government-owned, fully inclusive, social cash transfer programme in Zimbabwe. Inclusive social protection gives priority to reaching the poorest, most disadvantaged, and most vulnerable persons and households with transfers and basic social services that, together, significantly reduce their poverty and vulnerability, while empowering them to live a dignified life. In short, a cash transfer programme is inclusive if it targets the most excluded.

http://dx.doi.org/10.3362/9781780448435.003

The literature on targeting is preoccupied with the question of how to identify and reach the poorest persons or households in a specific region (e.g. Alviar et al., 2010; Grosh, 1997). A number of authors emphasize that targeting has to take the heterogeneity of poverty into account. In order to ensure that the poorest and most needy persons or households are not bypassed, they disaggregate the poor according to the degree of their poverty into different categories, e.g. moderate poverty and extreme poverty (Sen and Begum, 2010).

Policymakers and social protection experts in low-income countries like Zimbabwe have opted for a further disaggregation of target groups for their social protection interventions. Their unconditional social cash transfer programmes do not target all extremely poor households, but only those that, in addition to being extremely poor, also suffer from severe social and economic vulnerability. These are households that consist mainly, or exclusively, of elderly persons, disabled or chronically ill persons, widows, a large number of orphans, and other vulnerable children with no able-bodied adult household members, who are fit for productive work, or households with a very high dependency ratio. In Zimbabwe, the Harmonized Social Cash Transfer (HSCT) programme classifies these households as labour-constrained.

There are three reasons that countries such as Zimbabwe, Zambia, Malawi, Liberia, and Ethiopia focus their unconditional social cash transfers on extremely poor and, at the same time, labour-constrained households:

- By definition, low-income countries have a large number of extremely poor people and a small GDP. They find it difficult to provide social assistance to all extremely poor citizens. They therefore restrict unconditional cash transfers to those households that are not only extremely poor, but are also unable to fend for themselves or to benefit from labour-based programmes because they have no breadwinners.
- Low-income countries also suffer from weak institutional capacities. They find it easier to reach their most needy citizens through one inclusive programme compared to establishing categorical programmes for each vulnerable population group, such as orphans and vulnerable children, the elderly, disabled, HIV/AIDS-affected, etc.
- For extremely poor households that are labour-endowed, these countries offer programmes like Public Works (e.g. Food or Cash-for-Work) and livelihood programmes.

In summary, the targeting mechanisms of these countries have to go beyond poverty targeting. They have to identify the poorest households and, in addition, which of the poorest households are labour-constrained and which are labour-endowed.

To accomplish this task the Zimbabwe HSCT targeting and verification mechanism, resulting from a three-year learning process, is designed to avoid elite capture, while at the same time making full use of the community's local information and willingness to participate. Targeting is done by a census approach implemented by the Department of Social Services (DSS) in cooperation with the national statistics office (ZIMSTAT).

The census identifies the demographic structure and the poverty status of all households in the programme area using a proxy means test (PMT). The poverty scores of the PMT are aligned to the poverty indicators used in the PICES (Poverty, Income, Consumption, Expenditure Survey) national household survey.

The DSS's management information system (MIS) is used to process the social and demographic household data collected through the census, resulting in a preliminary list of households that meet the eligibility criteria. In a second step, community committees verify if households are left out and/or are wrongly classified. Based on the verification results, households are finally approved and registered. A full retargeting is implemented every second year.

The next section deals with the rationale behind the HSCT target group definition. It analyses to what extent this target group definition has contributed to reaching the poorest and most vulnerable population groups in Zimbabwe. The following sections document the three-year learning process to develop an effective targeting mechanism, while also describing the result of this process, i.e. the current HSCT targeting mechanism, before offering some conclusions and recommendations.

The HSCT target group

The poverty and vulnerability analysis leading to the definition of the HSCT target group

In early 2010 the DSS, in the Ministry of Public Services, Labour, and Social Welfare (MPSLSW), commissioned a study entitled *Child-Sensitive Social Protection in Zimbabwe* (Schubert, 2010). Based on all available documents on social protection needs and social protection interventions in Zimbabwe, and on discussions with a wide range of stakeholders, the study concluded that household poverty, combined with limited access to basic social services, is the main driver of vulnerabilities such as hunger, malnutrition, morbidity, child mortality, education deficits, early marriage, and risky coping strategies. Heads of extremely poor households are unable to care for the social protection needs of their household members, and especially the needs of the most vulnerable members like children, elderly persons, and persons living with disabilities or suffering from chronic illness.

Poverty in Zimbabwe is widespread and heterogeneous. In order to identify the most excluded categories of households, those that most urgently need social protection interventions, the study conducted a poverty and vulnerability analysis. Data from the most recent national household survey indicate that 16 per cent of all households in Zimbabwe live below the food poverty line (FPL), with a wide variation between urban areas (4 per cent food poverty prevalence) and rural areas (23 per cent food poverty prevalence).[1] According to the same household survey, 24 per cent of all households in Zimbabwe are labour-constrained (11 per cent in urban areas, and 27 per cent in rural areas). Six per cent of all households are food poor and, at the

Consumption
per person

Total consumption
poverty line: 63%

900,000	400,000
A	B

Food poverty line: 16%

C	D
300,000	200,000

Dependency ratio

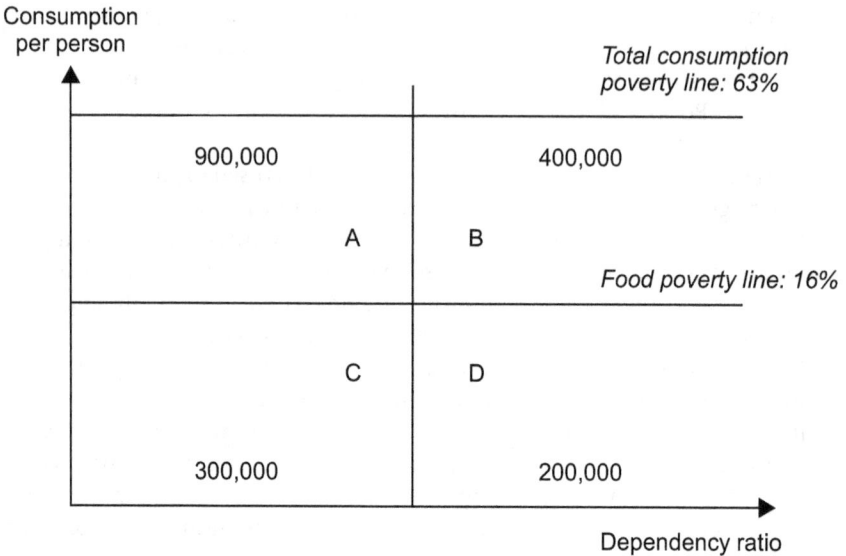

Figure 3.1 Households in Zimbabwe suffering from different categories of poverty (adapted from Schubert, 2010)

same time, labour-constrained (1 per cent in urban areas, and 7.5 per cent in rural areas). Figure 3.1 combines the data listed above into a poverty profile for Zimbabwe, and provides an analysis of the poverty dynamics among different categories of people in Zimbabwe.

From Figure 3.1 it is evident that, of the 3 million households in Zimbabwe, about 1.1 million (37 per cent) live above the total consumption poverty line (TCPL) – they are not poor; 1.4 million (47 per cent) live below the TCPL but above the food poverty line (FPL) – they are moderately poor; 500,000 households (16 per cent) live below the FPL – they are the poorest of the poor.

Figure 3.1 further distinguishes between labour-endowed households (those with a dependency ratio of 3 or lower) and labour-constrained households (those with no fit adult, or with a dependency ratio of more than 3). This results in four different categories of poverty:

1. Category A: labour-endowed, but moderately poor. The 900,000 households in category A are in a relatively favourable situation. They are just moderately poor, and include household members able to perform productive work. They are able to respond to self-help-oriented projects and programmes in order to overcome their poverty.
2. Category B: labour-constrained, and moderately poor. The 400,000 category B households are moderately poor, but because they are labour-constrained they are unable to respond to labour-based interventions. Households headed by a pensioner who receives a small pension, or households regularly supported by remittances, are typical for this group.

3. Category C: labour-endowed, and food poor. The 300,000 category C households suffer from extreme poverty despite the fact that they have household members able to perform productive work. Many small-scale farmers or former farmworkers fall into this category. To improve the economic situation of these households they have to be targeted by programmes that are specifically tailored to the needs of extremely poor but viable households.

4. Category D: labour-constrained, and food poor. The 200,000 households in category D are in the most unfavourable situation. They suffer from extreme poverty and hunger. At the same time, they cannot respond to development projects or programmes, or benefit from Public Works, because they do not have any, or have too few, household members able to perform productive work. They do not have any, or have little, self-help capacity. This group – the 6 per cent worst-off households in Zimbabwe – most urgently requires social protection interventions. Of category D households, 170,000 live in rural areas.

A review of ongoing social protection interventions revealed that category D households are bypassed by labour-based interventions because they lack capacity to work, and that only a few category D households are benefiting from any kind of social assistance. Government and NGOs implement categorical social assistance programmes for individual vulnerable persons, like orphans and other vulnerable children, the elderly, and the disabled. But these programmes are fragmented, cover only a small part of the population in need of social protection, lack coordination, and achieve little impact.[2] Only in times of emergencies, such as droughts and floods, do category D households, together with other poor households, receive temporary transfers, and mostly in kind (Schubert, 2010).

Hence, the 200,000 households that live below the FPL (extremely poor), and are at the same time labour-constrained (no or little self-help capacity), are the most excluded households in Zimbabwe, and most urgently require social protection interventions. At the same time, category D households have a higher percentage of children and of orphans compared to all other categories of households. Many of the category D households are generation-gap households headed by grandparents who care for HIV/AIDS orphans. The 2010 study on *Child-Sensitive Social Protection* therefore recommended giving priority to assisting all category D households with social assistance, and with access to basic social services. This recommendation formed the rationale for designing the HSCT programme.

The 300,000 category C households also live below the FPL, and also care for a high number of children. They need to be empowered to make more productive use of their work capacity. The study recommended targeting category C households with labour-based interventions, and to simultaneously improve their access to basic social services.

In summary, the review of social protection in Zimbabwe concluded that inclusive social protection policy should lift all the 500,000 food-poor households above the FPL. To achieve this objective, the 300,000 category C households should be provided with access to labour-based social protection interventions. The 200,000 category C households require social assistance. All food-poor households need access to basic social services. A second social protection objective is to protect moderately poor households from falling below the FPL. By ensuring that different categories of poor and vulnerable households are provided with social protection interventions that are tailored to their specific needs, Zimbabwe has established a systemic social protection approach.

The systemic approach described above has also been used for designing social protection policies and social cash transfer programmes in Zambia, Malawi, Ethiopia, and Liberia (Schubert, 2008).

An analysis of HSCT beneficiary households reached in the first 13 districts

After HSCT had been rolled out to the first, predominantly rural, 13 districts, the programme's MIS provided data on the profile of beneficiary households, and household members. The data show to what extent HSCT reaches the neediest and most excluded sectors of the population of Zimbabwe.

HSCT has approved 10 per cent of all the households living in the programme area. Because the prevalence of eligible households is much higher in rural areas compared to urban areas, the percentage of approved households exceeds the average percentage of 6 per cent classified as food poor and labour-constrained in Figure 3.1.

Table 3.1 shows that 64 per cent of beneficiary households are managed by the elderly, 63 per cent are female-headed, while 82 per cent of the beneficiary households care for children. In fact, most are generation-gap households headed by grandmothers, who are caring for orphans or other vulnerable children.

Table 3.2 shows that only 17 per cent of HSCT beneficiary household members are fit adults of working age, most of whom are single mothers – predominantly widows – caring for a large number of children. Thus, their dependency ratio is such that their households are considered labour-constrained. All other members of beneficiary households belong to the so-called 'vulnerable groups', like children, elderly persons, persons living with disabilities, or persons who are chronically ill.

Table 3.3 shows that HSCT households have a higher percentage of female-headed households compared to the national average. The percentages of elderly people, children, and orphans are also much higher compared with the national averages.

In summary, Tables 3.1, 3.2, and 3.3 show that, by targeting food-poor labour-constrained households, HSCT implements a life-cycle approach. The programme aims at reaching all children, including a high number of orphans, all elderly people, all disabled people, as well as all chronically ill, who live in households that are unable to care for them because of a combination of extreme poverty and lack of labour capacity.

Table 3.1 Profile of HSCT beneficiary households, June 2013

	Households living in 13 HSCT districts	HSCT beneficiary households	Elderly headed	Female headed	Child headed	Households with children
Rural households	256,554	30,894	19,777	19,699	776	25,516
Rural hhs (%)	82	12	64	64	3	83
Urban households	58,211	1,697	1,044	828	81	1,335
Urban hhs (%)	18	3	62	49	5	79
Total	314,765	32,591	20,821	20,527	857	26,851
Total (%)	100	10	64	63	3	82

Source: Compiled from HSCT statistics

Table 3.2 Members of HSCT beneficiary households, June 2013

Total number of HSCT household members	152,016	100%
Children (0–18) in HSCT households	97,166	64%
Orphans in HSCT households	35,544	35% of all children
Women of working age (19–59)	18,323	12%
Men of working age (19–59)	8,181	5%
Elderly persons (60+)	27,951	18%
Disabled or chronically ill	19,570	13%

Source: Compiled from HSCT statistics

Table 3.3 Comparison of general national demographic parameters (Demographic and Health Survey, 2010–11) with HSCT beneficiary households

Parameters		Rural	Urban	Total
Households headed by women (in % of all households)	HSCT households	64	49	64
	All households DHS 2010–11	44.1	45.3	44.6
Household members:				
Percentage of elderly (60+)	HSCT households	19	15	18
	All households DHS 2010–11	8	4	6.5
Percentage of children 0–18	HSCT households	64	61	64
Percentage of children 0–19	All households DHS 2010–11	56	45	53
Orphans as % of all children	HSCT households	36	35	36
	All households DHS 2010–11	22	18	21

Source: Compiled from HSCT statistics, and from the ZIMSTAT Demographic and Health Survey 2010–11 (ZIMSTAT, 2013a)

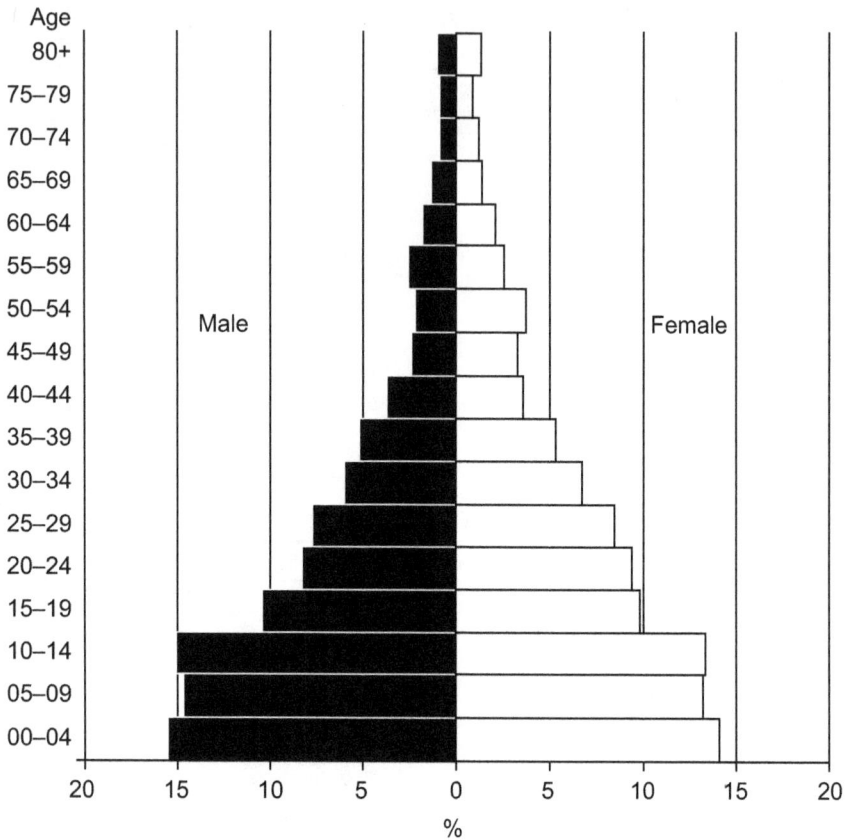

Figure 3.2 Age and sex structure of the general population of Zimbabwe (ZIMSTAT, 2013a)

This is confirmed by a comparison between the age and sex structure of the general population of Zimbabwe (Figure 3.2), and the age and sex structure of the members of HSCT beneficiary households (Figure 3.3). The age structure of the general population forms a pyramid with a broad base that progressively gets smaller at the top, while HSCT households are generation-gap households that consist nearly exclusively of children and elderly people. The few adults aged 19 to 59 are mostly female, and predominantly disabled or chronically ill.

Designing and progressively improving the HSCT targeting mechanism – a learning process

Lessons learnt from ongoing targeting activities in Zimbabwe

Targeting is the method that ensures the proper selection of the beneficiaries of a programme. In the case of HSCT it is the method to select labour-constrained food-poor households (for a classification of different targeting mechanisms see Alviar et al., 2010). As part of the preparation for designing the targeting

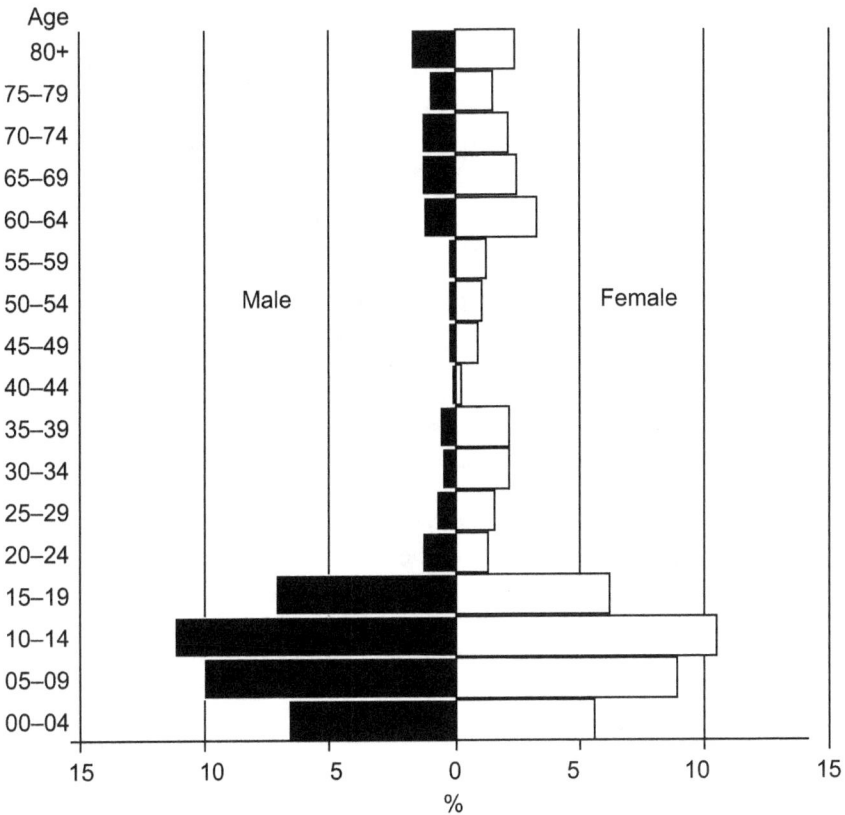

Figure 3.3 Age and sex structure of HSCT beneficiaries in 13 districts (June 2013)

method, and other features of HSCT, Zimbabwe's DSS, in cooperation with UNICEF, commissioned a study into the lessons learnt from ongoing social protection programmes in the country (MPSLSW, 2010). The study researched target groups, targeting criteria and methods, volume and frequency of transfers, delivery mechanisms, cost effectiveness, and also the concerns, risks, and challenges faced by government and NGO social protection programmes.

The three existing government social assistance programmes for extremely poor disabled persons, elderly persons, and destitute households use a categorical approach combined with a simple means test. In detail, this process works as follows.

An applicant must travel to their district social welfare office to fill in an application form, and provide a copy of their identity card, as well as a letter from their ward councillor confirming their residence. The welfare officer concerned is required to verify the information provided by the applicant. This is usually done at the district office itself, as verification through household visits is typically not possible due to a lack of transport. Once verification is completed, applications are forwarded to a provincial office for approval, and then passed to national level for registration.

This procedure is a difficult and costly one for the target group. Many eligible persons do not know how to apply, do not have the money to pay for transport to the district welfare office, or do not have an identity card. It is also cumbersome for the welfare officers, and is one of the reasons why, in 2010, the three programmes had only 11,655 beneficiaries in total. This mechanism is therefore unsuitable for a programme that aims to reach 200,000 eligible households.

Nearly all NGO food and cash transfer programmes employ a variety of tools for community-based targeting, such as community meetings for awareness raising, community committees, poverty mapping on a village level, and wealth-ranking exercises. The NGOs also verify the resultant lists generated through such methods by organizing household visits, and by establishing help desks to respond to complaints by community members who are dissatisfied with the results of the targeting process.

In summary, most NGO programmes are designed to ensure that participation and community ownership, complemented by verification exercises, are used in every possible manner so as to maximize transparency, and minimize inclusion and exclusion errors. Due to the high number of community visits by NGO officers necessary to organize and implement all the activities outlined above, the costs of these mechanisms amounted to, on average, 15 to 20 per cent of total annual programme costs.

Unfortunately, nearly all available evaluations and appraisals of community-based targeting in Zimbabwe indicate that the results of community-based targeting are far from satisfactory. It appears that shifting the responsibility of targeting to the community not only leads to high exclusion and inclusion errors, but also creates conflicts within the communities themselves.[3] During interviews with NGO personnel a community member was quoted as stating: 'You make us hate each other!' (Roman, 2010). The Zimbabwe experience is consistent with the more general observation that community-based targeting is open to nepotism and elite capture, while often eroding cohesion and breeding animosity within communities (Hanlon ct al., 2010).

The study on lessons learnt (MPSLSW, 2010) concluded that neither the ongoing DSS targeting mechanism nor the expensive, and at the same time ineffective, NGO mechanisms were appropriate for the HSCT programme. It therefore recommended designing and testing an alternative targeting approach, which is described below.

Most targeting mechanisms aim at selecting persons or households that meet one single criterion: poverty, as defined, for example, via absolute poverty, or food poverty, or being in the poorest quintile. Households eligible for the HSCT programme have to be food poor, but being that HSCT does not target all 500,000 food-poor households present in Zimbabwe, only those that are both food poor and at the same time labour-constrained are considered. This means that the HSCT targeting mechanism has to identify households that simultaneously meet two criteria. In order to properly select extremely poor labour-constrained households, the mechanism to be designed had to both accommodate the lesson learnt from ongoing programmes, and meet the following expectations:

- It had to be feasible within the limited implementation capacities of DSS at district, provincial, and central level;
- The percentage of approved households per district should be in line with the percentages of labour-constrained, food poor households identified by the national household survey (ZIMSTAT, 2013a);
- Inclusion and exclusion errors should be below 20 per cent;
- Costs of targeting should be below 10 per cent of total programme costs.

Designing and testing of a two-stage targeting mechanism

To meet these expectations, a two-stage census approach was managed via the DSS's MIS. Actual data collection, i.e. the census, was outsourced to a private service provider. This approach was operationalized by drafting a Manual of Operations (MPSLSW, 2013), and MIS Guidelines (MPSLSW, 2011b), which was subsequently tested in one ward of Goromonzi District (MPSLSW, 2013; Schubert, 2012).[4]

The first census stage looked to identify the demographic structure of all households living in the ward, and those households, considered labour-constrained, were then identified from the resultant data. The second stage saw all labour-constrained households interviewed for a second time. This second interview was designed to verify if the households classified as labour-constrained were indeed labour-constrained, as well as ascertaining the poverty status of the households via PMT.[5] Based on the second interview data, the labour-constrained households deemed extremely poor were finally identified. Households that met both criteria were subsequently approved.

The report on the test run drew a number of conclusions, not least of which was that the targeting mechanism is feasible and effective (MPSLSW, 2011a). Evident also was that the instrument resulted in low inclusion and exclusion errors, and has been accepted by the community. Moreover, the DSS's MIS had proved effective in assisting the targeting, approval, and payment process. The outsourcing of targeting and delivery to private service providers supervised by DSS officers was feasible and effective. It avoided the complications experienced in community targeting, and prevented DSS officers from getting involved in community politics. Child Protection Committees (CPCs) and headmen played an important and very positive role in the process. They informed programme beneficiaries, distributed beneficiary cards, and assisted beneficiaries in attending the pay day. The report also concluded that in order to be prepared for scaling up, the DSS district and ward level structures have to be strengthened, taking into account the fact that the HSCT programme involves a substantial additional workload.

Assessment of the 'rollout' to the first 10 districts

Based on the positive assessment of the test run, the MPSLSW decided to use the two-stage targeting approach for rolling out the HSCT in the first 10 of the 65 districts in Zimbabwe. The districts were selected by identifying the poorest district in each of the 10 provinces. After improving the operations manual as well as the MIS guidelines, and drafting a 'design report' that included a medium-term cost analysis and rollout plan, targeting and delivery of the transfers were tendered out.

A consortium consisting of a private sector company and ZIMSTAT won the tender. From October 2011 to January 2012 the consortium, in cooperation with UNICEF officers, implemented the two-stage census process supervised by DSS officers at national, provincial, and district level. By April 2012 the DSS's MIS had processed the census data, and approved households in the first 10 districts started to receive regular and predictable transfer payments.

The process and the results of targeting the first 10 districts have been thoroughly assessed. In summary, the assessment report concludes:

> The four factors that caused most of the challenges faced in the targeting and approval process were (1) the decision to conduct the targeting process simultaneously in all 10 districts with an army of about 500 enumerators, supervisors, and data input clerks. (2) To work under extreme time pressure. Reading through the reports on field visits by DSS and UNICEF officers it seems that most stakeholders involved in the targeting process were overwhelmed by the tasks they had to face and suffered from the stress they experienced. (3) DSS officers feel that not enough budgetary support was provided to the exercise. (4) Capacity at district level, as pronounced in the Manual of Operations, should have been strengthened before rolling out the programme (Schubert, 2012: 14).

Assessment of the rollout to the first three districts of phase two

The wealth of experience and lessons learnt from phase one was used to make substantial changes in the targeting mechanism for phase two (i.e. the next 10 districts):

- Instead of rolling out to 10 districts simultaneously, the rollout was staggered in a sequence of 3-3-4, with a month in between in order to assess, and further improve, the mechanism once a group of districts had been covered.
- Instead of conducting the census in two steps it was decided to collect a full set of demographic and socio-economic data from all households living in the respective districts in one single interview. This avoided having to visit households twice. It also ensured the MIS could produce a national household register that could be used not only for HSCT targeting, but also for other social protection programmes.

- To avoid communication and coordination problems experienced by using a consortium, and to reduce cost, the census was conducted by ZIMSTAT.
- A verification system was introduced that consisted of: 1) meetings with ward-level CPCs to check if any households had been missed out by the enumerators; and 2) randomized verification surveys of 10 households per ward that had been classified by the MIS as eligible, and 10 households that had been classified as ineligible.

After covering the first three districts during the period April to June 2013, the process and results of the targeting were again assessed. Based on the results of the verification activities, the assessment report concluded that, compared with phase one, the quality of targeting in terms of reducing inclusion and exclusion errors had improved (Schubert, 2013). At the same time, targeting costs were significantly lower, with a decrease from 6.5 per cent to 3.7 per cent of total programme costs, mainly due to shifting from two household visits to only one.

Lessons learned from external evaluations

HSCT is jointly funded by the Government of Zimbabwe and the multi-donor Child Protection Fund (CPF). From May to August 2013 the CPF underwent a mid-term review that included an evaluation of the HSCT programme (Ashley et al., 2013). The consultants gave HSCT an A+ score (moderately exceeding expectations), following the DFID guidance on project scoring. With regard to the HSCT targeting mechanism, they based their assessment on the preliminary results of the baseline report of an evaluation conducted by a consortium under the leadership of the American Institutes for Research (2013).

Both reports contain useful recommendations. They correctly observe that the verification process conducted by DSS district officers only verifies that the targeting methodology, as specified in the Manual of Operations, has been implemented correctly, but not if the methodology is appropriate. They recommend that the PMT should to be scrutinized to ensure that it correctly measures the degree of poverty. Both reports also state that HSCT needs a grievances system and community feedback loops.

The improved HSCT targeting mechanism resulting from the three-year learning process

The HSCT targeting and verification mechanism resulting from the three-year learning process was designed to avoid elite capture, while at the same time making full use of a community's local information and willingness to participate (see Figure 3.4). Targeting was done by a census approach, implemented by DSS, in cooperation with ZIMSTAT. The census identified the demographic structure and the poverty status of all households in the programme area using

1. Enumerators collect demo-graphic and socio-economic data from all households and fill in Form 1

2. Targeting agent ensures that data from Forms 1 are cleaned and transferred to MIS data bank

3. MIS unit processes census data and sends preliminary beneficiary list (Form 3.1) to DSSOs for verification by CPCs and runs exception reports to identify targeting errors

4. DSSOs visit households to verify inclusion and exclusion errors identified by CPCs and send results (Form 13) to programme manager

5. Programme manager instructs targeting agent to follow up on verification results and to provide improved data set to MIS unit

6. Based on improved data set from targeting agent programme manager approves eligible households (Form 3.2)

7. Programme manager prints beneficiary cards and transfers funds & payment schedule (Form 6) to delivery agent

8.DSSO gives beneficiary cards and information on venue and date of first payments to CPCs

10. DSSO and delivery agent organize launch and payment process and complaints desk

9.CPCs inform beneficiaries on approval and on first pay day

11. Beneficiaries access bi-monthly transfers monitored by external consultants

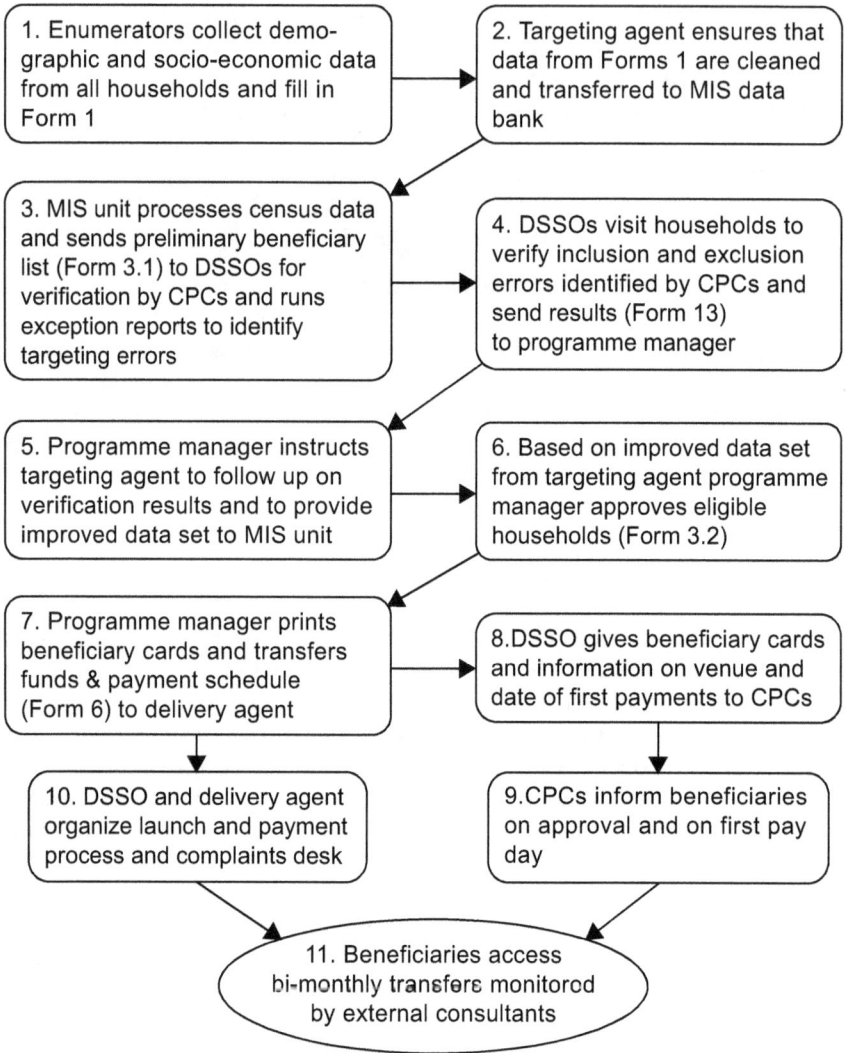

Figure 3.4 Flow chart of the HSCT targeting, verification, approval, registration, and payment process

a PMT. The poverty scores of the PMT were aligned to the poverty indicators used in the national household survey (ZIMSTAT, 2013a).

The DSS's MIS was used to process the social and demographic household data collected through the census resulting in a preliminary list of households that met the eligibility criteria. Following this, community committees verify if the preliminary household lists are complete, and if the classification of households, vis-à-vis their eligibility, is correct. Households that have been missed out, according to the community, are revisited by ZIMSTAT to integrate their data into the MIS. Households that are identified as incorrectly classified by the community are subsequently visited by a district social services officer (DSSO) in order to reassess their eligibility.

Based on this assessment, the preliminary list of eligible households is corrected and eventually used for the approval of all households that are food poor and at the same time labour-constrained.

The census-based targeting and verification approach described above accounts for 55 per cent of HSCT operational costs (Schubert et al., 2014). However, it is important to note that the census results are not only used for HSCT targeting and retargeting (conducted every two years), but the results will be incorporated into a national household register to be used in the future by other government and non-government programmes with respect to cooperation, harmonization, and targeting. These programmes will share the census costs, leading to a substantial reduction of HSCT operational costs.

Conclusions and recommendations

The analysis of the demographic structure of HSCT beneficiary households (Tables 3.1, 3.2, and 3.3 and Figures 3.2 and 3.3) shows that the programme is inclusive in the sense that it reaches members of all vulnerable groups. This includes children, the elderly, disabled persons, and the chronically ill who live in households that are unable to care for them due to the household being extremely poor while, at the same time, labour-constrained. This confirms what has already been learned from similar social cash transfer programmes in Zambia, Malawi, Liberia, and Ethiopia, that a low-income country does not necessarily need to establish separate categorical social assistance programmes for each of its vulnerable groups, which may in fact be beyond its financial and institutional capacity. Targeting extremely poor, labour-constrained households is an approach that can focus social assistance on those vulnerable groups that suffer from a double vulnerability: they are vulnerable as a result of their status, i.e. child, orphan, elderly, and they live in a socio-economically vulnerable household.

With regard to the mechanism used to target households that are simultaneously extremely poor and labour-constrained, the analysis reveals that different countries are using different approaches. Zambia and Malawi (Schubert, 2005) as well as Ethiopia (Ministry of Agriculture, 2015) are successfully using community targeting. Liberia and Zimbabwe, due to their previous experience with community targeting being negative, have established a census approach combined with community verification (Schubert, 2013). All of these countries used a systematic trial and error approach, combined with internal and external evaluations, to develop their targeting mechanisms and are satisfied with the cost-effectiveness achieved.

It may be concluded that the main factor for successfully establishing an effective and inclusive targeting system in a low-income country is first and foremost to ensure an appropriate definition of the target group.

The process to develop the targeting mechanism to reach the target group chosen should take previous experience from other programmes into account, and use a systematic and well-documented trial and error approach that leads to continuous improvements of the targeting effectiveness. This process may take a number of years.

Notes

1. Poverty data given in this paper are based on the Zimbabwe Poverty, Income, Consumption, and Expenditure Survey 2010/11 (ZIMSTAT, 2013b). The FPL represents the minimum consumption expenditure necessary (if all expenditures were devoted to food) to ensure that each household member can consume a minimum food basket representing 2,100 calories.
2. In 2010 the different Government Public Assistance Programmes reached the following number of people: maintenance of disabled persons 3,510; maintenance of elderly persons 4,015; and destitute households including child-headed households 4,140. The total of 11,655 represented coverage of 5.8 per cent of the 200,000 extremely poor labour-constrained households that urgently required social protection interventions.
3. Exclusion errors are usually expressed as the percentage of households or persons that meet the targeting criteria but are not approved by the respective programme. Inclusion errors are expressed as the percentage of households or persons that have been approved but do not meet the eligibility criteria.
4. The original Manual of Operations and the original MIS Guidelines have, in the meantime, been revised a number of times.
5. The PMT uses the following poverty indicators to determine the degree of poverty: number of meals per day; number of months the maize from last harvest has lasted; ownership of livestock, land, blankets, and other assets; main source of livelihood; type of toilet; if the household is child-headed or widow-headed; and household size.

References

Alviar, C., Ayala, F. and Handa, S. (2010) 'Testing combined targeting systems for cash transfer programmes: the case of the CT-OVC programme in Kenya', in D. Lawson, D. Hulme, I. Matin, and K. Moore (eds), *What Works for the Poorest: Poverty Reduction Programmes for the World's Extreme Poor*, pp. 97–114. Practical Action Publishing, Rugby <http://dx.doi.org/10.3362/9781780440439.006>.

American Institutes for Research (2013) *Targeting Report for Zimbabwe's Harmonized Social Cash Transfer Programme*. American Institutes for Research, Washington, DC.

Ashley, S., Ayliffe, T. and Chiroro, P. (2013) *Child Protection Fund (CPF): Mid-Term Review 2013 Final Report*. The IDL Group, Bristol.

Grosh M.E. (1997) *Administering Targeted Social Program in Latin America: From Platitudes to Practice.* World Bank, Washington DC <http://dx.doi.org/10.1596/0-8213-2620-1>.

Hanlon, J., Barrientos A. and Hulme, D. (2010) *Just Give the Money to the Poor: the Development Revolution from the Global South.* Kumarian Press, Sterling, VA.

Ministry of Agriculture (2015) *Productive Safety Net Programme Phase 4, Programme Implementation Manual.* Ministry of Agriculture, Government of Ethiopia, Addis Ababa.

MPSLSW (2010) *Lessons Learned from Ongoing Social Protection Programmes in Zimbabwe.* Ministry of Public Services, Labour and Social Welfare, Government of Zimbabwe and UNICEF, Harare.

MPSLSW (2011a) *Report on the Test Run of the Zimbabwe Harmonized Social Cash Transfer Programme in Ward 15 of Goromonzi District.* Ministry of Public Services, Labour and Social Welfare, Government of Zimbabwe, Harare.

MPSLSW (2011b) *Operational Guide for the Management Information System of the Zimbabwe Harmonized Social Cash Transfer Programme.* Ministry of Public Services, Labour and Social Welfare, Government of Zimbabwe, Harare.

MPSLSW (2013) *Manual of Operations of the Zimbabwe Harmonized Social Cash Transfer Programme, Fourth Edition.* Ministry of Public Services, Labour and Social Welfare, Government of Zimbabwe, Harare.

Roman, E.R. (2010) *Zimbabwe Emergency Cash Transfer Pilot Reports November, December 2009 and January 2010.* Concern Worldwide & World Food Programme, Harare.

Schubert, B. (2005) *The Pilot Social Cash Transfer Scheme Kalomo District Zambia. CPRC Working Paper 52.* Chronic Poverty Research Centre, University of Manchester, Manchester.

Schubert, B. (2008) 'Social cash transfers as a component of a comprehensive National Social Protection Programme: lessons learned from facilitating the process of designing, piloting and scaling up inclusive social cash transfer schemes in Zambia and Malawi', in *Social Protection for the Poorest in Africa: Learning from Experience* [online]. Available from: http://www.kulima.com/wp-content/uploads/2011/03/Conference-proceedings.pdf [accessed 14 January 2009].

Schubert, B. (2010) *Child-Sensitive Social Protection in Zimbabwe.* UNICEF, Harare.

Schubert, B. (2012) *Zimbabwe Harmonized Social Cash Transfer Programme: Analysis of the Process and Results of Targeting Labour Constrained Food Poor Households in 10 Districts.* Ministry of Labour and Social Services and UNICEF, Harare.

Schubert, B. (2013) *Process, Results and Costs of Targeting Cash Transfers to Labour Constrained Food Poor Households in 13 Districts of Zimbabwe.* Ministry of Labour and Social Services and UNICEF, Harare.

Schubert, B., Sammon, E., Hokoya, J. and Muwoni, L. (2014) *Value for Money. Cost Analysis of the Zimbabwe Harmonized Social Cash Transfer Programme.* Ministry of Public Services, Labour and Social Welfare, Harare.

Sen, B. and Begum, S. (2010) 'Identifying and targeting the extreme poor: a methodology for rural Bangladesh', in D. Lawson, D. Hulme, I. Matin, and K. Moore (eds), *What Works for The Poorest: Poverty Reduction Programmes for the World's Extreme Poor*, pp. 79–96. Practical Action Publishing, Rugby <http://dx.doi.org/10.3362/9781780440439.005>.

ZIMSTAT (2013a) *Poverty and Poverty Datum Line Analysis in Zimbabwe 2011/12*. Zimbabwe National Statistics Agency, Harare.

ZIMSTAT (2013b) *Poverty Income Consumption and Expenditure Survey 2011/12 Report*. Zimbabwe National Statistics Agency, Harare.

About the author

Bernd Schubert is a development researcher and practitioner. Since 1986 he has researched and worked in social protection and social transfers, designing social cash transfer schemes across sub-Saharan Africa. He also organized the 2006 Livingstone Intergovernmental Conference on Social Protection that resulted in the mushrooming of social cash transfer programmes across Africa.

PART B
Africa's children and youth

CHAPTER 4

Africa's extreme poor: Surviving early childhood

Lawrence Ado-Kofie and David Lawson

The chapter aims to provide a statistical orientation of different dimensions of extreme poverty in sub-Saharan Africa (SSA), with a particular focus on young children – first-day deaths and under-5 mortality – complemented by an analysis of maternal mortality. For the period 1990–2015, child and maternal mortality trends reveal that those countries with lower poverty levels appear to have made the most progress; however, child well-being and maternal health have widened over the last two decades, with 12 of the 13 countries that have made no progress in achieving under-5 mortality target reduction from SSA. If you are born in SSA, then the probability that you will die before your fifth birthday is almost 17 times greater than if you are born in a developed country, and 397,000 babies born in SSA die on their first day of life.

Keywords: first-day deaths, infant mortality, maternal mortality, health poverty, extreme poverty, Millennium Development Goals

Introduction

This chapter draws on currently available statistics on health poverty indicators to highlight the trend in child and maternal mortality in sub-Saharan African (SSA) countries, and to shed light on why some SSA countries have made progress in these health poverty indicators and others have failed to advance. In light of the finding that some of the worst health poverty statistics are recorded in SSA, despite more than decade-long international and national efforts to achieve the Millennium Development Goals (MDGs) 4 and 5, it is imperative to examine and understand these statistics in relation to other regions, and explore the reasons for the persistent health poverty in SSA. Consequently, the chapter examines countries in SSA that have made no or insignificant progress in MDGs 4 and 5 amidst the achievements of MDGs of other regions of the world. The chapter then synthesizes knowledge about what measures could improve the dire statistics on child and maternal mortality in SSA. Much of the measures could be national-level policymaking and investment in healthcare systems combined with international-level support of relevant actions.

http://dx.doi.org/10.3362/9781780448435.004

Evidence of extreme health poverty in SSA

An estimated 397,000 babies die each year in SSA on the day they are born. The region accounts for 12 per cent of the world's population but 38 per cent of the world's first-day deaths (Save the Children, 2013a: 27). As a region, SSA's under-5 mortality rate is 94 per 1,000 live births (the highest in the world) compared to 4 per 1,000 live births for industrialized countries. The lifetime risk of maternal death for a woman in SSA is 1 in 36 (the highest in the world) and 1 in 200 (the second highest in the world) for a woman in South Asia, compared to 1 in 6,400 for a woman in high-income OECD countries. In terms of income, the GNI per capita of SSA is about US$1,647 compared with $44,272 GNI per capita for high-income OECD countries (World Bank, 2016a).

The target for MDG 4 was to reduce the world's under-5 and infant mortality rate by two-thirds between 1990 and 2015. For MDG 5, the target was to reduce maternal mortality ratio by three-quarters over the same period. Statistics from Save the Children (2013a) show that, since 1990, the annual number of children under 5 who die each year has been reduced by 43 per cent (from 12 million to 6.9 million), and the number of maternal deaths has declined by 47 per cent (from 543,000 to 287,000 per year). Although these statistics indicate that substantial progress has been made in improving children's well-being and maternal health, there is evidence that these improvements were insufficient to achieve the targeted under-5 and infant mortality rates and the maternal mortality ratio (Save the Children, 2013a; WHO and UNICEF, 2012).

Under-5 mortality

There are 74 countries (42 from SSA) with available data on MDGs 4 and 5 that are classified as 'Countdown' countries (WHO and UNICEF, 2012). These countries were monitored in terms of on track, making progress, insufficient progress, and no progress towards achieving MDGs 4 and 5 by the 2015 deadline. Of the 23 Countdown countries that were on track to achieve MDG 4 (under-5 mortality), only four (i.e. Eritrea, Liberia, Madagascar, and Malawi) are in SSA. Furthermore, of the 74 countries overall, 38 made insufficient progress, of which 27 are in SSA, and of the 13 Countdown countries that made no progress, 12 are in SSA (ibid.).

The inability of the world to achieve these targets is further stressed by statistics compiled in the *State of the World's Mothers* report. The report estimates that 6.9 million children die before reaching their fifth birthday, and that the greater proportion of those deaths occurs in developing countries where children and mothers lack access to basic health care. In 2011, it was estimated that 3.4 million children in SSA died before reaching the age of 5, which is about 50 per cent of the world estimate (Save the Children, 2013a, 2013b). Although it has been estimated that newborn mortality rates, in particular, (43 per cent of the world's under-5 mortality rate) have been declining globally in recent decades, SSA countries have shown the least progress of any region trying to reduce newborn deaths over the past two decades (ibid.). SSA has the highest risk of death in the first month of life and is among the regions showing the least progress. In fact, statistics from the *State of the World's Mothers* report show that the newborn mortality rate in SSA has increased by 10 per cent, whilst in other regions it reduced by a minimum of 33 per cent to a maximum of 65 per cent between 1990 and 2011.

Furthermore, five out of nine developing regions show reductions in the under-5 mortality rate of more than 50 per cent over the period 1990–2011 (UNICEF, 2012). For example, while Eastern Asia (70 per cent reduction) and Northern Africa (68 per cent reduction) have achieved MDG 4, and Latin America and the Caribbean (64 per cent reduction) are close to achieving the MDG 4 target, SSA has reduced its under-5 mortality rate by only 39 per cent over the same period. The statistics imply that SSA is highly unlikely to achieve MDG 4. The highest rates of child mortality are in SSA, where one in nine children dies before age 5, compared to one in 152 on average for developed regions (ibid.). For example, one child in five in Sierra Leone, and one in six in Chad, Democratic Republic of the Congo, Mali, and Somalia, does not reach his or her fifth birthday, compared to Iceland where only one child in 400 dies before age 5. According to UNICEF's *Child Mortality Report* (2012), out of 24 countries with an under-5 mortality rate above 100 deaths per 1,000 live births in 2011, 23 are in SSA. This shows that under-5 mortality is more concentrated in SSA, while the share of the rest of the world dropped from 31 per cent in 1990 to 17 per cent in 2011 (Save the Children, 2013a, 2013b; UNICEF, 2012).

Although SSA has seen a faster decline in its under-5 mortality rate, with the annual rate of reduction doubling between 1990–2000 and 2000–15, the region still remains the one with the greatest burden of under-5 deaths. Nigeria, Democratic Republic of the Congo, and Ethiopia were among the five Countdown countries where most under-5 deaths occurred (WHO and UNICEF, 2012). Notwithstanding the dire statistics of under-5 mortality in SSA, some individual countries in SSA have made more progress in reducing child mortality. For example, in 1999, one in five Rwandan children died before reaching the age of 5. Since 1999, the country has made huge progress and, by 2011, the child mortality rate in Rwanda had fallen to one in 20. Eritrea, Liberia, Madagascar, and Malawi have also made significant progress. These four countries were on track to achieve the 2015 MDG 4 target of reducing under-5 mortality by two-thirds since 1990.

In terms of neonatal mortality, all regions have seen slower reductions in under-5 mortality since 1990. However, SSA records one of the slowest reductions (24 per cent) in neonatal mortality (just 1 per cent above the last placed Oceania region), while Eastern Asia records the fastest reduction (61 per cent) in neonatal mortality between 1990 and 2011 (UNICEF, 2012). The SSA region accounts for 38 per cent of worldwide neonatal deaths, and recorded 34 neonatal deaths per 1,000 live births in 2011, which is the highest neonatal mortality rate in the world (ibid.). Among the regions,

SSA has shown the least progress in reducing its neonatal mortality rate over the last two decades.

The disparity between SSA and other regions in terms of children's well-being has widened over the last two decades. In 1990, the probability of a child born in SSA dying before age 5 was 1.5 times higher than in Southern Asia, 3.4 times higher than in Latin America and the Caribbean, 3.7 times higher than in Eastern Asia, and 12.1 times higher than in developed regions. However, by 2011 the probability has increased drastically in comparison to other regions: 1.8 times higher than in Southern Asia, 5.7 times higher than in Latin America and the Caribbean, 7.4 times higher than in Eastern Asia, and 16.5 times higher than in developed regions (WHO and UNICEF, 2012).

Table 4.1 shows the incidence of child mortality in SSA between 1990 and 2015. Here, the top 16 countries have recorded, in 2015, the lowest under-5 mortality rates compared to the middle and bottom 16 countries in SSA. Eritrea and Madagascar, two of the four Countdown countries found in SSA that were on track to achieve MDG 4, are in the top 16 positions of the under-5 mortality ranking in 2015.

Among the four countries that were on track to achieve MDG 4, Malawi has been regarded as one of SSA's success stories in reducing its under-5 mortality rate from 244 per 1,000 live births in 1990 to 71 per 1,000 live births in 2012. In other words, the country has reduced its under-5 mortality by 46 per cent since 1990, which puts the country on track to meet MDG 4. However, the *State of the World's Mothers* report (Save the Children, 2013a) cautions that

Table 4.1 Incidence of child mortality in SSA, 1990–2015

Country*	Mortality rate, under-5 (per 1,000 live births)			Poverty level**
	1990	*2000*	*2015*	*2010*
Seychelles	17	14	14	0
Mauritius	23	19	14	–
Cape Verde	62	38	25	0
South Africa	61	74	41	29
Rwanda	151	182	42	14
Botswana	48	85	44	–
Namibia	73	73	45	20
Congo Rep.	100	118	45	13
Eritrea	150	89	47	63
Sao Tome & Principe	104	87	47	63
Senegal	142	139	47	81
Tanzania	166	132	49	30
Kenya	98	110	49	0
Madagascar	159	109	50	31
Gabon	92	86	51	34

Country*	Mortality rate, under-5 (per 1,000 live births)			Poverty level**
	1990	2000	2015	2010
Uganda	178	147	55	64
Ethiopia	204	146	59	22
Swaziland	71	121	61	40
Ghana	128	103	62	30
Malawi	244	174	64	19
Zambia	192	169	64	83
Gambia, The	170	116	69	48
Sudan	128	106	70	41
Liberia	248	176	70	24
Zimbabwe	74	102	71	74
Comoros	124	99	74	44
Togo	143	122	78	61
Mozambique	233	166	79	–
Burundi	164	150	82	9
Mauritania	128	111	85	30
Cameroon	135	150	88	48
Burkina Faso	202	186	89	36
Lesotho	85	114	90	–
South Sudan	251	181	93	38
Côte d'Ivoire	152	145	93	45
Guinea-Bissau	206	174	93	–
Equatorial Guinea	182	143	94	80
Guinea	241	171	94	23
Niger	326	227	96	44
Congo, Dem. Rep.	171	171	98	68
Benin	181	147	100	50
Nigeria	213	188	109	62
Mali	253	220	115	47
Sierra Leone	257	234	120	85
Central African Republic	171	164	130	–
Somalia	17	171	137	46
Chad	209	189	139	44
Angola	213	203	157	52

Source: Authors' compilation based on: 1) WDI online database (World Bank, 2016a); and 2) Poverty rates from PovcalNet (World Bank, 2016b)
Note: * Countries ranked by 2015 mortality rate; ** Poverty headcount ratio at $1.25/day (PPP) (5 of population)

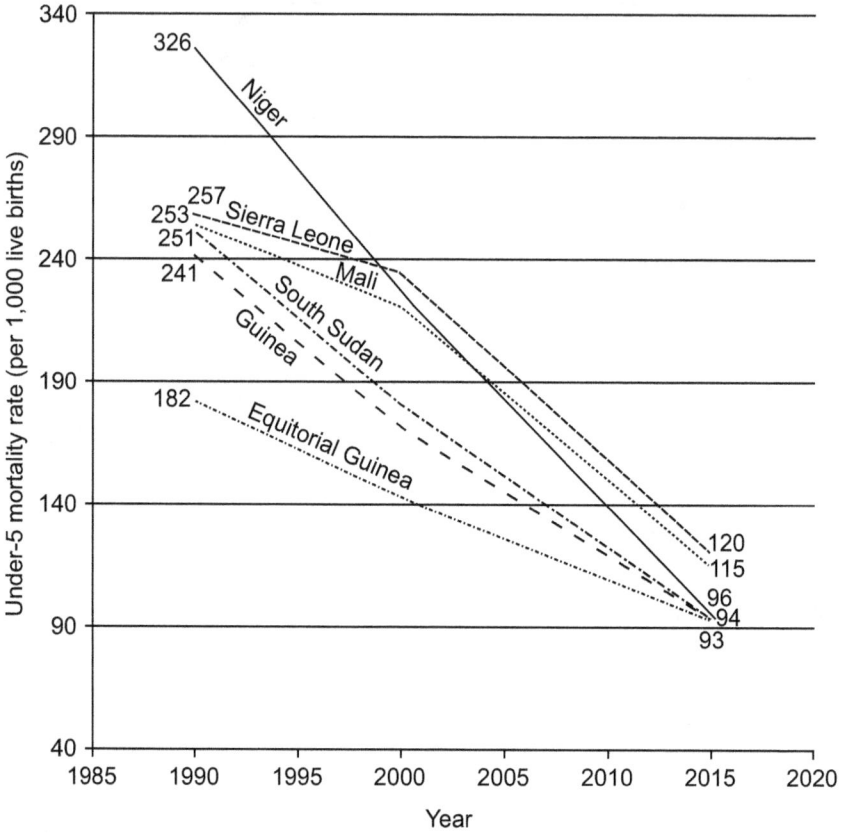

Figure 4.1 Under-5 mortality rate (per 1,000 live births)
Source: Authors' calculations based on WDI online database (World Bank, 2016a)

the country needs to increase its focus on childbirth and neonatal deaths in order to achieve MDG 4. Malawi's success in reducing its under-5 mortality rate has been achieved through high-level political commitment, help from international organizations, and a comprehensive national health sector approach (ibid.). Figure 4.1 shows the trend of under-5 mortality rates in the top 16 performing SSA countries ranked by 2015 mortality rate. The other SSA countries that have significantly reduced their under-5 mortality rate since 1990 include Madagascar, Tanzania, Rwanda, Ethiopia, Eritrea, and Senegal.

Considering under-5 mortality rates in the bottom 16 SSA countries ranked by 2015 mortality rate (Figure 4.1), Niger, South Sudan, Guinea, and Equatorial Guinea have made remarkable progress. For example, Niger has made the greatest strides in SSA, and worldwide, in reducing child mortality. Despite the country's scarce resources and recurring droughts, under-5 mortality rates in Niger fell by almost two-thirds after 1990 due to government policies to curb hunger and poor health care (Save the Children, 2013a). Although, in 2005, the country was hit by a severe drought, causing widespread hunger, international organizations (aid agencies) supported the country through the launch of an international campaign to feed hundreds of thousands of people. Thus, with political commitment, provision of free health care, and donor agencies' support, Niger has managed to reduce the deaths of children under the age of 5 from 326 per 1,000 in 1990 to 96 per 1,000 in 2015 (see Table 4.1).

At the lower end of the 16 bottom-ranked SSA countries, with slow reductions in under-5 mortality rates, lie Sierra Leone, Angola, Chad, Somalia, Democratic Republic of the Congo, Guinea-Bissau, Central Africa Republic, and Mali. These countries ranked by under-5 mortality statistics can be regarded as some of worst places in SSA to be born. Also, notable characteristics of most of these countries are conflicts and wars, which might have worsened the under-5 mortality rates in these countries.

Generally, Mauritius, Cape Verde, Seychelles, Namibia, South Africa, Madagascar, Gabon, and Senegal perform relatively well in children's well-being. Comparatively, Mali, Sierra Leone, Central Africa Republic, Somalia, Chad, and Angola perform very poorly in children's wellbeing. It has been shown that, in SSA, babies born in Sierra Leone, Guinea-Bissau, Somalia, Angola, Lesotho, Democratic Republic of the Congo, Mali, Central Africa Republic, Côte d'Ivoire, Chad, Nigeria, South Sudan, and Burundi have the highest risk of dying before their fifth birthday (Save the Children, 2013a).

Maternal mortality

Statistics from the *State of the World's Mothers* report (Save the Children, 2013a, 2013b) reveal that 800 women die daily during the course of pregnancy or childbirth globally. Furthermore, statistics from the *Child Mortality Report* also show that only nine out of 74 Countdown countries were on track to achieve MDG 5, while 40 made progress, and 25 have made insufficient or no progress. Of the nine countries that were on track to achieve MDG 5, only two are in SSA (Equatorial Guineas and Eritrea). Unsurprisingly, of the nine countries that have made no progress in achieving MDG 5, all are in SSA (Botswana, Cameroon, Chad, Democratic Republic of the Congo, Lesotho, Somalia, South Africa, Swaziland, and Zimbabwe). Twenty-four out of 40 countries that made progress, and eight out of 16 with insufficient progress, are in SSA (WHO and UNICEF, 2012).

The statistics clearly demonstrate that maternal deaths are more concentrated in SSA countries than in other developing countries. These statistics are an indication of global disparities in women's access to needed obstetrical care and other services, including family planning, and quality antenatal and postnatal care. It is estimated that an African woman's lifetime risk of dying from pregnancy-related causes in 2010 is 100 times higher than a woman in a developed country (UNICEF, 2012), and by 2015 it increased to 177 times higher (World Bank, 2016a). For example, it is also estimated that a woman in Chad has a one in 15 chance of dying of maternal causes during her lifetime. This risk is one in 16 in Somalia, one in 23 in Niger and Sierra Leone, and one in 30 in Democratic Republic of the Congo, compared to one in 3,800 for a woman in a developed country (UNICEF, 2012).

Also, the *State of the World's Mothers* report estimates that mothers in Somalia and Sierra Leone face, respectively, the second and third highest lifetime risk of maternal death in the world. The Mothers' Index computed by Save the Children (2013a), which highlights the regional dimension of women's health, shows that the bottom 12 countries are all in SSA, and the region also accounts for 26 of the 30 lowest-ranking countries. The index was based on lifetime risk of maternal death, under-5 mortality rate, expected years of formal schooling (for girls), GNI per capita, and participation of women in national government. The SSA region performs poorly on every indicator, except political status. For example, in SSA, one in 36 women is likely to die in pregnancy or childbirth, which is about five times the risk women in South Asia face (one in 200), and 177 times the risk faced by women in developed countries (one in 6,400) (World Bank, 2016a).

Tables 4.2a and 4.2b appear to show that there is some correlation between women's health status and their educational status, and also the economic status of the SSA countries. The top nine countries in Tables 4.2a and 4.2b have generally high GDP per capita, female primary school completion rate, and female life expectancy at birth (in years), and generally low poverty headcount ratio, number of maternal deaths, and lifetime risk of maternal death (in per cent). On the other hand, the bottom 16 countries overall, in the female life expectancy at birth ranking based on 2008 statistics, show the direct opposite of the economic status or conditions of the top 16 countries, and educational status of women in relation to women's health status. It is therefore possible from the statistics depicted in Table 4.2 to support the notion that high levels of poverty resulting in lack of adequate provision of health care and education contribute to the poor maternal health (see Box 4.1 case study) of women in most of the SSA countries.

Box 4.1 Uzazi Bora: Meeting maternal health needs in post-conflict environments of Kasongo and Lubero districts in the Democratic Republic of the Congo (DRC)

In DRC, the maternal mortality rate is 547 for 1,000 live births and the contraceptive prevalence is 6.7 per cent (EDS, 2010). The abortion rate for complicated pregnancies of adolescent girls is 30 per cent (EDS, 2007), the unmet need for family planning (FP) is 24 per cent (EDS, 2010), and the knowledge of FP methods is approximately 56 per cent. Furthermore, in DRC sexual violence against women averages just over 500 cases per month.

CARE DRC (in collaboration with 'Reproductive Health Access Information Services in Emergencies' (RAISE) Training Centre) secured funding for the implementation of the project related to FP and post-abortion care (PAC) that commenced in January 2013 for a period of three years. The project covered 19 structures of care in three health zones: five structures in the area of health, Kayna; five structures in the area of health, Lubero; and nine structures in the area of health, Kasongo (Maniema); covering a total population of 816,969 inhabitants. The project contributes to improving the health of mothers through health care accessibility, use of family planning methods, and post-abortion care in the three areas of intervention. This project, in a global context, acts as a tool to fight poverty.

Barriers to maternal health identified

Financial poverty: The IUD method costs about US$50, and given the high poverty rate in the country, the cost is beyond many women.

Geographic: Apart from the tropical climate and vast forests, which make target areas difficult to access, the nearest health centre in Kauli (near Lake Edward) is about 20km away from Mubana, with poor roads and no means of transport.

Socio-cultural: Women need to have their husband's approval before they can use FP methods. In addition, decision on rights for reproductive health is dictated by imams and priests.

Systems: Community structures (including Comité de Développement Sanitaire (CODESA)) are present, but not functional, and target groups are barely reached, particularly adolescents.

Target areas to improve maternal health

Primary targets include: women of reproductive age – the *misadi*, Village Savings and Loan Association (VSLA), religious communities, adult learning centres; men's groups such as *Barza* – parents' associations and community structures (CODESA, Comité de Développement Local (CDL), quality fora); and adolescent boys and girls such as football teams, youth centres, schools, meeting areas for youths, and sites (churches, theatre and cinema halls, areas for bicycle and motorcycle repairs).

Secondary targets include: health care service providers, and through exchanges in meetings on analysis of monthly health data and quarterly reviews.

Tertiary targets include: religious leaders to put in place an environment favourable for exchange of views (face-to-face with priests, bishops, etc.); young leaders through enter-tainment and sports activities; and traditional leadership through their involvement in decision-making with regard to quality fora (CDL, external supervision, CODESA).

Strategies adopted to achieve the targets

Mapping of social dynamics was undertaken, combined with a vulnerability analysis to support research on understanding power relations within households and identifying households' level of access to resources and services. Good governance is one aspect of achieving the targets, and this is done through increased use of PAC and PDQ (Partnership Defined Quality) databases based upon the identification of barriers related to the use of FP/PAC services. An enlargement of space for dialogue between community, service providers, and authorities was also included in the strategy.

Achievements

From 2007 to 2012, 3,500 new women clients, including 1,400 Method with Long Duration of Action (MLDA), were reached through the Kasongo RAISE Project; from January 2013 to April 2014, 9,293 new women clients, including 7,536 MLDA with 2,558 IUD, were reached under the Supporting Access to Family Planning and Post-Abortion Care in Emergencies (SAF PAC 2) programme. For the Kasongo RAISE Project, 3,460 new women clients, including 2,776 MLDA, were reached, 1,231 with IUD.

Impacts

There has been an increase in the number of qualified FP/PAC service providers, improved economic power of women (women on MLDA can easily meet their financial commitments in their VSLA), reduction of complications related to multiple pregnancies, and a clear trend showing a gradual decrease in maternal deaths recorded. Thus, the programme approach between UZAZI BORA and PAMOJA (CARE DRC governance project in Kasongo and Lubero) seems to have increased community involvement in the quality of family planning and PAC services in the Kasongo and Lubero districts in DRC.

Source: Based on RAISE Project DRC (CARE, 2011) and DR Congo CARE (2015)

Table 4.2a Women's education in comparison with economic status of SSA countries

Country	Rank*	Economic Status		Educational Status	
		GDP per capita (current US$)		Primary completion rate, female (% of relevant age group)	
		2008	2015	2008	2013
Seychelles	1	11,123	15,543	126	97.3
Cape Verde	2	3,222	3,641	102	93.6
Mauritius	3	7,600	10,017	–	103
Sao Tome & Principe	4	1,090	1,811	77	106.7
Senegal	5	1,094	1,067	59	–
Madagascar	5	471	449	69	70.2
Namibia	6	4,183	5,408	83	–
Eritrea	6	256	–	41	–
Sudan	6	1,242	1,876	48	–
Gabon	7	10,610	10,772	–	–
Mauritania	7	1,107	1,275	–	72
Rwanda	7	461	696	53	64.3
Comoros	8	817	810	66	75.8
Ghana	8	1,234	1,442	82	97.4
Ethiopia	8	325	574	48	–
Benin	9	739	904	55	68.4
Gambia, The	10	612	–	81	72.1
Liberia	10	231	458	57	–
Kenya	10	786	1358	–	–
Tanzania	11	504	955	–	79.8
Congo, Rep.	12	3,059	3,147	69	–
Togo	13	528	638	57	74.2
Niger	13	364	427	32	44
Uganda	13	454	715	57	53.9
Guinea-Bissau	14	556	568	–	–
Burkina Faso	14	570	713	33	62.9
Guinea	14	366	540	48	55.6
Somalia	14	–	543	–	–
South Africa	15	5,598	6,483	–	–
Cameroon	15	1,211	1,407	68	–
Burundi	16	187	286	42	72.4
Mali	16	665	705	44	–

Country	Rank*	Economic Status		Educational Status	
		GDP per capita (current US$)		Primary completion rate, female (% of relevant age group)	
		2008	2015	2008	2013
South Sudan	16	1,674	1,115	–	–
Equatorial Guinea	17	23,511	18,918	44	–
Zambia	17	1,175	1,722	91	82
Malawi	17	303	255	64	75.4
Angola	18	4,596	–	41	–
Nigeria	18	1,370	3,203	65	–
Côte d'Ivoire	19	1,282	1,546	–	53.5
Mozambique	19	435	586	52	45.7
Chad	19	758	1,025	–	30.1
Congo, Dem. Rep.	19	199	442	45	64.9
Zimbabwe	20	345	931	–	–
Central African Rep.	21	474	359	27	–
Swaziland	22	2,617	3,477	–	–
Botswana	23	5,747	7,123	97	–
Lesotho	23	827	1,034	78	83.9
Sierra Leone	24	453	766	–	–

Source: Authors' compilation based on WDI online database (World Bank, 2016a)
Note: * Countries ranked by 2015 mortality rate

Table 4.2b Women's health status in comparison with economic status of SSA countries

Country	Rank*	Economic Status		Health Status				
		GDP per capita (current US$)		Life expectancy at birth, female (years)		No. of maternal deaths	Lifetime risk of maternal death (%)	Lifetime risk of maternal death (1 in: rate varies by country)
		2008	2015	2008	2013	2015	2015	2015
Seychelles	1	11,123	15,543	79	77	–	–	–
Cape Verde	2	3,222	3,641	77	75	5	0.1	900
Mauritius	3	7,600	10,017	76	78	7	0.1	1300
Sao Tome & Principe	4	1,090	1,811	67	68	10	0.7	140
Senegal	5	1,094	1,067	64	68	1800	1.6	61

(Continued)

Table 4.2b Continued

Country	Rank*	Economic Status		Health Status				
		GDP per capita (current US$)		Life expectancy at birth, female (years)		No. of maternal deaths	Lifetime risk of maternal death (%)	Lifetime risk of maternal death (1 in: rate varies by country)
		2008	2015	2008	2013	2015	2015	2015
Madagascar	5	471	449	64	66	2900	1.7	60
Namibia	6	4,183	5,408	63	67	190	1	100
Eritrea	6	256	–	63	65	880	2.3	43
Sudan	6	1,242	1,876	63	65	4100	1.4	72
Gabon	7	10,610	10,772	62	64	150	1.2	85
Mauritania	7	1,107	1,275	62	64	810	2.7	36
Rwanda	7	461	696	62	67	1100	1.2	85
Comoros	8	817	810	61	65	88	1.5	66
Ghana	8	1,234	1,442	61	62	2800	1.3	74
Ethiopia	8	325	574	61	65	11000	1.6	64
Benin	9	739	904	60	61	1600	2	51
Gambia, The	10	612	–	59	61	590	4.1	24
Liberia	10	231	458	59	62	1100	3.6	28
Kenya	10	786	1358	59	63	8000	2.4	42
Tanzania	11	504	955	58	66	8200	2.2	45
Congo, Rep.	12	3,059	3,147	57	63	740	2.2	45
Togo	13	528	638	56	60	940	1.7	58
Niger	13	364	427	56	62	5400	4.4	23
Uganda	13	454	715	56	59	5700	2.1	47
Guinea-Bissau	14	556	568	55	57	370	2.6	38
Burkina Faso	14	570	713	55	60	2700	2.1	48
Guinea	14	366	540	55	59	3100	3.5	29
Somalia	14	–	543	55	57	3400	4.6	22
South Africa	15	5,598	6,483	54	59	1500	0.3	300
Cameroon	15	1,211	1,407	54	56	5100	2.9	35
Burundi	16	187	286	53	58	3500	4.3	23
Mali	16	665	705	53	57	4400	3.7	27
South Sudan	16	1,674	1,115	53	56	3500	3.9	26

Country	Rank*	Economic Status		Health Status				
		GDP per capita (current US$)		Life expectancy at birth, female (years)		No. of maternal deaths	Lifetime risk of maternal death (%)	Lifetime risk of maternal death (1 in: rate varies by country)
		2008	2015	2008	2013	2015	2015	2015
Equatorial Guinea	17	23,511	18,918	52	59	100	1.6	61
Zambia	17	1,175	1,722	52	61	1400	1.3	79
Malawi	17	303	255	52	63	4400	3.5	27
Angola	18	4,596	–	51	53	5400	3.1	32
Nigeria	18	1,370	3,203	51	53	58000	4.5	22
Côte d'Ivoire	19	1,282	1,546	50	52	5400	3.2	32
Mozambique	19	435	586	50	56	5300	2.5	40
Chad	19	758	1,025	50	52	5400	5.5	18
Congo, Dem. Rep.	19	199	442	50	60	22000	4.1	24
Zimbabwe	20	345	931	49	57	2400	1.9	52
Central African Rep.	21	474	359	48	52	1400	3.7	27
Swaziland	22	2,617	3,477	47	48	150	1.3	76
Botswana	23	5,747	7,123	46	67	72	0.4	270
Lesotho	23	827	1,034	46	50	300	1.6	61
Sierra Leone	24	453	766	44	51	3100	5.9	17

Source: Authors' compilation based on WDI online database (World Bank, 2016a)
Note: * Countries ranked by 2015 mortality rate

Why are all the statistics against SSA?

Poverty has been identified as one of the major factors contributing to these dire statistics. Most countries in SSA are constrained by financial resources when trying to address children's well-being and women's health issues (World Bank, 2013). Taking, for instance, Malawi, Burundi, Central African Republic, Liberia, and Democratic Republic of the Congo, World Bank statistics show that these countries are the poorest in the world, with an estimated GNI per capita of only US$250, $270, $320, and $380, respectively, in 2014 (World Bank, 2016a). In comparison with the GNI per capita of $103,630 of Norway, the difference and the impacts are clear. On average, most of the countries in SSA are poor. Other closely rated factors responsible for high under-5 mortality rates and maternal mortality ratios in SSA countries include: severe shortage of health workers; preterm birth; poor maternal health; malnutrition; low birth weight; insufficient health care for mothers; and lack of maternal education (Save the Children, 2013a, 2013b).

Closely related to the lack of economic resources is the severe shortage of health workers in SSA countries, which explains many of the poor statistics on child and maternal health. The SSA region as a whole has only 11 doctors, nurses, and midwives per 10,000 people (World Bank, 2016a), which is less than 50 per cent of the critical threshold of 23 generally considered necessary to deliver essential health services (Save the Children, 2013a). Guinea, Niger, Sierra Leone, and Somalia are all identified as the countries with the most severe shortages of health workers, where there are fewer than two skilled health workers for every 10,000 people. Out of the 48 countries in SSA, only eight are able to meet the minimum threshold for number of health workers (ibid.).

According to Save the Children (2013a, 2013b), many SSA countries have unusually high rates of preterm birth. As most mothers do not have access to skilled health workers and the necessary health care, the risk of neonatal and maternal deaths is more likely to be high. For example, Malawi has the highest prevalence of preterm birth in the world (18 per cent of babies are born too early). In Botswana, Mauritania, Mozambique, Zimbabwe, and several other SSA countries, more than 15 per cent of babies are born prematurely. Furthermore, 34 per cent and 27 per cent of babies born in Mauritania and Niger, respectively, are born with low birth weight (Save the Children, 2013b).

High rates of neonatal deaths have also been attributed to poor health among SSA mothers. Save the Children (2013b) estimates show that 10–20 per cent of women in SSA are underweight. Low body mass index and short maternal stature are also considered important risk factors for birth complications, low birth weight, and neonatal mortality in SSA. For example, 38 per cent of mothers in Eritrea, 28 per cent in Madagascar, and 24 per cent in Ethiopia are found to be underweight, while in Sierra Leone 13 per cent of women are stunted. Serious maternal undernutrition in SSA is considered one of the reasons for the regions' dire statistics on children's well-being and maternal health (Save the Children, 2013b).

Lack of sufficient health care for mothers in SSA countries also contributes to the poor statistics on under-5 and maternal mortalities. The worst place in terms of childbirth is Ethiopia, where about 90 per cent of women give birth at home without skilled care. In Mali and Niger, 13 per cent and 17 per cent of women, respectively, give birth alone. In Nigeria, one in five women has no one to help her during childbirth. It is estimated that, on average, only 50 per cent women in SSA receive skilled care during birth. For example, in Ethiopia, Niger, and South Sudan, more than 50 per cent of all women receive no skilled prenatal care (Save the Children, 2013a). Also in Niger and South Sudan, it is estimated that over 80 per cent of women are not attended to during childbirth. In Somalia, 74 per cent of pregnant women go without care during pregnancy (ibid.).

Conclusion

It is now clear that the region has failed to make significant progress in meeting MDGs 4 and 5. SSA governments, donor countries, and international agencies must be committed to providing stronger health systems for mothers and children under 5 in particular. Many socio-economic and cultural barriers that deter the seeking of health care must be addressed to ensure access to life-saving maternal and under-5 health care services. CARE DRC, through the Uzazi Bora case (Box 4.1), provides an interesting example of how practising good governance, through simple approaches of encouraging learning, sharing experiences, and empowerment of individuals and citizens, can improve the health of the mother through increased accessibility and use of planning and abortion care. However, we can see across SSA that poverty levels have been identified as one of the major factors contributing to these grim statistics. Most countries in SSA are constrained by financial resources when it comes to addressing children's well-being, women's health issues, provision of efficient health care systems, and the provision and maintenance of skilled health workers.

References

CARE (2011) 'Improving lives through CARE's sexual, reproductive, and maternal health programs. Uzazi Bora: meeting the maternal health needs of post-conflict Kasongo district, DRC', in *Voices from the Village*, Number 6, June. Care, Atlanta, GA.

DR Congo Care (2015) 'What Works for Africa's Poorest Background Note: Uzazi Bora – Meeting Maternal Health Needs in Post-Conflict Environments of Kasongo and Lubero Districts'.

EDS (2007) *Enquête Démographique et de Santé (Demographic and Health Surveys)*. MEASURE DHS de Macro International Inc. Calverton, Maryland, MD.

EDS (2010) *Enquête Démographique et de Santé (Demographic and Health Surveys)*. MEASURE DHS de Macro International Inc. Calverton, Maryland, MD.

Save the Children (2013a) *Surviving the First Day: State of the World's Mothers 2013*. Save the Children International, London.

Save the Children (2013b) *Nutrition in the First 1,000 Days: State of the World's Mothers 2012*. Save the Children International, London.

UNICEF (2012) *Levels and Trends in Child Mortality Report 2012: Estimates Developed by the UN Inter-agency Group for Child Mortality Estimation*. The United Nations Children's Fund, New York.

WHO and UNICEF (2012) *Countdown to 2015 – Maternal, Newborn & Child Survival: Building a Future for Women and Children: The 2012 Report*. World Health Organization and UNICEF, Washington, DC.

World Bank (2013) *World Development Indicators 2012*. World Bank, Washington, DC.

World Bank (2016a) *World Development Indicators* [online]. World Bank, Washington, DC. Available at: http://data.worldbank.org/data-catalog/world-development-indicators [accessed 4 January 2016].

World Bank (2016b) *PovcalNet: An Online Analysis Tool for Global Poverty Monitoring* [online]. World Bank, Washington, DC. Available at: http://iresearch.worldbank.org/PovcalNet/index.htm?1,0# [accessed 4 January 2016].

About the authors

Lawrence Ado-Kofie is a Research Associate at the Global Development Institute, University of Manchester.

David Lawson is a Senior Lecturer in Development Economics and Public Policy, Institute for Development Policy and Management, University of Manchester. He has worked extensively on SSA and specializes in poverty dynamics in African countries.

CHAPTER 5

Cash for care? Researching the linkages between social protection and children's care in Rwanda

Keetie Roelen, Helen Karki Chettri, and Emily Delap

Social protection is increasingly considered to be a powerful intervention for responding to concerns around children's care. This chapter considers the impact of social protection on child well-being, quality of care, family reunification, and the incentivization of foster or kinship care in Rwanda. The research focuses on the Vision 2020 Umurenge Programme (VUP) and two of its main components: 1) a regular cash transfer for those who are unable to work; and 2) a public works scheme for those who are able to work. Qualitative fieldwork was undertaken with children and their caregivers, as well as programme staff, to gain insight into the potential for social protection to support different elements of children's care.

Keywords: social protection, poverty reduction, care quality, child well-being, foster care

Introduction

Living in poverty can have wide-ranging and long-term adverse consequences for children (Brooks-Gunn and Duncan, 1997), thereby perpetuating the inter-generational transmission of poverty. As Corak points out (2006), poor children are more likely to become poor adults. Inadequate care can also impair children's education, health, and emotional and physical development, and can lead to a vicious cycle of harm when poorly cared-for children pass those patterns on to their own children (Csáky, 2014). There is a strong interplay between poverty and care for children: poverty can greatly undermine the quality of care, can compromise children's abilities to stay with their parents, and may also affect the ability of extended or other families to offer homes for children. Efforts towards poverty reduction and improved quality of care for children should, therefore, go hand in hand. Both of these factors are imperative in improving children's lives now and in the future.

The increased acknowledgement of childhood as a crucial time for breaking intergenerational transmissions of poverty can be seen reflected in the rapid expansion of social protection in the last decade, and particularly in social

http://dx.doi.org/10.3362/9781780448435.005

protection programmes that aim to improve children's outcomes. Recent years have seen a push towards more 'child-sensitive social protection' (Roelen and Sabates-Wheeler, 2012), aiming to make programmes recognizant of children's particular needs and vulnerabilities, and to maximize the potential benefits for children. Evidence regarding the positive impacts of social protection, and cash transfers in particular, is expanding rapidly, pointing towards significant reductions in poverty and large beneficial effects on nutritional, educational, and health outcomes (DFID, 2011; Hanlon et al., 2010). Many of these efforts, and subsequent evidence, come from sub-Saharan Africa (SSA), with many social protection programmes being piloted, rolled out, and scaled up across the region.

Nevertheless, understandings of the links between social protection and children's care are limited (Barrientos et al., 2013; Sanfilippo et al., 2012), and little guidance is offered on how to ensure that social protection promotes better care for children. The majority of programmes (and, therefore, their evaluations) focus on the role that programmes can play in improving observable and measurable outcomes, and pay little attention to wider impacts related to non-material, psychosocial, or societal well-being (Roelen, 2014). This presents us with an important knowledge gap, as social protection programmes may have unforeseen positive and negative effects beyond programmes' theories of change and lists of observable outcomes (Devereux et al., 2013). In reference to the impact on child well-being and care, this lack of knowledge is a missed opportunity at best, and a cause for harmful practices at worst; see, for example, Roelen (2014) for a discussion of unintended adverse side-effects of conditional cash transfer programmes. This chapter aims to begin filling this knowledge gap by presenting research that considers adults' and children's perceptions of the linkages between social protection and quality of care, family separation, and incentives for foster/kinship care in Rwanda.[1]

This chapter is framed around three research questions: 1) what are the linkages between social protection and the quality of children's care? 2) what is the link between social protection and the loss of parental care or family separation? and 3) how can social protection influence decisions about foster or kinship care? These questions are considered with respect to the Vision 2020 Umurenge Programme (VUP) in Rwanda, providing insights into programme-specific lessons learned and challenges ahead, but also allowing for more general reflections about the role of social protection in promoting children's care in sub-Saharan Africa.

The remainder of this chapter is structured as follows. We first of all describe the VUP programme and research methodology in more detail. Second, we present findings with respect to the three different research questions. Third, we summarize the main research findings, and conclude with lessons learned and recommendations for programming in Rwanda and social protection more broadly.

VUP and research methodology

VUP

The VUP is integral to Rwanda's *Economic Development and Poverty Reduction Strategy III* (EDPRS), and is targeted at the extreme poor based on community-based targeting using the local Ubudehe household wealth categories (MINALOC, 2011). The programme consists of four pillars, of which the largest two are Direct Support (DS), and Public Works (PW). DS consists of unconditional cash transfers targeted at extremely poor households without an adult who is able to work. PW offers paid employment on community asset-building projects, and is targeted at extremely poor households with at least one adult who is able to work. Financial services (FS) is the third pillar, and includes providing access to savings, credit, and financial institutions. The fourth pillar of training and sensitization is currently being rolled out, and focuses on creating awareness within the community on the VUP and how it can support households to improve their lives.

This study focuses primarily on the DS and PW components of the programme, and its linkages to children's well-being and care. It also considers the current, and potential, role of training and sensitization in future efforts to strengthen linkages between the VUP and child well-being, children's care, and family reunification. Although the research did ask research participants about challenges with respect to programme implementation, the discussion of findings is restricted to issues that are of direct relevance to the research questions.

Research methodology

The findings in this chapter are based on analysis of primary qualitative data. Qualitative fieldwork for this research took place in two different localities – Kibilizi and Rwabicuma – in Nyanza district in Southern Province in Rwanda. Rwabicuma is an accessible sector with a relatively good level of services, whereas Kibilizi is a more remote sector with weaker access to services. In 2008–9 Kibilizi was part of the first cohort of sectors in which the VUP was rolled out, and Rwabicuma was included in the fourth cohort of sectors for VUP rollout in 2011–12. The sample for this study includes 120 adults and 90 children, including programme staff, programme partici-pants, and community members. The findings reflect the opinions and perceptions of those directly and indirectly benefiting from the VUP. They also provide benchmark information regarding issues of child well-being and children's care. Qualitative techniques employed in the research sought to tap into the perceptions, opinions, and experiences of different individuals, and as such included key informant interviews, focus group discussions, case studies, and participatory techniques. Codes of conduct and ethical protocols were developed and observed throughout the research.

VUP and quality of care

We analyse the links between VUP and the quality of children's care from two different perspectives: effects on material and non-material aspects of well-being and care. This distinction follows from discussions with research participants about what constitutes child well-being, and what it means for a child to be 'happy, healthy, and well cared for'. Whilst material aspects focus primarily on basic needs such as food, education, shelter, clothing, and health care, non-material aspects encompass psychosocial elements including feelings of respect, confidence, love, and affection. The qualitative nature of this research allows for considering observable and verifiable outcomes, as well as wider and more subjective impacts of the VUP from the perspectives of those directly and indirectly affected by this programme.

Positive effects: material aspects of well-being and care

As indicated in the introduction, a wide and growing body of evidence is available regarding the positive effects of cash transfers and other social protection programmes. Regular and reliable assistance helps to reduce economic vulnerability in the household, to strengthen livelihoods, and to avoid the need for adverse coping strategies, such as sending children to work (Jones and Marquez, 2014). Programmes have been found to reduce poverty, improve nutritional outcomes, allow more children to go to and stay in school, and strengthen access to health services (Hanlon et al., 2010; Sanfilippo et al., 2012). We find similar positive effects on the fulfilment of children's basic needs, and subsequent outcomes with respect to the VUP in Rwanda.

Findings point towards a considerable income effect with cash transfers received through the VUP, improving carers' abilities to provide for children's basic needs. Respondents, both adults and children, indicate how participation in the VUP improves children's diets, helps children go to school, allows for buying health insurance, and supports general development of household livelihoods. A girl from Kibilize living in a household receiving DS said: 'We were living in poverty, we were not having a place to stay in, but VUP gave us money; now we have bought iron sheets to build a beautiful home, we get sufficient food, school materials, and health insurance.' A girl from Rwabicuma, living in a household participating in PW, said: 'It has a big importance because when our parents get paid we get what we need – school materials, uniforms – and we cannot miss the food when we come back from school. They also buy for us health insurance, and we can get medical care when we are sick.'

Findings suggest that sensitization meetings around activities within the VUP can compound this positive effect. Respondents in Rwabicuma discussed how meetings before and after the PW activities provide advice on how to improve children's diet, health, and other aspects of their well-being. In addition to the positive effects of the VUP for households directly participating in the programme, transfers are found to have positive spillover effects for children who are part of non-participating households. As mentioned by an adult respondent not participating in the VUP: 'When the participants get the money they can give jobs to neighbours who are not participants. This helps them to get the money or any compensation, and they can feed their families.' Spillover effects from the VUP were mentioned by both participants in the VUP and those who did not participate in the programme. The most common effects that were mentioned referred to milk or food given or sold to other households, as well as giving jobs to other households, for example, working on their field when working on PW, and fertilizer. Positive spillover effects also included improvements to local infrastructure, such as roads, and schools.

Positive effects: non-material aspects of well-being and care

Evidence of the impact of social protection and cash transfers on other aspects of child well-being, including family relations, domestic abuse, or neglect, is less widely available (Barrientos et al., 2013). Where such evidence is available, effects are limited or absent (Fiszbein and Schady, 2009). For example, in their study of Peru's Juntos programme, Jones and Marquez (2014) conclude that the programme's performance in terms of realizing children's rights to care and protection has been relatively weak.

Findings in this research clearly point towards the positive role that the VUP plays in strengthening family relations through supporting carers' abilities to provide for children's basic needs. The inflow of cash makes parents feel more confident, and the improved economic resilience reduces stress levels within the family. Many carers indicate that they feel better able to fulfil their duties. A better ability to provide for children's material needs was also said to lead to improvements in non-material aspects of children's care, as it reduces conflicts between carers and children, and helps to avoid children engaging in risk-taking behaviour. A male participant in DS mentioned: 'The VUP helps to get free from conflict, and parents can help each other in caring for their children', whilst a male PW participant also said:

> It helped us a lot because when children are not getting what they need, they can decide to look for it in bad ways. For example, girls can run after sexual intercourse thinking that they can get money and the boys leave their families. This programme supported us so that we could give our children what they need, and continue studying without other bad thoughts.

Parents and carers also indicated that participation in the VUP helps to improve the relationships between them and their children. Parents feel more comfortable talking to their children and giving them advice. A male DS participant mentioned: 'When children find out that you have the means to give them what they want, they also become free, and want to discuss with you about their problems, what they need. They also feel free to relax with other children, as they have been fed with healthy meals.' Respondents suggest that the VUP programme not only helps to instil confidence in carers and parents, but also has positive effects on children's psychosocial well-being, as they are better fed, have better clothes, and experience less stress in the household. As indicated by a female DS participant:

> [T]he programme helped us a lot because when you don't have means, and you are not able to get things that your child needs, you cannot even approach her and talk about the life or share views. Sometimes you are even dirty, and you cannot say anything in front of her. The VUP has built in us the abilities to fulfil our responsibility towards our children [...]. This time you can now converse with your children, share views, and give her advices on how she has to behave.

The relevance of this finding should not be underestimated; Harper et al. (2003) found that social relations and connectedness are enabling factors in breaking poverty cycles through their positive effects on self-confidence and stress at the family level.

Unforeseen adverse consequences

Despite these diverse positive effects, adults and children also identified a number of unforeseen negative effects following participation in the VUP programme. These include: the balance between informal work, and care duties and work responsibilities as part of PW; perpetuation of differences in quality of care for biological and non-biological children; and the misuse of money, particularly in relation to alcohol. Although evidence of such adverse effects of social protection is generally less widely available, a number of studies have pointed towards the need for greater scrutiny (Roelen, 2014) and have warned against the risk of basing decisions about 'child-sensitive' social protection on assumptions rather than in-depth and context analyses (Roelen and Sabates-Wheeler, 2012).

Participation in PW programmes creates challenges in balancing informal work and care duties with formal work requirements. Evidence from around the world on the impact of PW programmes on children's outcomes, particularly child labour, is mixed. Whilst evidence of some programmes shows that they reduce the occurrence of child labour, other studies point towards an increase or a substitution effect, whereby children take on tasks from adult household members, such as care responsibilities or housework (Barrientos et al., 2013; Roelen, 2014).

Findings for the VUP confirm the challenges posed by PW programmes in terms of balancing care and PW responsibilities, particularly with respect to women's absence from the household following participation in PW activities. Respondents indicated that they take young children with them to work sites, leave young children in the care of older children, or, in some cases, lock them in the house. PW activities were also mentioned as interfering with the preparation of food in the household, resulting in women getting up early to prepare food before going to work, or sometimes leading to children going without food. As indicated by an adult woman participating in PW: 'As I worked very far from home I had to leave the children alone, and close the door so that they cannot go outside and I left food for them.' Likewise, a young boy living in a household receiving DS observed: 'There are parents who choose to sacrifice some children for being able to go to work in VUP. [...] these children stay home, and are refused to go to school for taking care of his/her siblings.'

Furthermore, these challenges are not specific to women. While many female respondents pointed towards juggling work activities with care duties as the biggest difficulty in relation to PW, male PW participants also suggested that the PW activities interfere with their ability to care for their children. Some respondents mentioned how DS is therefore preferable to PW, as one participant stated: 'The Direct Support benefit more than others, because they get the time to care for their children, whereas the Public Works participants spend much time in works.'

A second, unforeseen, adverse consequence concerns the programme's interplay with pre-existing differential levels of care and well-being for biological and non-biological children across and within households. Both adults and children indicated that biological children often receive better care than non-biological children, both in material and non-material terms. Non-biological children were also instructed to serve as domestic servants or houseworkers in their respective host families, as illustrated by a quote from a child household head from Rwabicuma: 'Most non-biological children raised in families are not treated on the same level as biological children. The parents give much [more] care to their biological children than their non-biological children. Those non-biological [children] don't study, but they stay at home doing the housework.' Although it should be noted that the VUP is not the cause of these inequalities, the programme can perpetuate and compound inequalities if households are considered a single entity, and the situation and needs of their individual children are not taken into account or pre-existing inequalities not addressed. A similar observation was made in the VUP gender audit (FATE Consulting, 2013), which suggested that, in some households, women and older people may not benefit from the VUP, as the household head does not look after their needs.

Finally, concerns exist over the use of transfers, and the items on which cash is spent. In particular, children and women respondents were concerned with the way money, largely VUP transfers, was being misused by men as a means to purchase alcohol. The potential negative use of transfers was also acknowledged by VUP staff. It was stated that village chiefs are involved where money is not being spent properly (such as on alcohol), and that people are removed from the programme in severe cases. Again, the use of cash to purchase alcohol is not a problem triggered by participation in the VUP per se; the issue of alcoholism often preceded participation in the programme. However, a failure to address these spending patterns not only lessens the potential beneficial impact on child well-being and care due to less cash being available, but it can also cause considerable intra-household tensions that lead to poor-quality care.

VUP, prevention of family separation, and family reunification

Factors leading to family separation and loss of parental care vary by context, and may include poverty, violence, abuse, or neglect in the household, a lack of access to basic services including education and health care, the impacts of HIV and AIDS and conflict, and climate change (EveryChild, 2009). Poverty is the most commonly cited factor contributing to the loss of parental care and the institutionalization of children (EveryChild, 2011; UNICEF, 2010). It can result in children having to leave home to work, or to go and live with richer relatives to ease the burden on households. Poverty can also encourage adult migration, leaving children in the care of family members, foster care, or residential care. Poverty can exacerbate other factors which lead to family separation or a loss of parental care. The stress of trying to make ends meet can put a great strain on intra-household dynamics, and be a cause of tension and conflict (EveryChild, 2010). As such, social protection programmes can play a role in preventing family separation through poverty reduction. The effect can take the form of a direct income effect, such that more resources can prevent the need to engage in coping strategies that would result in family separation. The effect can also be indirect, in that the ability to provide for children's basic material needs has the potential to improve parent–child relationships and reduce family conflicts. Such positive effects could be underlined by a complementary package of social support (Csáky, 2014).

Respondents in this research listed a range of different causes for family separation, including poverty, lack of basic needs, alcoholism, family conflicts, and unequal treatment of children in the same household. A child heading a household said: 'Poverty is amongst the reason of separation because some children have left their families, and they went to seek jobs in Kigali, as they could not go to school due to poverty.' A female DS participant said: 'There are many reasons, but the key reasons are poverty and conflicts between parents. For example, in this village there are some girls who went in Kigali, because their families are poor. They become sex workers.' Family separation can be initiated by parents and children, although most examples refer to children leaving the household in search of work or to escape conflict at home. When asked about what could prevent families from breaking up, respondents pointed towards the importance of alleviating poverty, reducing family conflict, and improving communication within the family. Other important factors included the avoidance of drunkenness, family planning, love and affection for children, freedom of expression for children, and good behaviour of children.

Given these causes and preventive factors, the VUP has a positive role to play in preventing family separation. The inflow of cash directly reduces poverty, and improves the ability to provide for basic needs. Subsequent improvements in household dynamics address various non-material concerns, such as family conflicts and tensions. The beneficial role of the VUP was highlighted by a woman participating in DS as follows:

> [T]he thing that causes the separation is poverty and VUP has come to solve this problem. It also helped the beneficiaries to have enough abilities to use the money that they are given. The VUP helped families to stay together, and think about how they can use the money that they get to develop their lives.

Findings were more explicit in terms of how participation in the VUP can support family reunification. Respondents refer to how the programme improved households' abilities to send children to school, and how this often goes hand in hand with a reduction in child labour, including sex work. One male participant in PW pointed out: 'We know families where children have left before due to the poverty and hunger, but after participation in VUP by those families the children came back, and they are studying well.' A female DS participant shared her own experience:

> After getting poor, my husband has left me with my three children, and the last child was three months, but now she is three years; till now I don't know where my husband is. One time I have decided to commit a suicide with my children, but other people were informed, and they stopped me before I get to Mwogo River. After the children were separated they get into different directions, they never get into schools; they had bad behaviour. But, when I get support from VUP, the children came back home, and they can go to school.

Notwithstanding the positive effects, findings suggest that unintended adverse consequences can also have repercussions in terms of family cohesion. First, the misuse of VUP cash was thought to lead to undesirable behaviour such as drunkenness, conflicts, and domestic violence that caused children to leave the household. As indicated by a boy living in a household participating in PW: 'There comes a time when a parent works in VUP, for instance a father, and after getting paid he got the whole money wasted because of the drunkenness, and disputes come from there which leads to a separation.' Second, issues surrounding the balancing of care responsibilities for children with participation in PW activities were also mentioned as a potential cause for family separation, and for children leaving their families. A young boy stated: 'It is possible [for VUP to cause family separation] because sometimes parents spend much time in VUP, and children don't have someone adult to look after them; therefore, parents don't get time to take care of them.'

Incentives for foster care

With respect to those cases where children are in need of alternative care options, there is widespread consensus that kinship support, foster care, or formal adoption are more appropriate and preferable to (temporary) residential care (Shibuya and Taylor, 2013; Thompson, 2014). The 'overextension' of already poor host households is considered one of the major constraints in terms of the provision of informal care for children (Roby, 2011). As such, the provision of support to kinship or foster carers, in the form of cash transfers or sponsorships, can form much needed support to families in enabling them to care for non-biological children. As observed by Duflo (2003), the social pension scheme in South Africa is crucial in supporting grandmothers taking care of single or double orphans following the HIV pandemic. A cash transfer programme in Goma, DRC directed at supporting foster families in caring for separated and unaccompanied children, many of whom were previously members of armed groups, was found to be successful in providing children with family-based care (CaLP, 2012). Findings from other contexts, however, indicate that motives behind the provision of kinship or foster care may not always be benevolent. Roelen et al. (2011) refer to the 'commodification of children', where findings from Botswana suggested that carers are largely motivated by monetary incentives, rather than an intrinsic interest in caring for a child. Experiences in Goma also revealed that an important element to success was the training of carers, and families' agreement to a code of conduct. In settings where such additional measures were not taken, children were more likely to become the victims of abuse and exploitation (CaLP, 2012).

Although the VUP is not a scheme that specifically seeks to support foster/kinship care or aims to be an incentive for households to care for non-biological children, this research provides valuable insight into how the VUP supports those caring for non-biological children and more general perceptions regarding the use of transfers as an incentive for foster care. Adult respondents – including carers for non-biological and biological children – suggest that there are two main reasons that motivate care for a non-biological child: one is based on feelings of love, affection, and compassion; the other is based on more instrumental reasons, with the child being considered a labour resource. A female DS participant stated: 'There are some people who feel love and compassion towards children who don't have families, or those who are not well cared in the families, then you decide to take the child at your household. There [are] others who took those children so they have part of the properties which belonged to the parents of those children.' Furthermore, a male participant in PW said:

> There are a lot of reasons behind raising a non-biological child: everyone with good heart and kindness is touched by the situation of homeless children; there is the family relation which can push the members of same family to take care of children when one of parents

dies; another reason is when the children own properties, and other person fight for raising those children, so that they will share with them those properties.

The presence of materially motivated reasons to take care of a non-biological child underlines the differential levels of care that biological and non-biological children receive, as discussed earlier.

Given this duality of reasons, the potential role of cash transfers or a sponsorship for supporting and incentivizing foster/kinship care can be both positive and negative. When asked about the potential impact of a transfer to support kinship or foster care, both carers of non-biological children and other respondents indicated that it provides much needed support in providing foster/kinship care for children. As indicated by a male participant in DS: 'For those who receive support it gets easier, as they can find means to take care of those children.' Respondents in our sample, who are caring for non-biological children, indicated that they started to care for those children prior to becoming a VUP participant, and so the receipt of VUP was not part of the decision-making process, as demonstrated by a female DS participant: 'The decision to take kids at home came before VUP. Indeed this programme was implemented here while we had taken children within our households.' However, participation in the VUP greatly facilitated their practice.

Other respondents refer, quite explicitly, to how transfers can encourage both positive and negative intentions in people with regard to whether or not they care for non-biological children, including, for example, this male respondent from Kibilize: 'On one hand, the support is a good thing because it will improve the care of children and the family. On the other hand, it would be a bad thing because it can be like a trading business, where a parent will take the child so that he can get the money to solve his problems.' Some adults warn specifically against the negative effects of attaching financial incentives to the provision of foster care: '[a cash transfer] would not be a good idea, as there are some people who take those children as they want to get the sponsorship, and could be like a trading business as they want to gain money, and once the sponsorship is stopped they can fire the children.'

Conclusion and lessons learned

This research's findings provide certain key insights into the role of the VUP in Rwanda, and social protection in the region more broadly, with respect to issues affecting child well-being, children's care, and family reunification. Below, we summarize the key findings, before reflecting on the lessons learned as they relate to positive effects, missed opportunities, and unintended adverse consequences. This chapter then concludes by providing suggestions for the way forward.

Key findings

- The VUP plays a positive role in improving child well-being and quality of care.
- The VUP can support family reunification.
- Benefits from the VUP do not benefit all children equally.
- The VUP PW component may compromise carers' abilities to provide high-quality care.
- The potential spending of cash on alcohol may negatively affect household relations and children's care.
- Cash transfers, as an incentive for foster care, can have positive and negative effects.

Findings point towards overwhelmingly positive effects of the VUP on both material and non-material aspects of care for children. Carers are better able to provide for children's basic needs, instilling confidence and making them feel more able to fulfil their care responsibilities. The subsequent reduction in household tension and conflict improves intra-household relationships between adult household members, and between carers and children. Children feel more appreciated and respected by their caregivers and peers, and are more likely to confide in their caregivers. Findings also suggest that participation in the VUP, and subsequent improvements in living conditions, can support family reunification. Children who were living elsewhere or with other family members to attend school or to work have returned home after households started participating in the VUP. The VUP may also prevent family separation or loss of parental care through its poverty-reducing effect.

Furthermore, these positive findings support the recognition, expressed in Rwanda's 2011 National Social Protection Strategy, that the VUP can 'reach children effectively by providing financial assistance to their carers and other household members who have their best interests at heart' (MINALOC, 2011: 23). More generally, this research corroborates other widespread findings showing the positive effects of social protection programmes on material well-being in sub-Saharan Africa. In addition, this research strongly indicates that social protection programmes can reduce stress and tensions, promote psychosocial well-being of children and carers, and improve family relationships.

We can also identify a number of missed opportunities whereby the VUP appears unable to address pre-existing inequalities and non-conducive behaviour. First, the programme is not well equipped to address the disadvantaged position of non-biological children. Although the VUP is not the cause of this disadvantage, acknowledging differential needs within the household, offering social support services to raise awareness, or referring specific cases of abuse, neglect, or exploitation, present opportunities for reducing, rather than perpetuating, such circumstances. Second, the potential spending of cash transfers on alcohol negatively affects household relations and can undermine children's care, while, in the most extreme cases, it can lead to family separation. Again, the problem of alcoholism is not caused by the VUP, but the programme currently has limited mechanisms to sensitize participants about the use of cash transfers for non-productive purposes, or for responding to individual cases.

Adverse consequences of the VUP were observed, particularly in terms of the PW component, as it was found to compromise the ability of carers to provide high-quality care. The requirement to work, in order to receive transfers, can add to the already existing and pronounced strain on the ability of households to provide care for children. It can also result in children being left unsupervised or assuming the role of a substitute adult, vis-à-vis work and care responsibilities, at the expense of their own schooling and leisure time. Although the tension between care and work duties holds more generally, and is not specific to participation in a PW programme, the additional burden that participation in PW activities poses, over and above existing formal and informal work and care responsibilities, can compromise the quality of care for children, may reinforce inequalities of care between children, and, in extreme cases, can cause family separation.

Cash transfers, as an incentive for foster care, were found to have both positive and negative implications. Transfers can provide much needed support for households caring for non-biological children when such care is principally motivated by feelings of affection, compassion, and humanity. Findings also give rise to concern in terms of the 'commodification of children', in that the financial incentive may be the sole reason for households to care for non-biological children. This can result in children receiving low-quality care, or being exploited as labourers. Although the extent of perverse incentives cannot be established on the basis of this research, the potential of cash transfers to generate atypical incentives is important to keep in mind in the current context of child care reform in Rwanda, and elsewhere in the region. In moving from residential care to family-based care, foster care grants or scholarships are increasingly considered as options for incentivizing families to care for children that are not their own.

These insights begin to address the knowledge gap relating to the wider linkages between social protection and children's care, and generate recommendations for improving the VUP. Recommendations for the VUP following this research also echo those from other sources, including VUP reviews (Devereux, 2012; VUP, 2011) and the VUP gender audit (FATE Consulting, 2013). They also tie into current developments in Rwanda that aim to make the programme more gender- and child-sensitive, including the rollout of the training and sensitization manual as part of the fourth pillar of the VUP, and the assessment of options for linking early childhood development (ECD) to the VUP. These recommendations are also more widely relevant, as they feed into discussions and commitments coming from many other sub-Saharan African countries that are making social protection more child- and gender-sensitive (AU, 2014).

Policy recommendations

- Strengthen the link between the VUP and social work or child protection services.
- Firmly integrate solutions for child care and care responsibilities into the VUP, and particularly into its PW component.
- Use training and sensitization within the VUP more strategically to address issues around children's care and well-being.

One key implication is the requirement for a stronger link between social protection and social work or child protection services. This would allow for the maximization of the programme's positive impacts, while minimizing its negative side effects and perverse incentives. As suggested by a 14-year-old boy from Kibilizi, in response to the question of what should be in place to prevent family separation or to motivate families to care for children who are not their own: 'Regular visits of people from the sector's office to make sure children are alright at home.' Although a certain degree of advice and support already appears to be in place around VUP PW activities, this focuses on a more general use of funds, rather than being particularly child-focused. Stronger advice and support services, and closer monitoring by trained (professional or voluntary) social workers, can create awareness about improving quality of care for children, address intra-household conflict and tensions, respond to misuse of money, and support kinship or foster caregivers.

A second key implication is that solutions for child care and care duties need to be more firmly integrated into social protection programmes, parti-cularly those providing transfers conditional on work or other activities. In Rwanda, UNICEF is currently leading efforts to identify and develop options for making the VUP more sensitive to the needs of early childhood development (UNICEF, 2014). These options include solutions for child care, such as child care facilities at PW sites, or making child care and ECD services an element of PW activities. In terms of the specific case of pregnant and lactating women, it is suggested that women could be temporarily moved into DS, or be relieved of their work requirement. Improved child care options and provisions for pregnant and lactating women would improve the quality of care for children, and can help avoid family separation. As indicated by Devereux (2012) and FATE Consulting (2013), such solutions can also address gender inequities and reduce women's exclusion by making PW programmes more accessible for them, by offering both a solution to their care burden and activities that are more physically feasible. Such initiatives have to be undertaken with due caution, however, as they build on women's existing roles as main caregivers, and may therefore reinforce, rather than lessen, gender inequities.

A third key implication refers to optimizing the opportunities offered by social protection programmes to provide sensitization and training to programme participants, staff, and the wider community. With respect to the VUP in Rwanda, sensitization and training services are already being undertaken, but could be used more strategically to address issues around children's care and well-being. Strengthening and widening the coverage of these sensitization efforts could help further improve the quality of care, but also avoid family separation. Improvements should be made in terms of standardizing sensitization efforts across all sectors included in the VUP, and strengthening the capacity of the staff and volunteers involved. Current developments in terms of the rollout of the fourth pillar of the VUP are promising, with sector leaders around the country being trained in using the training and sensitization manual. Strong monitoring of these efforts, and continued support for ongoing skills training and capacity building, particularly in terms of more complex issues around child well-being and children's care, will be imperative to make these efforts effective. This holds particularly true as a number of problems identified in this report (unequal care between biological and non-biological children, gendered patterns of care, misuse of money on alcohol) are largely caused by socio-cultural factors.

Note

1. The research in Rwanda is part of a multi-country research project that is a joint initiative of Family for Every Child, and the Centre for Social Protection at the Institute of Development Studies (IDS).

References

AU (2014) *Recommendations of the African Union Expert Consultation on Children and Social Protection Systems: Building the African Agenda. Fourth Session of the AU Conference of Ministers of Social Development (CAMSD4)*. African Union, Addis Ababa.

Barrientos, A., Byrne, J., Villa, J.M. and Peña, P. (2013) 'Social transfers and child protection', *Working Paper 2013-05*. UNICEF Office of Research, Florence.

Brooks-Gunn, J. and Duncan, G. (1997) 'The effects of poverty on children', in *The Future of Children 7*(2), pp. 55–71 <http://dx.doi.org/10.2307/1602387>.

CaLP (2012) *What Cash Transfer Programming Can Do to Protect Children from Violence, Abuse and Exploitation. Review and Recommendations*. The Cash Learning Partnership: Save the Children and Women's Refugee Commission, Oxford, London, and New York, NY.

Corak, M. (2006) 'Do poor children become poor adults? Lessons from a cross-country comparison of generational earnings mobility', *Discussion Paper No. 1993*. Institute for the Study of Labor, Bonn.

Csáky, C. (2014) *Why Care Matters: The Importance of Adequate Care for Children and Society*. Family for Every Child, London.

Devereux, S. (2012) *Third Annual Review of DFID Support to the Vision 2020 Umurenge Programme (VUP), Rwanda*. Institute of Development Studies, Brighton.

Devereux, S., Roelen, K., Béné, C., Chopra, D., Leavy, J. and McGregor, A. (2013) 'Evaluating outside the box: an alternative framework for analysing social protection programmes', *IDS Working Paper 431/CSP Working Paper 010*. Institute of Development Studies and Centre for Social Protection, Brighton.

DFID (2011) *Cash Transfers Evidence Paper*. Department for International Development, London.

Duflo, E. (2003) 'Grandmothers and granddaughters: old-age pensions and intrahousehold allocation in South Africa', *The World Bank Economic Review* 17(1): 1–25 <http://dx.doi.org/10.1093/wber/lhg013>.

EveryChild (2009) *Every Child Deserves a Family: EveryChild's Approach to Children Without Parental Care*. EveryChild, London.

EveryChild (2010) *Positively Caring: Ensuring that Positive Choices Can Be Made About the Care of Children Affected by HIV*. EveryChild, London.

EveryChild (2011) 'Scaling down: reducing, reshaping and improving residential care around the world', *Positive Care Choices: Working Paper 1*. EveryChild, London.

FATE Consulting (2013) *Vision 2020 Umurenge Programme (VUP) Gender Equity Assessment*. Rwanda Local Development Support Fund, Kigali.

Fiszbein, A. and Schady, N. (2009) *Conditional Cash Transfers: Reducing Present and Future Poverty. A World Bank Policy Research Report*. World Bank, Washington DC <http://dx.doi.org/10.1596/978-0-8213-7352-1>.

Hanlon, J., Barrientos, A. and Hulme D. (2010) *Just Give Money to the Poor: The Development Revolution from the Global South*. Kumarian Press, Sterling, VA.

Harper, C., Marcus, R. and Moore, K. (2003) 'Enduring poverty and the conditions of childhood: lifecourse and intergenerational poverty transmissions', *World Development* 31(3): 535–54 <http://dx.doi.org/10.1016/S0305-750X(03)00010-X>.

Jones, N. and Marquez, E.V. (2014) 'Is cash the answer? Lessons for child protection programming from Peru: the Juntos (Together) program has the potential to improve children's care and protection', *Child Abuse & Neglect* 38(3): 383–94 <http://dx.doi.org/10.1016/j.chiabu.2014.01.015>.

MINALOC (2011) *National Social Protection Strategy*. Ministry of Local Government, Kigali.

Roby, J. (2011) *Children in Informal Alternative Care*. UNICEF, New York, NY.

Roelen, K. (2014) 'Sticks or carrots? Conditional cash transfers and their effect on child abuse and neglect: researchers observe both benefits and harms of CCT programs', *Child Abuse & Neglect* 38(3): 372–82 <http://dx.doi.org/10.1016/j.chiabu.2014.01.014>.

Roelen, K., Edstrom, J., Sabates-Wheeler, R. and Davies, M. (2011) *Lessons from the Children and AIDS Regional Initiative (CARI): Child- and HIV-Sensitive Social Protection in Eastern and Southern Africa*. Centre for Social Protection, Institute of Development Studies, Brighton.

Roelen, K. and Sabates-Wheeler, R. (2012) 'A child-sensitive approach to social protection: serving practical and strategic needs', *Journal of Poverty and Social Justice* 20(3): 291–306 <http://dx.doi.org/10.1332/175982712X657118>.

Sanfilippo, M., De Neubourg, C. and Martorano, B. (2012) 'The impact of social protection on children: a review of the literature', *Working Paper 2012-06*. UNICEF Office of Research, Florence.

Shibuya, T. and Taylor, V. (2013) 'Alternative care options and policy choices to support orphans: the case of Mozambique in the context of the SADC',

International Social Security Review 66(1): 71–95 <http://dx.doi.org/10.1111/issr.12003>.

Thompson, H. (2014) 'Cash for protection: cash transfer programs can promote child protection outcomes', *Child Abuse & Neglect* 38(3): 360–71 <http://dx.doi.org/10.1016/j.chiabu.2014.01.013>.

UNICEF (2010) *At Home or In a Home? Formal Care and Adoption of Children in Eastern Europe and Central Asia*. UNICEF, Geneva.

UNICEF (2014) 'Child-sensitive social protection: linking ECD to VUP', paper presented at roundtable discussion *Protection and Children's Care*, Kigali, 13 March 2014.

VUP (2011) *Vision 2020 Umurenge Programme. Annual Report 2009/10*. VUP/Rural Local Development Support Fund/MINALOC, Kigali.

About the authors

Keetie Roelen is a research fellow at the Institute of Development Studies and Co-Director of the Centre for Social Protection. Her research and work focus on the dynamics of (child) poverty, the linkages between child protection and social protection, intergenerational graduation out of poverty, and mixed method evaluations of social protection programmes in sub-Saharan Africa and Asia.

Helen Karki Chettri is a Nepal-based social policy research consultant currently working with the Institute of Development Studies and the Centre for Social Protection. She has several years of grass-roots experience with South American and Nepali NGOs working in research, education, child protection, and alternative care, and has advised on NGO-level policy for child protection issues including alternative care and reunification.

Emily Delap is Head of Technical Support at Family for Every Child, a network of national NGOs promoting family strengthening and alternative care. She has over 20 years' experience in the field of child protection and alternative care.

CHAPTER 6

Promoting employment, protecting youth: BRAC's Empowerment and Livelihoods for Adolescent Girls Programme in Uganda and Tanzania

Nicola Banks

How can development policies and programmes better address the multiple needs of vulnerable youth populations? This case study of BRAC's Empowerment and Livelihoods for Adolescent Girls Programme in Uganda and Tanzania emphasizes that integrated programmes are necessary to reach deeper transformative goals of youth empowerment. Programmes that combine life skills and livelihoods training, and generate strong peer support networks, can go beyond improved employment outcomes to also improve social conditions and health outcomes for participants and the broader community.

Keywords: protecting youth, employment promotion, empowerment, sexual and reproductive health

Introduction

Global youth unemployment has reached unprecedented levels. Latest figures highlight a 'Generation at Risk' from unemployment (ILO, 2013). Labour market difficulties for young people go beyond unemployment: as many as two-thirds of youth populations in developing economies (where 90 per cent of the global youth population live) are under-utilized (ILO, 2013). These dangers are particularly pronounced in sub-Saharan Africa (SSA), where youth constitute large proportions of national populations and where economic growth has been fuelled by natural resource extraction rather than industry, limiting the job-creating potential of growth in towns and cities (Kessides, 2007; Potts, 2013; World Bank, 2014).

This chapter highlights the need, on multiple grounds, to target Africa's youth in poverty reduction programmes. First, young people constitute large proportions of national populations: over 40 per cent of the population in all but three African countries (Guengant and May, 2013). The term 'youth bulge' has become synonymous with large youth populations in some policy circles, raising fears of large frustrated youth cohorts on national development

http://dx.doi.org/10.3362/9781780448435.006

outcomes (Urdal, 2008). Second, young Africans suffer disproportionately from development challenges, such as higher rates of under-employment and unemployment and HIV/AIDS infection (Garcia and Fares, 2008b; Garrett, 2005). The third reason that warrants specific programmatic attention for youth is that it constitutes such a critical period in the lifecycle. It is a period when young people become increasingly independent and household support is reduced (Juarez et al., 2013). As well as its financial implications, long periods of under-employment and unemployment have devastating results throughout the lifecycle, reducing human capital accumulation and impairing future job prospects (Garcia and Fares, 2008a; Godfrey, 2003).

In this chapter we explore how BRAC's Empowerment and Livelihoods for Adolescent Girls (ELA) programme in Uganda and Tanzania has been designed to assist young people into better employment and address broader social development. We begin by introducing the context in which ELA operates, looking at the key social and economic challenges facing young people – and young women in particular – in Uganda and Tanzania. Then we outline how programme objectives and components are designed to address the key vulnerabilities young women face in these two contexts. Findings from a first-round impact evaluation of ELA in Uganda find that it increases labour force participation and income, improves health-related knowledge, and reduces risky behaviours (Bandiera et al., 2012). We explore the channels through which these outcomes are realized, before concluding with some important lessons for other NGO programmes aimed at young people's social and economic development.

Youth employment in sub-Saharan Africa: economic vulnerability in Uganda and Tanzania

Work is critical to income generation, but also to securing status, acceptance, and self-confidence (Bryceson, 2010). Yet the labour market prospects of Africa's youth populations are bleak. The informal sector is the major source of job creation, accounting for 90 per cent of all new jobs created across Africa in the 1990s (Brown et al., 2010). Africa's youth unemployment rate of 11.8 per cent is below the global average of 12.6 per cent, but is accompanied by a high dependence on irregular and informal opportunities, and high levels of working poverty (ILO, 2013; World Bank, 2014). This makes youth employment an increasingly pressing policy priority across the continent, requiring action from governments, the private sector, NGOs, communities, and young people themselves.

Uganda and Tanzania are the focus of this paper. In both countries, young people constitute large and increasing proportions of the population. Uganda had the world's youngest population in 2010, as well as the highest prevalence of poverty among its youth (World Bank, 2008). Latest census figures indicate that 78 per cent of Uganda's population is under the age of 30 (UBOS, 2010). Likewise, with 66 per cent of its population under the age of 25, Tanzania is fast approaching a 'youth bulge' that is expected to last for the next 30 years (Restless Development, 2013).

The different structure of these two economies and labour markets results in varying employment opportunity landscapes and poverty statuses for youth in Uganda and Tanzania. While the majority of Ugandan youth are employed in agriculture, over half of young people in Tanzania are employed in services (Elder and Koné, 2014). Cross-country surveys reveal that nearly 60 per cent of Ugandan youth report living in 'poor' or 'fairly poor' households. In Tanzania, just under 60 per cent of young people report their household economic status as being 'average', and only around 30 per cent report it as being 'poor' or 'fairly poor' (Elder and Koné, 2014).

Young people suffer disproportionately from deteriorating labour market outcomes in both countries. Tanzania has the highest average youth unemployment rate of 42 per cent, well above sub-Saharan Africa's average rate of 22.8 per cent (Elder and Koné, 2014). Long-term unemployment is a serious problem: more than 40 per cent of unemployed youth in Tanzania have been unemployed for more than two years, and more than 70 per cent have been unemployed for more than a year (Garcia and Fares, 2008a). One-quarter and 67 per cent of young men and women, respectively, are 'discouraged workers', that is, inactive members of the labour force who have been discouraged from their job search (Godfrey, 2003).

Young people make up 80 per cent of Uganda's unemployed (IYF, 2011). They take an average of three years before finding employment (Garcia and Fares, 2008c). Over 90 per cent survive through irregular and informal employment, compared with just under 60 per cent of adults (Garcia and Fares, 2008a). Only 12 per cent of Ugandan youth receive stable monthly incomes (Banks and Sulaiman, 2012), highlighting the difficulties they face meeting their basic needs.

Concerns about the long-term implications of young people's risky behaviours on well-being and mortality are frequently expressed (Furlong, 2009). Transactional sexual relationships are one option young women resort to in order to meet their basic needs (Samara, 2010). As young women in Uganda highlighted, 'It is poverty at home that forces one to give into the demands of the opposite sex ... Once a girl has dropped out of school she will be tempted by all avenues to survive. A girl may decide to have sex with a man just to earn 5,000 shillings to buy essentials' (Banks and Sulaiman, 2012: 96).[1] Young women face marked gender inequalities due to their lower economic and socio-cultural status. They spend a disproportionate amount of time caring for other family members, engaged in domestic responsibilities, and/or working as unpaid family labourers (Godfrey, 2003). A nationally representative survey in Uganda found that young women receive, on average, 0.7 years less schooling than young men, are disadvantaged in ownership of physical assets and land, and have less access to finance both in terms of cash incomes and the ability to borrow money (Banks and Sulaiman, 2012). Tanzanian young women are also less likely to be in school than young men of the same age

(Kondylis and Manacorda, 2008), underscoring discrepancies in literacy rates of 83 and 78 per cent for Tanzanian young men and women (aged 15–24), respectively (NBS, 2011). Early pregnancy or marriage leads to early withdrawal from schooling and entry into the labour market. When girls fall pregnant they face an even bigger set of challenges that influence their ability to stay in school, achieve positive health outcomes, and avoid social and economic threats (Bangser, 2010). It is unsurprising then, that 30 per cent of Ugandan youth identify early pregnancy as the biggest health risk for young women (Banks and Sulaiman, 2012).

Young women are also particularly vulnerable to HIV/AIDS. Both Uganda and Tanzania display significantly higher rates of HIV/AIDS infection than Africa's average: 7.2 per cent and 5.8 per cent of their populations (aged 15–49), respectively, are HIV positive, in comparison with 4.9 per cent across sub-Saharan Africa (PRB, 2014). In Tanzania, young women are at a higher risk of infection from an earlier age, accounting for 45 per cent of new HIV/AIDS infections (TACAIDS, 2008). Understanding how risky behaviours are driven in part by economic insecurity highlights that programmes to improve health outcomes through increasing sexual and reproductive health knowledge cannot on their own address the root economic causes resulting in risky behaviours and negative health outcomes. We have to see these behaviours and practices as outcomes of a much broader set of constraints and challenges facing young women (Banks and Sulaiman, 2012). Behavioural change within this context is dependent on transforming opportunities for young women, giving them the economic power they require for making informed decisions and withstanding social pressures.

This is the philosophy that underpinned the design of BRAC's ELA programme, which the following section discusses. Crucially, it recognizes the inter-linkages between young women's economic, social, and health vulnerabilities, and that the programme's impact can be maximized by pursuing social and economic objectives simultaneously.

BRAC's ELA programme

BRAC is a Bangladeshi NGO that has received global acclaim for its work in poverty reduction. It expanded internationally in 2002, and began operations in Uganda and Tanzania in 2006. Recognizing the multiple challenges of school dropout, early pregnancy, poverty, and unemployment faced by young women in East Africa, the ELA programme was designed and implemented from 2008, with an initial 100 clubs opened in both countries (Yam, 2013). The programme seeks the social and economic empowerment of school-going and out-of-school young women (aged 13–25) through an integrated programme of life skills and livelihoods training, complemented by access to microfinance. This is delivered through a club-based platform that provides peer support and a place for activities like music, dance, drama, and sports. In doing so, it joins a calibre of development programmes in trying to reverse the cycle of intergenerational poverty by putting girls first in an attempt to overcome problems of early school dropout, early marriage, and motherhood that lead to long-term social and economic insecurity, and to realize their role as important agents of change in the community.[2] In partnership with the MasterCard Foundation, ELA has scaled up dramatically in Uganda, now reaching 1,285 clubs and around 50,000 girls across the country (BRAC, 2012a). In neighbouring Tanzania the programme has grown more slowly, with 180 clubs reaching around 7,400 girls (BRAC, 2012b). The ELA programme follows an integrated approach, recognizing that the key to transforming opportunities and creating behavioural change among young women will be dependent on improved sexual and reproductive health (SRH) knowledge *and* improved incomes. Table 6.1 presents a breakdown of the programme and its components.

Economic components include financial literacy training, vocational training, and microfinance, while social components include the provision of a safe space for socializing, playing, and learning, life skills training, and mentoring. Recognizing the importance of institutional support to young people's acceptance and development in the community, BRAC also mobilizes parent support committees. Individually, each component plays an important role. Furthermore, they combine to create an enabling environment that protects investments gained as young women become equipped with the skills, support, confidence, and access to finance they need to become socially and economically empowered. Findings from a recent impact evaluation in Uganda indicate that this goal is more than just a dream (Bandiera et al., 2012). Alongside economic improvements of club members, results show improvements in health behaviours and outcomes that spill over to other young women in ELA communities (YEN, 2013). Here we explore how Uganda's programme has achieved these results, giving young women the economic power to make good decisions, and transforming social norms and practices in the community.

Social components of the ELA programme

As Table 6.1 illustrates, ELA follows a graduated approach, starting with the social components of activities and building towards the introduction of livelihood and financial literacy training and microfinance. At the centre of the programme is the provision of adolescent development clubs. These offer a platform of service delivery that provides a safe physical space for programme activities, and creates a supportive environment to fulfil the programme's transformative objectives. Clubs are open every weekday afternoon, and are led by a female mentor who is selected by the community as a responsible young woman with leadership potential (Yam, 2013). Members are offered a variety of club activities including reading, board games, sports, singing, drama, and dancing. Alongside these, mentors facilitate a programme of life skills discussions that cover: the key health-related risks issues facing young women (puberty, menstruation, family planning, sexually transmitted infections and HIV/AIDS,

Table 6.1 BRAC's Empowerment and Livelihoods for Adolescent Girls Programme: Components, purpose, and timeline

Programme component	Purpose	Project timeline
Club house	To provide a safe space for learning, socializing, and supporting one another, as well as an enabling environment that helps maximize returns to social and economic investments.	From club opening
Mentor	Appointed by community to facilitate club activities and act as role model to members.	From club opening
Life skills training	To improve SRH knowledge and reduce risky behaviours, early pregnancy, and transmission of STDs and HIV/AIDS.	From club opening
	To improve life skills such as leadership, negotiation, and improved knowledge on rights. Building confidence and solidarity.	
Various activities (sports, games, books, music, dance, drama)	To build confidence and solidarity and provide an opportunity for members to be 'young' amidst adult responsibilities.	From club opening
Livelihoods skills training (and inputs)	To build skills that members can translate into income-generating opportunities. (For training in agriculture and poultry this is accompanied by inputs to increase skills utilization.)	Six months after club opening
Financial literacy training	To enhance financial literacy, maximize the impact of livelihood training, and prepare members for possibility of taking microfinance loans.	Seven months after club opening
Microfinance	To provide start-up capital for self-employment. Loans start at the local equivalent of around US$100, increasing by around US$60 each cycle.[3]	Eight months after club opening
Parent/support committees	To build a supportive environment for the club and help achieve the programme's transformative objectives.	From club opening

Source: adapted from Yam (2013)

sexual and reproductive health issues, and rape); life skills (management skills, negotiation, leadership, and conflict resolution); and legal issues affecting women (bride price, child marriage, and violence against women) (Bandiera et al., 2012). The club space enables privacy, which is critical when discussing sensitive topics and in creating a space where young women feel comfortable sharing and discussing personal issues and problems.

There are two important processes at play here. The first is the process of education itself, that is, the transmission of relevant information about the key issues young women are facing in their day-to-day lives. Second, and perhaps more crucial for the programme's transformative goals, is the creation of a strong peer support network. Research in both countries highlights the limited material and emotional support young people receive from their parents, making peer support one of their most valuable assets (Banks, forthcoming; Banks and Sulaiman, 2012). Regular interactions allow club members to create strong networks that offer support and advice in all aspects of their lives. It provides opportunities to collectively discuss and solve problems that girls come across in their daily lives. One young woman in Uganda highlighted that of all the things the ELA club had contributed to her success, the most important was neither the training nor the microfinance that had helped her run a thriving business, but the support and guidance she had received from her ELA friends. Through this support she no longer has to 'go it alone'. Rather, she has a close-knit group of friends in similar positions with whom she discusses how best to survive and support their dependents, how best they can sustain their businesses, and how they can live well with others without conflict, including how to resist the advances of the opposite sex (Banks and Sulaiman, 2012).

Differences across Uganda and Tanzania highlight two important aspects of these processes of change. One is the socio-cultural context which directly influences the effectiveness of the life skills component in building a network of solidarity. In Uganda, the peer support platform is harnessed because Ugandans are typically open and free in their discussions of personal and intimate lives, and this leads to frank discussions in which members are happy to share their personal experiences (Yam, 2013). In contrast, cultural characteristics dampen the impact of these activities, with members reluctant to discuss their private lives and personal experiences for fear of judgement (ibid.). Second is the importance of a distinct girls-only space that allows ELA members to feel ownership over club activities, and to attend regularly. This is evident in one particular region in Tanzania where the programme was facing implementation and retention problems. Here, the programme had been unable to secure clubhouses in many of the villages, with meetings switching between different members' houses or open spaces around town (ibid.). This caused multiple problems; for example, if it rained clubs could not open, materials got lost and damaged moving around regularly, and girls got tired of moving from place to place (ibid.). In contrast, all Ugandan ELA clubs have their own prescribed space that can be decorated by members with posters, paintings, and drawings from their life skills sessions (ibid.).

It is easy to underestimate the importance of the 'social' side of club activities. Time use allocations in Uganda highlight that large proportions of young people's time are taken up by work, study, and domestic responsibilities, leaving little time for entertainment or escaping the pressures of everyday life (Banks and Sulaiman, 2012). Parents or husbands frown upon time that is not spent 'productively' away from household obligations, but young people see social activities as critical to developing their talents. Group participation in activities like ELA assists with the development of a range of social competencies such as self-esteem, communication skills, and confidence. It also builds social assets through expanding friends and social networks, engaging with young people from other backgrounds and communities, and promoting positive perceptions of young people in the community (Banks and Sulaiman, 2012; Tanti et al., 2011).

A diverse selection of activities is also central to regular participation and member retention. Evaluation of Uganda's ELA programme two years after initiation revealed that most members attended club meetings for an average of one or two times a week, representing a significant time investment (Bandiera et al., 2012). Retaining regular attendance, therefore, requires ongoing activities that members continue to find enjoyable and attractive. Again, comparisons across Uganda and Tanzania illustrate this fact. Where the programme struggled in Tanzania, clubs lacked a variety of functioning materials to attract girls, which mentors blamed for low attendance rates (Yam, 2013). ELA clubs were more successful in a second region of Tanzania, but even here, where there was a variety of books and games, members complained about the repetitiveness of activities (ibid.). Uganda's programme has responded to these challenges by diversifying and improving club activities, holding regional sports, music, and talent competitions across clubs, encouraging members to perform at community forums to share the life skills training they have used, and developing their artistic talents through handicraft production (ibid.).

Economic components of the programme

The outcomes of ELA's economic components are more direct in terms of increasing employment and income-generating activities (IGAs). It is these economic benefits that are the key attraction to club membership and central to generating parental and community support for the programme (Yam, 2013). The programme generally attracts young women who place a high value on financial independence (such as single mothers or those alienated from their families) and those who are most likely to benefit from economic activities, namely those who believe they could be successful entrepreneurs but who lack the skills for this prior to joining (Bandiera et al., 2009).

ELA's economic components are not introduced until the club has been open for six months, and after the life skills education is completed. In the sixth month, a range of livelihood training is made available, followed by financial literacy training in the seventh. The staggered introduction of these two components aims to prepare members for the introduction of microfinance in the eighth month, theoretically equipping members with the skills they need to expand IGAs, financial know-how on how to manage small businesses as well as increased incomes, and then finally, the access to capital they need to fulfil this.

Members can self-select onto a variety of livelihood training on offer. Beneficiaries of the training are primarily non-school-going members.[4] BRAC agriculture staff teach short courses on agriculture, poultry, and livestock-rearing, and local experts are hired to teach short introductory courses in hairdressing, food-processing, and tailoring, amongst others. In both contexts, members, parents, and trainers have voiced concerns about the livelihood training (Yam, 2013). Most take place in under a week, giving insufficient exposure to the concepts and skills being learned, or the practical experience necessary for utilizing them for income generation (ibid.). Microfinance is introduced to ELA clubs after members have completed financial literacy training. This component of the ELA programme is the most recent, but also one of the most popular. Attendance registers show that club attendance rebounds after microfinance is introduced (ibid.). Alongside low and irregular incomes, limited access to financial services means that young women struggle to accumulate start-up capital. Only 9 per cent of young Ugandans have loans, with young women half as likely to have borrowed money as young men (Banks and Sulaiman, 2012). This makes ELA's microfinance programme one of the few places where young women can access lump sums of capital when they lack financial support from their parents. Starting at the local equivalent of around US$100, loans increase by around US$60 with each cycle (Yam, 2013), allowing members to access greater sums once they have proven their ability to invest and manage funds. While some members express dissatisfaction with the size of new and repeat loans in both countries (ibid.), loan ceilings do minimize the likelihood of encountering repayment problems or over-indebtedness.

Programme impacts: social and economic empowerment for young women?

Since inception, the ELA programme in Uganda and Tanzania has been subject to a rigorous multi-stage impact evaluation based on a randomized control trial (RCT). This tracks 4,800 girls in 100 treatment and 50 control villages, and is being carried out in collaboration with a team of researchers led by University College London and the London School of Economics. After a baseline survey in 2008, Uganda's first follow-up survey was conducted in 2010. The evaluation in Tanzania started slightly later in 2009, with a first-round follow up in 2011.[5] The results of this analysis in Tanzania are not yet available, but early analysis suggests that it has had negligible impact (Yam, 2013). In contrast, Ugandan results show that ELA has achieved significant impact in social and economic indicators (Bandiera et al., 2012). A greater number of young women in ELA villages are engaged in IGAs and earning higher incomes, while health knowledge has improved across a number of indicators, and this is feeding into behavioural change and improved health outcomes at the village level (ibid.). Table 6.2 illustrates a selection of some of the key indicators of change. This first-round follow-up took place before microfinance was introduced. This means economic improvements can only be considered in relation to livelihood and financial literacy training, and the programme's social components.

One of the most visible improvements is in the number of girls involved in IGAs. The likelihood of a young woman being involved in an IGA (predominantly self-employment) showed an increase of 32 per cent over baseline levels (Bandiera et al., 2012).[6] Improvements in economic empowerment are evident

Table 6.2 Impact evaluation of the ELA programme in Uganda: Selected indicators

Income-generating activities (IGAs)	
Engagement in IGAs	32% increase in girls engaged in IGAs
Cash incomes	Girls are four percentage points more likely to earn income from self-employment
	Average increase of 14.8% in earnings from self-employment relative to baseline
Health-related behavioural change	
Fertility rates	Treatment villages display a 26% drop in fertility rates
Self-reported condom usage	Treatment villages display a 12.5% increase in sexually active young women who always use a condom
Sexual coercion	Number of girls who report having sex unwillingly decreases by 16.1 percentage points in treated communities

Source: adapted from Bandiera et al. (2012)

across a variety of indicators including engagement in IGAs, personal income, financial literacy, entrepreneurial ability, financial market participation, and personal savings. The programme significantly increases self-reported entrepreneurial skills along nearly every dimension of an entrepreneurial skills index (ibid.).[7] The authors report that these economic impacts are particularly encouraging since RCT evaluations of standalone financial and entrepreneurship training have generally found weaker impacts (ibid.). The results suggest, however, that economic improvements are confined to ELA club members and do not spill over to other young women in ELA villages, that is, non-participants in ELA villages were no more likely to be earning an income than young women in control villages (YEN, 2013).

In contrast, the evaluation finds significant improvements in reproductive health knowledge and practices that spill over to other young women in ELA communities (YEN, 2013). This means that girls are not only more aware and knowledgeable about issues such as STIs, HIV/AIDS, and early pregnancy, but are also more likely to follow safe practices (Bandiera et al., 2012). In comparison with control villages where only 38 per cent of young women report always using a condom during sexual intercourse, 16 per cent more young women report this behaviour in ELA villages (ibid.). This effect is even stronger among ELA members, 67 per cent of whom report consistent condom usage (ibid.). Similar direct and indirect impacts are observed in the prevalence of early motherhood. Girls living in ELA villages are three percentage points less likely to report having a child, corresponding with a 28.6 per cent decrease in fertility rates among the target population (ibid.). Young women in ELA villages are also more likely to seek health services when they have an STD. Another startling result is the reduction in the number of girls reporting having had sex unwillingly, which dropped by around 16 percentage points from the baseline level of 21 per cent, and this represents a 76 per cent reduction in such incidents (ibid.).

Other indirect impacts of participation in ELA activities are likely to play a role in improved health-related behaviours, including increases in self-confidence and self-esteem, and greater hopes and aspirations for the future. Furthermore, greater economic security gives young women the opportunity to enter relationships out of choice rather than necessity, and gives them greater autonomy and negotiating power over the terms of sexual relations. Common in discussions with ELA members in Uganda is a heightened determination to forge their own paths away from the manipulations of men. As one programme beneficiary in Uganda revealed: 'Of course I get advances like all other young women here, but I just turn them away. Both younger and older women are constantly complaining about their boyfriends and husbands mistreating them, so why would I want to put myself through this?' (Banks and Sulaiman, 2012: 111). That social improvements have reached outside club boundaries shows that young people's social networks are not confined to the club, and that new social norms are starting to be established where ELA mentors and members come to be seen as role models in the community. The programme has taken steps to catalyse this spillover effect, with ELA members in both countries taking peer education outside of club members to reach more young women in the community through drama performances and networks of friends (Yam, 2013).

We see, therefore, that the ELA programme in Uganda has achieved remarkable success in its early stages, even prior to the addition of microfinance. Yet as we saw earlier, tentative results from Tanzania's impact evaluation do not show the same level of success. Cultural differences, in terms of willingness to discuss personal issues, influence the ability of members to draw upon each other for support. These are exacerbated in the region where the programme struggled to secure clubhouses, with clubs unable to build social cohesion and strong relationships given the lack of active participation in club activities (Yam, 2013). Different cross-country outcomes also highlight the importance of strong programme management, implementation, and two-way processes of accountability. Geographic difficulties made this difficult in Tanzania. The region where ELA clubs were struggling was 450km away from BRAC's Head Office. This makes communication with programme management difficult, and dampens accountability processes, both in terms of ensuring staff are implementing the programme in line with the model and that the demands of ELA members are fed back to programme management (ibid.). These problems were intensified by the fact that the programme's Area Manager post had been vacant for one year in this area, leaving other supervisory staff stretched and unable to control programme staff (ibid.). Underperforming staff, who were often absent from work and were not adhering to guidelines, feed directly into the motivations of mentors, and through them, ELA members (ibid.). In Uganda, by contrast, monthly management meetings provide an opportunity for ELA staff from across the country to come to Kampala to be updated with management and operational requirements, review programme rules and procedures to ensure adherence to the same, and to feed back issues from the field (ibid.).

Staff are motivated, engaged, and visiting the clubs frequently to supervise, and to see whether the programme continues to meet members' needs (ibid.).

Conclusions and lessons learned

As we have seen, risky sexual behaviours and poor sexual and reproductive health outcomes are symptomatic of a broad set of constraints and challenges facing young people in all aspects of their lives. Central to this is limited financial independence, and the difficulties young women face meeting their basic needs when economic opportunities are so scarce. The ELA programme recognizes that changing these behaviours requires building and expanding economic opportunities for young women. It does so through creating an enabling environment in which the benefits can be realized through a supportive peer network, in the process allowing young women to be change agents in their lives and communities. In doing so, the programme triggers a process of institutional change, creating a more supportive environment for youth by slowly reshaping the institutions that play a key role (and often a key constraint) in their lives. Given the widespread negative stereotypes of young people, attitude changes across parents, communities, employers, politicians, and even young people themselves, help to create more supportive environments. This is the case not only in terms of financial and material support, but also with respect to the emotional support necessary to give young women the range and depth of assets they need to turn their dreams into reality and negotiate a successful transition to adulthood (Banks and Sulaiman, 2012).

BRAC's ELA programme illustrates the return to this two-pronged approach to youth development: that of increasing young women's access to the assets and skills they need while, at the same time, improving the institutional environment in which they are situated. Positive effects, as seen from Uganda's impact evaluation, suggest that combining these social and economic objectives and interventions proves especially effective when it comes to reducing risky sexual behaviours (Bandiera et al., 2012; YEN, 2013). In doing so, the programme recognizes and 'treats' both the 'symptoms' and root causes of risky sexual behaviours. These findings emphasize that risky behaviours should not be viewed independently of the limited economic opportunities, poverty, and financial dependence that increase young women's vulnerability.

BRAC's ELA programme seeks development as transformation, and not only of individual lives and outcomes, but also of the social and economic environment that disadvantages and constrains young women. The programme's success in Uganda, along with lessons from Tanzania where it has been less successful, has important implications for other programmes assisting young people's development, which we conclude with here.

Programmes must take a holistic approach to young women's development: Making a successful transition to adulthood as healthy, happy, and productive citizens requires young people to take control of their own lives and futures. Programmes focusing on narrower outcomes (such as awareness campaigns or vocational training) are not addressing the multitude of constraints young women face, which include: a lack of institutional support and social assets; a lack of role models in the community; a lack of economic opportunities, poverty, and financial insecurity; and limited means through which they can escape the realities and responsibilities of their everyday lives. The deeper transformative goals of social and economic empowerment – enabling young women to become change agents in their lives and communities – would not be possible from the economic or social components individually.

Securing and retaining member participation and commitment is critical: Parents and members are attracted to the club primarily for its economic components, since these meet their most urgent needs. BRAC's graduated approach, delaying economic components until social interventions are completed, is critical in meeting the broader goals of the programme. The programme's social benefits in terms of improved knowledge and behavioural change, and increased confidence, self-esteem, and leadership skills, are dependent on receiving life skills training, and strong peer support networks developing between members. Continued investments in and diversification of club activities are necessary to maintain membership and participation and the club's social impacts. If girls get bored, or if parents and/or guardians see club activities as a waste of time, they may become demotivated and stop participating, since commitment to the club comes at a cost of other competing demands on time. Uganda's ability to meet demands for new activities helps to drive the success of the programme there and must be maintained.

What about young men? The ELA programme focuses on young women because of their relative disadvantage, and their high risk of early pregnancy, school dropout, and exposure to STDs and HIV/AIDS. Yet the pressure and influence from young men continues to be a key driver of the vulnerabilities facing young women when it comes to their sexual and reproductive health outcomes (Banks and Sulaiman, 2012). Under-employment and unemployment lead to specific forms of anxiety for young men when it comes to marriage and family formation, who are expected to be financially responsible for providing housing and living costs after marriage, despite their struggles to meet their basic needs in the present (Banks and Sulaiman, 2012). Pursuing multiple sexual relationships is one means through which young men attempt to redefine their masculinity in the face of unemployment, increasing young women's exposure to STDs and HIV/AIDS (Joshi, 2011). Unless young men work alongside young women to challenge unequal relationships, progress in reducing gender inequalities will continue to be slow (Plan International, 2011). Despite the importance of a specific focus on young women and the benefits that can be reaped in doing so, this must not come at the cost of overlooking the social and economic needs and vulnerabilities of young men in different contexts.

Ongoing learning and evaluation leads to innovation: Given the centrality of young people's development outcomes in Africa, as well as its programme portfolio, BRAC has made young people's lives a core theme of its research portfolio in

East Africa. In 2012 this included the first in a series of reports on young people's social and economic lives in Uganda. A number of complementary pilot programmes have been implemented as a result of on-the-ground learning and research and evaluation work, including the appointment of Adolescent Health Promoters in ELA villages, and of young men beginning to be included in their programme portfolio, primarily through vocational training. The ability of BRAC to innovate and build on successes is down to the strong emphasis it places on research and evaluation, both internally through its Research and Evaluation Unit, and externally through its partnerships and collaborations with universities across the globe. This not only allows BRAC to monitor progress, test pilot projects, and make changes based on findings, but making these findings accessible also generates important lessons for other organizations aiming to further young people's development.

Notes

1. GB£1 = 4,720 Ugandan Shillings (UGX) (as of 3 June 2015).
2. See www.thegirleffect.org
3. US$1 = 3.075 UGX (as of 3 June 2015).
4. Bandiera et al. (2012) explore whether this targeting has any influence on school-going members in terms of encouraging school dropout. Reassuringly, they find no significant impact of the programme on school dropout among ELA members.
5. Second-round follow-ups were conducted in 2012 and 2013 in Uganda and Tanzania, respectively. Results are in the final stage of analysis and will be available soon.
6. Encouragingly, there is no evidence that this influences negatively on school enrolment, suggesting that there is little trade-off in promoting the empowerment of girls through health and vocational skills-based interventions and their current incentives to invest in human capital (Bandiera et al., 2012).
7. This asked respondents to rank their ability on how well they can: identify business opportunities; obtain credit; save for investment; manage employees; manage finances; bargain for inputs; bargain for selling outputs; protect their assets; collect money; and run their own business (Bandiera et al., 2012).

References

Bandiera, O., Buehren, N., Burgess, R., Goldstein, M., Gulesci, S., Rasul, I. and Sulaiman, M. (2012) 'Empowering adolescent girls: evidence from a randomized control trial in Uganda', *Mimeo*, available from: http://econ.lse.ac.uk/staff/rburgess/wp/ELA.pdf [accessed 11/08/2014].

Bandiera, O., Gulesci, S., Burgess, R., Rasul, I., Goldstein, M. and Sulaiman, M. (2009) 'Intention to participate in adolescent training programs: evidence from Uganda', *Mimeo,* available from: http://www.povertyactionlab.org/sites/default/files/publications/Project%20111%20-%20Intentions%20to%20participate%20in%20adolescent%20training%20programs.pdf [accessed 01/09/2014].

Bangser, M. (2010) *Falling through the Cracks. Adolescent Girls in Tanzania: Insight from Mtwara*. Dar es Salaam: USAID, Tanzania.

Banks, N. (forthcoming) 'Youth poverty, employment and livelihoods: Living with insecurity in Arusha, Tanzania', *Environment and Urbanization* 28(2), October 2016.

Banks, N. and Sulaiman, M. (2012) *Youth Watch 2012: Problem or Promise? Harnessing Youth Potential in Uganda*. BRAC International, Kampala.

BRAC (2012a) *BRAC Uganda Annual Report 2012*. BRAC International, Dhaka.

BRAC (2012b) *BRAC Tanzania Annual Report 2012*. BRAC International, Dhaka.

Brown, A., Lyons, M. and Dankoco, I. (2010) 'Street traders and emerging spaces for urban voice and citizenship in African cities', *Urban Studies* 47(3): 666–83 <http://dx.doi.org/10.1177/0042098009351187>.

Bryceson, D.F. (2010) 'Africa at work: transforming occupational identity and morality', in D.F. Bryceson (ed.), *Africa at Work: Occupational Change, Identity and Morality*, pp. 3–26. Practical Action Publishing, Rugby.

Elder, S. and Koné, K.S. (2014) 'Labour market transitions of young women and men in sub-Saharan Africa', *Work4Youth Publication Series No. 9*. ILO, Geneva.

Furlong, A. (2009) 'Physical and mental health', in A. Furlong (ed.), *Routledge Handbook of Youth and Young Adulthood: New Perspectives and Agendas*. Routledge, Oxon and New York, NY, pp. 320–30.

Garcia, M. and Fares, J. (2008a) 'Working in bad jobs or not working at all', in M.H. Garcia and J. Fares (eds), *Youth in Africa's Labor Market*. World Bank, Washington DC <http://dx.doi.org/10.1596/978-0-8213-6884-8>.

Garcia, M. and Fares, J. (2008b) 'Why is it important for Africa to invest in its youth?', in M.H. Garcia and J. Fares (eds), *Youth in Africa's Labor Market*. World Bank, Washington, DC.

Garcia, M. and Fares, J. (2008c) 'Transitions to working life for Africa's youth', in M.H. Garcia and J. Fares (eds), *Youth in Africa's Labor Market*. World Bank, Washington, DC.

Garrett, L. (2005) 'The lessons of HIV/AIDS', *Foreign Affairs* 84(4): 51–64.

Godfrey, M. (2003) 'Youth employment policy in developing and transition countries – prevention as well as cure', *Social Protection Discussion Paper Series No. 0320*. World Bank, Washington, DC.

Guengant, J. and May, J.F. (2013) 'African demography', *Global Journal of Emerging Market Economies* 5(3): 215–67 <http://dx.doi.org/10.1177/0974910113505792>.

ILO (2013) *Global Employment Trends for Youth 2013: A Generation at Risk*. International Labour Organization, Geneva.

IYF (2011) *Navigating Challenges, Charting Hope. A Cross-Sector Situational Analysis on Youth in Uganda*. International Youth Federation, Baltimore MD.

Joshi, A. (2011) 'Multiple sexual partnerships: perceptions of young men in Uganda', *Journal of Health Organization and Management* 24(5): 520–7 <http://dx.doi.org/10.1108/14777261011070547>.

Juarez, F., LeGrand, T., Lloyd, C.B., Singh, S. and Hertich, V. (2013) 'Youth migration and transitions to adulthood in developing countries', *The ANNALS of the American Academy of Political and Social Science* 648: 6–15 <http://dx.doi.org/10.1177/0002716213485052>.

Kessides, C. (2007) 'The urban transition in sub-Saharan Africa: challenges and opportunities', *Environment and Planning C: Government and Policy* 25(4): 466–85 <http://dx.doi.org/10.1068/c3p>.

Kondylis, F. and Manacorda, M. (2008) 'Youth in the labour market and the transition from school-to-work in Tanzania', in M.H. Garcia and J. Fares (eds), *Youth in Africa's Labor Market*. World Bank, Washington, DC.

NBS (2011) *Youth in Tanzania: Data from the 2010 Tanzania Demographic and Health Survey*. National Bureau of Statistics, Dar es Salaam.

Plan International (2011) *Because I Am a Girl: The State of the World's Girls 2011: So, What About Boys?* Plan International, Surrey.

Potts, D. (2013) 'Urban economies, urban livelihoods, and natural-resource based economic growth in sub-Saharan Africa: the constraints of a liberalized world economy', *Local Economy* 28(2): 170–87 <http://dx.doi.org/10.1177/0269094212466040>.

PRB (2014) *2014 World Population Data Sheet*. The Population Reference Bureau, Washington, DC.

Restless Development (2013) *Youth in Tanzania Today: The Report 2012/13*. Restless Development, Dar es Salaam.

Samara, S. (2010) 'Something-for-something love: the motivations of young women in Uganda', *Journal of Organization and Management* 24(5): 512–19 <http://dx.doi.org/10.1108/14777261011070538>.

TACAIDS (2008) *Tanzania: HIV/AIDS and Malaria Indicator Survey 2007/08*. Tanzania Commission for AIDS (TACAIDS), Zanzibar AIDS Commission, National Bureau of Statistics, Office of Chief Statistician, and Macro International Inc., Dar es Salaam.

Tanti, C., Stukas, A., Halloran, M.J. and Foddy, M. (2011) 'Social identity change: shifts in social identity during adolescence', *Journal of Adolescence* 34: 555–67 <http://dx.doi.org/10.1016/j.adolescence.2010.05.012>.

UBOS (2010) *Uganda National Household Survey 2009/2010: Socioeconomic Module Abridged Report*. Uganda Bureau of Statistics, Kampala.

Urdal, H. (2008) 'A clash of generations? Youth bulges and political violence', *International Studies Quarterly* 50(3): 607–29 <http://dx.doi.org/10.1111/j.1468-2478.2006.00416.x>.

World Bank (2008) *Africa Development Indicators 2008/2009: Youth and Employment in Africa: The Potential, the Problem, the Promise*. World Bank, Washington DC <http://dx.doi.org/10.1596/978-0-8213 7787-1>.

World Bank (2014) *Youth Employment in sub-Saharan Africa*. World Bank, Washington, DC.

Yam, V. (2013) 'One design producing different outcomes: comparative analysis of BRAC's ELA programme in Tanzania and Uganda', *Mimeo*. BRAC Research and Evaluation Unit, Kampala.

YEN (2013) 'Empowering girls: better impact from combined interventions', *YEN Briefs Issue 2, May 2013*. International Labour Organization, Geneva.

About the author

Dr Nicola Banks is an ESRC Future Research Leader (funded under grant reference number ES/K009729/1) at the University of Manchester. Her research explores young people's experiences of urban poverty in Tanzania. She was previously Head of BRAC's Research and Evaluation Unit in Uganda, managing research operations in East Africa.

PART C
Getting Africa to 'work'

CHAPTER 7

Female engagement in commercial agriculture, interventions, and welfare in Malawi

Ralitza Dimova and Ira N. Gang

The poverty and extreme poverty-alleviating potential of female empowerment through agricultural commercialization has been an increasing focus of much of the recent development literature and policy discourse. Using representative data from Malawi, this chapter looks at the role of key policy interventions on the probability for women to enter the commercial agricultural sector and the impact of agricultural commercialization on (extreme) poverty. We find that: a) most interventions had a positive impact on female food commercialization, but either did not affect or affected negatively female entry into high-value agriculture; and b) female empowerment through high-value agriculture benefited the (extreme) poor. We conclude that gender norms in food commercialization and high-value agriculture should be understood for female empowerment interventions of the type implemented in Malawi to have the desired effect.

Keywords: female empowerment, commercial agriculture, policy interventions, household welfare

Introduction

Throughout sub-Saharan Africa (SSA), lucrative commercial crops are typically perceived as 'male crops', while lower-value crops for home consumption are perceived as 'female crops' (Duflo and Udry, 2004; Kasante et al., 2001). However, the potential for engaging female agricultural producers in high-value crop activities has received increasing attention in the academic literature and policy discourse. The argument is that female cultivation of 'male crops' should not only bolster women's economic empowerment, but also improve overall household welfare and nutrition, especially that of children (Dolan and Sorby, 2003; Haddad and Hoddinott, 1994). There is related evidence that cash crop production is superior to reliance on subsistence farming, even in the context of rising food prices (Dimova and Gbakou, 2013; von Braun and Kennedy, 1994; Wood et al., 2013).

Malawi is one of the poorest countries in the world, and is predominantly agricultural. It shares key characteristics with many other poor, tropical African economies, namely, a comparative advantage in tropical cash crop activities, and it is threatened by food insecurity, especially in an environment of rising food prices and potential droughts. Children are among the most high-profile victims of food insecurity. According to ORC Macro (2006), about half of the children aged 0–59 months are chronically stunted, and the proportion of stunted children is 24 times the level expected in a healthy, well-nourished population. Furthermore, about one-third of all under-5 deaths in Malawi are related to moderate or severe malnutrition. Exploring 1) the choice across food and cash crops among farmers – in particular, female farmers – and the effect of policy interventions that facilitate the latter, and 2) the impact of this choice on poverty and extreme poverty indicators, is therefore of utmost importance.

While we know that significant barriers, such as lack of access to production inputs, especially fertilizers, credit, and technology, prevent women from cultivating higher-value cash crops, we know less about the consequences of interventions that remove these barriers and allow women to cultivate more lucrative commercial crops. The positive implications of removing barriers to female engagement in commercial agriculture tend to be taken for granted. However, von Braun et al. (1989) document a counter-intuitive effect of one such intervention. In Gambia, where women were traditional rice growers, it was assumed that introduction of better technology for rice production, in the form of pump irrigation, would enhance their income-generating potential. But, faced with constraints on access to credit and hired labour, women failed to adopt the new technology and remained traditional rice producers. In contrast, men moved into the irrigated rice sector. This attempt at female economic empowerment played no role in household welfare enhancement. We do not know to what extent this result is generalizable. There are significant gaps in the literature related to understanding both the determinants of female empowerment through high-value agriculture and the effect on household welfare indicators, such as overall household poverty. Research on whether the poorest are completely excluded from this process is even rarer.

Using a representative household survey from Malawi, we look at policy-based determinants of female engagement in commercial agriculture and at the effect of such engagement on poverty (and extreme poverty) measures. We explore both the potential transition from purely subsistence-oriented staples into higher-yielding food varieties, such as hybrid maize, and the entry of females into high-value crops such as tobacco, which have traditionally been a high-income-generating male prerogative. Entry into higher-value activities like tobacco, while profitable, has unclear implications for household poverty and nutrition. In a context like Malawi, where production is rain-fed and not mechanized, this is an inherently risky and expensive venture, potentially open to only those households that have crossed a certain asset (particularly land size) threshold (Dimova et al., 2015; Wood et al., 2013). Given incomplete markets, high population density, and shrinking land sizes, this transition often comes at the expense of staple crop production on the farm. This potentially exposes uninsured smallholders to unexpected food price increases that limit their purchases of additional food required after foregoing staple food production, and is of particular significance to the ultra-poor (Sahn and Arulpragasam, 1991; Dimova et al., 2015).

Furthermore, the literature concurs that entry barriers to both the agricultural input market and (thereafter) to high productivity agricultural sector niches continue to be highest for women. Latest research attributes most of the productivity, and hence income, gender gap in Malawi to low access to higher-value activities like tobacco production and to inputs in the production process (Kilic et al., 2013a). At the same time, we do not know whether these identified constraints to female entry into both the input and output agricultural markets matter for household welfare, and how effective government action may be in dismantling these barriers.

On the one hand, differential spending behaviour on the part of men and women, with women presumably devoting larger proportions of their incomes to nutrition and household (in particular, child welfare enhancing expenditure categories), is expected to have positive implications for household welfare (Duflo and Udry, 2004). On the other hand, barriers to complementary resources like land, labour, and relevant networks may make females less productive than males within the same agricultural niches (Udry, 1996; Udry and Goldstein, 2008), and hence, prioritizing female as opposed to male entry into the highest income niches may lead to lowering the income status of households as a whole. To the best of our knowledge, there is as yet no unambiguous answer to the question of whether the types of agricultural interventions implemented in Malawi are effective in assuring successful (female) entry into higher income niches, and in turn, whether entry into higher value niches has necessarily resulted in the alleviation of poverty and under-nutrition. We address this question, with a specific focus on the issue of gender, and those belonging to the poor and ultra-poor percentiles of the income distribution.

Context and policy environment

Predominantly agricultural, Malawi is one of the poorest countries in the world, ranking 174 out of 187 countries, according to the 2014 Human Development Index (UNDP, 2014). Between 2007 and 2011, 61.6 per cent of the population on average fell below the international poverty line of US$1.25/day (ibid.). According to Malawi's third *Integrated Household Survey 2010–2011*, as used in this chapter, 18.97 per cent of the population are ultra-poor or falling below the internationally accepted nutritional minimum (NSO, 2012).

Malawi shares key characteristics with many other sub-Saharan African economies, for example, a comparative advantage in tropical cash crop activities, and it is threatened by food insecurity in an environment of rising food prices and occasional severe droughts. While the poorest (subsistence) farmers have typically been shown to restrict themselves to low-risk and low-return subsistence activities, there are significant entry constraints in pursuing more lucrative crop choices, including tobacco, hybrid maize, and groundnuts. These constraints are a historical legacy of the 1970s to 1990s policy environment characterized by heavy government involvement and stimulation of the large-scale, estate-based, high-value sector (predominantly tobacco) at the expense of the food crop sector.

Between independence in 1964 and the late 1990s, all key agricultural decisions, such as extension, technological development, and the marketing of agricultural output, were taken by the Agricultural Development and Marketing Corporation (ADMARC), which sold inputs to and bought produce from farmers. The corporation divided agriculture into two subsectors: a smallholder sector made up of predominantly subsistence-oriented producers, and a cash crop sector with production concentrated in estates. These two subsectors contribute 70 per cent and 30 per cent of the agricultural GDP, respectively. The prices of key staple crops such as maize were kept artificially low, while all revenues were channelled into the development of the cash crop estate sector, viewed as the engine of growth.

As in other similar sub-Saharan economies, the dramatic change in the terms of trade during the 1970s (together with other external shocks, such as the war in Mozambique and a severe drought in 1979–80) highlighted the failure of government-led, agricultural export-based policies. A series of food crises paved the way for the IMF and the World Bank to introduce adjustment programmes. These included active encouragement of smallholder involvement in the production of exportable cash crops, such as tobacco and groundnuts, as well as the adoption of higher-value hybrid maize varieties. Together with a discontinuation of maize fertilizer subsidies, these policies contributed to a significant reallocation of food crops into cash crops among smallholders (Harrigan, 2003). But, severe drought in 1992–4 and a renewed food crisis contributed to a further rethinking of input-based government strategies for poor smallholders, among the most prominent being the (pro-poor) allocation of fertilizer subsidies and credit to Malawian households.

Box 7.1 highlights the timeline of agricultural policy developments in Malawi since independence. One of the most highly discussed elements in the post-1990s policy timeline is the fertilizer input and subsidy programme (FISP), which started in the late 1990s and continued through the 2000s. The programme was developed out of the Starter Pack Programme of 1998. It was administered through a series (and multi-period) of sub-programmes of coupon voucher allocations, enabling households to purchase fertilizer, hybrid seeds, and pesticides at reduced prices (Dorward and Chirwa, 2011). The four criteria to identify beneficiaries were that: 1) households should own land, which is cultivated in the relevant season; 2) households should be bona fide residents of the village; 3) only one beneficiary should be eligible in a household; and 4) vulnerable groups, especially households headed by women, should be given priority.

Box 7.1 Agricultural policy timeline

1964   *1987–95*   *1998 onwards*

| ADMARC dual agro sector of food-producing smallholders and cash crop (tobacco-producing estates) | • Liberalization of output markets
• Abolition of fertilizer subsidies
• Relaxation of tobacco quota | Fertilizer/seeds subsidy programmes
• 1998/2001: starter pack
• 2005/6–2008/9; 2009/10: FISP | Microcredit MRFC, PMREW, MMF, MUSCCO, Only MUSCCO and MRFC |

Selected impact evaluation studies:

- Coady et al. (2002); Holden and Lunduka (2010); Kilic et al. (2013b): redistribution of coupons in favour of relatively better-off and male-headed households.
- Diagne and Zeller's (2001) series of papers on access to credit: no direct effect on income and nutrition; targeted credit may have negative impact on food security.
- More recent gender-related studies – Kilic et al. (2013a) – male–female productivity gap mostly explained by endowments, especially access to cash crop production.

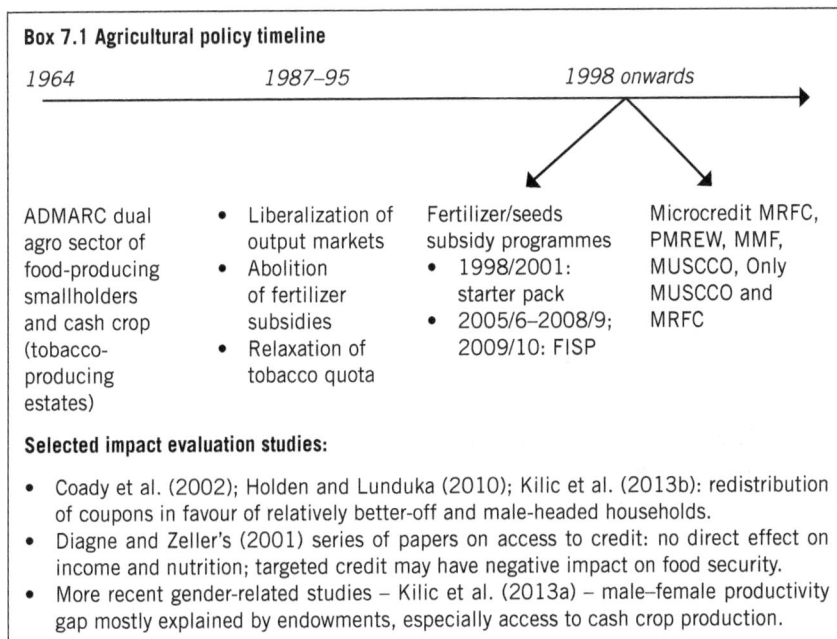

The prolific literature evaluating either the direct or indirect (via enhancing the potential of smallholder entry into higher-productivity income-generating niches in the agricultural market and their subsequent productivity) effects on poverty and nutrition is inconclusive. If anything, the dominant view appears to be that, contrary to programme design and intentions, coupons for seeds and fertilizers tended to be allocated in favour of relatively better-off households (Coady et al., 2002; Holden and Lunduka, 2010; Kilic et al., 2013b).

Complementary programmes aimed at encouraging diversification and enhanced productivity of the rural sector (though receiving significantly less attention in the literature) have emerged in the form of a proliferation of rural (micro)finance credit and corresponding institutions, aimed at enhancing access to credit for smallholders (see Box 7.1). These include: the Malawi Rural Finance Company (MRFC), a state-owned and nationwide agricultural credit programme; the Promotion of Micro Enterprises for Rural Women (PMERW), a programme explicitly targeting women; the Malawi Mudzi Fund (MMF), a replica of the Grameen Bank; and the Malawi Union of Savings and Credit Cooperatives (MUSCCO), a local saving and credit union. Among the numerous programmes and credit allocation institutions, only MRFC and MUSCCO have national coverage. Once again, as in the case of the FISP, the results of impact evaluation studies are inconclusive. In fact, Diagne and Zeller (2001) argue that, by promoting the reallocation of smallholder land from food to cash crop production, micro-credit programmes may have had a negative impact on food security.

Furthermore, the literature concurs that entry barriers to both the agricultural input market and (thereafter) high-productivity agricultural sector niches continue to be highest for women. The most recent research attributes most of the productivity, and hence income, gender gap in Malawi to low access to higher-value activities like tobacco production and to inputs in the production process (Kilic et al., 2013a). At the same time, we do not know whether these identified constraints to female entry into both the input and output agricultural markets matter for household welfare, and how effective government action may be in dismantling these barriers.

Empirical methodology and specification

We model stylized measures of poverty and extreme poverty as depending on female engagement in commercial agriculture, where female engagement in commercial agriculture is, in turn, a result of a set of government policies, such as access to credit, extension services, and other inputs in the production process, and household endowments including land and human capital.

In doing so, we employ sophisticated econometric techniques that allow us to produce unbiased estimates of the effect of female engagement in commercial agriculture on poverty, or other measures of household welfare. Specifically, we acknowledge the fact that women engaged in commercial agriculture are unlikely to be a randomly selected sample. If women from households with either genuinely higher or genuinely lower welfare are self-selected into commercial agriculture, estimates that do not take this into account would be biased. For our purpose, we estimate a treatment effect model of household welfare, which accounts for the possibility of non-random female selection into commercial agriculture. Appendix 1 offers a brief, and fairly non-technical, outline of this empirical procedure, while a more technical description of the model can be found in Dimova and Wolff (2008) and Guo and Frazer (2010).

In our baseline estimation we use per adult equivalent food consumption as a poverty measure, which also implicitly takes into account potential under-nutrition. To assess explicitly the impact of female entry into commercial agriculture on the poorest, we re-estimate the model using the incidence of extreme poverty as a dependent variable. Since extreme poverty takes the value of one, if the household is extremely poor and zero otherwise, we estimate a biprobit model, which is appropriate for this case's empirical version of the treatment effect model described earlier. The results that we report in the next section only account for the direction of different economic relationships explored. The full set of empirical results is presented in Appendix 1.

In each estimation we take into account human capital characteristics, distinguishing between households whose head has tertiary, secondary, or primary education, with the baseline variable being no education. In keeping with the literature, we expect higher levels of education to be associated with both higher probability of entry into commercial agriculture and lower probability for the household to be ultra-poor or constrained in its food consumption. We also control for the age and marital status of the head of households, as well as for the gender of the head of household. Female-headed households are expected to face higher probability of female entry into commercial agriculture, but also lower probability than male households of being lifted out of poverty.

To avoid reverse causality issues with the policy-related variables (namely, the possibility that relatively better-off households may have a better access to productivity and welfare-enhancing policy interventions), we experiment with relevant variables at the village as opposed to the household level. In particular, we look at the female empowerment implications of village-level access to either extension services or capital. To explicitly capture the access by women to coupons for the purchase of seeds, fertilizers, or credit, we also control for the share of females in the village who were able to obtain coupons in the reference period, and the share of females in the village who were able to obtain a loan for use in agricultural production.

Data

We perform our empirical estimations using Malawi's third *Integrated Household Survey (IHS3)*, conducted between March 2010 and March 2011; this is a representative survey for the country as a whole, conducted by the National Statistical Office of Malawi (NSO, 2012), and which received technical support from the World Bank as part of the World Bank's Living Standards Measurement Study (LSMS). After accounting for missing observations, and restricting the sample to those households who had access to land and derived income from agricultural production during the reference period, we are left with a sample of 9,025 observations.

The survey is informationally rich. Aside from the LSMS survey's typically detailed information on consumption, income, and human capital and household characteristics, there is detailed information on ownership and engagement, in different agricultural and non-agricultural activities, such that we are able to identify the owner of assets (such as land), and determine whether the person responsible for commercial agricultural production is male or female. In addition, there is rich information on access to all relevant services (credit, coupons for agricultural inputs, and extension services) used by the government as a means to encourage commercial agricultural production.

To start with, we take a brief look at the links between commercial agriculture, which, given the specific Malawian context, we proxy with the probability of producing either tobacco or hybrid maize, and the probability of households to be engaged in commercial agriculture. We focus explicitly on female engagement in commercial agriculture, which is proxied by female control over the cash crop production and marketing process.

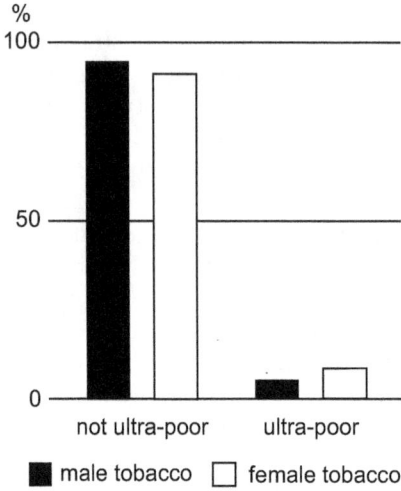

Figure 7.1 Commercial agricultural engagement (tobacco), and the probability of being ultra-poor

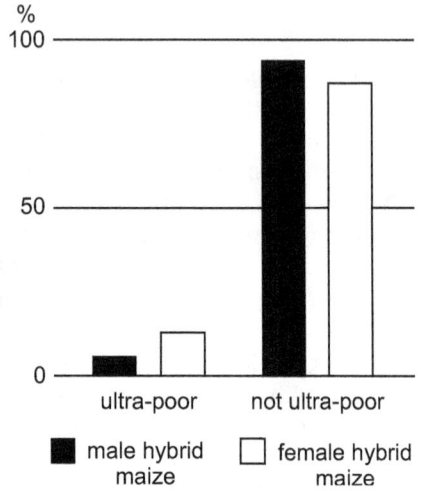

Figure 7.2 Commercial agricultural engagement (hybrid maize), and the probability of being ultra-poor

The cross-tabulations in Figures 7.1 and 7.2 indicate that there is strong association between the probability of engaging in either tobacco or hybrid maize production, and the probability of not falling into the category of ultra-poor households. Note that in our definition of the ultra-poor category, we use the methodology adopted by the World Bank in the collection of the IHS3 data. Specifically, the survey defines a total poverty line, which has two principal components: a food component and a non-food component. The food poverty line is the amount of expenditure below which a person cannot meet the WHO recommended calorie requirements of 2,400 calories a day. This amounts to approximately (Malawian Kwacha) MWK27.50 per person per day.[1] Households falling below the food poverty line, defined this way, are considered ultra-poor. By contrast, the non-food component of the poverty line is calculated as the weighted average of non-food expenditures of people that are either 5 per cent below or 5 per cent above the food poverty line. The total poverty line (defined as the sum of food and non-food poverty lines described above) is estimated as MWK44.30 per person per day, and households falling below this line are considered poor.

The results are not significantly driven by the gender of the household member responsible for either type of commercial agriculture. At the same time, we see a significant gender gap in engagement in commercial agriculture (Figure 7.3). While 15.28 per cent of male agricultural producers are engaged in tobacco production, the corresponding female sample is less than 2 per cent. Similarly, 46.69 per cent of the male agricultural producers are engaged in hybrid maize production, while the corresponding female sample is only 15.86 per cent. As indicated in Figure 7.4, males are also more likely to receive

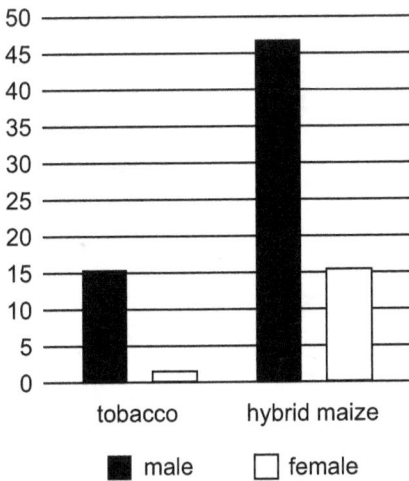

Figure 7.3 Commercial agricultural engagement by gender

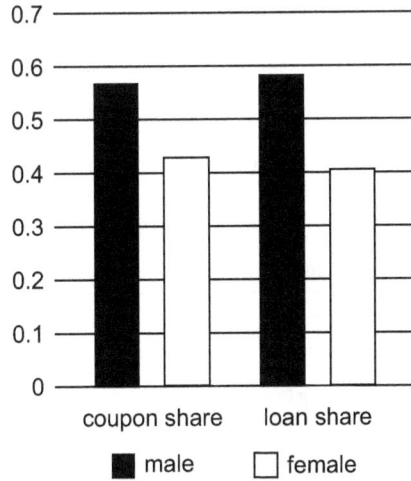

Figure 7.4 Gender differences in the receipt of coupons and credit

either loans or coupons for seeds and fertilizers than females, although the gap is not as large as the gender gap in engagement in commercial agriculture.

Empirical findings

In Table 7.1 we highlight the direction of the relationship between the various policy interventions and female entry into commercial agricultural activities, while in Figure 7.5 we plot the coefficients of the impact of female agricultural commercialization on our two measures of household welfare.

The results indicate that, while female ownership of land and extension services has an unquestionable positive impact on the probability of women being involved in commercial agriculture, the effect of alternative intervention is ambiguous, and is dependent on the type of agricultural commercialization. Village-level access to finance, as well as coupons for agricultural inputs and targeted allocation of loans to women, have a positive impact on the probability of women adopting higher-value hybrid maize production. However, village-level access to finance and targeted allocation of loans do not have any impact on the involvement of women in tobacco production, while allocation of coupons has a negative impact on the probability of women entering the highest value tobacco sector. The results, highlighted in Figure 7.4, indicate that female agricultural commercialization reduces significantly the probability for the household to be ultra-poor, and increases significantly its per adult equivalent food consumption. The effect of food commercialization, in the form of adopting hybrid maize production on the latter, is almost twice as strong as the effect of commercialization through adopting tobacco production.

Table 7.1 Direction of impact of policy interventions on female agricultural commercialization

	Female high-value crops	Female hybrid maize
Female land size	Positive	Positive
Male land size	Negative	Negative
Extension services	Positive	Positive
Village-level access to finance	Insignificant	Positive
Female share coupons	Negative	Positive
Female share loans	Insignificant	Positive

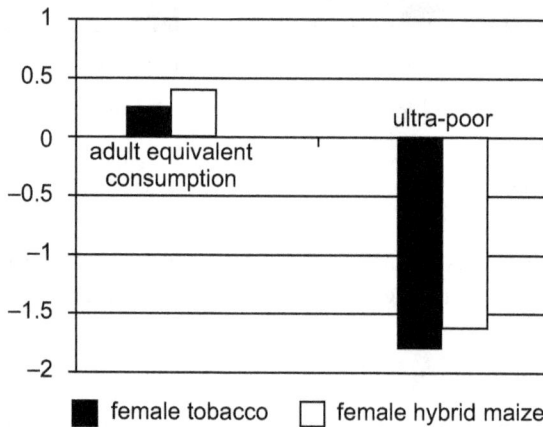

Figure 7.5 Impact of female engagement in commercial agriculture on poverty and extreme poverty

Taken together, these observations are consistent with the evidence from The Gambia's case as presented by von Braun et al. (1989), in the sense that perceptions on gender roles in specific crop production need to be properly understood for the intended intervention to have the desired effect. In the case of Malawi, we see that policy-based encouragement of a technologically more advanced version of food production had the desired effect on women, but did not enhance their involvement in the 'male crop' production sector. It is also important to note that, while female ownership of land encourages female entry into higher-productivity niches, male ownership of land discourages it. This feeds into the ongoing debate on envisaged land reforms in Malawi (Peters and Kambewa, 2007).

Conclusions and policy implications

The focus of this chapter is on disentangling the impact of policies aimed at encouraging poor (especially female) farmers' entry into lucrative agricultural niches, and in turn, the effect of female entry into these niches on household welfare (proxied with per adult equivalent consumption) and the probability to be ultra-poor. Overall, the policy implications of our empirical analysis are mixed. On the one hand, our descriptive statistics do not highlight any substantial gender differences in the welfare consequences of engagement in either type of commercial agriculture examined, such as higher-value crops like tobacco or technologically more advanced food crops like hybrid maize. However, we see that females face a significantly lower chance of being engaged in commercial agriculture, and a slightly lower chance of receiving access to productivity-enhancing interventions.

The statistical analysis confirms the significant positive impact of female engagement in commercial agriculture on the household's chance to escape extreme poverty. Furthermore, our empirical analysis confirms that greater access to credit, fertilizer, and seed coupons for women enhances their probability of entering the more profitable food production niches. However, we do not see any indication that they enhance their chance of entering higher-value cash crop niches of the agricultural market, such as tobacco, which have historically been considered a 'male' domain.

Indeed, when we perform the same rigorous regression analysis on the male sample (results available upon request), we see that greater availability of coupons and credit for males in the cluster enhances significantly their chance of entering the tobacco sector. Male entry into the tobacco sector, in turn, has stronger positive welfare implications on poor households than female entry into the tobacco sector.

Overall, our conclusions echo the message of related research (Udry, 1996; Udry and Goldstein, 2008; von Braun et al., 1989), and indicate that gender norms in cash crop production and the availability of complementary production resources, including, among others, land and appropriate networks, should be properly understood for female empowerment interventions of the types implemented in Malawi, so as to have the desired empowering and poverty-alleviating effect.

Appendix 1: brief description of the empirical methodology

Heuristically, we model household welfare as being dependent on female engagement in commercial agriculture, where female engagement in commercial agriculture is, in turn, a result of a set of government policies, such as access to credit, extension services and other inputs in the production process, and household endowments including land and human capital. In other words, we estimate the following system of equations:

$$Welfare = X_c \beta_c + \delta_c FemaleCommercial + \varepsilon_c, \tag{1}$$

$$FemaleCommercial^* = Z_{HV} \theta_{HV} + \mu_{HV} \tag{2}$$

Table A.1 Empirical results

	Food_adulteq		Food_adulteq		Ultra-poor		Ultra-poor	
Constant	10.76***	-3.0C***	10.73***	-2.10***	-1.48***	-3.10***	-1.21***	-2.12***
	(0.04)	(0.22)	(0.03)	(0.11)	(0.09)	(0.21)	(0.08)	(0.11)
Head age	-0.00***	-0.00	-0.00**	-0.00**	-0.00***	-0.00	-0.00***	-0.00**
	(0.00)	(0.00)	(0.00)	(0.00)	(0.00)	(0.00)	(0.00)	(0.00)
Female head	-0.13***	1.26***	-0.31***	1.67***	0.37***	1.23***	1.04***	1.68***
	(0.03)	(0.13)	(0.05)	(0.07)	(0.07)	(0.13)	(0.08)	(0.07)
Married monogamous	-0.03	0.23***	-0.00	-0.10	0.02	0.24*	-0.12*	-0.10
	(.03)	(0.13)	(0.03)	(0.08)	(0.07)	(0.13)	(0.06)	(0.07)
Married polygamous	-0.04	0.58***	-0.03	0.26***	0.08	0.52***	0.00	0.22**
	(0.03)	(0.15)	(0.03)	(0.09)	(0.08)	(0.15)	(0.07)	(0.09)
Household size	-0.10***	0.04**	-0.10***	0.04***	0.18***	0.03*	0.17***	0.04***
	(0.00)	(0.02)	(0.00)	(0.00)	(0.01)	(0.02)	(0.01)	(0.01)
Primary education	0.23***	0.13	0.22***	0.12*	-0.49***	0.12	-0.40***	0.08
	(0.02)	(0.14)	(0.02)	(0.07)	(0.06)	(0.13)	(0.05)	(0.07)
Secondary education	0.39***	0.03	0.37***	0.31***	-0.77***	0.05	-0.58***	0.26***
	(0.02)	(0.14)	(0.02)	(0.06)	(0.06)	(0.14)	(0.06)	(0.06)
Tertiary education	0.98***	0.44*	0.94***	0.51***	-1.74***	0.37	-1.29***	0.49***
	(0.05)	(0.27)	(0.05)	(0.14)	(0.33)	(0.27)	(0.28)	(0.14)
Female land size		0.22=**		0.08***		0.21***		0.08***
		(0.02)		(0.02)		(0.02)		(0.01)
Male land size		-0.08**		-0.18***		-0.05		-0.12***
		(0.03)		(0.03)		(0.03)		(0.02)

	Food_adulteq	Food_adulteq	Ultra-poor	Ultra-poor
Extension services	0.30**	0.33***	0.39***	0.37***
	(0.12)	(0.06)	(0.11)	(0.06)
Access to finance	−0.10	0.16***	0.06	0.23***
	(0.14)	(0.06)	(0.14)	(0.05)
Female share coupons	−0.70***	0.45***	−0.47***	0.47***
	(0.16)	(0.07)	(0.16)	(0.06)
Female share loans	−0.07	0.21***	−0.00	0.19***
	(0.11)	(0.05)	(0.10)	(0.04)
Female tobacco	0.24**		−1.74***	
	(0.09)		(0.21)	
Female hybrid maize		0.42***		−1.56***
		(0.08)		(0.07)
N Observations	9025	9025	9025	9025

Note: The figures in brackets are standard errors. ***, **, and * indicate significance at the 1%, 5%, and 10%, respectively.

In equation [1] we successively proxy *Welfare* with a range of stylized welfare measures for the ith household, including per adult equivalent food consumption and child anthropometric characteristics, X_c are a set of j variables, β_c is the associated vector of coefficients, and δ_c captures the effect of female engagement in commercial agriculture. The residual ε_c is assumed to follow normal distribution $\varepsilon_c \sim N(0, \sigma^2)$. In equation [2] *FemaleCommercial** is a latent variable measuring the likelihood of female engagement in commercial agriculture, Z_{HV} is a vector of explanatory variables, θ_{HV} is the associated vector of coefficient estimates, and μ_{HV} is the error term. The latent variable *FemaleCommercial** is unobserved, but we observe *FemaleCommercial* = 1 when *FemaleCommercial** > 0 and *FemaleCommercial* = 0 otherwise. Under the assumption that μ_{HV} follows a normal distribution such that $\mu_{HV} \sim N(0,1)$, the corresponding specification is a probit model. Hence, $\Pr(HV = 1) = \Phi(Z_T\theta_T)$ and $\Pr(T = 0) = \Phi(-Z_T\theta_T)$, where $\Phi(.)$ is a normal distribution function. As argued in the main body of the chapter, we estimate the related model where ultra-poor is a dependent variable as a biprobit model, which is the conceptually analogical equivalent of the treatreg model for the case of a limited dependent variable.

Note

1.   GB£1 = 693.93 Malawian Kwacha (MWK) (as of 30 June 2015).

References

Coady, D., Grosh, M. and Hoddinott, J. (2002) 'Targeting outcomes redux', *World Bank Research Observer* 19(1): 61–86 <http://dx.doi.org/10.1093/wbro/lkh016>.

Diagne, A. and Zeller, M. (2001) 'Access to credit and its impact on welfare in Malawi', *Research Report 116*. International Food Policy Research Institute, Washington, DC <http://www.ifpri.org/sites/default/files/publications/rr116.pdf> [accessed 23 June 2016], <http://dx.doi.org/10.2499/0896291197rr116>.

Dimova, R. and Wolff, F.C. (2008) 'Are private transfers poverty and inequality reducing? Household level evidence from Bulgaria', *Journal of Comparative Economics* 36(4): 584–98 <http://dx.doi.org/10.1016/j.jce.2008.05.002>.

Dimova, R. and Gbakou, M.P.B. (2013) 'The global food crisis: disaster, opportunity or non-event? Household level evidence from Côte d'Ivoire', *World Development* 46: 185–96 <http://dx.doi.org/10.1016/j.worlddev.2013.02.007>.

Dimova, R., Gangopadhyay, S., Michaelowa, K. and Weber, A. (2015) 'Off-farm labor supply and correlated shocks: new theoretical insights and evidence from Malawi', *Economic Development and Cultural Change* 63(2): 361–91 <http://dx.doi.org/10.1086/679193>.

Dolan, C. and Sorby, K. (2003) 'Gender and employment in high-value agriculture industries', *Agriculture and Rural Development Working Paper 7*. World Bank, Washington, DC.

Dorward, A. and Chirwa, E. (2011) 'The Malawi agricultural input subsidy programme: 2005–6 to 2008–9', *International Journal of Agricultural Sustainability* 9(1): 1–21 <http://dx.doi.org/10.3763/ijas.2010.0567>.

Duflo, E. and Udry, C. (2004) 'Intrahousehold resource allocation in Côte d'Ivoire: social norms, separate accounts and consumption choices', *NBER Working Paper 10498*. National Bureau of Economic Research, Cambridge, MA <http://www.nber.org/papers/w10498>.

Guo, S.Y. and Frazer, M.W. (2010) *Propensity Score Analysis: Statistical Methods and Applications*. SAGE Publications, Thousand Oaks, CA.

Haddad, L. and Hoddinott, J. (1994) 'Women's income and boy–girl anthropometric status in Côte d'Ivoire', *World Development* 22(4): 543–53 <http://dx.doi.org/10.1016/0305-750X(94)90110-4>.

Harrigan, J. (2003) 'U-turns and full circles: two decades of agricultural reform in Malawi 1981–2000', *World Development* 31(5): 847–63 <http://dx.doi.org/10.1016/S0305-750X(03)00019-6>.

Holden, S. and Lunduka, R. (2010) 'Impacts of the fertilizer subsidy programme in Malawi: targeting, household perceptions and preferences', *Noragric Report 54*, Department of International Environment and Development Studies, Noragric, Norwegian University of Life Sciences, Aas <http://www.umb.no/statisk/noragric/publications/reports/2010_nor_rep_54.pdf> [accessed 23 June 2016].

Kasante, D., Lockwood, M., Vivian, J. and Whitehead, A. (2001) 'Gender and the expansion of non-traditional agricultural exports in Uganda', in S. Razavi (ed.), *Shifting Burdens: Gender and Agrarian Change under Neo-liberalism*. Kumarian Press, Bloomfield, CT.

Kilic, T., Palacios-Lopez, A. and Goldstein, M. (2013a) 'Caught in a productivity trap. A distributional perspective on gender differences in Malawian agriculture', *Policy Research Working Paper 6381*. World Bank, Washington, DC <http://www-wds.worldbank.org/external/default/WDSContentServer/WDSP/IB/2013/03/11/000158349_20130311112435/Rendered/PDF/wps6381.pdf> <http://dx.doi.org/10.1596/1813-9450-6381>.

Kilic, T., Whitney, E. and Winters, P. (2013b). 'Decentralized beneficiary targeting in large scale development programs: insights from the Malawi farm input subsidy program', *Policy Research Working Paper 6713*. World Bank, Washington, DC <http://www-wds.worldbank.org/servlet/WDSContentServer/WDSP/IB/2013/11/26/000158349_20131126152801/Rendered/PDF/WPS6713.pdf> [accessed 23 June 2016], <http://dx.doi.org/10.1596/1813-9450-6713>.

NSO (2012) *Integrated Household Survey 2010–2011: Household Socio-Economic Characteristics Report*. National Statistical Office of Malawi, Zomba.

ORC Macro (2006) *Africa Nutrition Chartbooks: Nutrition of Young Children and Mothers in Malawi. Findings from the 2004 Malawi Demographic and Health Survey*. ORC Macro Inc., Calverton, MD.

Peters, P. and Kambewa, D. (2007) 'Whose security? Deepening social conflict over "customary" tenure in the shadow of land tenure reform in Malawi', *Journal of Modern African Studies* 45(3): 447–72 <http://dx.doi.org/10.1017/S0022278X07002704>.

Sahn, D. and Arulpragasam, J. (1991) 'The stagnation of smallholder agriculture in Malawi: a decade of structural adjustment', *Food Policy* 16(3): 219–34 <http://dx.doi.org/10.1016/0306-9192(91)90088-2>.

Udry, C. (1996) 'Gender, agricultural production and the theory of the household', *Journal of Political Economy* 104(5): 1010–46 <http://dx.doi.org/10.1086/262050>.

Udry, C. and Goldstein, M. (2008) 'The profits of power: land rights and agricultural investment in Ghana', *Journal of Political Economy* 116(6): 981–1022 <http://dx.doi.org/10.1086/595561>.

UNDP (2014) *Human Development Report 2014. Sustaining Human Progress: Reducing Vulnerabilities and Building Resilience*. United Nations Development Programme, New York, NY.

von Braun, J. and Kennedy, E. (1994) *Agricultural Commercialization, Economic Development and Nutrition*. International Food Policy Research Institute, The John Hopkins University Press, Baltimore, MD.

von Braun, J., Puetz, D. and Webb, P. (1989) 'Irrigation technology and commercialization of rice in the Gambia: effects on income and nutrition', *Research Report 75*. International Food Policy Research Institute, Washington, DC <http://www.ifpri.org/sites/default/files/publications/rr75.pdf> [accessed 23 June 2016].

Wood, B., Nelson, C., Kilic, T. and Murray, S. (2013) 'Up in smoke? Agricultural commercialization, rising food prices and stunting in Malawi', *Policy Research Working Paper 6650*. World Bank, Washington, DC <http://dx.doi.org/10.1596/1813-9450-6650>.

About the authors

Ralitza Dimova is a Senior Lecturer in Development Economics at the School of Environment, Education, and Development at the University of Manchester. She is an applied microeconomist with a main interest in food security and labour markets in developing countries, especially in Francophone West Africa.

Ira N. Gang is a Professor of Economics at Rutgers University in the USA, where he has been since 1986. His recent research interests involve both theoretical and empirical aspects of economic development, with a specific focus on labour markets in developing countries.

CHAPTER 8

Effects of food assistance: Evaluation of a food-for-training project in South Sudan[1]

Munshi Sulaiman

Food assistance programmes are often criticized for their possible effects of creating disincentives to work and crowding out private transfers. On the other hand, nutrition-based efficiency wage theory predicts that food assistance can increase ability to work and the labour supply of the poor. This experimental research assesses the effects of a food-for-training programme on household labour supply, informal transfers, and welfare in South Sudan. We do not find any significant effect on the hours of work or the type of economic activities undertaken by adult members. However, there was a significant negative impact (about 20 per cent) on per capita household income. This decline came about mostly through reduction in child labour, coinciding with positive impacts on school enrolment of girls. Furthermore, we find positive impacts on consumption of durable goods, especially on housing.

Keywords: food assistance, incentive effects, crowding-out, household income, South Sudan

Introduction

Food assistance is one of the most common forms of safety net programmes for the poor in developing countries. Besides the humanitarian objective, it is often believed that such assistance may work as a livelihood promotional mechanism by providing the poor with an opportunity to save and build a stronger asset base. Food assistance can also enable them to fulfil their nutritional requirement, and thereby work harder. On the other hand, there is widespread scepticism regarding different forms of food assistance since such transfers can create disincentives to work among those participating, generate dependency, and crowd out private transfers.

There is considerable literature on the field of social protection that discusses different aspects of food assistance. This includes, but is certainly not limited to, incentive effects of such transfers on labour supply (Abdulai et al., 2005), changes in local production through price effects (Tadesse and Shively, 2009), crowding out of informal assistance (Dercon and Krishnan, 2003), effects on productivity through improved nutritional status, effects on asset accumulation to break poverty traps (Dalgaard and Strulik, 2011; Gilligan and Hoddinott, 2007),

http://dx.doi.org/10.3362/9781780448435.008

appropriate forms of transfers (cash vs. in kind) (Basu, 1996), and efficacy of conditionality. Most empirical studies, especially those based on microdata, are limited to relatively stable contexts, and the results are often ambiguous. For example, in a review of 25 years of literature, Lentz (2003) did not find any instance whereby evidence clearly demonstrated (dis)incentive effects of food assistance. Moreover, despite the lack of rigorous evidence, food transfers are often assumed to have positive effects on peace-building by materializing developmental effects in post-conflict settings (Bailey and Harragin, 2009). Barrett and Maxwell (2005) describe these two roles of food assistance as 'emergency' and 'developmental'.

This paper, using a randomized evaluation of a programme in South Sudan, investigates two key aspects of food transfers: influence on incentive to work; and effects on crowding out informal private transfers. The programme evaluated in this paper is called Food for Training and Income Generation (FFTIG), and was implemented by BRAC for the 'ultra-poor' living in Juba.[2] Along with food transfers, this programme provided training on income-generating activities (IGAs) (mostly in the agriculture sector) and offered credit services. We used over-selection of potential beneficiaries to construct a randomized control group. Following a baseline survey in 2008, randomly selected households were provided with a monthly food package for nine months. One adult woman from each beneficiary household also participated in 5–20 days of training on an IGA. BRAC also offered credit services, although only 6 per cent of the treatment households availed of this facility.

Using a panel data collected at one-year intervals, our results show that the programme did not make any substantial change in the amount of time spent on earning activities by adult members of the participant households. We also do not observe any significant impact on the types of their economic activities. The participants did not start the activities that they received training on, indicating that the training component of programme did not have any significant influence.

The programme had reduced the extent of child labour in the beneficiary households by about 85 hours a year, which is about 60 per cent of average hours of total child labour, per household, in the baseline. We also find about 20–25 per cent reduction in the per capita income of the participant households, and about 10 percentage points increase in school enrolment of girls. There is also no evidence of crowding out of informal private transfers, which is probably due to very limited informal transfers to begin with. Interestingly, we find that programme participation increased the likelihood (and amount) of transfers being given out.

In terms of effects on welfare, food assistance helped the participants to improve their housing conditions, e.g. homestead ownership increased by about eight percentage points, and use of better construction materials increased by nine percentage points compared to the control group. These changes in housing are consistent with positive effects on annual non-food expenditures of the participants. No major impact is observed on accumulation of other physical assets, except marginal increases in ownership of sheds for livestock, electric fans, and bed nets. Since many of the households were recent returnees from camps and were living in makeshift houses, this priority of investment in housing is understandable. This also shows that the households spread the gain from a short-term food transfer over a long term by investing in housing, instead of reducing current labour supply, as the permanent income hypothesis predicts (Imbens et al., 2001).

Findings from this study indicate that food transfers do not necessarily lead to reduced labour supply by participants, and households may smooth their consumption from this gain by investing in durable goods. The results cannot be generalized to all forms of food transfers, but to transfers that are for a specified period. Although the training and credit components of the programme seem to have been ineffective, reflected through the very low uptake of the activities they received training on and of credit, we cannot completely rule out the effects of these additional services. As far as improving livelihood strategy and productivity of the poor is concerned, food-for-training programmes are not sufficient to bring any substantial change. Other forms of transfers, e.g. productive assets, could be tested as possible means of bringing sustainable changes in the livelihoods of the poor.

The next section gives a brief description of the context, the programme, and the data. Impact findings are discussed in the subsequent section, followed by the chapter's conclusion.

Programme description and the experiment design

BRAC-South Sudan (BRAC-SS) initiated the FFTIG pilot programme in Juba in collaboration with the World Food Programme (WFP) and the Consultative Group to Assist the Poor (CGAP). The objective of the programme was to combine the 'protection' and 'promotion' aspects of safety nets (Matin and Hulme, 2003), with food transfer being the protection component, and training in IGAs and access to credit containing promotional aspects. Programme expectations were such that households would be enabled to move into a situation where they retain a regular source of income and build an asset base through the combination of food transfers with skill development and financial services.

The context

A good description of the context is important given the uniqueness of South Sudan. As such, the results may not be generalizable for most food transfer programmes. South Sudan went through five decades of civil conflict that took a serious toll on the lives and livelihoods of the people. Over 2 million people have died of famine and conflict since 1983 (USAID, 2004), over 4 million were displaced within Sudan, and over half a million people took refuge in neighbouring countries (UNDP, 2004). These figures are enormous

Table 8.1 Selected social indicators for South Sudan

Social indicators	Central Equatoria in South Sudan (2006)[a]	Sub-Saharan Africa (2006)[b]
Infant mortality (per 1,000)	107	89
Life expectancy at birth	42	51
Maternal mortality (per 100,000 live births)	1,867	900
Contraceptive prevalence (%)	7.5	22.8
Net primary enrolment	43	72
Primary completion rate	1.6	60
Access to improved water sources (%)	36	58

Source: [a]Sudan Household Survey 2006 (MoH-GOSS and SSCCSE, 2008); Juba is located in the Central Equatoria region; [b]World Bank Database (World Bank, 2010)

in relation to South Sudan's population of 8 million. Though the situation started to improve with the 2005 peace agreement, conditions in South Sudan remain some of the harshest in the world.[3]

The first official statistical record in 50 years in South Sudan reveals only a glimpse of this state of affairs (SSCCSE, 2009). One in every 10 children in the Central Equatoria state of South Sudan does not survive their first year (Table 8.1). Average life expectancy at birth was only 42 years in 2006. South Sudan also has one of the highest maternal mortality rates in the world, with 1,867 deaths per 100,000 live births compared to a sub-Saharan average of 900. Although poverty in South Sudan cannot easily be measured in economic terms, UNDP (2004) estimates show that over 90 per cent of its population lives on less than a dollar a day. According to more recent statistics, more than half of the population is living below the poverty line (SSCCSE, 2010). Livelihoods in rural areas consist almost entirely of agriculture and livestock. Even in Juba, the capital and a county of Central Equatoria, livestock rearing is the major economic activity and the most commonly used indicator of wealth (SSCCSE, 2010; WFP, 1999).

Given the circumstances in South Sudan, food aid has been one of the key factors of development and famine control in this region for almost half a century (Gelsdorf et al., 2007). Food has been a key facet of the politics of Sudan as well. Keen (2008) argues that famines in Sudan have sometimes been generated by deliberate obstruction of aid efforts, and as a result of food and aid being plundered. Following the peace agreement in 2005, Sudan has become one of the top three countries for WFP interventions (WFP, 2015). In 2008 Sudan alone received more than 11 per cent of the total food aid delivered by WFP. However, food aid in South Sudan is often criticized for failing to embed any 'exit strategy' (Pantuliano, 2007). Consequently, WFP's food assistance in South Sudan started to shift towards making it a means of reintegration by enhancing 'the ability of returnees to secure the political, economic and social conditions to maintain their life, livelihood and dignity' (Bailey and Harragin, 2009: 1).

The intervention

Each participant household received food for a period of nine months starting from 30 March 2008. The amount of food transferred followed the WFP guidelines for food rations for training programmes. The ration includes 450 grams of cereals, 50 grams of pulses, 30 grams of vegetable oil, 10 grams of iodized salt, 30 grams of sugar, and 50 grams of corn soy blend for one person per day. The participants received their monthly allocation of food based on the initial size of their households. To minimize the cost of collection, the transfers took place at BRAC branch offices, which are within walking distance of the participants' houses.

From mid-April 2008 adult women from each participant household (either the head or spouse of the head) were mobilized into small groups. In group meetings, alternative training opportunities were described, and each participant chose one IGA on which to receive training. Though five different IGA trainings were provided as choices, almost 80 per cent of the participants opted for vegetable cultivation. The other training options included setting up a nursery, tailoring, petty trade, and cattle rearing. One agriculture sector specialist conducted the training sessions. The training courses included both classroom discussion in the branch offices and working in the fields. A typical training period lasted for two hours per day for five days. Although food aid was designed to allow the households to become engaged in new earning activities, the actual transfer was not conditional on engaging in the trained activity.

Among the three components, food transfer, in terms of cost, comprised the majority of the programme. Over 90 per cent of the total cost of the programme was associated with the food transfers.[4] The training courses were for too short a duration, and food transfers were not conditional on uptake of the activity. We also found that the training courses were ineffective (discussed in the Labour supply section below). The credit component was available for all the households in those communities. However, the uptake of loans was very low: only 2 per cent in the baseline for both the treatment and control groups, which increased to 6 per cent during the follow-up period for the treatment group, while uptake remained the same for the control group. Because of this low uptake, participation in credit is also unlikely to drive the main results of this evaluation.

Targeting beneficiaries

The programme provided support to 500 households from six branch offices in Juba. We over-selected the number of potential participants to construct a control group. Selection of potential beneficiaries started in December 2007, and followed three distinct steps to ensure effective targeting. In each branch office, a list of very poor households was prepared by consulting village elders, local chairpersons, and microfinance group members.[5] Describing the characteristics of 'very poor' in a post-conflict setting such as Juba was quite challenging. BRAC staff therefore often started by asking the community to identify the poorest households in the village. They stopped collecting names when around 10 households had been identified in a village. In subsequent meetings with other people of the same village, the staff used the prior list of names as a reference group, and asked for any other households whom they consider to be poorer or equally poor.

Once the household list of a village was prepared, BRAC staff visited each household to collect information on a few basic characteristics including female headship, whether they own/rent the house, main material of the wall of their house, number of dependents, and number of regular earners (a regular earner was defined as someone who had been involved in any earning activity for at least 24 days in the past month). This information was used to assign a poverty score to each household. The score was the sum of four variables:

1. female headship [score 2];
2. house wall made of sticks/hay [score 1];
3. living in other's house as charity [score 1];
4. at least three dependents per earner [score 1].

All of the households with a score of at least 3 were primarily selected by staff at the branch office. The programme manager from the country office visited each of the primarily selected households to verify their status and made the final selection. Those households already participating in microfinance were excluded in the final selection. Out of 1,250 primarily selected households, 1,049 households were finally selected and were eligible to participate in the programme.

Almost all of the households in our sample are female-headed. About 80 per cent did not own any cattle in the baseline. While SSCCSE (2010) defined the national poverty line at a per capita annual income level of (Sudanese pound) SDG874 (US$380), average per capita income of the sample households in 2008 was SDG595 ($259). According to a multidimensional poverty measure, a baseline report by BRAC-SS found that the households in our study were worse off than the general population of Juba, showing effective targeting by the programme (BRAC-SS, 2008). About 44 per cent of these households had no other earner in the household except the female head. In the baseline, only 4 per cent of them were engaged in cultivation. Their primary activity was self-employment in the non-farm sector; this mostly included activities such as collecting wild food or fruits, charcoal making, collection and sale of firewood, home-based brewery, and baking breads. Wage employment opportunities were extremely scarce, and only 12 per cent of the female heads were involved in any work for a wage in the baseline.

Table 8.2 Actual participation in the intervention by random assignment

Group assigned to	Full sample	Branch					
		Atlabara	Munuki	Hai-gabat	Jabel Kujur	Buluk	Katun
Treatment (%)	88	89	87	90	63	94	99
Control (%)	14	7	19	9	36	11	7

Source: 2008–9 panel data for impact evaluation

Evaluation strategy and data

Once the eligible households were selected by BRAC-SS, 500 households were selected randomly for the intervention, and the other 549 households were assigned to the control group. A baseline survey was conducted in March 2008, just before the intervention started. Out of the 1,049 households, 994 households could be interviewed in the baseline. The follow-up survey took place a year later, and 943 households were interviewed. This 5 per cent attrition rate is reasonable given that many of the households were recent returnees from internally displaced people (IDP) camps. Comparisons of the households that could and could not be followed up in the survey do not reveal major differences in their baseline characteristics. Moreover, treatment status did not have any statistically significant effect on the likelihood of being interviewed in the follow-up survey. Therefore, sample attrition is unlikely to have introduced any major bias in the evaluation.

The extent of non-compliance (households assigned for treatment not participating) and contamination (control households participating in the intervention) is an important determinant of the reliability of a randomized evaluation. The actual intervention did not fully comply with the random assignment to treatment and control groups. Among the households in the panel, 12 per cent of the treatment group did not receive the food transfers, and 14 per cent of the control group received intervention (Table 8.2). There is also considerable variation across the branches in the level of non-compliance. Jabel Kujur branch had the lowest compliance (and highest contamination), followed by Munuki. It is interesting to note that both these branches, among the six, are located the furthest away from the central office where the programme manager was based. In the four other branches, non-compliance was very low. Because of the high level of non-compliance/contamination, the observations from Jebel Kujur branch have been excluded from the analysis, resulting in a panel of 814 observations (391 treatment households and 423 control households).

Programme impact

In this section we discuss the main findings from the evaluation. Detailed discussions of econometric methods, full estimates, and robustness checks of the findings are available in Sulaiman (2010).

Labour supply

In terms of impact on hours spent by the adult household members, we do not find any statistically significant effect. We looked into this labour supply indicator separately for the respondent adult male members and other adult female members. The respondents are the women who were selected from each household to participate in the programme. The respondents are also usually the main earner for their households. Total hours worked by these respondents remained unchanged between baseline and follow-up, and there is no difference between the treatment and control groups either at baseline or endline. Similarly, we do not find any evidence of food transfers affecting labour supply of the other adult male or female members. A common concern in interpreting such zero effect is the precision of the measurement. We collected total work hours by recalling for the 12 months prior to the survey. There is a risk that measurement errors can yield statistically not significant results, even if there is true effect. One approach to deal with this concern is to look at the confidence interval. Based on our data, we can reject the possibility of disincentive effect in labour hours being more than 15 per cent for the respondents. Consistent with these null effects on respondents' work hours, we find no impact on the income earned by the adult members. Therefore, we conclude that there is no strong disincentive effect of food transfer in our study sample.

A large part of the empirical research on incentive effects of transfer programmes has utilized experiments with welfare reforms in the US. The evidence in general suggests that participation in welfare programmes reduces labour supply, and welfare reforms reduce participation in such programmes and increase labour supply (Moffitt, 2002). The evidence of such disincentive effects in developing countries is often based on anecdotes (Lentz, 2003). Sahn and Alderman (1996) find that food subsidy in rural Sri Lanka reduced work effort and income. However, Abdulai et al. (2005) argue that most of those evidences suffer from their failure to take endogeneity in programme placement and participation into account. Using cross-sectional data from Ethiopia, they find no evidence of disincentive effects after controlling for the household and local-level factors of participation. They also rely on endogenous programme participation to identify impact estimates. In a randomized evaluation of cash and in-kind (food) transfer in Mexico, Skoufias et al. (2008) find no effect of either form of transfers on labour market participation. Therefore, this evaluation contributes to the empirical literature with a robust assessment of the effect of a short-term food transfer programme on labour supply of the poor, and the main findings are consistent with the other empirical literature in developing countries.

Unlike the zero effects on hours worked by the adult members, we find significant effects on total hours worked by children and on income from their activities. Programme participation reduced total amount of work done by the children by 85 hours, which is about 60 per cent of the 142 hours spent by children on economic activities per household at baseline. Reduction in income earned by children due to programme participation is of similar magnitude, and statistically significant. These findings are in line with the 'luxury axiom' of child labour (Basu and Van, 1998), where children's non-work is a luxury in the household's consumption basket. Therefore, this cannot necessarily be interpreted as disincentive to work. Separating these estimates by sex reveal reduced labour supply by both male and female, although the effects are not statistically significant for male children. Results on school enrolment, presented later in this chapter, show significant effects on enrolment for girls, but not for boys, which correspond to this gender difference in effects on child labour.

By looking into the types of activities that the respondents are engaged in, we also do not observe any significant change in the composition of earning activities. Non-farm self-employment (petty trading of different sorts) was the major activity of the respondents, and their involvement in cultivation remained minimal. Proportions of respondents engaged in farming during the baseline period were 4 per cent for both the treatment and control groups; this did not change significantly during the follow-up period (5 per cent). This lack of change in farming activities shows that the trainings were ineffective, and these results are unlikely to be the product of the training component of the FFTIG programme.[6]

Another form of potential disincentive effect is reduction in work intensity. The hours of work may not fully capture the incentive effect, as it does not measure the intensity of work. Since self-employment is by far the major activity, it is plausible that the negative effect on income is driven by reduction in work intensity. We, however, do not observe any significant impact on the productivity of respondents (measured as income earned per hour worked) in non-farm self-employment activities.

Informal private transfers

Informal transfers play critical roles in risk-sharing strategies of poor households in developing countries, especially in the absence of formal safety net programmes. Public transfers are highly likely to create crowding-out effects if private transfers are motivated by pure altruism. However, the theoretical predictions are ambiguous when private transfers are considered to embed elements of risk-sharing or reciprocity (Cox et al., 1998). In post-war and fragile settings, such informal insurance can be almost non-existent, as conflict and displacement usually reduce informal risk-sharing mechanisms of consumption smoothing (Ibañez and Moya, 2010). In such situations, formal transfers can play a complementary role to informal transfers, and facilitate risk-sharing by allowing the poor households to invest in rebuilding these networks.

As expected, the extent of private transfers (either received or given out) was very low among our sample households in the baseline. Only 9 per cent of households reported receiving any transfer/gift, and 3 per cent of households reported making such transfers during the year preceding the baseline. We do not find any impact of programme participation on the likelihood of receiving transfers or the value of transfers received. We observe a significant positive trend in transfer receipts by both treatment and control households; the likelihood of receiving transfers increased by about four percentage points between the baseline and the follow-up. The value of transfers received also increased by SDG14 per household, which is about 58 per cent of baseline level of per-household transfer receipts. These changes probably reflect the fact that these households started developing risk-sharing as the wider situation was settling down.

Unlike zero effects on transfers received, there is a positive impact on both likelihood and value of transfer *given out* by the treatment households. Programme participation increased the probability of transfers given out by about six percentage points, which is quite substantial, given that only 3 per cent of households reported making such transfers during the baseline period. The impact on the value of transfers given out in one year is about SDG15 ($6.50), which is three times the size of the annual transfers made by these households at baseline. The types of transfers indicate that the majority of the increased transfers came from in-kind rather than cash transfers.

These results of informal transfers contrast with most of the empirical literature on this issue. Existing evidence in general demonstrates significant crowding-out effects, though they differ regarding the magnitudes of these effects. One dramatic example is presented in Cox and Jimenez (1995). According to their estimates in urban Philippines, a transfer of 100 pesos from public programmes reduced informal support by 92 pesos, resulting in only 8 pesos of net gain. Jensen (2003) finds that public transfer for the elderly in South Africa was counterbalanced by a 20–40 per cent decline in private transfer. Albarran and Attanasio (2004) present strong evidence of public safety nets undermining the informal support system in Mexico.

Despite these effects on the number of transfers, an ethnographic study by Heemskerk et al. (2004) shows important qualitative change in informal safety net mechanisms. Crowding out can be considered an acceptable cost for public transfers, since reduced private transfer is not pure wastage (Morduch, 1999). Hoff and Sen (2005) even argue that crowding out informal transfers can be desirable if it helps to break poverty traps arising from ethnic or social class solidarity. Our results indicate that the households started rebuilding their risk-sharing networks relatively quickly in post-conflict situations. The transfers observed in our study could also be pure altruism. However, there is a strong positive correlation between the likelihood of receiving and giving out transfers by households, which suggests reciprocity.

Per capita household income

There was a general decline in per capita income of the households over the one-year period, though the coefficients for follow-up are not always significant. According to a monthly Juba consumer price index (Sulaiman, 2010),

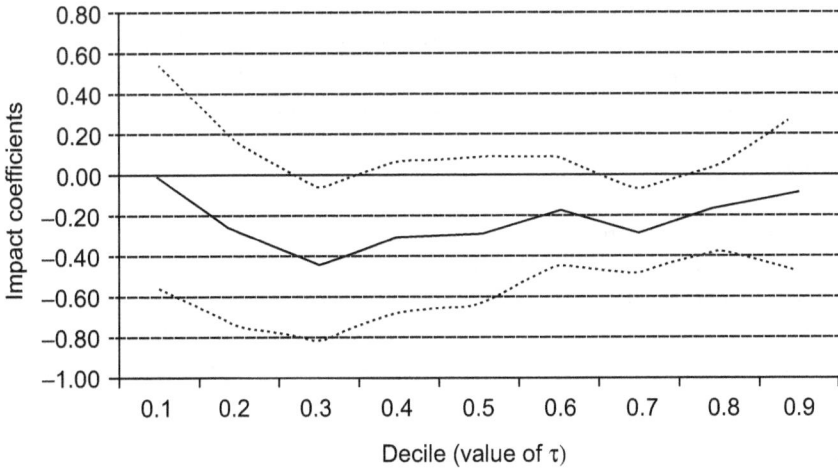

Figure 8.1 Quantile regression of log of per capita income
Source: 2008–9 panel data for impact evaluation

prices declined marginally after September 2008 (six months after initiation of food transfers). More importantly, there had been a surge of returnees from IDP camps during this period. According to Bailey and Harragin (2009), only 13 per cent of the returnees come through the official reintegration process, and the rest are spontaneous returnees. Most of these returnees were flocking into the urban areas, including Juba. There have also been reports of violence between the returnees and settled inhabitants, as the unskilled returnees were intensifying pressure on the already saturated labour market. These situations explain the general reduction in income. Participation in the programme appears to have reduced per capita annual income by SDG120 ($52), which is about 20 per cent of the baseline average. The effect size varies between 14 per cent and 26 per cent depending on the estimates, and is not always significant. This negative effect on per capita income is also concentrated among the households who relied on child labour at baseline.

Barrett (2002) argues that much of the observed negative impact of food transfers on labour supply and household income is primarily due to targeting errors. According to this argument, negative impact on income should be higher for higher-income households. Though the study sample consists of extremely poor households, quantile regression shows impact estimates on per capita income (log) at different deciles (Figure 8.1). Though the coefficients have relatively large confidence intervals, this does not reveal any wealth effect.

Consumption expenditure

For impact on consumption, we estimated out-of-pocket expenses on food and non-food items. Food expenditure data were collected by the three-day recall method. Since the food transfers ended about three months before the follow-up survey, any impact on food consumption is likely to reflect the indirect effect of food assistance through changed income and/or taste instead of its direct effect. Any impact on food consumption and reallocation of expenses across different food items *during* the food assistance period cannot be observed from this data. No impact on current per capita food consumption is observed.[7]

The non-food consumption items are divided into monthly and annual expenditures. Monthly items include transportation, fuel, and toiletries; annual items are education, clothing, durables, dowry, or other ceremonial expenses. There is no impact observed on per capita expenditure on monthly non-food items. However, we find significant effect on annual non-food expenses. The recall period for these non-food expenses was the year between baseline and follow-up, and overlaps with the food transfer period. Estimated effect on total expenses on annual non-food items was SDG117 ($51), which is 47 per cent of total expenses on these items during the baseline period. It appears that households have reallocated their income to more non-food items, especially on durables. The positive effect on education expenses is quite large (SDG122 or 34 per cent of baseline mean), but this effect was imprecisely estimated and hence statistically not significant.

School enrolment of children

Since we observe reduction in child labour and an indication of an increase in education expenses, it is possible to have an increase in enrolment rates. In fact, we find a significant increase in enrolment rates of girls but not for boys. Estimated impact on enrolment rates of girls is about 10 percentage points. This impact on enrolment rates is consistent with the results reported earlier, that the reduction in child labour was higher for girls than for boys.

Housing and other assets

One of the arguments for food transfer is that it helps to prohibit distress sale of assets, and thereby protects households from becoming trapped in poverty. There is some evidence of this protective role of food transfers in Africa (Gilligan and Hoddinott, 2007). The promotional argument for food transfer is that it can help households to build an asset base.

Since many of these respondents are returnees from different camps, and housing quality was one of the key indicators used by the programme to identify their potential participants, their housing condition was quite poor. Almost all the households in our sample lived in a single-room makeshift hut with an earthen floor and walls made of rudimentary materials. About 60 per cent of the households owned homestead land. We did not collect data on house improvement expenses. However, there is general improvement on different housing indicators (Figure 8.2). This is expected, given the poor state of housing in the baseline. There are some positive effects of programme participation on

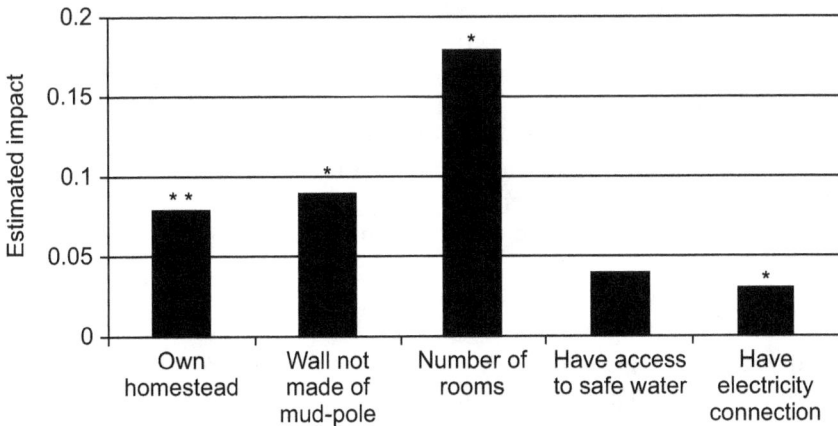

Figure 8.2 Impact on housing
Source: 2008–9 panel data for impact evaluation
Note: * significant at 10%; ** significant at 5%; and *** significant at 1%

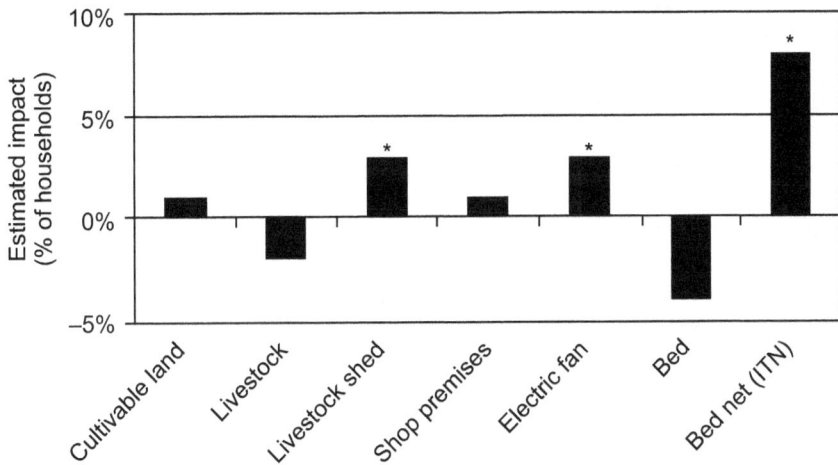

Figure 8.3 Impact on asset ownership
Source: 2008–9 panel data for impact evaluation
Note· * significant at 10%; ** significant at 5%; and *** significant at 1%

housing quality. However, the participants were more likely to have acquired homestead land and to have replaced their mud-pole walls with unburned bricks. Significant impact is observed on housing space (number of rooms) as well. Only 5 per cent of households had an electricity connection in the baseline, and there is a positive effect (three percentage points) of programme participation.

There is no major impact observed on different types of other household assets (Figure 8.3). Programme participation did not necessarily lead to any significant accumulation of physical assets. Significant positive effects, albeit relatively small, are observed on the probability of ownership of a shed for livestock (three percentage points), electric fans (three percentage points), and insecticide-treated nets (eight percentage points). The impact on ownership of a shed for livestock is in line with the homestead/housing improvement. Similarly, the impact on owning electric fans is aligned with higher access to electricity. It seems that the beneficiaries improved housing quality by reallocating their income from food expenses to investment in housing.

Conclusion

Food assistance programmes such as direct food distribution, food-for-training, food-for-work, school feeding, or many other forms are widespread in every country of the world. There is very little rigorous evidence on the impacts of these food transfer programmes, especially in developing countries. On the other hand, skills training programmes are abundant, and there could potentially be complementarities between the two. This paper has evaluated the impact of a food-for-training programme in South Sudan (which included training and access to credit in addition to food transfers) on labour supply, informal transfers, and several welfare indicators.

We do not find any evidence of disincentive or crowding out effects in this study. However, we find a significant negative impact (20–25 per cent) on per capita income. The major driver of this effect on per capita income is reduction in child labour in the beneficiary households. There is also a positive effect on school enrolment of girls, indicating that children's non-work and schooling is a luxury for these households. There is also a small but significant impact of transfers given out by the participants. This indicates the possibility of short-term targeted aid recreating risk-sharing networks of the poor households.

In terms of effects on welfare, food assistance helped the participants to improve their housing conditions, e.g. homestead ownership increased by about eight percentage points, and use of better construction materials for houses increased by nine percentage points. These changes in housing are consistent with positive effects on annual non-food expenditures of the participants. However, no impact is observed on accumulation of other major productive assets. Since many of the households were recent returnees from camps and many of them had been living in makeshift houses, this priority of investment in housing is understandable. This also shows that the households spread the gain from a short-term food transfer over a lifetime by investing in housing, instead of reducing current labour supply, as the permanent income hypothesis predicts.

These findings support food transfer programmes as a short-term solution by making it clear to the participants about the duration of support. This could allow the poor households to invest in durables such as housing, which are necessary conditions for a sustainable livelihood. However, such programmes may not be successful in affecting the productivity and/or income of the participants. Given that food transfer programmes are quite costly, alternative transfer programmes (such as transfer of productive assets) need to be piloted in such contexts.

Notes

1. I thank the research unit of BRAC-South Sudan for their part in implementing the evaluation project. I have greatly benefited from regular discussions with Oriana Bandiera on the analysis. I also thank Robin Burgess, Imran Matin, Imran Rasul, Markus Goldstein, and Selim Gulesci for their suggestions, and Proloy Barua for his critical assistance with field work. This research benefited from funding by the World Bank, and the UK Department for International Development (DFID). DFID funding was part of the iiG, a research programme to study how to improve institutions for pro-poor growth in Africa and South Asia. The views expressed are not necessarily those of DFID. All remaining errors are mine.
2. BRAC is an NGO originating in Bangladesh and currently implementing various development initiatives (such as microfinance, primary health care, agriculture extension, education, youth development) in several Asian and African countries. For more information, visit www.brac.net
3. More recently the situation worsened, with internal conflicts escalating in late 2013.
4. Total amount of transfer in the programme was 198 metric tonnes of cereal and 56 metric tonnes of other food items. According to WFP costing reports in May 2008, the costs of procurement and transportation of these foods to Juba was US$192,000, with a per household cost of $384. Including the cost of distributed food, transportation, storage, training, and BRAC staff expenses, the per beneficiary cost is over $425.
5. BRAC-SS had been operating microfinance programmes in these study villages for almost two years when this study was initiated.
6. A qualitative assessment of a similar food transfer programme by BRAC called Income Generation for Vulnerable Group Development (IGVGD) showed that beneficiary households participated primarily to receive food transfers, and they were not interested in the training or credit components (Webb et al., 2002).
7. A small decline in alcohol consumption is also observed, though the amount spent on this item was very small on average.

References

Abdulai, A., Barrett, C.B. and Hoddinott, J. (2005) 'Does food aid really have disincentive effect? New evidence from sub-Saharan Africa', *World Development* 33(10): 1689–704 <http://dx.doi.org/10.1016/j.worlddev. 2005.04.014>.

Albarran, P. and Attanasio, O.P. (2004) 'Do public transfers crowd out private transfers? Evidence from a randomized experiment in Mexico', in S. Dercon (ed.), *Insurance Against Poverty*. Oxford University Press, Oxford. <http:// dx.doi.org/10.1093/0199276838.003.0014>.

Bailey, S. and Harragin, S. (2009) *Food Assistance, Reintegration and Dependency in Southern Sudan. A Report Commissioned by the World Food Programme.* Humanitarian Policy Group, Overseas Development Institute, London.

Barrett, C.B. (2002) 'Food aid effectiveness: "It's the targeting, stupid!"', *Working Paper 2002-43*. Department of Applied Economics and Management, Cornell University, Ithaca NY. <http://dx.doi.org/10.2139/ssrn.431261>.

Barrett, C.B. and Maxwell, D.G. (2005) *Food Aid After Fifty Years: Recasting Its Role.* London: Routledge <http://dx.doi.org/10.4324/9780203799536>.

Basu, K. (1996) 'Relief programs: when it may be better to give food instead of cash', *World Development* 24(1): 91–6 <http://dx.doi.org/10.1016/0305-750X(95)00110-X>.

Basu, K. and Van, P.H. (1998) 'The economics of child labor', *American Economic Review* 88(3): 412–27.

BRAC-SS (2008) *Baseline Report on Food Distribution, Skill Development, and Financial Services: An Evaluation of BRAC South Sudan's FFTIG Program* [online]. Oxford, iiG. Available from: http://www.iig.ox.ac.uk/output/reports/pdfs/iiG-report-FFTIG_baseline_report-Draft-22-12-2008.pdf [accessed 13 October 2010].

Cox, D., Eser, Z. and Jimenez, E. (1998) 'Motives for private transfers over the life cycle: an analytical framework and evidence from Peru', *Journal of Development Economics* 55: 57–80 <http://dx.doi.org/10.1016/S0304-3878(97)00056-4>.

Cox, D. and Jimenez, E. (1995) 'Private transfers and the effectiveness of public income redistribution in the Philippines', in D. van de Walle and K. Nead (eds), *Public Spending and the Poor: Theory and Evidence.* John Hopkins/World Bank, Baltimore MD.

Dalgaard, C.J. and Strulik, H. (2011) 'A physiological foundation for the nutrition-based efficiency wage model', *Oxford Economic Papers* 63(2): 232–53 <http://dx.doi.org/10.1093/oep/gpq031>.

Dercon, S. and Krishnan, P. (2003) 'Risk sharing and public transfers', *Economic Journal* 113(486): C86–C94 <http://dx.doi.org/10.1111/1468-0297.00116>.

Gelsdorf, K., Walker, P. and Maxwell, D (2007) 'Editorial: the future of WFP programming in Sudan', *Disasters* 31(s1): s1–s8 <http://dx.doi.org/10.1111/j.1467-7717.2007.00345.x>.

Gilligan, D.O. and Hoddinott, J. (2007) 'Is there persistence in impact of emergency food aid? Evidence on consumption, food security, and assets in rural Ethiopia', *American Journal of Agricultural Economics* 89(2): 225–42 <http://dx.doi.org/10.1111/j.1467-8276.2007.00992.x>.

Heemskerk, M., Norton, A. and de Dehn, L. (2004) 'Does public welfare crowd out informal safety nets? Ethnographic evidence from rural Latin America', *World Development* 32(6): 941–55 <http://dx.doi.org/10.1016/j.worlddev.2003.11.009>.

Hoff, K. and Sen, A. (2005) 'The kin system as a poverty trap?' *Policy Research Working Paper 3575*. World Bank, Washington, DC <http://dx.doi.org/10.1596/1813-9450-3575>.

Ibañez, A.M. and Moya, A. (2010) 'Vulnerability of victims of civil conflicts: empirical evidence for the displaced population in Colombia', *World Development* 38(4): 647–63 <http://dx.doi.org/10.1016/j.worlddev.2009.11.015>.

Imbens, G.W., Rubin, D.B. and Sacerdote, B.I. (2001) 'Estimating the effect of unearned income on labor earnings, savings and consumption: evidence from a survey of lottery players', *American Economic Review* 91(4): 778–94 <http://dx.doi.org/10.1257/aer.91.4.778>.

Jensen, R.T. (2003) 'Do private transfers "displace" the benefits of public transfers? Evidence from South Africa', *Journal of Public Economics* 88: 89–112 <http://dx.doi.org/10.1016/S0047-2727(02)00085-3>.

Keen, D. (2008) *The Benefits of Famine: A Political Economy of Famine and Relief in Southwestern Sudan, 1983–1989*. Ohio University Press, Athens, OH.

Lentz, E. (2003) 'Annotated bibliography of food aid disincentive effects', *Mimeo*. Cornell University, Ithaca, NY.

Matin, I. and Hulme, D. (2003) 'Programs for the poorest: learning from IGVGD program in Bangladesh', *World Development* 31(3): 647–65 <http://dx.doi.org/10.1016/S0305-750X(02)00223-1>.

Moffitt, R. (2002) 'Welfare programs and labor supply', in A.J. Auerbach and M. Feldstein (eds), *Handbook of Public Economics, Volume 4*. Elsevier, New York, NY: pp. 2393–430 <http://dx.doi.org/10.1016/S1573-4420(02)80013-1>.

MoH-GOSS and SSCCSE (2008) *Southern Sudan Household Health Survey*. Ministry of Health, Government of Southern Sudan and the Southern Sudan Commission for Census, Statistics and Evaluation, Juba.

Morduch, J. (1999) 'Between the market and state: can informal insurance patch the safety net?', *World Bank Research Observer* 14(2): 187–208 <http://dx.doi.org/10.1093/wbro/14.2.187>.

Pantuliano, S. (2007) 'From food aid to livelihood support: rethinking the role of WFP in eastern Sudan', *Disasters* 31(s1): s77–s90 <http://dx.doi.org/10.1111/j.1467-7717.2007.00350.x>.

Sahn, D.E. and Alderman, H. (1996) 'The effect of food subsidies on labor supply in Sri Lanka', *Economic Development and Cultural Change* 45(1): 125–45 <http://dx.doi.org/10.1086/452260>.

Skoufias, E., Unar, M. and González-Cossío, T. (2008) 'The impacts of cash and in-kind transfers on consumption and labor supply: experimental evidence from rural Mexico', *Policy Research Working Paper 4778*. World Bank, Washington, DC <http://dx.doi.org/10.1596/1813-9450-4778>.

SSCCSE (2009) *Statistical Yearbook of Southern Sudan 2009*. Southern Sudan Centre for Census Statistics and Evaluation, Juba.

SSCCSE (2010) *Poverty in Southern Sudan: Estimates from NBHS 2009*. Southern Sudan Centre for Census Statistics and Evaluation, Juba.

Sulaiman, M. (2010) 'Incentive and crowding out effects of food assistance: evidence from randomized evaluation of food-for-training project in Southern Sudan', *Paper No. EOPP 019*. London School of Economics and Political Science, London.

Tadesse, G. and Shively, G. (2009) 'Food aid, food prices and producer disincentive in Ethiopia', *American Journal of Agricultural Economics* 91(4): 942–55 <http://dx.doi.org/10.1111/j.1467-8276.2009.01324.x>.

UNDP (2004) *Millennium Development Goals: Interim Report for South Sudan*. The New Sudan Centre for Statistics and Evaluation and UNDP, Juba.

USAID (2004) 'Sudan: complex emergency', *Situation Report No. 4* [online]. U.S. Agency for International Development, Washington, DC. Available from: http://www.usaid.gov/our_work/humanitarian_assistance/disaster_assistance/countries/sudan/fy2004/Sudan_CE_SR04_06-21-2004.pdf [accessed 10 July 2010].

Webb, P., Coates, J. and Houser, R. (2002) 'Does microcredit meet the needs of all poor women? Constraints to participation among destitute women in Bangladesh', *Discussion Paper No. 3*, Medway, MA: Food Policy and Applied Nutrition Program, Tufts Nutrition, Tufts University.

WFP (1999) *Monitoring Assessment Report.* World Food Programme, Sudan.

WFP (2015) *The World Food Programme in 2014: Facts and Figures.* World Food Programme, Rome.

World Bank (2010) *World Bank Open Data Online Database* [online]. World Bank, Washington, DC. Available from: http://data.worldbank.org/ [accessed 12 May 2010].

About the author

Munshi Sulaiman is a Postdoctoral Associate in the Economic Growth Center, Yale University.

CHAPTER 9

The role of public works in addressing poverty: Lessons from recent developments in public works programming

Anna McCord

This chapter explores recent innovations in public works (PW) programming in sub-Saharan Africa to address the challenge of social protection provision in contexts of chronic mass under- and unemployment. Three ongoing national programmes introduced in the mid-2000s are explored: the Ethiopian Productive Safety Nets Programme, the Rwandan Vision 2020 Umurenge Programme, and the South African Expanded Public Works Programme (PWP). These have introduced a variety of innovations relating to the scale and duration of employment provided, the sectors in which employment is provided, the creation of performance incentives, and coordination with complementary interventions. While they aim to provide social protection which enables participants to graduate out of poverty, they are designed in recognition of the fact that mass graduation is unlikely in the short term given the structural determinants of poverty and under- and unemployment. The programmes still face challenges in providing effective social protection for the working-age poor, but nonetheless they offer valuable options for future programming and differ significantly from the conventional PWP approach adopted in the region.

Keywords: public works, social protection, graduation, productive safety nets, unemployment

Introduction: the growing importance of PWP in the international discourse

Public works programmes (PWPs) are becoming increasingly popular as one component of the social protection 'package' promoted by UN agencies, bilateral development agencies, and international financing agencies in low- and middle-income countries. These are often linked to realization of the employment component of the social protection floor. The package typically constitutes demographically targeted cash transfers for poor households containing the elderly or children and with limited labour capacity, together with PW for poor households with working-age members.

http://dx.doi.org/10.3362/9781780448435.009

At the heart of the conventional PWP model is a set of assumptions which anticipate that the intervention will address poverty in three ways: providing income to meet immediate consumption needs; work experience/training to enhance labour market performance; and assets which contribute to medium-term production gains.

Beyond the social protection objectives of relating to the provision of income, PWPs have become linked in the international discourse with growing interest in 'productive safety nets', 'transformative' social protection, growth, and graduation, particularly in the sub-Saharan Africa region, which forms the main focus of this chapter. This interest in the productive safety net approach and the role of social protection in promoting labour market participation is linked with the increasingly 'productivist' focus of many governments in the region (Golooba-Mutemi and Hickey, 2013), with growth identified as the preferred driver of poverty reduction, and the associated desire to identify social protection which can contribute to this priority.

Similarly, there is a demand for PW (and social protection more widely) to contribute at an individual level to 'graduation' out of 'dependence' on social protection support by enhancing livelihoods, productivity, and labour market engagement (McCord and Slater, 2015). Furthermore, such PW can also play a 'transformative' function (see Devereux and Sabates-Wheeler, 2004; applied in the South African context in Philip, 2013), with partici-pation actively shifting the social and economic status of participants, and PWP playing a role as one component of active labour markets programmes to promote labour activation and engagement (McCord and Slater, 2015). These extended aspirations for social protection have become increasingly common following the shock of the 2008/9 triple financial, food, and fuel crisis (the Triple F crisis). This is in line with the growing recognition of the chronic labour market challenges of under- and unemployment in the region, the slower than anticipated process of structural economic transformation (Filmer and Fox, 2014), and the emergence of a pattern of growth offering aggregate GDP gains with the simultaneous occurrence of increasing inequality and absolute numbers of poor.

In the wake of the Triple F crisis, multiple new PWPs were introduced in the region. Many were financed through the newly formed Rapid Social Response trust fund, administered by the World Bank, set up to address the immediate labour market challenges arising from the economic slowdown, and the associated risks of social destabilization (McCord, 2013).

Simultaneously, the popularity of PWPs has been enhanced by a number of recent institutional developments. Included in this has been the transfor-mation of the World Food Programme (WFP), a key player in the PWP sector, from a food aid-to a food security-oriented agency: '[the] modern WFP not only delivers food – it delivers hunger solutions' (WFP, 2010: 3).[1] Accordingly, WFP has become increasingly concerned with promoting economic and social development through the use of food aid interventions, using PWPs to create assets to enhance livelihoods on a sustainable basis, contributing to the resolution, rather than temporary amelioration, of food security challenges (WFP, 2004; WFP, 2008). The rise of financing for climate change has also promoted increased donor financing flows to the instrument with a focus on the creation of assets, which contribute to environmental protection and rehabilitation ('adaptive social protection').

These developments have also coincided with a conceptual reorientation within the humanitarian sector, resulting in major programming shifts in a number of countries from repeated 'emergency' responses to more systematic developmental programming. The objective here is to address the causes of repeated crises through tackling poverty via the promotion of food security (see, for example, Raisin, 2001). In this context, PW have become a key policy instrument, and have assumed increasing importance as both a responsive and a pre-emptive instrument for addressing latent and patent humanitarian crises. PWPs have been implemented in a number of countries both to provide social protection and to pre-empt social tension and destabilization, which could result in the need for further humanitarian support. Financing for such programming is protected, even in a context of development-financing challenges, due to geopolitical interests in maintaining regional political stability.

Associated with this increase in interest in PW programming is a simultaneous expansion of the range of expectations of what the instrument can achieve (a tendency in social protection in general, and PW in particular, given their focus on the working-age poor), with PW identified, or at least publicly conceptualized, as an instrument able to promote movement out of poverty. In this context, PW, as the major instrument for addressing the needs of the working-age poor, has been identified as a primary instrument for promoting graduation and transformation.

This chapter attempts to explore lessons relating to how PW work for the poorest, and the extent to which they can contribute to the expectations outlined above. We will be primarily focusing on performance in relation to their social protection function, but other anticipated benefits will also be discussed, including impacts resulting from the assets created, the social capital developed, and the social or political stabilization resulting from employment creation.

This chapter first provides an overview of the developing role of PW vis-à-vis social protection and development. A brief summary of the prevailing PWP critique is then outlined, and three innovative programmes discussed – the South African Expanded Public Works Programme (EPWP), the Ethiopian Productive Safety Nets Programme (PSNP), and the Rwandan Vision 2020 Umurenge Programme (VUP) – focusing on the design and implementation innovations each has introduced. An overview of each programme is provided, followed by key achievements and challenges. The insights from these programmes are summarized in terms of the implications for both policy and programme design and implementation.

Changing labour market challenges

Recent analysis indicates over one billion workers globally are either unemployed or employed and living in poverty (ILO, 2013). Internationally, and particularly in low-income countries (LICs), economies are not generating sufficient employment for the growing labour force, and the work that is generated is failing in the most part to conform to the 'decent work' standard, which provides adequate remuneration for workers to support their families. Employment growth is decelerating, resulting in a rise in global unemployment and persistent under-employment, which together are threatening the progress in poverty reduction achieved over the past decade (ILO, 2013).

One consequence is the growing numbers of youth not in education, employment, or training, and another is the persistence of significant numbers of working-age poor. In part this is an artefact of the changing nature of many LIC economies, with aggregate growth taking place alongside urbanization, migration, and the breakdown of traditional economic relationships. In sub-Saharan Africa, this is also the result of slow economic transformation, with under-employment and low productivity in the agricultural sector – still the dominant sector in terms of employment – remaining two of the key factors underlying persistent rural poverty (ILO, 2012; Filmer and Fox, 2014). In this context, unemployment is typically not structural, cyclical, or frictional, but rather may be described as 'transformational', resulting from incomplete economic transformation, and creating a major labour demand deficit. Accordingly, the poverty resulting from this is not transient but chronic, reflecting the nature of economic development across the region, and the existence of significant 'surplus' labour.

Prevalent under- and unemployment has a potentially significant social and economic cost, which goes beyond the tragedy of household-level poverty, being linked to social and geopolitical instability. Hence, recent years have seen an increasing focus on sponsored employment as a solution, and a merging of the social protection and labour debates. As such, PW has increasingly been seen as a tool not only to provide temporary income to enable consumption smoothing, but also to promote 'activation', enhancing worker skills and stimulating workers to look for employment.

Review of PWP critique

The key design critique of most PWPs in the region is that they offer partial coverage (being implemented in localized areas, and providing support only to a subset of those eligible) and only temporary employment (providing a single episode of short-term employment). Most donor-supported PWPs fall into this category, in that they are small in scale with low coverage, and are supply rather than demand driven (McCord and Slater, 2009). They tend to offer short-term and one-off employment opportunities, adopting a model designed to address temporary unemployment, in a regional context characterized by chronic under- and unemployment, limiting the direct social protection impact in terms of improving consumption. The efficacy of the life skills/experience/training component of programmes has not been systematically examined, and, similarly, the quality and functionality assets created in most programmes have gone without being evaluated, as has their relevance in terms of sustained impact on livelihoods (see McCord et al., 2015). In the few cases where livelihoods impacts over time have been examined, the findings have been negative or ambiguous (Ludi et al., 2016; WFP, 2011).

Where examined in detail, many programmes have been found to be poorly fitted to purpose in terms of overall social protection provision for the working-age poor at both individual and community levels, due to sub-market wage rates, late and unpredictable payments, the provision of only temporary support, and the highly rationed nature of access. Typically, these programmes are subject to implementation challenges relating to the high levels of managerial and technical inputs. These are required to administer and execute PWPs, handle financial challenges linked to the associated capital input costs, and manage institutional coordination challenges, where attempts are made to integrate programming with, for example, training or agricultural extension activities. Where such inputs and coordination are limited, the quality of programming outcomes tends to be significantly compromised.

Finally, for the reasons outlined above, PWPs have a high cost-per-dollar transfer relative to alternative social protection instruments, such as cash transfers. The actual cost to the national and international fiscus can often be obscured, however, such as in the case of concessional loan-funded programmes by the deferment of national payment, and in the case of donor-funded programmes by the provision of technical and administrative support, in additional to financing or uncosted food inputs. These factors lessen domestic (and international) potential for fiscal accountability, and value for money analysis.

To date, there is little evidence of the anticipated medium-term programme impacts in terms of the greater objectives of sustainable graduation out of poverty, transformation, or contribution to economic growth (see Hagen-Zanker et al., 2011; Holmes et al., 2013; McCord et al., 2015). Recent research initiatives have started to explore these research gaps (see, for example, Berhane et al., 2011; McCord et al., 2015), reflecting a growing interest in exploring the 'productive safety nets' concept, and the impact of social protection interventions on growth more generally, as illustrated by the recent regional 'Protection to Production' research initiative implemented by a group of international donors in the region.[2] In the case of PW, however, such research has been primarily limited to a small number of the large, and somewhat atypical, PWPs, notably the PSNP in Ethiopia, and the Mahatma Gandhi National Rural Employment Guarantee Scheme in India.

Over the last decade, there has been significant rethinking and innovation in a small number of influential PWPs in response to the challenges outlined above. Since 2005, a number of innovative programmes, which diverge from the dominant PWP model in terms of both conceptualization and design, have played a significant role in reshaping the PWP debate in the region from the standpoints of both aspirations and language, although not necessarily in design, and three of these programmes are the subject of this chapter: the public works components of the Ethiopian PSNP; the Rwandan VUP; and the South African EPWP.

The novel aspect central to the emerging debate is the notion of the productivity-enhancing PWP, with the potential to contribute to both micro- and macro-level growth, thus characterizing the PWP as an instrument to facilitate movement out of poverty and instrumental in the process of poverty reduction and transformation, rather than just a tool to facilitate temporary consumption smoothing and the associated programming innovations. This thinking informed the development of the PSNP in Ethiopia in 2005 and, based on same model, the VUP in Rwanda soon thereafter and also the simultaneous implementation of the EPWP in South Africa.

Case studies overview

The PSNP, VUP, and EPWP are briefly summarized in Table 9.1, and their innovations and key achievements are discussed below, together with the factors promoting positive outcomes and the challenges experienced. The insights they offer to the broader social protection discourse are then set out.

Productive Safety Nets Programme (PSNP) Ethiopia

PSNP overview

The PSNP, initiated in 2005, is one of four components of the Ethiopian national Food Security Programme (FSP).[3] The second phase of the programme was completed in 2015.

The PSNP was intended to replace the annual appeal and short-term donor-funded humanitarian food security intervention approach, largely based on PW, which had been in place for several decades, supporting a core chronically food-insecure population in the context of declining overall food security (Hilhorst and van Uffelen, 2013). The PSNP was innovative in this attempt to promote a shift away from ad hoc annualized humanitarian interventions to a proactive pre-planned multi-year programme response, which aimed to address immediate food security needs, while at the same time promoting food security and graduation out of poverty, thus reducing future demand for international humanitarian support. The programme was developed jointly by the Ethiopian government and the donor community, drawing on decades of humanitarian PW experience.

The PSNP includes both PW and cash transfer components, targeted to food insecure households with and without labour, respectively, previously reliant on humanitarian provision. The programme, depending on the locality, is implemented variously by civil society, INGO, and government actors.

Table 9.1 Summary of case study PWPs

Country	Programme Name	Programme Type	Year Initiated	Budget	Scale (est. no. of beneficiaries)*	Geographical Coverage	Innovations	Challenges
Ethiopia	Productive Safety Nets Programme	PWP and cash transfer package (85% of beneficiaries are PWP) forming part of larger Food Security Programme	2005	£1.4 billion (2010–15)	7 million beneficiaries (25% of the poor)	370 food insecure districts (out of a total of 770 in eight out of nine regions)	• Mass coverage • Shift from annual humanitarian response to multi-year programming • Multi-year participation • Addressing causes of food insecurity • Integration with development interventions (microfinance and agricultural extension) • Indexing of transfer level	• Limited likelihood of mass graduation • Pressure to exit participants and reduce beneficiary caseload • Assets not necessarily contributing to sustainable changes • Reliance on external financing • Not able to address structural drivers of food insecurity
Rwanda	Vision 2020 Umurenge Programme	PWP and cash transfer package with microfinance	2008	£27 million (2013/14)	520,000 beneficiaries (10% of the poor)	180 out of 416 sectors	• Mass coverage • Wage levels commensurate with social protection objectives • Multi-year participation • Integration across line ministries • Accountability through performance incentives	• Difficulty creating sufficient employment • Falling labour intensity • Geographical extension without matching budget • Rationed access • Limited likelihood of mass graduation • Focus on workday creation targets, rather than social protection outcomes • Tension between infrastructure creation and social protection objectives • Decentralization and public-sector reform increase training needs • Reliance on external financing

(Continued)

Table 9.1 Continued

Country	Programme Name	Programme Type	Year Initiated	Budget	Scale (est. no. of beneficiaries)*	Geographical Coverage	Innovations	Challenges
South Africa	Expanded Public Works Programme	Cross-sectoral PWP	2004	£1 trillion (2013/14)	5 million beneficiaries (1 million work opportunities) (2013/14)	National coverage	• Mass coverage • Extended employment beyond infrastructure sector into environmental and social sectors • Promote labour intensification across ministries • Create financial incentives (job subsidies) for employment creation • Recognize systemic nature of employment challenge and limits of market capacity to absorb surplus labour • Recognize trade-offs between skills development, asset creation, and social protection objectives	• Implemented through ministry with limited convening power • Limited capacity to deliver quality training on mass scale • Focus on 'work opportunity' targets, rather than number of days provided per beneficiary or social protection outcomes • Provision of one-off 'work opportunity' • Rationed access • Market not able to absorb workers exiting EPWP • Creation of a two-tier labour market

Sources: DFID (2014), McCord and Shenge (2014), Department of Public Works (2014b)

Note: * Estimates for illustrative purposes only, based on the simplifying assumption that five household members benefit per person employed

PSNP achievements

The PSNP has achieved much since shifting to a national multi-year initiative. Most notable successes are the scale of implementation, and the fact that beneficiaries may be retained within the programme if they remain food insecure. During the first round many beneficiaries were 'rotated' out of the programme each year, but, by 2012, almost 90 per cent had been in the programme for three years or more (DFID, 2014). There were a number of payment-related successes. The fact that the wage level is set on the basis of household size with the aim of ensuring basic consumption needs are met, means that payment may be provided either in cash or food, with a degree of beneficiary choice, and attempts have been made to index the cash value in order to retain the real cash value in a context of inflation.

A key design innovation, included from the initiation of the programme, is that the PW component of the FSP is one part of a medium-term goal to promote food security. This stemmed from the recognition that the approach adopted with donor support for more than two decades (prior to the introduction of the PSNP, and dominant throughout PWPs in the region) was the provision of sponsored employment, and that this alone, on an annual ad hoc basis as a response to periodic food insecurity, was unlikely to promote sustained food security benefits. As such, the programme is now explicitly linked to complementary agricultural extension and microfinance interventions.

In this context, receipt of the PSNP wage has been found to have a beneficial impact on nutrition, and there is also some evidence of a positive impact in terms of accumulation of benefits over time, in the form of asset accumulation (Berhane et al., 2011). The recognition of the need to provide multi-year support for participating households in an attempt to increase the potential for sustained graduation out of poverty, and the retention of households in the programme on a multi-year basis if necessary, represents a significant positive shift in conventional PW thinking. This is significant given such PW approaches often provide only one-off short-term employment, whilst retaining an aspiration of graduation. This shift was inspired by the food insecurity of participants, and the humanitarian risk inherent in premature programme withdrawal, which was perhaps more extreme in Ethiopia than in development contexts characterized by lower levels of food insecurity.

Another achievement has been the attempt to promote the value and relevance of assets created through the programme. This includes a greater focus on asset quality in the second phase in response to critiques of the first, along with increased investment in the administrative resources required to promote the quality of asset selection and construction. These, together with increased PSNP investment in support for extension workers, enable households to capture the potentially positive impacts on production. This has included integration of the PSNP with district infrastructure planning processes and agricultural extension programming, and also the provision of complementary inputs. While the design innovation of this programming is noted here, the efficacy of these initiatives in terms of outcomes remains open to question, as they did not, in all cases, result in the anticipated programme impacts.

The programme was significant in implicitly recognizing the existence of a sub-population of beneficiaries experiencing chronic food insecurity, who, by virtue of their lack of labour or high-dependency ratios, are unlikely to graduate from programme dependence, even with significant additional support. In recognition of this challenge, the cash transfer component of the PSNP is currently being transformed into a separate institutional entity (Pearson et al., forthcoming). This is so that it will be managed separately from the PW component, providing ongoing social assistance without the underlying assumption of graduation.

PSNP challenges

However, despite these highly significant design innovations in the PSNP, key programming challenges remain:

- The limited likelihood of mass graduation, even among non-labour-constrained households participating in the PW component, due to confounding external factors, such as constrained per capita land availability, production constraints linked to rainfall deficits, national policies limiting opportunities for outmigration, and in the problematic nature of agricultural production (Lavers, 2013; McCord et al., forthcoming). The development model underlying the programme does not take into account broader structural factors driving and maintaining poverty and food insecurity, and overestimates the potential impact of the PW wage and assets in promoting graduation or transformative outcomes.
- In order to meet programme targets, there is pressure for beneficiaries to be 'graduated' or 'exited' from the programme before achieving food security (Dagnachew, 2013). Accompanying this is the fact that the criteria for achieving graduation are often being contested among the PSNP supporter community, rather than transparently reflecting sustainable graduation out of poverty.
- The assets created may not necessarily directly contribute to livelihoods development as anticipated. While some may make a significant contribution to medium- to long-term natural resource management, with medium-term environmental benefits, they may not necessarily impact significantly on production and livelihoods (McCord et al., forthcoming). To date, there is no widespread evidence of the PSNP resulting in significant productivity enhancement or livelihoods diversification.
- The programme remains reliant on external financing, although the significant management and administrative inputs on the part of the government, and the ongoing institutionalization of the cash transfer component of the programme, all indicate that this is not inconsistent with significant government commitment.

PSNP reasons for success

The reasons for the achievements of the PSNP, noted above, are largely related to decades of experience of PWP implementation prior to programme initiation, along with the associated development of processes, institutions, and systems for delivery. In addition, government commitment to the programme is key given the PSNP is too important to fail, being the primary instrument in preventing excess mortality each year among chronically food-insecure sub-populations. The high opportunity cost of programme failure in human terms is associated with high levels of political support from the government, and also ongoing financial and technical support from the donor community. Delivered in the form of medium- to long-term financing commitments means donors are unable to withdraw without significant adverse humanitarian consequences. This has resulted in a security of external financing, which is unusual in an aid context more usually characterized by medium- to long-term financing uncertainty.

Associated with this financial commitment has been keen donor and government interest in performance, and monitoring and evaluation scrutiny, which has contributed to significant learning cycles and ongoing programme redevelopment over the cycles of implementation (Devereux and Teshome, 2013). This has enabled the programme to address design weaknesses which characterize other PWPs, for example, by integration with other components of the FSP, such as the Household Asset Building Programme and Complementary Community Investment Programme, although this has not necessarily yet resulted in the benefits anticipated.

Vision 2020 Umurenge Programme (VUP) Rwanda

VUP overview

The VUP, launched in 2008, is a joint donor and Rwandan government initiative. The programme offers, through donor financial and design support (including conceptual input from the PSNP), a combination of PW, cash transfers, and microfinance. The programme further aims to provide temporary social protection for the poorest, while at the same time promoting graduation out of poverty for participating households within a five-year period through capital accumulation and investment in livelihoods diversification.

The PW and cash transfer components are targeted to the poorest, with and without labour, respectively, with the cash transfer component being presented as an entitlement for all those who were eligible, and PW employment being discretionary. Targeting is based on self-reported poverty status under the community-based Ubudehe targeting system.[4] Members of the bottom two Ubudehe categories were eligible for inclusion in the VUP (and also entitled to multiple other poverty-related benefits) until 2015 when the system was revised. Each participating household is eligible to receive 100 days of employment on the programme per annum. While the government makes a substantial financial contribution to the programme and aspires to increase domestic funding, it remains dependent on external financing (McCord and Shenge, 2014). The programme is implemented exclusively by local government actors.

VUP success

The main areas of VUP success are: 1) the mass coverage which has been achieved, both in terms of the absolute numbers of beneficiaries and also the geographical spread; 2) the level of remuneration, which is commensurate with social protection objectives; 3) the accommodation of multiple-year participation in the design; 4) integration across line ministries, with technical staff to promote the quality of infrastructure produced; and 5) the creation of incentives to promote performance of implementing actors. The programme is also currently exploring the potential to include social service provision as means for creating additional PWP employment and simultaneously expanding Early Childhood Development (ECD) provision.

The programme has high coverage, which is expanding annually, and has credible plans for nationwide extension, although progress was slowed by the 2008/9 financial crisis and periodic diplomacy-driven donor suspensions of financing. The PW is part of a set of interventions, which together contribute to an integrated system of social protection provision, entailing cash transfers and subsidized health insurance, although there are multiple additional state-funded initiatives in the sector which are not yet part of a harmonized system. The wage level, chosen in order to ensure a significant poverty reduction impact (unlike many other PWPs, where the adequacy of the wage in relation to needs is not a design consideration), was, in some cases, higher than the prevailing agricultural daily wage rate. This approach enables recipients to hire additional labour with their PWP wages to substitute for or complement their own labour with respect to domestic production. This system means that recipients are not forced to make a choice between domestic production and PWP participation for immediate cash income with potentially adverse medium-term production implications.

Most importantly, ongoing multiple-year support for participating households is accommodated within the programme, enabling those who are consistently ranked in the eligible Ubudehe categories to be re-employed. This, however, is subject to the limitations inherent in a rationed system, as the amount of employment provided is not adequate to absorb all those eligible.

The assets created under the programme – in particular, those relating to terracing and irrigation – are reported to be of appropriate quality technically, are impacting positively on soil conservation and production, and are being implemented in close coordination with agricultural sector staff, enabling integration with agricultural extension, and infrastructure programming and policies.

Finally, the quality of VUP implementation is enhanced by the focus on accountability in the performance contracts, or *imihigo*, which govern the actions of civil servants at all levels of the administration (and also households), and under which performance against certain VUP targets is closely monitored.

VUP challenges

Despite these significant achievements, the VUP faces some major challenges:

- The difficulty of supplying sufficient employment to meet the commitment to provide 100 days each year for participating households, with actual provision averaging 48 days.
- The inability to create sufficient days of employment undermines the social protection function of the VUP, and means that households cannot be guaranteed ongoing employment over multiple years.
- The preference to extend geographical coverage, without commensurate budget increases, has resulted in a reduction in the number of households participating in each district.
- Employment is not based on an entitlement, and the limited amount of employment created results in the exclusion of a significant number of those technically eligible for support.
- The labour intensity of employment has decreased over time as opportunities for labour-intensive terracing activities diminish, resulting in increasing capital–labour cost ratios, and a reducing share of the budget being spent on PW wages.
- This limits the value of the total transfer to poor households, constraining the social protection and 'productivity enhancing', 'transformative', and 'graduation' benefits of PWP participation, and there is little evidence of the programme meeting its graduation objectives.
- Local officials focus on the aggregate number of workdays created, aiming to meet VUP performance targets rather than social protection outcomes, and ensuring that sufficient days are provided for each participant to generate the requisite income on an ongoing basis.
- There is a tension between infrastructure creation objectives and welfare objectives at the local level, with social protection being just one component of the local government mandate. Since employment-based social protection is a relatively unfamiliar concept, incentives to use the VUP to deliver on infrastructure, rather than poverty-related outcomes, can distort local project choice and decision-making, with potentially negative implications for employment creation.
- Finally, political decentralization and public sector reform, relating to local government structures, represent a challenge to future implementation and programme expansion, as the employment of new cadres unfamiliar with the VUP, and social protection programming in general, require national training programmes.

VUP reasons for success

The reasons for the success of the VUP in terms of its expansion and performance are instructive. In terms of programme performance, effective field implementation is enabled by adequate staffing levels, programme training, availability of skills at local level, and also the fact that performance incentives are in place through the *imihigo*.

The inclusion of VUP objectives within civil servants' *imihigo* is one indicator of the importance given to the programme by the government. This attests to the extent of government ownership of the programme, which is identified as a key part of the national strategy for addressing the economic inequities perceived to be one of the multiple factors underlying the genocide. As such, the programme is publicly endorsed by senior politicians as a priority instrument to address poverty and equity challenges, and promote stabilization as a key part of the current state–citizen compact.

In addition, the consistent leadership and management of the programme over time by a team of skilled and dedicated civil servants, and ongoing support from key members of the donor community who have provided secure funding and a range of technical inputs over time, have also enhanced the quality of programming. The need for ongoing financial and technical support, as well as collaboration between the government and the donor community, is mutually recognized.

Recognition of the challenge represented by the aspiration to achieve graduation in a short timeframe has been accommodated by the acceptance of multi-year programme participation. Hence, although the programme retains the language of graduation, and had sought explicitly to promote movement away from ongoing reliance on social protection, analysis of performance to date has resulted in a greater realism regarding the need for ongoing PW support through multiple years of programme employment, particularly given the limited number of days of employment provided.

Expanded Public Works Programme (EPWP) South Africa

EPWP overview

The South African EPWP is a nationally developed initiative launched in 2004. Its design was based on the institutionalization of pre-existing small-scale project-based initiatives, and the incorporation of lessons from the International Labour Organization (ILO). Such lessons drew notably from the Employment Intensive Infrastructure Programme (EIIP) model. The EIIP looked to promote the labour intensification of infrastructure expenditure, together with the innovative additional element of extending beyond the traditional construction sector focus based around the creation and maintenance of physical assets, and into the social and environmental sectors.

The programme had its origins in the 2003 national Growth and Development Summit which aimed to promote 'More jobs, better jobs, decent work for all', and adopted PW as the key instrument to 'provide poverty and income relief through temporary work for the unemployed to carry out socially useful activities' (Department of Public Works, 2014b). The EPWP is implemented in four 'sectors' – infrastructure, social, environmental, and culture and 'non-state' (promoting employment through non-profit organizations) – and a community-based work programme. The programme aimed to provide 100 workdays per beneficiary on a one-off 'work opportunity' basis. It created approximately 1 million 'work opportunities' per annum in its second phase, between 2009 and 2014. This was achieved, with government financing, through the creation of additional employment by public bodies from all spheres of government.

EPWP achievements

The programme has been highly successful in terms of its own objective of creating mass employment. The programme is politically popular, retaining a high profile in terms of the national priority of addressing poverty among the working poor. The programme has been innovative inasmuch as it has promoted employment, by requiring the labour intensification of infrastructure expenditure across government agencies in order to increase aggregate employment. In addition, it has attempted to extend PW employment beyond the conventional infrastructure sector, notably into the environmental and social sectors. In the environmental sector, this has included clearing millions of hectares of alien invasive plants, and providing services to respond to and prevent forest fires through the 'Working on Fire', 'Working for Wetlands', and 'Working for Water' programmes, thus realizing considerable savings for the forestry and agriculture industries. In the social sector, the programme has supported a range of activities including ECD, and Home and Community-Based Care (Skosana, 2012).

Hence, the programme has found new ways to absorb labour, attempting to stimulate employment across sectors, and finding experimental ways of creating additional employment. This has been done, in part, by mandating all ministries to contribute additional jobs, while also attempting to innovate by absorbing surplus labour in programmes to address a range of societal challenges. These include, in an attempt to increase aggregate employment, addressing environmental and security-related challenges. Included in this is increased NGO employment, through the promotion of a shift from voluntary to remunerated employment. In this way, PW employment has been linked to the realization of other government objectives, and the promotion of a range of national policies, including the National Integrated Plan for ECD.

As well as finding ways to create additional employment, the EPWP has also sought to create financial incentives for agencies conforming to these requirements, for example, by creating an 'incentive grant' available to both government departments and non-state employers, to reward the creation of EPWP employment (Philip, 2013). The government has also developed a new initiative, the Community Works Programme (CWP), to explore additional community-based options for employment innovation (Philip, 2013).

In the first phase of the EPWP, it was expected that those exiting the programme would go on to find market-based employment due to increased labour demand resulting from economic growth, and the EPWP explicitly linked PW employment with skills training in order to enhance employability (McCord, 2012). However, by 2011 realism regarding limits to the growth-based employment creation replaced this optimism, and the need for continued mass state sponsored employment was recognized. In the second phase of the EPWP (2009–14), it was acknowledged that market-based solutions would not be possible for the South African unemployment challenge, given the systemic challenges within the mainstream economy (Government of South Africa, 2010, cited in Department of Public Works, 2014a). As such, there was a need for ongoing, rather than one-off, employment provision, which was a radical insight within the region.

> The problem of unemployment and underemployment has become too big for market-based solutions to solve in the next 10 to 20 years. There is no doubt that market-based employment is the most sustainable source of job creation, but in even the most optimistic of scenarios, many people are likely to remain out of work. [...] The public employment programmes should target the creation of 2 million opportunities annually by 2020 or earlier, if possible (National Planning Commission, 2011: 153).

EPWP managers have also formally recognized that there are trade-offs between the three anticipated outcomes of the programme: 1) the provision of social protection transfers on an ongoing basis; 2) the creation of assets; and 3) the provision of training and skills development. Furthermore, enhancing performance in one area 'is likely to result in decreases in the others' (Department of Public Works, 2014a). This is another fundamental insight not widely recognized in the region, where PWPs are often perceived as able to deliver on these three key areas simultaneously, with the result that attempting to promote skills and asset creation often compromises social protection outcomes.

EPWP challenges

While positive developments in the EPWP may be characterized by mass provision, the incentivization of employment creation, innovation in the sectors and activities providing employment, and realism regarding the limits to market capacity, it remains subject to several key challenges, which it is still struggling to address.

- Institutionally, the EPWP is implemented under the auspices of the national agency for PW, and, given that this agency is traditionally mandated to manage public assets rather than provide social protection or create employment (and with commensurately low cross-sectoral convening power), this hinders its performance.

- Institutional constraints relating to national training and management capacity were a challenge when the programme was implemented to scale. The emphasis on training and skills development became a challenge to programme delivery due to insufficient trainers and quality-control mechanisms.
- The requirement to create employment and ensure skills development represented an additional burden on line ministries already struggling to deliver on their core mandates, which compromised implementation.
- The programme was not able to provide 100 days of work to each participant as intended.
- The market is not able to absorb the labour exiting from EPWP employment, with beneficiaries returning to their unemployed status after PWP employment due to the oversupply of low- and semi-skilled labour (Philip, 2013).
- Despite the insight regarding the need for ongoing employment provision outlined above, the programme has not responded by adopting a policy of ongoing or repeat employment, although some agencies covertly provide ongoing employment in recognition of the fact that workers would not find alternative work after exiting.
- The focus on performance against 'work opportunity' targets has promoted incentives to create EPWP jobs, resulting in some substitution of EPWP workers for workers displaced from existing formal jobs, the renaming of pre-existing jobs as EPWP jobs, and the re-categorization of voluntary workers receiving sub-market rate stipends as 'EPWP employees', which does not necessarily contribute to additional employment.
- The creation of a two-tier labour market, identified as a risk at the start of the EPWP by South African unionists (McCord, 2012), with PWP employees as alternative workers with inferior terms and conditions (not conforming to the 'decent work' terms of employment negotiated by unions in South Africa), is problematic and potentially also risks a deterioration in the services provided (Philip, 2013).

The EPWP was originally intended to provide social protection provision for the working-age poor, and the PWP instrument was selected in preference to cash transfer alternatives for the unemployed by the Taylor Commission, charged with designing the social protection system for the new, post-1994, democratic South Africa. However, the social protection function of the programme is significantly compromised by the challenges outlined above. Similarly, the focus on proximate goals, notably the creation of 'workdays' as the fundamental indicator against which performance is measured, has meant that the programme has lost the broader vision of creation of employment as a means to provide social protection for the working-age poor.

Community Works Programme (CWP)

South Africa is continuing to innovate in the sector by developing experimental community-based PWPs, which attempt to match needs and available
labour in new ways, including the provision of subsidies for communities
to initiate activities according to priority needs (such as construction or the
provision of security personnel). This approach does not differ significantly
from conventional PWP community projects implemented in the region by
the WFP or ILO, or as part of World Bank-funded Social Action Funds, except
in the critical dimensions of: 1) the priority accorded to community ownership
at key junctures (identification of activities, financial management, etc.);
and 2) integration with local government. Such intent is often nominally
included in programme design, but in the CWP this aspect of programming is
prioritized with explicit investment in facilitation, training, skills, and accountability mechanisms; these being the core developmental processes which are
essential to address the development deficits at local level (community and
local government), which serve as key constraints to effective implementation
in many 'community-led' PWP initiatives (see, for example, McCord et al., 2013
with reference to the impact of developmental deficits on PWP asset selection
in Northern Uganda).

EPWP reasons for success

Government 'job creation' through investment in EPWP employment is
central to the policy discourse in relation to the challenge of the working-age
poor, with unemployment being recognized as a major social, economic, and
political problem, and also one with potentially destabilizing consequences.
As such, the EPWP, as a key programme, is part of the national vision and
policy discourse that addresses national priorities. It is exclusively financed
domestically, and has secure medium-term financing. The government has
promoted and invested in innovation, adaptation, and reflexivity in the
programme.

Once it was recognized that programme participation was unlikely to result
in improved labour market performance given the scale of the unemployment
challenge, the idea of 'massifying' state-sponsored employment through the
EPWP was developed. Although massification has not been successful (in terms
of providing a sufficient number of days of employment, thus ensuring social
protection objectives are met for a significant portion of the unemployed),
programme targets have been met. The recognition of the ongoing need for
mass provision and the divestment of the graduation objective was a mark of
realism and candour in government analysis of the labour market context,
which is unusual within the region.

Finally, in recognition of the challenges in delivering adequate quality
training on a mass scale, and providing meaningful training inputs during
the short interface provided by the period of EPWP employment, the EPWP

removed training as a formal requirement of implementation, delinking training and skills development from EPWP employment.

Summary and conclusions

Over the last decade, these three programmes have attempted to address serious limitations inherent to the dominant model of PW programming by developing a range of innovations during successive phases of programme implementation.

The key innovations are based on an emerging set of insights, which may be summarized as:

- Recognition of the limits of market absorption of surplus labour, and the mass scale of the challenge of under- and unemployment.
- Acknowledgement that programme design needs to respond to under- and unemployment as a chronic, rather than transient, problem.
- Recognition of the limits to graduation as a route out of poverty, and attempting to develop design options accordingly, with extended/ open-ended employment.
- The extension of PWP employment beyond conventional infrastructure sector activity in an attempt to relieve the labour demand constraints to programme implementation, and also to address social and environmental as well as infrastructure needs.
- The implementation of complementary interventions to increase the potential for PW employment to relieve poverty on a sustained basis, such as microfinance, training, and agricultural extension. Although not widely successful due to the many implementation and coordination challenges it entails, and the essentially structural and/or political determinants of poverty which a PWP cannot address, this insight is important in terms of its recognition that PW participation alone is not sufficient to promote significant sustained poverty reduction or graduation. This challenges a common assumption informing much PW programming in the region.

These programmes have had considerable success in terms of the provision of social protection, due to these innovations, and flexibility in programming, recognizing, and addressing institutional, design, and implementation challenges during successive phases of programme execution. In this way, PWPs are explicitly being integrated into longer-term development processes, and are taking account of the broader context, rather than being implemented in isolation as standalone, 'off the peg', interventions. The need to ensure PW remains rooted in the development approach may be summarized thus:

> In making the case for a longer-term development approach, [...] such an approach would not only allow these programmes to act as shock absorbers without being 'too little, too late' but would also enable

the state to strengthen its capacities to provide support to livelihood strategies of the poor through addressing critical public goods and service deficits while creating jobs (Lal et al., 2010: 3).

Despite these innovations, however, the programmes outlined above remain subject to a range of significant challenges, which continue to constrain performance. Perhaps the most binding challenge is the struggle to create sufficient employment to meet programme objectives. This is a significant challenge throughout the region, with provision of employment falling far below demand for employment across all programmes. Even in India, under the celebrated Mahatma Gandhi National Rural Employment Guarantee Scheme, this challenge represents a major threat to programme performance. The consequence is strict rationing of access and limited days of employment for participants, reducing the social protection impact significantly.

There is a linked administrative issue which exacerbates this challenge. The focus on performance monitoring, in terms of the aggregate number of 'work opportunities' or 'workdays' created, is distorting performance in favour of achieving process indicators relating to proximate objectives, and moving away from the ultimate objective of social protection provision (IEG, 2011; McCord and Shenge, 2014). This shifts the focus in monitoring and, hence, programme implementation to the prioritization of jobs or workday creation, rather than focusing on the social protection objectives and outcomes of PW, as well as the need to ensure sufficient workdays per beneficiary. The social protection function risks being compromised by the focus on the number of jobs created and the need to provide support, which conforms to the basic principles of social protection (being regular, reliable, and ongoing), can remain forgotten.

Conclusion

The driving factors behind the success of these programmes are political commitment, adequate and secure financing, and the high cost of failure (notably social unrest, political instability, and famine). In the case study countries, PW are key to political settlement in the context of strong states which provide space for policy innovation, which is not constrained by the application of conventional or external models of programme design.

The key shift in terms of social protection provision is from one-off to ongoing provision, representing a deviation from the regional norm. This has stemmed from the desire for programme impact, and the recognition of limits to poverty reduction and graduation, likely to accrue from programme participation.

The perception of PW as a means to promote graduation out of poverty has been associated with an increasing ambition in the PW discourse over the last decade throughout the region. This has extended beyond social protection to graduation and transformation, but without associated revisions to programme conceptualization or design. These three programmes challenge conventional thinking and the approaches promoted in prevalent donor models. This has been achieved through adopting innovations to improve performance, adapting programming to fit the reality of labour market challenges in the twenty-first-century in terms of social protection provision, and implicitly denoting the limits to what this instrument can achieve in terms of wider graduation aspirations.

Notes

1. WFP provided over 0.5 million metric tonnes of food through Food for Work and Food Assistance for Assets programmes in 2010, at a direct cost of US$400 million (WFP, 2011).
2. The From Protection to Production project is a collaborative multi-country impact evaluation of cash transfers in sub-Saharan Africa involving the FAO, UNICEF, and seven governments in sub-Saharan Africa. It is part of the larger FAO, UNICEF, Save the Children UK, and the University of North Carolina Transfer Project, which promotes the design and implementation of cash transfer impact evaluations in sub-Saharan Africa (FAO, 2015).
3. The other three components are the Household Asset Building Programme, the Complementary Community Investment Programme, and the Resettlement Programme.
4. Under the original Ubudehe system, the whole population was self-classified into six income categories. The system was revised in 2015 to address inclusion error due to excess self-allocation into the categories eligible for VUP participation, and a range of additional poverty-related benefits.

References

Berhane, G., Hoddinott, J., Kumar, N., Taffesse, A., Diressie, M., Yohannes, Y., Sabates-Wheeler, R., Handino, M., Lind, J., Tefera, M. and Simma F. (2011) *Evaluation of Ethiopia's Food Security Program: Documenting Progress in the Implementation of the Productive Safety Nets Programme and the Household Asset Building Programme.* International Food Policy Research Institute, Washington, DC.

Dagnachew, S. (2013) 'Household experiences of graduation from the PSNP: implications for food security', in D. Rahmato, A. Pankhurst, and J.G. van Uffelen (eds), *Food Security, Safety Nets and Social Protection in Ethiopia.* Forum for Social Studies, Addis Ababa.

Devereux, S. and Sabates-Wheeler, R. (2004) 'Transformative social protection', *IDS Working Paper 232.* Institute of Development Studies, Brighton.

Devereux, S. and Teshome, A. (2013) 'From safety nets to social protection: options for Direct Support beneficiaries of the Productive Safety Net Programme', in D. Rahmato, A. Pankhurst, and J.G. van Uffelen (eds), *Food Security, Safety Nets and Social Protection in Ethiopia.* Forum for Social Studies, Addis Ababa.

Department of Public Works (2014a) *Expanded Public Works Programme (EPWP) Phase 3 Green Jobs Summit 09 April 2014* [online]. Department of Public Works,

Republic of South Africa, Pretoria. Available from: https://www.environment.gov.za/sites/default/files/docs/greenjobsdialogue_epwp_phase3.pdf [accessed 26 March 2014].

Department of Public Works (2014b) *Annexures A–E. EPWP Quarterly Report. Report for the Period 1 April–31 March Financial Year 2013/15.* Department of Public Works, Republic of South Africa, Pretoria.

DFID (2014) *Ethiopia Productive Safety Net Programme (PSNP) Annual Review. ARIES Project 200762.* Department for International Development, London.

FAO (2015) *From Protection to Production: Exploring the Linkages and Strengthening Coordination Between Social Protection, Agriculture and Rural Development* [online]. Rome: Food and Agriculture Organization. Available from: http://www.fao.org/economic/ptop/home/en/ [accessed 26 March 2014].

Filmer, D. and Fox, L. (2014) *Overview: Youth Employment in Sub-Saharan Africa.* World Bank, Washington, DC.

Golooba-Mutebi, F. and Hickey, S. (2013) 'Investigating the links between political settlements and inclusive development in Uganda: towards a research agenda', *ESID Working Paper No. 20.* Effective States and Inclusive Development Research Centre, Manchester.

Hagen-Zanker, J., McCord., A. and Holmes, R. (2011) *Systematic Review of the Impact of Employment Guarantee Schemes and Cash Transfers on the Poor* [online]. London: Overseas Development Institute. Available from: http://www.odi.org/sites/odi.org.uk/files/odi-assets/publications-opinion-files/7161.pdf [accessed 2 June 2014].

Hilhorst, D. and van Uffelen, J.G. (2013) 'Introduction to the LEAFS program', in D. Rahmato, A. Pankhurst, and J.G. van Uffelen (eds), *Food Security, Safety Nets and Social Protection in Ethiopia.* Forum for Social Studies, Addis Ababa.

Holmes, R., McCord, A. and Hagen-Zanker, J. (2013) *What is the Evidence on the Impact of Employment Creation on Stability and Poverty Reduction in Fragile States: A Systematic Review* [online]. London: Overseas Development Institute. Available from: http://r4d.dfid.gov.uk/pdf/outputs/systematicreviews/What_is_the_evidence_on_the_impact_of_employment_creation_on_stability_and_poverty_reduction_in_fragile_states.pdf [accessed 2 June 2014].

IEG (2011) *Social Safety Nets: An Evaluation of World Bank Support, 2000–2010.* Independent Evaluation Group, World Bank, Washington, DC.

ILO (2012) *Global Employment Trends 2012: Preventing a Deeper Jobs Crisis.* International Labour Office, Geneva.

ILO (2013) *Global Employment Trends 2013: Recovering from a Second Jobs Dip.* International Labour Office, Geneva.

Lal, R., Miller, S., Lieuw-Kie-Song, M. and Kostzer, D. (2010) 'Public works and employment programmes: towards a long-term development approach', *Working Paper Number 66.* International Policy Centre for Inclusive Growth and UNDP, Brasilia.

Lavers, T. (2013) 'Food security and social protection in highland Ethiopia: linking the productive safety net to the land question', *Journal of Modern African Studies* 51(3): 459–85 <http://dx.doi.org/10.1017/S0022278X13000402>.

Ludi, E., Levine, S., McCord, A., Duvendack, M., with Agol, D., Njigua, J., Amsalu, A. and Tefera, M. (2016) *Approaches to Evaluating the Impacts of Public Works Assets on Livelihoods: A Case Study of NRM Assets.* Overseas Development Institute, London.

McCord, A. (2012) *Public Works and Social Protection in sub-Saharan Africa. Do Public Works Work for the Poor?* United Nations University Press, Tokyo.

McCord, A. (2013) *Review of the Literature on Social Protection Shock Responses and Readiness* [online]. Overseas Development Institute, London. Available from: http://www.odi.org/publications/6495-shockwatch-social-protection-responses-readiness-food [accessed 24 March 2014].

McCord, A., Ludi, E., Duvendack, M. and Levine, S. (2015) 'Developing practical methodologies to assess the spatial, temporal and socio-economic distribution of public works programme impacts', paper prepared for conference on *Measuring the Social, Economic and Political Effects of Social Protection: How to Overcome the Challenges?* German Development Institute, Bonn 15–17 April 2015.

McCord, A., Ludi, E., Duvendack M., Levine, S., Tefera, M., Aklelu, A., Agol D. and Njigua, J. (forthcoming) *Livelihoods Impact of Public Works Assets (LIPA) Report (Ethiopia and Kenya).* Overseas Development Institute, London.

McCord, A., Onapa, P. and Levine, S. (2013) *NUSAF 2 PWP Design Review.* Overseas Development Institute, London.

McCord, A. and Shenge, S. (2014) *Social Protection Support to the Poorest in Rwanda Annual Review Report.* Department for International Development, London.

McCord, A. and Slater, R. (2009) *Overview of Public Works Programmes in sub-Saharan Africa.* Overseas Development Institute, London.

McCord, A. and Slater, R. (2015) 'Social protection and graduation through sustainable employment', *IDS Bulletin Special Issue: Graduating from Social Protection?* 46(2): 134–44 <http://dx.doi.org/10.1111/1759-5436.12136>.

National Planning Commission (2011) *National Development Plan 2030: Our Future – Make it Work* [online]. Pretoria: National Planning Commission. Available from: http://www.poa.gov.za/news/Documents/NPC%20National%20Development%20Plan%20Vision%202030%20-lo-res.pdf [accessed 11 July 2014].

Pearson, R., Afaw, S., Baschieri, A., Birru, B., Berhane, G., Chaiba, T., Davis, B., Devereux, S., Hoddinott, J., Hoel, J., Kagin, J., Ledlie, N., Lemma, H., Mahonde, D., Pigois, R., Pozarny, P., Roelen, K., Schwab, B., Salama, P., Sessay, I., Taylor, E., Tegebu, F.N., Tsegay, N. and Webb, D. (forthcoming) 'The role of the Tigray Pilot Social Cash Transfer Programme and its evaluation in the evolution of the Tigray social protection policy', in B. Davis, S. Handa, N. Hypher, N. Winder-Rossi, P. Winters, and J. Yablonski (eds), *The Promise of Social Protection: Social and Productive Impacts of Cash Transfer Programmes in Sub-Saharan Africa.* Oxford University Press, Oxford.

Philip, K. (2013) 'The transformative potential of public employment programmes', *Occasional Paper Series No.1/2013.* Graduate School of Development Policy and Practice, University of Cape Town, Cape Town.

Raisin, J. (2001) *Beyond the Merry-Go-Round to the Relief-Development Continuum: Prospects for Linking USAID Relief and Development Resources in Amhara National Regional State (ANRS).* USAID Ethiopia, Addis Ababa.

Skosana, N. (2012) 'The role of Expanded Public Works Programme in ECD provisioning', paper prepared for conference on *Early Childhood Development,* East London International Convention Centre, 26–30 March 2012.

WFP (2004) *World Food Programme Policy Framework*. World Food Programme, Rome.

WFP (2008) *WFP Strategic Plan 2008–2011*. World Food Programme, Rome.

WFP (2010) *Revolution: From Food Aid to Food Assistance: Innovations in Overcoming Hunger*. World Food Programme, Rome.

WFP (2011) *Evaluation Top Ten Lessons. WFP Evaluations Concerning Safety Nets* [online]. World Food Programme, Rome. Available from: documents. wfp.org/stellent/groups/public/documents/reports/wfp247636.pdf [accessed 14 January 2015].

About the author

Dr Anna McCord is an Honorary Research Fellow in ESID at the University of Manchester, an ODI Research Associate, and a Research Affiliate of SALDRU at the University of Cape Town. She is an economist and social scientist specializing in research into the role of PW in the provision of social protection.

CHAPTER 10

Exploring potentials and limits of graduation: Tanzania's Social Action Fund

Usha Mishra and Emmanuel J. Mtambie

African Union states have repeatedly emphasized the capability of social protection in delivering multiple benefits to national economies. As such, they also highlight the necessity of supporting this endeavour through building human capital, breaking the intergenerational poverty cycle, and reducing growing socio-economic inequalities. Social protection programmes have therefore seen a growth in number, across the continent, from 25 in 9 countries in 2000, to 254 in 41 countries in 2012. Nevertheless, despite the growth of such programmes, numbers of poor have, at the same time, increased in certain regions in Africa. Tanzania is one such area, where, despite the country experiencing a high rate of GDP growth as well as having a history of commitment to social protection, results in poverty and inequality reduction have been far lower. In this light, this chapter looks to explore Tanzania's Social Action Fund's productive social safety net programme and its goal of 'threshold graduation'. Specifically, the variety of enabling and constraining factors are looked at, as well as the range of mechanisms that contribute to, or hinder, the success of this programme. Conclusions indicate that, in order to help ensure its success, the Tanzanian programme must learn to embrace in-course adaptation and revisions as evidenced in several of its African neighbours.

Keywords: social action fund, graduation, social protection, conditional cash transfers, Tanzania

Introduction

Tanzania's heightened commitment to social protection needs to be placed within a similar growing regional and pan-African interest, enthusiasm, and dedication, thus underscoring the relevance of regional and international efforts towards addressing some complex, and intractable, development and human rights issues. Over the last decade, African Union member states have emphasized the multiple beneficial impacts that social protection has on national economies, as well as its essential role in building human capital, breaking the intergenerational poverty cycle, and reducing the growing inequalities that constrain Africa's economic and social development (Pearson, 2014). Tanzania has been a regular party to such deliberations and declarations,

http://dx.doi.org/10.3362/9781780448435.010

including the 2004 Ouagadougou Declaration that urged member states to recognize, among other things, the centrality of social protection for social policy enhancement. The agreed plan of action committed governments to 'improving and strengthening the social protection schemes and extending them to workers and their families currently excluded' (African Union, 2004: 2). Following that commitment, a number of policy activities, statements, and recommendations have been developed. These include the 2006 Livingstone and Yaoundé Calls for Action, agreements reached during the 11th African regional meeting of the International Labour Organization held in Addis Ababa in April 2007, and the recommendations of the 2008 Regional Meetings on Investing in Social Protection in Africa (Livingstone 2) process (ibid.).

Most recently, the Addis Ababa Ministerial Declaration at the Fourth Session of the Ministers of Social Development, from 26 to 30 May 2014, committed members to the expansion and scale-up of social protection programmes to operationalize comprehensive social protection systems, and to the allocation (and ring-fencing) of national resources for social protection (African Union, 2015). Africa has seen an expansion from 25 programmes in nine nations in 2000, to 254 programmes in 41 nations in 2012 (Garcia and Moore, 2012). More specifically, in 2013 the number of countries implementing cash transfers stood at 37, whereas approximately 10–15 years previously, only three African countries – South Africa, Mauritius, and Botswana – were engaged in this activity.

Paradoxically, and unfortunately, this expansion has coincided with a sharp increase in the number of poor in certain regions of Africa (sub-Sahara in particular), where such numbers have increased from 290 million in 1990, to 408 million in 2014 (World Bank, 2014a). Overall, the rate of poverty reduction, as estimated by household budgeting/consumption surveys, in Africa remained low (World Bank, n.d.).

In 2014, Tanzania's population stood at 51.8 million with a per capita GNI of US$920, placing it in the category of low-income countries (World Bank, 2014b). Over the past decade it has made remarkable progress towards meeting its Millennium Development Goal (MDG) targets; specifically, it was on track to achieve five of the eight MDGs by early 2015. However, Tanzania is currently not on target to meet the first MDG goal of eradicating extreme poverty and hunger. Despite the progress that has been made, poverty is prevalent, with 28.2 per cent of the population still living under the national poverty line, using a basic needs poverty measure of (Tanzanian Shillings) TZS36,482 equivalent to $1.36 per adult per day at 2005 purchasing power parity (Ministry of Planning, 2012).[1] Although the Household Budget Survey 2011–12 results indicate that poverty and inequality have declined at less than one percentage point per year (ibid.), this reduction is still troubling against a background of a steady 6–7 per cent GDP growth rate attained by Tanzania (excluding the 2008–9 financial crisis period), which is the ninth highest in Africa, putting it in the same league as such high-performing economies as Angola, Ethiopia, Uganda, and Mozambique (World Bank, 2014a).[2] While it is possible for a country to experience faster growth over an extended period of time, a large segment of its population, especially those subsisting on farming, small-scale informal activities, and other labour-intensive activities, could be left behind, as they are stuck in various poverty traps. Such is the reality confronting most low-income African countries (Shimeles, 2014). This may go some way towards explaining the apparent inconsistency between high economic growth and low pace of poverty reduction, not only in Tanzania but in many other African countries as well.

As per growth-incidence analysis, the poorest 10 per cent are benefiting least from growth. The impact of the 2008–9 crisis, and food price inflation, in particular, resulted in a deep deterioration of the well-being of the poorest (Adam et al., 2012). Furthermore, there has been an unquestionable increase in inequality as in many other countries globally (Samson, 2014). However, inequality in Tanzania is still not as acute as in some other African countries, such as South Africa, Botswana, Namibia, Nigeria, or the Central African Republic (World Bank, 2014a)·

To its credit, Tanzania has had a track record of higher commitment to social protection, as evidenced from its financial outlay in this regard, which, standing at 4–5.9 per cent, is on the higher side when compared with other nations across the African continent. Inspired and guided by Julius Nyerere's socialistic vision, Tanzania has had a tradition of social safety nets and social funds. As one of the initiatives to accelerate progress towards meeting the first MDG, the Tanzanian government established the Tanzania Social Action Fund (TASAF) in 2000 (see Figure 10.1). TASAF interventions have demonstrated notable achievements, particularly in terms of facilitating increased access to improved social services by ultra-poor households and communities (TASAF, 2013). In 2012, the prevalent political disposition, when faced with the impending failure of missing the first MDG, was open to accelerating and intensifying its efforts, and to utilizing technical advice from development partners such as UNICEF, the World Bank, DFID, and SIDA. As such, the country set about expanding TASAF, its mainstay poverty reduction programme, into a fully fledged productive social safety net programme.

This chapter aims to explore the underlying notions of graduation within the latest TASAF programme – TASAF III: Productive Social Safety Net (PSSN) – and the range of enabling and constraining factors that facilitate or undermine this change process. It emphasizes the existence of multiple factors working at different levels beyond the household, such as sectoral responses and investments, and community investment, and scale effects that work to constrain or complement each other and support graduation, or lack of the same. Graduation, in this case, is defined as a 'threshold graduation', which still remains to be determined clearly with respect to TASAF III (Devereux and Sabates-Wheeler, 2011).[3] For TASAF, it is linked to a recertification measure every three years, which is essentially a re-application of the proxy means test (PMT) to determine whether a household has reduced its poverty and vulnerability. However, the scope of this verification PMT

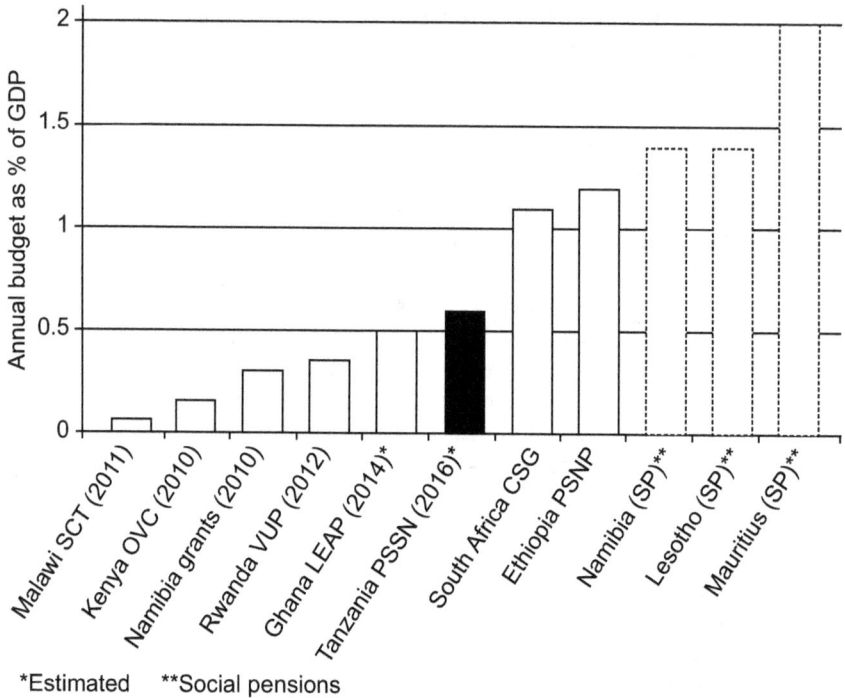

*Estimated   **Social pensions

Figure 10.1 Annual cost of cash transfer programmes as a per cent of GDP
Source: TASAF calculations 2014

and the criteria for this 'threshold graduation' were yet to be determined at the time of publication.

TASAF III/PSSN: an overview

The Tanzanian Social Action Fund III is a social safety net that emerged from previous iterations of Tanzanian social funds. Begun in 2000, TASAF has passed through at least three incarnations.[4] Up to 2007, it was largely a community-based public works (PW) programme providing one-off opportunities for cash- and food-strapped households through supplementing their incomes during the lean agricultural season. Livelihoods enhancement (LE), or savings group and income generating activities (IGA), components were subsequently added to the programme. In 2010, cash transfer was piloted among 40,000 households and, following an evaluation, was set to expand to cover 275,000 households to complement the earlier PW and LE elements. The incorporation of these components is a specific attempt to release the poorest families, dependent largely on farming and casual labour, set on the path of breaking free from the above-mentioned poverty traps.

Box 10.1, adapted from the World Bank project appraisal document, outlines the evolution of the programme from TASAF I through to TASAF II (World Bank, 2012a).

Box 10.1 TASAF II Evolution from a social action fund to a productive safety net

With support of the World Bank, TASAF I was rolled out on 22 August 2000. That year the Government of the United Republic of Tanzania had established TASAF as one of the instruments for operationalizing its poverty reduction strategy. This strategy targeted 40 project administrative areas (PAAs) in the 16 poorest regions on the mainland, plus Unguja and Pemba in Zanzibar. The main purpose was to support communities with a need for service delivery in health, education, water, and community roads and bridges. TASAF I focused on construction of such infrastructure, responding directly to community demands. Support to food-insecure households, through the PW programme, was a small part of the project. TASAF was also used as a vehicle for empowering communities through a community-driven development approach.

After a mid-term review, TASAF began to be piloted in four PAAs trialling support to vulnerable groups, an intervention that was scaled up under TASAF II. TASAF had staff in each PAA directly overseeing its operations, and it reached 7 million direct beneficiaries.

Improving upon the experience of TASAF I, TASAF II was rolled out in 2004. This programme was nationwide, having being scaled up geographically, but also including those vulnerable groups targeted under TASAF I. While TASAF II was a follow-on project, providing resources for responding to community demands, it had additionally responded to the need for operating through government structures to ensure sustainability. Both TASAF I and TASAF II supported communities in a one-off manner with respect to infrastructure, public works support to insecure households, and the provision of support to the vulnerable through income-generating activities. TASAF II also supported communities by instilling a culture of accumulating one's own savings, and investing through the Community Savings and Investment Promotion programme (COMSIP). While TASAF's main interventions were targeted at poor households, the COMSIP was available to support groups of poor savers in urban and rural areas.

Source: World Bank PSSN Project Assessment Document, March 2012

In 2012, TASAF III was launched, with a scaling up of PSSN from 275,000 households to an estimated 900,000, covering approximately 7 million of the poorest below the food poverty line, an estimated 16.5 per cent of the population (Ministry of Planning, 2012). The key elements of this scaled-up PSSN are:

1. A national safety net incorporating transfers linked to participation in PW, and adherence to co-responsibilities (in health and education).
2. Cash transfers at a basic rate of $5 per eligible household plus another $5 if they had children younger than 18 and had met the health and education conditionalities. Their benefits have been recently revised, with an additional allowance for secondary school provided.[5]
3. Community-driven interventions that enhance livelihoods and increase incomes through community savings and investments, as well as specific livelihood-enhancing grants.
4. Targeted infrastructure development (education, health, and water) to enable poor communities to realize the objectives of the safety net.
5. Capacity building to ensure adequate programme participation by communities, project area authorities/districts, and at the national level.

The programme is unique in several ways, not least due to the sheer ambition of its rapid scaling up. The programme was set to cover 900,000 to 1 million households by the end of 2015, with cash transfers as well as (optional) components of the PW programme now operating as a compulsory IGA component during the lean agricultural season. There is, furthermore, an understanding that the programme will gradually enhance the capacity of the participants to take risks, and start saving and investing.[6] Thus:

- The programme is expected to assist households to move out of poverty and away from dependency on assistance transfers to an independent and sustainable livelihood, in addition 'to increas[ing] income and consumption and improv[ing] the ability to cope with shocks among targeted vulnerable population groups, while enhancing and protecting the human capital of their children' (World Bank, 2012b: 5). In this context, the expected outcomes from this government strategy can be summarized as follows:
    - Vulnerable populations protected from severest consequences of poverty.
    - Vulnerable populations better able to support themselves through enhanced and diversified livelihoods.
    - Access to an enabling environment being enhanced, including access to key services in targeted communities.

Though the programme has been subjected to limited rigorous evaluation, positive results have been reported with respect to human capital accumulation, risk mitigation, and livelihoods (World Bank, 2011, 2012b). However, the impacts have not been measured for sustainability or for graduation. It is not clear how many households from the first and second phases have been moved out of poverty, but many assume that their resilience has been enhanced, with many being set on a path to graduation (World Bank, 2012b).

Each participating household receives a basic transfer of $5 per month, plus an additional $5 if they have children younger than 18, and also if they meet the conditionalities of education (school attendance, including pre-school, enrolment, and 80 per cent attendance), and health care, which involves regular health check-ups, including once a year for the elderly, and antenatal care and postnatal care for pregnant mothers and infants.

Exploring graduation potential and challenges

The remainder of this chapter will be devoted to examining the context, design features, and implementation arrangements that have the potential to facilitate, as well as constrain, threshold graduation.

Targeting and Implementation

TASAF III is timely in terms of its very clear ambition to drive Tanzania towards meeting the first MDG. This ensures a strong political buy-in, as is evident from the government-funded pledge increase from $44 million in 2015, to $100 million by 2016. According to World Bank estimates, the non-scaled-up version of PSSN, and allowing for an estimated error of 30–40 per cent from the PMT targeting model, where 900,000 households would be identified for participation (covering 16.5 per cent of the population), a combination of a basic transfer of $5 per month, plus a variable cash transfer of $5 per month with $1.35 per day for 60 days of PW, would lead to a poverty headcount and poverty gap reduction of 8–9 per cent and 18 per cent, respectively. Current estimates show that the annual cost of the PSSN, once it has reached full coverage and implemented all interventions, including PW and LE, would be between $270 million and $295 million. The total cost of the PSSN for the period of the fiscal years 2015–19 is between $960 million and approximately $1.12 billion. In total, the PSSN transfer amounts to 30 per cent of average per capita consumption of the food-poor population.

Tanzania faces the same dilemma as many low-income countries: there are many poor; resources are scarce; it is difficult to determine who should benefit from safety net programmes; and identifying the ultra-poor is problematic. A common problem across sub-Saharan Africa is the acquisition of reliable and up-to-date data on people's income, thus limiting the application of adminis-trative targeting measures. Proxy identifiers, such as assets, are commonly used, but there is little difference in ownership of basic assets, land, or housing conditions among the bottom 60 per cent of the population (Booysen et al., 2008). Consequently, this can lead to misidentification of the very poorest. Increasingly, general programmes need to be self-targeted (for example, by offering employment on PW only at a low wage rate). For the cash transfer component, this necessitates the use of community-based targeting, under which village committees use local knowledge to identify who is most vulnerable.

In the context of the scarcity of resources, concerns regarding 'dependency' and non-productive investments become more acute. Inclusion of productive elements, such as PW, as well as the positioning of education within social safety net measures, are also more often a political response than purely a technical one.

The programme has evolved from PW to also include IGAs, and now combines bi-monthly cash transfers with the conditionality focused on health and education. It is an old programme that is being re-modelled on the strengths, or the tried and tested elements, of PW, IGAs, and cash transfers contributing to productiveness. The cash transfer component of PSSN is the backbone or catalytic input for human capital accumulation (see Box 10.2).

If a vision of graduation within this programme is contingent on the accumulation of human capital, poor sectoral take-up and ownership threatens this worthy goal. This, it appears, is not a limitation of the programme design, but of implementation arrangements, which can compromise the results from this rapidly scaled-up programme. In terms of sustainability of impact, the programme is clear that interventions covered by the programme will not,

---

Box 10.2 Evaluation of Community-Based Conditional Cash Transfer (CB-CCT)

The impact evaluation of TASAF's pilot shows important gains with respect to education, health, and nutrition outcomes (Evans et al., 2014). On average, children from beneficiary households, in the 15–17 age bracket, are 15 per cent more likely to complete Standard 7 grade compared to non-beneficiaries. The difference is even higher among girls (24 per cent). Furthermore, the CB-CCT seems to be responsible for significant increases, particularly among the poorest beneficiaries, in non-banking savings, and in the diversification of productive assets, with this diversification serving as a self-insurance mechanism in case of shocks affecting regular incomes. The pilot has also resulted in the increased use of insurance by households, thereby reducing their vulnerability. On average, the rate of use of medical insurance was significantly higher amongst participating households than non-participating households. Specifically, the rate of use was 28 per cent higher for medical insurance to finance medical care for children younger than 18, and 17 per cent higher for medical insurance to finance medical care for the elderly. The difference in the level of utilization of medical insurance is even higher among the poorest households in the programme (53 per cent for children requiring health attention).

---

by themselves, result in significant levels of graduation out of poverty, but should enable benefiting households to take advantage of other opportunities, reverse any decline in livelihoods, and move on to a positive trajectory. Furthermore, the PSSN programme actively supports households to invest in the future through investments in health and education for children (via the variable conditional transfer), investment in labour-intensive PW (through the PW component), and savings (through the community savings promotion sub-component). The results of these investments should continue to have positive impacts on households and their communities after they exit the programme.

In essence, the assumptions that are underlying graduation are:

- human capital accumulation through adherence to education and health co-responsibilities.
- start of IGAs, signifying a fundamental risk-taking and resilience-enhancing attitude of households.

Limits on graduation: can everyone graduate?

PSSN is intended to cover an estimated 16.5 per cent of the poorest. Unsurprisingly, this means that many of these households are labour-constrained due to old age, disability, etc. Increasingly, as a result of rural–urban migration in Tanzania, a growing number of elderly are being excluded and therefore often form the poorest of the poor in the community (Lindeboom and Leach, 2010; Rwegoshora, 2015). Forty per cent of all orphans in Tanzania are cared for by older people, usually their grandmothers. Households with elderly and children are by far the poorest (43 per cent in urban areas and 46 per cent in rural areas) (Lindeboom and Leach, 2010). Eleven per cent of project beneficiaries are children under 5, and 32 per cent are aged 6–18

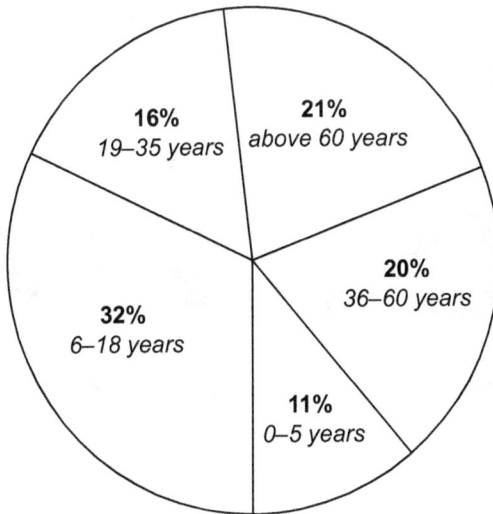

Figure 10.2 Beneficiary age groups, TASAF estimates 2014
Source: TASAF, 2014

(see Figure 10.2). The largest programme age bracket is for participants aged 19–60, comprising 36 per cent of beneficiaries. Thus, this programme has, in theory, a high dependency ratio of 64 per cent, constraining opportunities simply through its 'productiveness'. So, even if all able-bodied individuals were capable of engaging in PW and set up IGAs, which is highly unlikely, there would still be significant sections of dependent beneficiaries.

With respect to the elderly, not all live in houses that have children. It was widely recognized that graduation for such households would be more difficult, as there is no family support. However, such transfers will enhance their purchasing power, and should also contribute to spillover effects by contributing to local demand and multiplier effects with the strengthening of local markets.

Overall, when we consider limits to graduation, we must recognize that both TASAF I and TASAF II supported communities in a one-off manner regarding infrastructure, PW support to insecure households, and support to food for the vulnerable, as well as through IGAs. Support to household consumption was improved for a short time, but it decreased for most beneficiaries after the sub-project implementation was completed, leaving most of the beneficiaries generally in the same state they were before the intervention.

Graduation pillars: promises and challenges

To complement the critique of graduation we focus briefly on certain promises and challenges facing some of the graduation pillars. From an educational perspective, the World Bank-supported randomized control trial

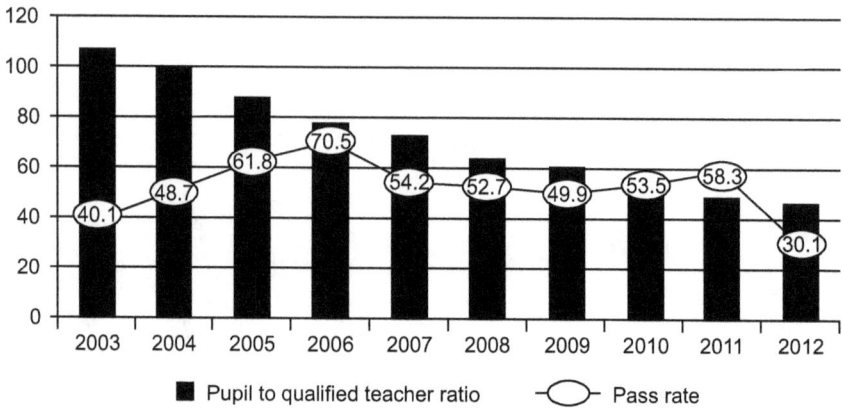

Figure 10.3 Pupil to qualified teacher ratio and pass rate 2003–12
Source: Basic Education Statistics Tanzania (PMORALG, 2014)

of the CB-CCT programme showed some positive impacts regarding whether children had ever attended school or if they completed Standard 7. There were no clear impacts on school attendance, although only 12 per cent of children reported being absent the previous week at baseline, so student absenteeism may not be a major problem. In education, the primary school completion effect is particularly striking for girls, and literacy rates increase particularly for children who were poor school attenders at the beginning of the study.

Though the programme is expected to result in enhanced enrolment (and is already being reported by the communities as per the preliminary data from TASAF III), this poses additional potential challenges regarding the quality of learning. Tanzania has a rather poor pupil–teacher ratio, and any expansion in enrolment and attendance poses a risk of further deterioration. In Figure 10.3 we note that the pupil to qualified teacher ratio in primary schools ranged from 107:1 in 2003 to 47:1 in 2012. This could be explained by the rapid expansion of enrolment in 2001, which was not matched by the number of qualified teachers.

This conditionality also monitors school attendance, which is of higher significance than just getting children into school. The programme is still developing management information systems with respect to compliance, but if this is indeed enforced, the pressures on school facilities and teaching staff will be yet higher and risk affecting the quality of learning. In Bagamoyo district, where the field research was conducted and TASAF III is being implemented, the qualified teacher to pupil ratio stands far higher than the national at 90:1.[7]

However, results at other levels of education might be different. Early childhood schooling is notoriously underutilized in Tanzania, where less than 40 per cent of 4–5 year-olds are in school (UNICEF, 2011). The programme's insistence on pre-schooling will contribute to the creation of awareness as well

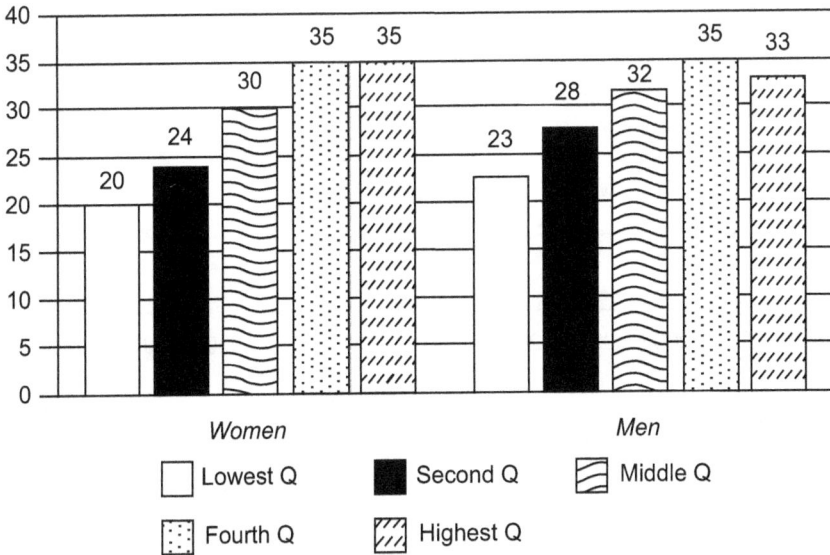

Figure 10.4 Percentage of population completed primary school by wealth quintile, 2010
Source: Basic Education Statistics Tanzania (PMORALG, 2014)

as demand and hopefully strengthen response, which is more easily delivered at this level than in primary and secondary schools.

Similarly, secondary education stands to benefit strongly, according to the evaluation of 2011 and 2014 (Evans et al., 2014; World Bank, 2011). In a recent simulation carried out by the World Bank, a new additional transfer of $1 for lower secondary and $3 for upper higher secondary is expected to result in a 50 per cent increase in secondary school enrolment (in places that have a secondary school in the vicinity). In secondary education, the constraints to attaining enhanced educational outcomes also stem from the sheer paucity of school numbers. The number of, and average distance to and from, secondary schools is just not sufficient to meet the demand should the transition rate from primary to secondary school increase. The current rates, especially for the poorest, are somewhat low (see Figure 10.4) and have also unfortunately witnessed a downward trend (see Figure 10.5).

In almost all the villages visited by the TASAF III assessment mission in April 2014, secondary schools were at least 5 kilometres away. This poses significant transaction costs in both time and money (for transport), on the one hand, and security, especially for girls, on the other.

Despite these challenges and risks, the programme is undeniably laying the groundwork for community demand for various forms of education, perhaps for the first time for pre-school and secondary levels, and has the potential to extract a response from the education sector to enhance the supply of these basic services. Such an achievement would be considered remarkable.

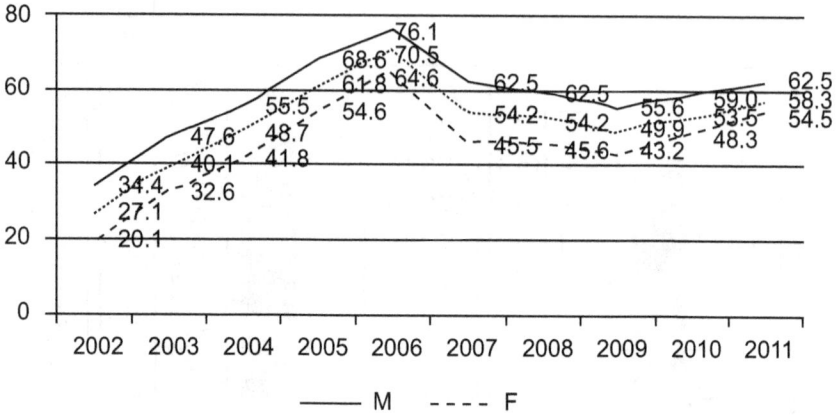

Figure 10.5 Primary school leaving examination (PSLE) results
Source: Basic Education Statistics Tanzania (PMORALG, 2014)

How health may impact on graduation

According to the randomized control trial of the CB-CCT programme, impacts on health, though less than that of education, have been encouraging, especially for younger children (Evans et al., 2014). After an initial surge in clinic visits among treatment households, 34 months into the programme participating households were attending clinics less often but were healthier: 5 per cent were less likely to be sick at all ages, and 11 per cent less likely for children under 4 (ibid.). Besides the conditionality of attending health clinics and the uptake of insurance, the Community Health Fund is expected to have contributed strongly to health and nutrition outcomes.[8] The participating households are much more likely to finance medical care with insurance and to purchase insurance than their comparison counterparts. Insurance is also the one category of spending that households in every sub-group increase expenditures on.

Public work livelihoods and other factors

The potential for improved productivity via community assets is also a significant factor. Apart from those projects that involved the construction of classrooms and health centres, which were subsequently subsumed within the sectorial infrastructure, many other structures, such as small irrigation projects, pools, etc., fell largely into disuse, and hence did not result in any sustainable enhancement in productivity. Furthermore, participation in PW programmes is often seen as a way of ensuring additional transfers through lean seasons, rather than necessarily creating productive assets. Thus, a sizeable potential goes largely unrealized. PSSN must remain cognizant of these pitfalls, and put structure, procedures, and mechanisms in place to address this early on.

Conclusion

The TASAF programme leaves significant scope for adaptation and refining, which, it must be reiterated, for national social protection programmes seems to be the norm rather than an exception, especially in Africa (Samson, 2014). There seem to be several opportunities for cross-learning, in-course corrections, and adaptations. Few sectors of social or economic policy depend so constrictively on evidence-informed approaches for the design and implementation of strategies. For example, the Productive Safety Net Programme in Ethiopia added the household asset-building programme and a microcredit component (Mishra, 2010). The Rwanda Vision 2020 Umurenge Programme redefined and re-scheduled recertification after being implemented. The challenge and the opportunity for TASAF are to be cognizant of this need for programme adaptation and revisions, and to achieve this with a clear understanding of the theory of change, the larger economic and market context, and the availability of resilience or vulnerability, and above all to do so within a larger developmental response within the education and health sectors. The latter is of paramount importance, as the notion of graduation hinges on the accumulation of human capital.

Notes

1. A decline in poverty incidence from 33.6 per cent in 2007 appears; however, changes to the survey instruments and poverty estimation methodologies mean that caution should be applied when comparing the two sets of figures, with further analysis required to evaluate changes in poverty between the two points in time.
2. Inequality in Tanzania Mainland declined slightly, with the Gini coefficient at 0.35 in 2007 and 0.34 in 2011/12 (World Bank, 2014b).
3. Graduation from a programme after reaching a certain threshold level of asset/human capital or livelihoods accumulation as defined by the programme (Devereaux and Sabates-Wheeler, 2011).
4. Transfers to the poor, including PW employment, subsidies, food distribution programmes, cash and in-kind transfers, vouchers, and exemptions: it does not look at formal pensions, insurance, income-generating schemes, or credit programmes.
5. As per TASAF's papers from December 2014, the conditional cash transfer benefits are as follows (TZS10,000 (equivalent US$5) per month):

   - Basic benefit
     - Children under 18 years: $2 per month
   - Health variable benefit
     - Children under 5 years: $2 per month
   - Education variable benefit
     - Primary school: $1 per month (with CAP $4)
     - Junior Secondary: $2 per month (with CAP $6)
     - Senior Secondary: $3 per month (with CAP $6)

6. One of the main 'shocks' faced by the poor is seasonality in food stocks and price. Subsistence households run out of grain about five to eight months after the harvest each year, and then enter a 'lean season' before the next harvest. But this is also the time when market prices for grain are highest – typically 50 per cent higher than in the post-harvest period – placing tremendous hardship on the poorest. Any safety net or policy intervention that can help ameliorate this seasonal food shock will be an important part of the safety net solution. Examples include seasonality in PW employment and transfers (World Bank, 2011).

7. The standard norm is to have a pupil–teacher qualified teacher ratio of 40:1; that is, 40 pupils in a class, this being the set target to be achieved by 2015.

8. 'The [Community Health Fund] is a form of pre-payment scheme designed for rural people in Tanzania. It is based on the concept of risk sharing whereby members pay a small contribution on a regular basis to offset the risk of needing to pay a much larger amount in health care user fees if they fall sick' (Munishi, 2001 as cited in Mtei and Mulligan, 2007: 2).

References

Adam, C., Kwimbere, D., Mbowe, W. and O'Connell, S. (2012) 'Food prices and inflation in Tanzania', *Working Paper Series No. 163*, African Development Bank, Tunis.

African Union (2004) *Assembly of the African Union Third Extraordinary Session on Employment and Poverty Alleviation. 3–9 September 2004. Ouagadougou, Burkina Faso (Ext/Assembly/AU/4 (III) Rev.3*. African Union, Addis Ababa.

African Union (2015) *Addis Ababa Declaration on Social Development for Inclusive Development*. African Union, Addis Ababa.

Booysen, F. le R., Van der Berg, S., Burger, R., Von Maltitz, M. and Du Rand, G. (2008) 'Using an asset index to assess trends in poverty in seven sub-Saharan African countries', *World Development* 36(6): 1113–30 <http://dx.doi.org/10.1016/j.worlddev.2007.10.008>.

Devereux, S. and Sabates-Wheeler, R. (2011) 'Transforming livelihoods for resilient futures: How to facilitate graduation in social protection programmes', *CSP Working Paper Number 003*, Centre for Social Protection and Future Agricultures, Institute of Development Studies, Brighton.

Evans, D.K., Hausladen, S., Kosec, K. and Reese, N. (2014) *Community-Based Conditional Cash Transfers in Tanzania: Results from a Randomized Trial*. World Bank, Washington, DC <http://dx.doi.org/10.1596/978-1-4648-0141-9>.

Garcia, M. and Moore, C.M.T. (2012) *The Cash Dividend: The Rise of Cash Transfer Programs in Sub-Saharan Africa*. World Bank, Washington, DC <http://dx.doi.org/10.1596/978-0-8213-8897-6>.

Lindeboom, W. and Leach, V. (2010) *Poverty Among the Elderly and Children in Mainland Tanzania: Volume 23 of REPOA Brief*. Research on Poverty Alleviation, Dar es Salaam.

Ministry of Planning (2012) *Housing Budget Survey 2012*. Ministry of Planning, Dar es Salaam.

Mishra, U. (2010) 'Policy advice vs. implementation: Optimization of results. A case of PSNP in Ethiopia', paper prepared for the *UN Knowledge Fair on Policy Advice vs. Implementation: How to find the right positioning for UN development activities at the country level?* Austria Vienna Center, Vienna, 28–30 September 2010.

Mtei, G. and Mulligan, J.A. (2007) *Community Health Funds in Tanzania: A Literature Review.* Ifakara Health Institute, Dar es Salaam.

Pearson, R. (2014) 'Child focused social protection strategies across Africa: Trends, innovations and organizing principles', paper prepared for the *International Social Protection Conference*, International Conference Centre, Simba Hall, Arusha, 15–17 December 2014.

PMORALG (2014) *Pre-Primary, Primary and Secondary Education Statistics 2013.* Prime Minister's Office Regional Administration and Local Government, The United Republic of Tanzania, Dar es Salaam.

Rwegoshora, H. (2015) 'The plight of social pension provision to older people in Tanzania', *Huria: Journal of the Open University of Tanzania* 19(1): 105–18. The Open University of Tanzania, Dar es Salaam.

Samson, M. (2014) 'Developing a social protection agenda for equitable growth: Perspectives, policies and best practices', paper prepared for the *International Social Protection Conference*, International Conference Centre, Simba Hall, Arusha, 15–17 December 2014.

Shimeles, A. (2014) 'Growth and poverty in Africa: Shifting fortunes and new perspectives', *IZA Discussion Paper No. 8751.* Institute for the Study of Labor, Bonn.

TASAF (2013) *Qualitative Assessment of Conditional Cash Transfer and Complementary Components Under the Productive Social Safety-Net Project: Institutional, Capacity, and Strategic Issues.* Tanzania Social Action Fund, Dar es Salaam.

TASAF (2014) 'Tanzania Social Action Fund. Government of Tanzania, President's Office, Dar Es Salaam.' Available from: http://www.tasaf.go.tz/index.php/reports.

UNICEF (2011) *Children and Women in Tanzania, Volume I Mainland, Volume II Zanzibar.* UNICEF Tanzania, Dar es Salaam.

World Bank (2011) *Tanzania: Poverty, Growth, and Public Transfers, Options for a National Productive Safety Net Programme.* World Bank, Washington, DC.

World Bank (2012a) *Project Appraisal Document on a Proposed Credit in the Amount of SDR 141.9 Million (US$220 Million Equivalent) to the United Republic of Tanzania for a Productive Social Safety Net Project (APL I).* World Bank, Washington, DC.

World Bank (2012b) *Tanzania: Productive Social Safety Net Project. Project Appraisal Document.* World Bank, Washington, DC.

World Bank (2014a) *World Bank Indicators 2014.* World Bank, Washington, DC. <http://dx.doi.org/10.1596/978-1-4648-0163-1>.

World Bank (2014b) *World Bank Data: Tanzania* [online]. World Bank, Washington, DC. Available from: http://data.worldbank.org/country/tanzania.

World Bank (n.d.) *PovcalNet: An Online Analysis Tool for Global Poverty Monitoring* [online]. World Bank, Washington, DC. Available from: http://iresearch.worldbank.org/PovcalNet/

About the authors

Usha Mishra is the Chief of Social Policy, Planning, and M&E for UNICEF Afghanistan. She has researched extensively and presented papers on safety net programmes in Africa and Asia.

Emmanuel J. Mtambie is the Principal Officer – Training and Capacity-Building – for the CRDB Microfinance Services Company Ltd in Tanzania. He holds an MA in Development Management and is completing a degree in Business Administration focusing on financial sustainability.

CHAPTER 11

Do 'graduation' programmes work for Africa's poorest?

Stephen Devereux

Graduation model programmes offer an innovative approach to poverty reduction. By delivering a sequenced package of support that includes cash and asset transfers, access to savings, training, and coaching, participating households embark on an upward trajectory out of extreme poverty. This chapter reviews the adaptation of graduation thinking from Bangladesh by national programmes in Ethiopia and Rwanda, and smaller pilot projects in Rwanda and Burundi. Evaluations are generating evidence of significant positive impacts across a range of indicators, from household food security and asset ownership, to access to health services. Several factors are identified that enable or constrain sustainable graduation at several levels: programme (design and implementation); community; market; and environment. The assumption of a smooth linear 'graduation pathway' is questioned, as is the graduation potential of labour-constrained households. Finally, graduation programmes risk diverting the focus of social protection away from managing risk and vulnerability towards achieving poverty reduction targets.

Keywords: graduation, social protection, food security, poverty reduction, targeting

Introduction

Increasingly, social protection programmes in Africa are incorporating 'graduation' as an explicit objective, where graduation is usually defined as a sustainable move by participating households out of extreme poverty or chronic food insecurity (Hashemi and Umaira, 2011). These interventions are modelled on an approach pioneered by BRAC in Bangladesh in the early 2000s (Matin et al., 2008; Hulme and Moore, 2010), and subsequently replicated through 10 pilot projects in 8 countries, including Ethiopia and Ghana in Africa, to test whether the 'graduation model' can be successfully adapted to different contexts (de Montesquiou and Sheldon, 2014).

This chapter reviews the experience of four ongoing graduation-oriented programmes in Ethiopia, Rwanda, and Burundi. The Productive Safety Net Programme (PSNP) in Ethiopia evolved out of the government's dissatisfaction with annual emergency appeals for food aid; the overarching objective

http://dx.doi.org/10.3362/9781780448435.011

was to 'graduate' the country off food aid dependency, and out of chronic and acute food insecurity. The Vision 2020 Umurenge Programme (VUP) in Rwanda follows a similar design to the PSNP, but was conceptualized more as a rural poverty reduction programme with environmental sustainability considerations. Concern Worldwide's graduation model programmes in Burundi and Rwanda are small-scale livelihood promotion projects that are direct adaptations of the BRAC approach.

The review of programmes raises four 'discussion points': 1) The assumption of linearity versus the reality of variability; 2) Is graduation possible for the labour-constrained 'poorest of the poor'? 3) How do we know if graduation is sustainable? 4) If graduation does not happen, has the programme failed?

Conceptualizing and operationalizing graduation

The 'graduation model' was originally developed by BRAC in Bangladesh for its 'Challenging the Frontiers of Poverty Reduction/Targeting the Ultra Poor Programme' (CFPR/TUP). BRAC recognized that its microfinance and Income Generation for Vulnerable Group Development programmes either were not reaching the 'ultra-poor', or were not meeting their needs (Hulme and Moore, 2010). Launched in 2002, the CFPR/TUP was conceptualized as an innovative way of supporting economically active ultra-poor households to develop sustainable livelihoods.

The BRAC approach has several components that are delivered in a specific sequence over a period of 24 months (Hashemi and Umaira, 2011). The first step is identification of eligible 'ultra-poor' households – those living in extreme poverty that are food insecure with no regular employment – which is undertaken using participatory community-based targeting techniques. All households selected receive a 'stipend' for the two-year duration of their participation in the programme in the form of cash or food transfers, to stabilize their consumption and to protect their assets against having to be sold to meet urgent cash needs. Next, these households receive a productive asset such as a cow or access to land for farming, and training in financial literacy and how to manage the asset to maximize the income it generates. Life-skills coaching is also provided on issues such as good hygiene practices and women's empowerment. Participants are encouraged, or even required, to save with local microfinance institutions; one ultimate objective is to facilitate access to microcredit.

A defining feature of graduation model programmes is that they provide an integrated package of support to poor households over a prolonged period of time. This differentiates them from conventional developmental interventions that identify a binding constraint which they attempt to alleviate by transferring a single resource, such as fertilizer or food aid or microfinance. Graduation programmes adopt a more holistic view of the causes of poverty, and recognize that multiple forms of assistance are needed. Although cash transfers are one component of graduation programmes, it is not sufficient to 'just give money to the poor' (Hanlon et al., 2010). In particular, the regular, personalized coaching and mentoring that each participant receives is sometimes described as the 'X factor' that explains much of the success of the CFPR/TUP. In addition, value chain analysis and market assessments are conducted to ensure that participants adopt livelihood activities that are viable and sustainable.

After receiving support for about two years, CFPR/TUP households are assessed on a number of criteria, including having diversified sources of income, owning productive assets, eating at least two meals a day, using safe drinking water and sanitary latrines, and whether their children are going to school. Early results of the CFPR/TUP were very encouraging. Evaluations conducted by BRAC's Research and Evaluation Department found that programme participants increased their asset-holdings (land and livestock), income, savings, and food consumption both absolutely and compared to an 'ultra-poor' control group. No less than 92 per cent of participating households crossed the extreme poverty line of US$0.50 per person per day, and this was sustained three years after programme support ended (Hashemi and Umaira, 2010). More recent evaluations, involving independent researchers, confirmed these impressive results, whereby a four-year randomized control trial found that 95 per cent of participants graduated, and stayed out of ultra-poverty (BRAC, 2013).

Graduation must be distinguished from exiting a programme, which Samson (2015) describes as 'endogenous' and 'exogenous' graduation, respectively. 'Exogenous exit' occurs when a sequenced set of benefits are provided for a defined period, and all support ceases automatically at the end of the programme cycle. 'Endogenous graduation' occurs when the household reaches a predefined threshold in terms of income, assets, or food security indicators based on an individual assessment of progress by administrators or the local community. Graduation can also be 'developmental', meaning that households move from one type of support to another (Samson, 2015) – e.g. from cash and asset transfers to subsidized and then commercial financial services, or from social assistance to employment-related social security – rather than being summarily ejected from a programme and receiving no further support.

Four implications follow from graduation model thinking, which will be explored in this chapter. First is the assumption that people can be supported to move from below the (extreme) poverty line to above this line, on a linear pathway of progress. The second is that graduation programmes need to target individuals and households that have graduation potential, meaning that they should have the resources and capacities necessary to sustain an independent livelihood. A third implication is that graduation needs to be sustainable; graduates must remain above the graduation threshold even after support is withdrawn. A final implication is the risk that graduation programmes might be assessed as having failed if a high proportion of participants do not graduate out of extreme poverty.

Four graduation programmes in Africa

The Food Security Programme (FSP) in Ethiopia is the longest-running and largest of the four programmes discussed in this chapter. The first five-year cycle ran from January 2005 to 2009, and the second cycle was completed in 2014. At inception it reached 5 million Ethiopians; this number was expected to fall year by year, but instead it increased steadily, and the second cycle was launched in 2010 with almost 8 million participants.

The FSP consists of a set of linked interventions dominated by the Productive Safety Net Programme (PSNP), which is subdivided into public works (PW) (temporary employment on community infrastructure activities) for food-insecure households with labour capacity, and Direct Support (unconditional cash transfers) for food-insecure households without labour capacity. It also includes a Household Asset Building Programme (HABP), which supports secondary livelihood activities. Districts and households are targeted if they are 'chronically food insecure', defined as having received food aid for three consecutive years. By providing cash or food transfers, building community assets through PW, and promoting livelihoods through credit-based asset transfers, the FSP aims to graduate participants out of these programmes and off 'dependence' on food aid within three to five years. Graduation is defined in terms of both food self-reliance and resilience: '[a] household has graduated when, in the absence of receiving PSNP transfers, it can meet its food needs for all 12 months and is able to withstand modest shocks' (GFDRE, 2007: 2). Operationally, graduation is assessed in terms of the household's asset portfolio, that is, whether it owns sufficient land, labour, farm tools, and other productive assets (benchmarked at the district level) to sustain a livelihood and resist shocks.

In Rwanda, the Vision 2020 Umurenge Programme (VUP) was launched in 2008 in the poorest sector in each of the country's 30 districts, and has been rolled out to progressively less poor sectors each year. The VUP has a similar design to the PSNP, and has four 'pillars': PW (temporary employment on community infrastructure activities) for extremely poor households with labour capacity; Direct Support (unconditional cash transfers) for extremely poor households without labour capacity; Financial Services (dominated by the Ubudehe Credit Scheme (UCS)) that gives small enterprise loans to individuals and groups; and Training and Sensitization (community sensitization about VUP, and community mobilization to promote graduation). Conceptually, the Government of Rwanda's second Economic Development and Poverty Reduction Strategy defines sustainable graduation as 'viable pathways out of poverty that enable people to exit core social protection support and progress to complementary social development programme that build skills and resilience' (Government of Rwanda, 2012a: 49). Operationally, the VUP's *Targeting, Exit and Graduation Manual* draws a distinction between 'exit' from the programme – which occurs when the community-based social mapping classifies a household during a retargeting round as having moved from Ubudehe category #1 or #2 (extreme poverty) to #3 or #4 (moderate poverty) – and 'graduation' out of poverty, which occurs only when the household moves to category #5 or #6 (non-poor). Households that reach Ubudehe category #3 are no longer eligible for Direct Support or PW, but they can continue to access Financial Services until they reach category #5 (Government of Rwanda, 2012b). In practice, because the programme has been scaling up, coverage has increased rather than fallen each year, from 18,000 PW participants in 2008 to 89,000 PW, 44,000 Direct Support, and 55,000 Financial Services participants in 2013.

Also in Rwanda, Concern Worldwide introduced a graduation model programme called 'Enhancing the Productive Capacity of Extremely Poor People' in two southern districts in 2011. The programme delivers a sequenced package of support that starts with the delivery of regular cash transfers (average value equivalent to US$26 per month) and coaching, then promotion of savings, followed by training for livelihood activities and the transfer of productive assets. The expectation is that this package will launch participating households onto an upward trajectory out of extreme poverty, although exit occurs automatically after the project cycle ends, and there are no criteria for assessing whether households have graduated in terms of reaching predefined benchmarks or thresholds. Coverage is low, with only 400 households in the first cohort and 800 in the second. Households were targeted if they were classified in the bottom two Ubudehe categories (as on VUP), but had at least one adult member able to work, they were landless or near-landless and homeless, they had no cattle and no IGA, and they were not supported by other projects, including VUP (Devereux, 2014).

In Burundi, Concern Worldwide's 'Graduation Model Programme' – or 'Terintambwe', meaning 'step forward' – follows a similar design to the programme in neighbouring Rwanda. Launched in 2013, it delivers a sequenced package including consumption support (regular cash transfers), microfinance (through savings and credit groups), skills training and regular coaching, and asset transfers (including mobile phones as part of the cash delivery mechanism). Terintambwe targets 2,000 poor households with productive capacity – one category above the 'poorest of the poor' in local social mappings – in two of Burundi's poorest provinces. A unique feature of the programme is that participants were divided into 'high treatment' (T1) and 'low treatment' (T2) groups. Both received the same level of cash and asset transfers, but T1 households received more home visits and more intensive coaching and mentoring than T2 households, with the objective of testing the hypothesis that life-skills coaching or mentoring is 'perhaps the most critical success factor for the Graduation Approach' (de Montesquiou and Sheldon, 2014: 84).

There are important comparisons and contrasts across these four programmes. The PSNP and VUP are national government-run programmes reaching tens of thousands or millions of people, but the Concern Worldwide projects are small-scale NGO projects reaching only a few thousand people each. Their smaller scale and stronger community presence allow Concern to deliver intensive mentoring visits and regular coaching sessions to each participating household, which is arguably beyond the capacity of the large-scale government-run PSNP and VUP programmes. Is this trade-off between scale and intensity of support inevitable? Can the PSNP and VUP be labelled 'graduation model' programmes even though they do not deliver the crucial personalized coaching component? Another difference is in how graduation is operationalized. The PSNP and VUP practise 'endogenous graduation' – each household's progress is assessed against graduation benchmarks – but both of the Concern projects practise 'exogenous exit', whereby households receive support for a predetermined period.

Evidence on graduation impacts in Africa

This section reviews available evidence on the impacts of graduation programmes in Ethiopia, Rwanda, and Burundi. Several evaluations have been conducted on the FSP/PSNP since its launch in 2005, mostly assessing its impact on household food security and other indicators of well-being, rather than quantifying how many participants have achieved graduation benchmarks. The VUP's monitoring and evaluation (M&E) system has functioned sporadically, but has not yet generated credible data on graduation outcomes; for instance, the management information system compiles total numbers of Direct Support beneficiaries and PW participants each year, but provides no disaggregation of how many have left the programme and how many are newly registered.

Concern Worldwide's graduation programmes in Rwanda and Burundi both built in semi-randomized, controlled trial, M&E methodologies from the outset. As part of this approach, a set of key outcome indicators was identified and, in order to establish the pre-intervention values of these indicators, baseline surveys were conducted. A control group of equally poor but excluded households was also surveyed to ensure that changes observed in participating households could be attributed to the programme and not to other factors operating in the wider environment. Participants and control group households are re-interviewed two or three times during and after the programme period; a standard difference-in-differences impact evaluation methodology.

Ethiopia (FSP/PSNP)

The Government of Ethiopia aimed to graduate all 5 million chronically food-insecure participants out of the FSP/PSNP and off the annual food aid list during its first five-year cycle. In the second cycle, the objective was to graduate 80 per cent of participants into self-reliant and resilient livelihoods. However, official sources and survey evidence confirm that actual graduation has been 'minimal' (White and Ellis, 2012: 28). According to government records, only 58,000 of more than 1 million participating households graduated out of the FSP/PSNP between 2005 and 2009, or less than 5 per cent (MoARD, 2009). Between 2009 and 2011, as political pressure to speed up graduation intensified, approximately 270,000 households were graduated, or 17 per cent of the 1.6 million households registered for the second cycle (White and Ellis, 2012: 28). It is likely that a significant proportion of this was 'political graduation' or 'premature graduation'. A community survey undertaken as part of an evaluation in 2010 found that no graduation had occurred in nearly half of all communities visited, and less than 5 per cent of communities reported graduation rates above 10 per cent (Berhane et al., 2011: 197).

Sabates-Wheeler and Devereux (2013) identify a range of factors at several levels, mostly beyond the control of participants – programme (design and implementation), community, market, and environment – that might enable or constrain graduation. In Ethiopia, explanations for the failure of the FSP/ PSNP to achieve substantial rates of graduation have been identified in each of these areas.

In terms of programme design, the cash and food transfers provided through Direct Support and PW are expected to stabilize consumption and provide a safety net against shocks, but the main pathway to graduation is through the livelihoods support provided by the HABP. However, many of the HABP packages selected were inappropriate. One researcher found that 'livestock packages failed to make positive contributions to the incomes of any of my respondents', and a local official asserted that 'there is no possibility of graduation through agriculture' (Lavers, 2013: 18–19).

At programme implementation level, a major challenge to graduation followed from failures to implement 'full family targeting', meaning that PSNP transfers should be directly proportional to household size, but often are not due to budget constraints at the local level, leaving participants with no resources to invest after meeting their family's basic needs. Also, relatively few households had access to HABP livelihood packages, but those that did were, on average, more food secure and invested more in productivity-enhancing inputs than those that did not (Berhane et al., 2011).

At the community level, PSNP households, especially those in pastoral areas, faced 'intense pressure to give and support within horizontal networks' (Sabates-Wheeler et al., 2013: 10), which resulted in transfer dilution, that is, PSNP transfers were spread more thinly across poor households, including many who were not targeted by PSNP. This reduced the resources available to targeted households to build their asset base and graduate into more lucrative livelihood activities.

Market factors also undermined the impact of the FSP/PSNP; in particular, food price inflation (notably during the food price crisis of 2007/8) and price seasonality have been significant since the PSNP started in 2005, eroding the purchasing power of PSNP transfers. By mid-2008, the retail price of staple grains in Ethiopia had, since 2005, increased threefold, but the payment for working on PSNP PW was raised by only 33 per cent during this period (Sabates-Wheeler and Devereux, 2010).

An analysis of shocks experienced by PSNP households identified numerous events that resulted in loss of income or assets. Three of the five most common shocks reported in the period 2004–8 were environment-related – drought (57 per cent of households surveyed), loss of crops to disease, pests, frost, or hail (36 per cent), and loss of livestock to disease or accident (20 per cent) – while the other two were serious illness of a family member (26 per cent), and high food or input prices (22 per cent) (Béné et al., 2012). Households responded to such shocks by either reducing consumption (eating less food), or smoothing consumption by selling assets (such as livestock) and reducing non-food spending (including on education). These coping strategies all have the effect of reducing the household's productive capacity, and undermine its ability to either achieve or sustain graduation. One encouraging finding is that PSNP households maintained higher levels of food security than non-PSNP households when both were exposed to a shock (Figure 11.1).

On the other hand, among PSNP households, those exposed to shocks were more food insecure than those that were not (Figure 11.2), suggesting that the programme does not insulate households fully against the impact of shocks.

Overall, the FSP/PSNP has succeeded in improving the well-being of participants and reducing their food insecurity, and it has provided a safety net against the many shocks they face. However, it has not managed to make households food secure – even while receiving PSNP transfers, the average food gap in participating households fell only from 3.6 months in 2006 to 2.3 months in 2010 – and it provides only partial protection against shocks. On both components of the Government of Ethiopia's definition of graduation, self-reliance, and resilience, the FSP/PSNP has therefore failed, and most households have not in fact graduated out of the programme.

Rwanda (VUP)

There is only circumstantial evidence on how many participants have graduated from the VUP. A household survey conducted in 2010 found that, across Rwanda, the total net movement out of 'extreme social poverty' between 2007 and 2009 (measured as the percentage of households that progressed out of categories #1 and #2, minus the percentage that fell into these categories) was 17.8 per cent (Asselin, 2010). However, in sectors where the VUP was operational the figure was higher, at 26.2 per cent (ibid.). This suggests that almost a third of the total graduation recorded (i.e. 8.4 per cent) was attributable to the VUP. This survey also found that graduation was higher among male- than female-headed households, at 20.1 per cent and 12.8 per cent, respectively (ibid.). Two plausible explanations for this are supported by the fact that more women than men are Direct Support beneficiaries: on average, female-headed households are poorer so need more support, and they are also more labour- and time-constrained, so are less able to take advantage of opportunities to enhance their livelihoods.

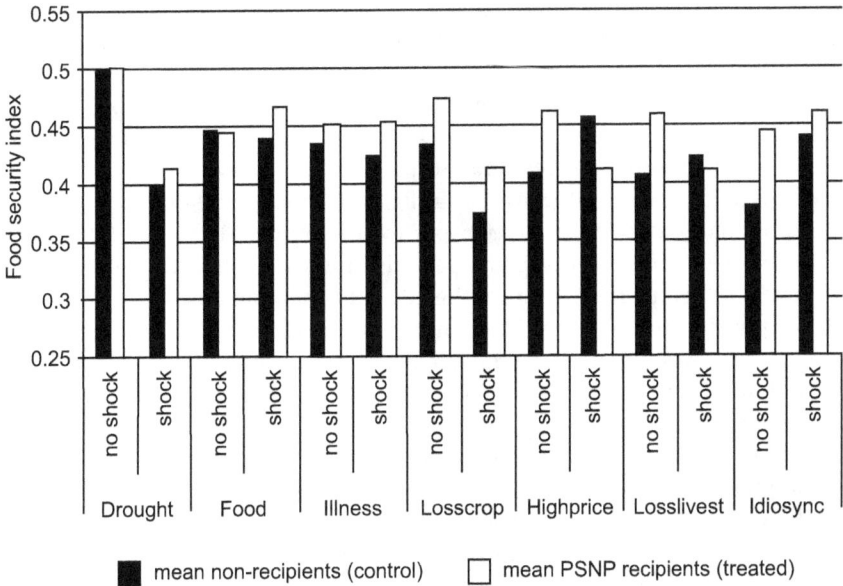

Figure 11.1 Impact of PSNP on household food security index, shock-affected and non-shock-affected households, Ethiopia
Source: Béné et al., 2012: 22

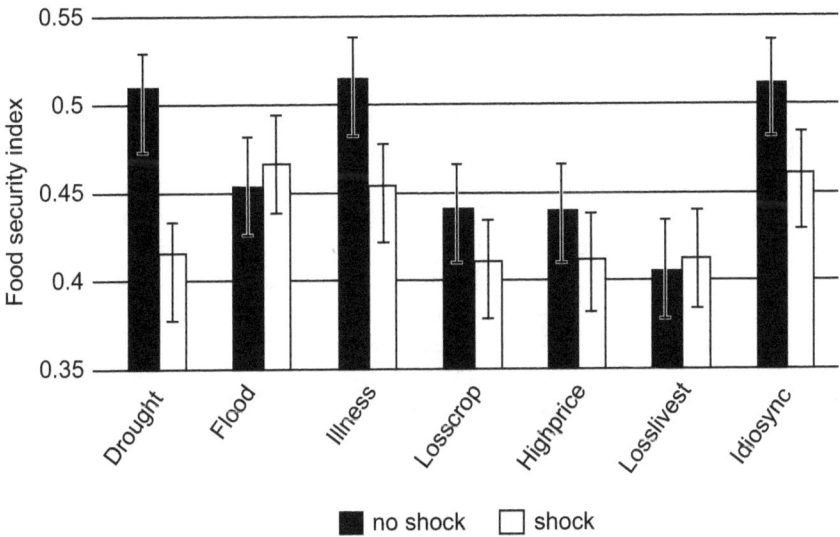

Figure 11.2 Impact of shocks on household food security index, PSNP recipients, Ethiopia
Source: Béné et al., 2012: 23

A more recent survey found that 41 per cent of Direct Support recipients in 2011 were in a higher Ubudehe category in 2014, but so were 35 per cent of control group households that were eligible but did not receive Direct Support. In this case, only one graduated household in six (i.e. 6 per cent) can be attributed to the VUP. Among PW households, very few of those that participated for only one year, but 30 per cent of those that participated for more than one year, had moved to a higher Ubudehe category by 2014. On the other hand, almost the same proportion of households surveyed that were eligible for PW but did not participate also improved their Ubudehe status, which 'is probably a reflection of the general economic growth that Rwanda has enjoyed in recent years' (Gahamanyi and Kettlewell, 2015: 55). Overall, graduation rates appear to be higher on Rwanda's VUP than on Ethiopia's PSNP, but only a fraction of the graduation recorded in Rwanda can be directly attributed to the VUP.

The main constraints to graduation from the VUP arise from challenges in programme design and implementation. For instance, it seems anomalous that more Direct Support beneficiaries than PW participants have graduated, when households undertaking PW have, by definition, more labour capacity and Direct Support households are not expected to graduate. The explanation lies in the fact that higher levels of resource transfers are made to Direct Support households, which are entitled to receive a regular cash transfer each month for six months of the year. Many use some of this cash to purchase small livestock, which reproduce and generate flows of income and animal products (e.g. eggs, meat, and manure) that cause the community to promote these households to a higher Ubudehe category.

By contrast, PW households are also entitled to six months of paid work in theory, but, in practice, creating enough work opportunities on community infrastructure projects (such as building feeder roads or school classrooms) has become increasingly difficult each year, so periods of employment are typically shorter than six months, available workplaces are rotated among eligible households, and many are told to wait until next year. In 2011, for example, the average PW household worked for only 68 days and earned a third of what Direct Support households received for free, while 43 per cent of households that were eligible for PW were not offered any employment at all (Devereux, 2012). Moreover, PW households tend to be larger than Direct Support households (which are often single persons living alone, notably elderly widows), so payments need to be shared among more people. There is no 'full family targeting' as in Ethiopia.

However, the main VUP pathway to graduation is through support to livelihoods, which is delivered by the Financial Services component, and includes microcredit, matching-grant challenge funds, and financial literacy training. Unfortunately, the UCS faced several difficulties, which resulted in delayed repayments or high levels of defaults. The repayment rate in 2011 was only 39 per cent (Arora et al., 2011: 7). Challenges included inadequate support to the development of business plans (no value chain or market analysis, unrealistic profit forecasts), unfeasible repayment schedules (UCS loans should be repaid in full within 12 months, but many businesses – such as rearing livestock – take longer than a year to generate economic returns), and a credibility gap around enforcing repayment, since the VUP was simultaneously handing out free cash transfers and disbursing interest-bearing loans.

Some important lessons have emerged from the VUP experience to date. One is that the likelihood and sustainability of graduation are enhanced the longer the duration of support: 'progress towards graduation does not appear to be sustainable for many when benefits have been received only for a short time' (Gahamanyi and Kettlewell, 2015: 61). Many households that received Direct Support cash or PW employment for only one year before being 'graduated' fell back into eligibility one or two years later. Another lesson is the importance of delivering the full package of support. Cash transfers, whether given freely as Direct Support or as wages for PW, are only the safety net component of the graduation model, but participants should not be expected to graduate without complementary measures that support livelihoods and provide insurance against shocks. 'Access to VUP's financial services, insurance, education, and training are elements to take into consideration for sustainable graduation in the long run' (Gahamanyi and Kettlewell, 2015: 62).

Rwanda (graduation programme)

Concern Worldwide's Graduation Programme in Rwanda follows the 'exogenous exit' approach. Cohorts of households receive assistance for a fixed period – cash transfers and coaching for 12–18 months, then livelihoods support for a further 12–18 months – after which they leave the programme. No benchmarks have been set to determine whether participants have graduated out of income poverty or social poverty, but their performance against a range of indicators, and in comparison to a control group, is monitored over time using difference-in-differences methodology.

Three quantitative surveys have been conducted on the first cohort of households. A baseline survey recorded the situation of households before the programme started, and verified that there were few statistically significant differences between participants and control group households. A survey after one year of operations revealed how 12 months of cash transfers and coaching had affected participants' lives. A third survey, 18 months after the last cash transfer was paid, captured the impacts of other programme activities, notably IGAs and skills training. A final survey round was conducted in late 2015, to assess whether improvements observed during the programme were sustained.

A 'deprivation index' was constructed, based on indicators of household food security (meals per day) and access to health care (ability to pay for health insurance and medicines). Results suggest a substantial reduction in

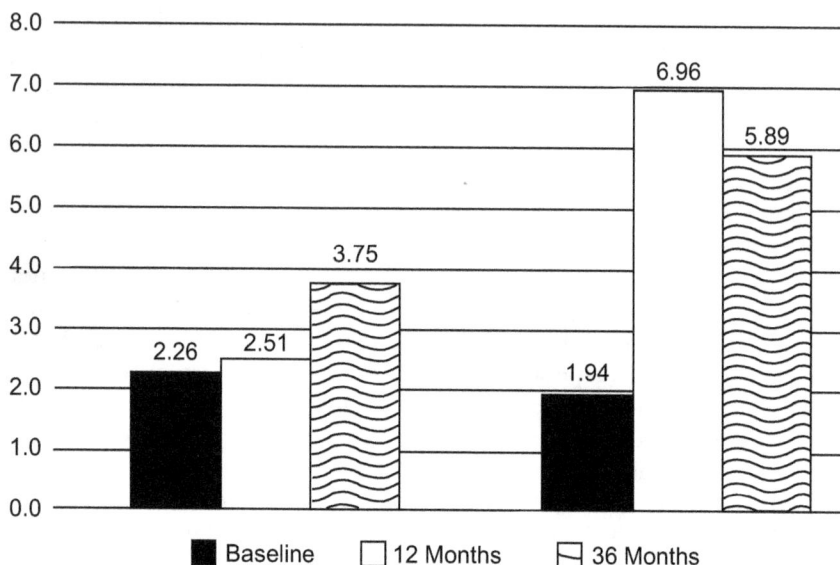

Figure 11.3 Changes in well-being indicators, Graduation Programme, Rwanda: Deprivation index
Source: Sabates et al., 2015: 17

deprivation for participants. On a scale from 0 (worst) to 8 (best), the first cohort improved their average score from 1.9 to 7.0 after receiving 12 months of support, while control group households improved only marginally, from 2.3 to 2.7. After cash transfers stopped, levels of deprivation among participants started rising slightly – their average score dropped from 7.0 to 5.9 between 12 and 36 months, but remained much higher than at baseline – while control households enjoyed an improvement in their deprivation score, from 2.5 to 3.8, still substantially below the level attained by participants (Figure 11.3).

An index ranging from 0 to 9 was constructed for ownership of consumer goods, including kitchen utensils, furniture, and radios. First cohort participants reported a doubling of the number of distinct goods they owned, from 3.4 to 6.9, while control group households registered a small decline, from 4.5 to 3.7. During the next 24 months participants continued to acquire more consumer goods, while control households saw little change (Figure 11.4). For both indices, the difference-in-differences results are statistically significant.

The first cohort of participants significantly increased their ownership of productive assets, between baseline and 12 months later, and relative to control group households, including farm tools, bicycles, and mobile phones, and these gains were retained two years later (Figure 11.5). The proportion of participants owning livestock increased dramatically, from no households owning a cow at baseline to 7 per cent and 16 per cent after one and three years, respectively, and, for other domesticated animals, from 7 per cent to 81 per cent in the first year, dropping slightly to 74 per cent in the next two years (Figure 11.6).

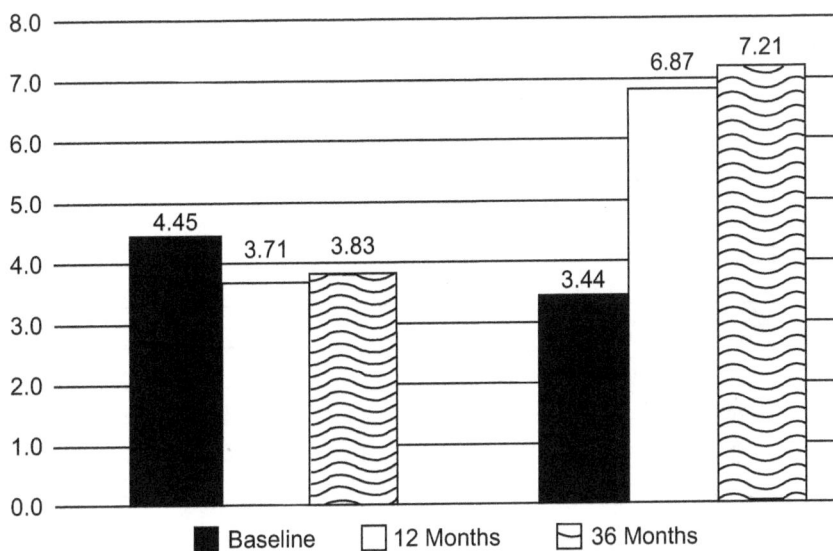

Figure 11.4 Changes in well-being indicators, Graduation Programme, Rwanda: Consumer goods index
Source: Sabates et al., 2015: 17

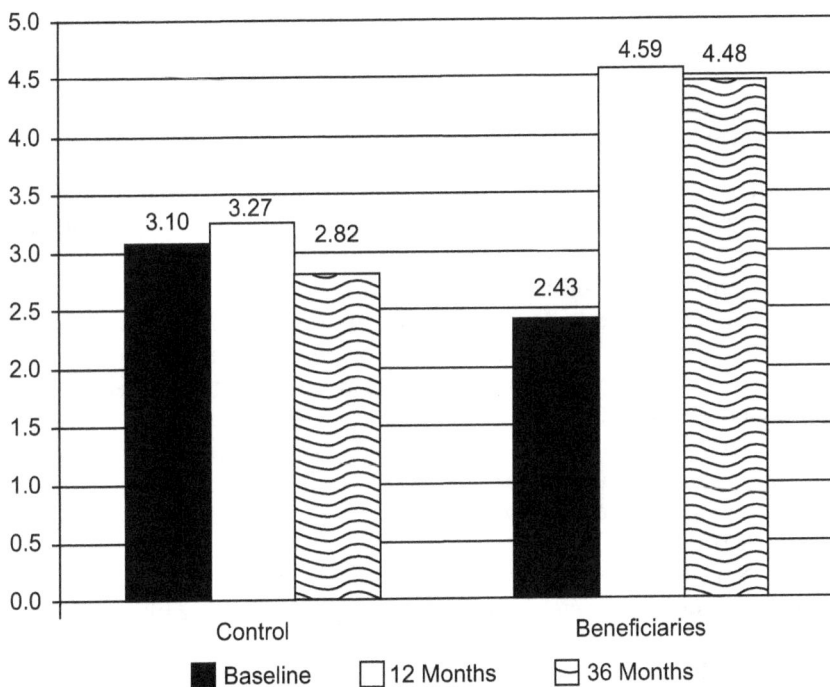

Figure 11.5 Changes in asset ownership, Graduation Programme, Rwanda: Productive assets index
Source: Sabates et al., 2015: 12

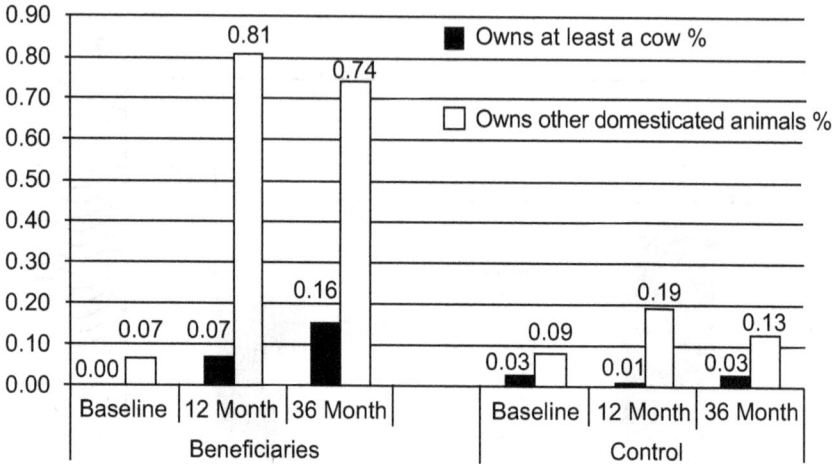

Figure 11.6 Changes in asset ownership, Graduation Programme, Rwanda: Livestock ownership
Source: Sabates et al., 2015: 15

Changes in ownership of productive assets and livestock are significant because they represent an enhanced capacity of the household to generate income and achieve self-reliant livelihoods. It remains to be seen whether this capacity actually translates into graduation out of extreme poverty that is sustained over time, even in the absence of programme support.

Burundi (Terintambwe)

The M&E component of the Terintambwe programme monitors 2,600 extremely poor households that were identified using community-based targeting, and then randomly assigned to a high treatment group (T1=1,000), a low treatment group (T2=1,000), or a control group (C=600 households), allowing for a quasi-experimental evaluation design. A baseline survey was implemented in late 2012, before the programme started, and a 'midline' survey was implemented in mid-2014, when the cash transfers ended and the asset transfer phase was about to begin. The midline survey allows the impacts of the cash and asset transfers to be disentangled from each other. An endline survey will be conducted when all programme support ends in mid-2015 and a follow-up survey will be implemented 18 months later, in late 2016.

Between the baseline and midline surveys, the well-being of Terintambwe participants improved across a diverse range of indicators, relative to control group households (Devereux et al., 2014). Attributable improvements were observed in housing quality (e.g. better roofing materials), sanitation facilities (upgrading of pit latrines by installing slabs), and lighting sources (more use of battery lamps and less use of firewood). Participants acquired numerous assets, including domestic items (kitchen utensils and furniture), consumer durables (radios and mobile phones), farming assets (hoes, ploughs, and machetes), and livestock (especially goats, pigs, and chickens).

Participants used some of the incremental income they received from the programme to increase food consumption, leading to dramatic improvements in household food security. At baseline, only 19 per cent of all adults and 34 per cent of all children surveyed were eating at least two meals a day, but when the midline survey was conducted (in a more favourable season) these figures had risen to 87 per cent and 94 per cent, respectively in Terintambwe households, but only to 34 per cent and 54 per cent, respectively in control group households.

Access to education, health care, and medicines improved, as did hygiene practices and knowledge about HIV and AIDS. Terintambwe participants were also more likely to save and to borrow, partly because the programme encouraged the formation of SILC groups (Savings and Internal Lending Communities), so this was a programme effect rather than an impact.

Some of these improvements – such as asset acquisition and food security – can be explained by the material resources transferred, especially cash, but others – such as hygiene and savings behaviour – are behavioural changes related to the messages delivered by Concern case managers in training, mentoring, and coaching sessions. On the other hand, very few significant differences were found between high and low treatment participants (T1 and T2 households), either because the support provided was not sufficiently differentiated, or because of spillover effects; low treatment and control group households learning about good practices from high treatment households living in the same community. A better survey design would have been to provide no coaching or mentoring at all to T2 households (this was rejected by the NGO on ethical grounds), or to select T1, T2, and control households from contiguous communities, rather than from within the same community.

Discussion points

Many intriguing issues have been raised by the first generation of graduation programmes in Africa, a few of which are touched upon here.

The assumption of linearity versus the reality of variability

Diagrammatic representations of the theory of change of graduation programmes all depict a linear trajectory out of extreme poverty or food insecurity over time, with different components of the support package being introduced at key moments to push participants up to the next level. For instance, the putative 'graduation pathway' in Ethiopia meanders steadily upwards, with households benefiting from various forms of support until they graduate, first from the PSNP and ultimately from the FSP altogether (Figure 11.7).

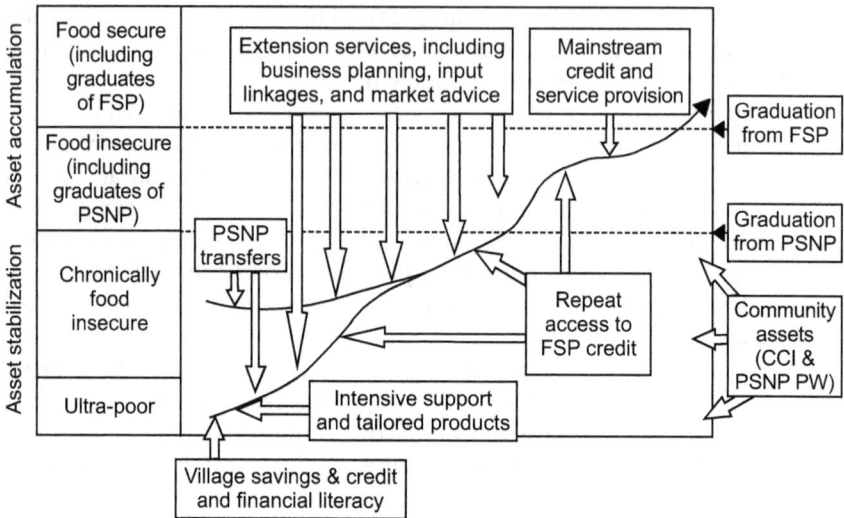

Figure 11.7 Graduation pathway from the Food Security Programme, Ethiopia
Source: MoARD, 2009: 17

As was seen above, this assumption of linearity is naïve and unrealistic, given the harsh agro-ecology and unpredictable climate of highland Ethiopia, where rainfall is so variable and harvests fluctuate so dramatically that the numbers of people requiring assistance can exceed a quarter of the population in bad years. In 2008, for instance, two major shocks – food price spikes and rain failures – combined to cause a food crisis in parts of Ethiopia, obliterating the gains made by participants during the PSNP's early years. Partly for this reason, contingency funds and risk financing were introduced, which allow for partici- pants in drought-affected districts to receive additional support, e.g. eight months of Direct Support and PW employment rather than six (White and Ellis, 2012). Strengthening the safety net function of the FSP/PSNP in this way is intended to ensure that the programme delivers both livelihood protection and livelihood promotion for food-insecure families, and that shocks do not derail completely their progress towards graduation.

Is graduation possible for the labour-constrained 'poorest of the poor'?

A distinction is often drawn in social protection systems between providing social welfare assistance to people with no labour capacity (Direct Support in the PSNP and VUP), and providing livelihoods support to people who have labour capacity (PW employment, asset packages, training, and microfinance). The assumption is that only individuals or households with labour capacity have graduation potential, since graduation implies self-reliance. However, graduation is possible for people with limited labour capacity, bearing in mind

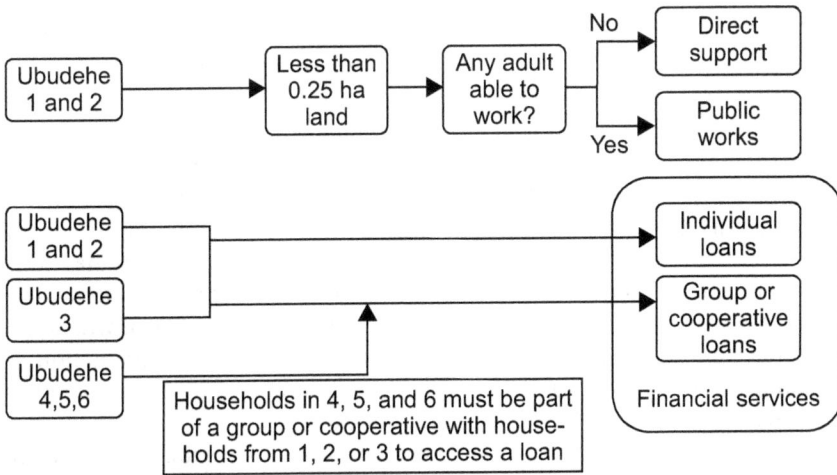

Figure 11.8 Eligibility for VUP by component, Rwanda
Source: MINALOC, 2010: 13

the risk that political pressure to demonstrate 'success' might prompt artificial or premature exits from the programme.

Exit from Rwanda's VUP occurs when a community-level social mapping exercise classifies a household in Ubudehe category #3 or higher. Many Direct Support recipients (who qualified for VUP support because they were initially classified as Ubudehe #1 or #2) have been promoted to category #3 after one or two years because they used their VUP cash transfers to purchase assets like small livestock, which is enough to move them out of extreme poverty, according to their neighbours, but not according to these 'graduates' themselves. In 2010, I interviewed a widow in her 70s who used her Direct Support cash to buy saucepans, blankets, the first shoes she had ever owned, and a sheep. She was removed from the VUP beneficiary list, even though there was no transformative change in her livelihood situation, and she argued passionately that she needed one more year of support.

A second pathway out of extreme poverty for the poorest VUP participants is via the microcredit component. The UCS introduced an innovative targeting model whereby richer individuals (from Ubudehe categories #4, #5, and #6) can form groups with their poorest neighbours (Ubudehe categories #1 and #2) to access 'group loans' for small businesses (Figure 11.8). The wealthy group members benefit by accessing credit at a subsidized interest rate of 2 per cent, while poor members gain access to business expertise and working capital. There is anecdotal evidence that this strategy worked well for some groups, but not for all. An official audit reported a case of one group whose president absconded with the loan money: 'the group may not be able to accomplish the planned activities because of misappropriation of some funds' (Office of the Auditor General of State Finances, 2011: 12).

How do we know if graduation is sustainable?

A distinction should be drawn between 'threshold graduation', meaning that a household is assessed as having passed a level of income or assets at a point in time, and 'sustainable graduation', meaning that the household is likely to remain above the threshold level indefinitely and require no further support, except perhaps following a major emergency (Devereux, 2010). Sustainability is implicit in the Government of Ethiopia's definition, which has two components – one indicating that household food security has been achieved ('the household is able to meet its food needs for 12 months'), the other indicating that the household is resilient ('the household can withstand moderate shocks'). But how can it be determined whether graduation is sustainable? What is a 'moderate shock', and how can we assess whether a household is able to 'withstand' such a shock?

As we have seen, one approach to measuring sustainability is to track participants' progress against indicators of graduation before, during, and also after their involvement in a programme, compared to a control group. An independent evaluation of BRAC's Challenging the Frontiers of Poverty Reduction/Targeting the Ultra-Poor programme, for instance, found that, between joining the programme and exiting two years later, participating households improved their scores on several indicators, including livestock ownership and incomes both in absolute terms and relative to a control group. A follow-up survey two years later confirmed that these gains were maintained or, in many cases, continued to improve after exit (BRAC, 2013). This provides strong evidence of sustainability of impacts over time. Early results from Concern Worldwide's M&E systems in Rwanda and Burundi look similarly encouraging, with positive results for several 'difference-in-differences' hypotheses, including that participating households will register lower levels of deprivation and higher levels of productive assets ownership after receiving programme support than at baseline, in comparison to control group households.

On the other hand, Roelen (2015) argues that the standard timeframe for assessing sustainability is too short, and that 'true sustainable graduation should be about achieving long-term improvements in livelihoods and living conditions that are maintained across generations' (Roelen, 2015: 25). 'Intergenerational graduation' requires investing in children, but the risk is that the immediate demands of graduation programmes could divert household's monetary and time resources away from children, and might even incentivize contributions by children. Examples of potential trade-offs include: participants investing in asset acquisition rather than children's needs; caregivers working and neglecting their children; older children being removed from school to care for younger siblings while caregivers work on graduation programme activities; and children themselves working on programme-supported livelihood activities. All of these possible outcomes could undermine children's immediate well-being and threaten their future well-being, even if participants graduate and their graduation is assessed as sustainable in the short to medium term.

If graduation does not happen, has the programme failed?

If graduation programmes are seen as 'livelihood promotion programmes, pure and simple' (Freeland, 2013: 1), then it is appropriate to measure their success by their ability to promote improved – higher income, self-reliant, resilient, and sustainable – livelihoods. But, if they are seen as social protection programmes with livelihood-promoting components, then it is more important that they provide an effective safety net against shocks; insurance first, investment second.

At a workshop in Addis Ababa in 2011, an Ethiopian government official stated that the purpose of the PSNP was to move millions of Ethiopians off dependence on annual emergency food aid appeals. What actually happened is that PSNP participants increased from 4.8 million to 7.5 million between 2005 and 2009 (Figure 11.9). The government official was disappointed. 'Instead of the numbers going down we are seeing them going up every year', he said. 'Instead of ending dependency we are creating it.' In his opinion, the PSNP was a failure. In their 'value for money assessment', White and Ellis (2012: 28) are equally pessimistic: 'While past research has rightly highlighted positive impacts on household consumption and distress sales of productive assets, the FSP has had little success in achieving graduation and finding a sustainable solution to food insecurity.'

On the other hand, we saw earlier that PSNP participants are better able to withstand moderate shocks than non-participants. But is 'graduation' off

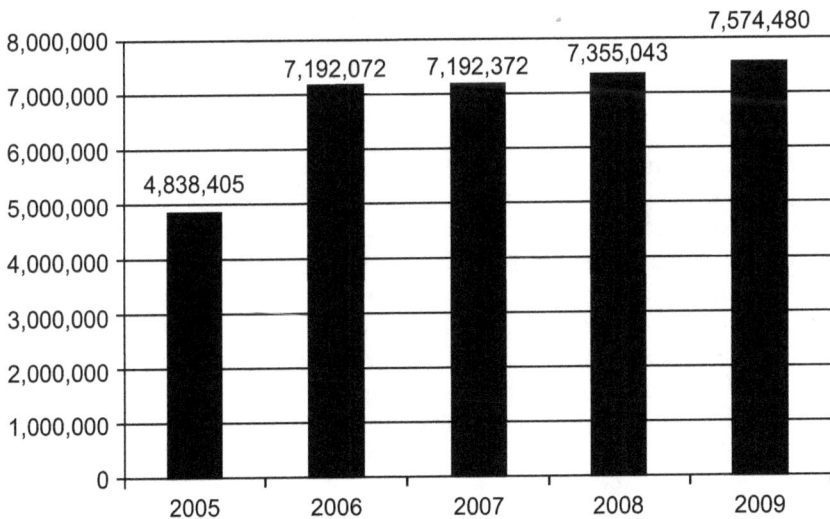

Figure 11.9 PSNP participants, 2005–9, Ethiopia
Source: White and Ellis, 2012: 19

dependence on damaging coping strategies, such as distress sale of assets to smooth consumption, enough indication of success? The answer depends on whether the focus of the PSNP is on the 'Productive' aspect or the 'Safety Net' objective. Any intervention that protects vulnerable farmers against risks such as drought is an effective social protection measure, and the extension of social protection to more food-insecure farmers in Ethiopia should surely be interpreted as evidence of success, not failure.

It seems that how success is assessed depends on how graduation is defined. In phase 2 of the Chars Livelihoods Programme (CLP-2) in Bangladesh, multiple indicators are applied to assess households' progress, and the graduation threshold was set at achieving six out of ten key indicators. Although 85 per cent of participants achieved this, and were classified as having graduated by the time they exited the CLP, this figure is extremely sensitive to the cut-off level set (arbitrarily) by administrators. If the bar were raised to eight out of ten indicators, the CLP-2 graduation rate would fall to 37 per cent, whereas lowering the bar to four indicators would raise the graduation rate to 99 per cent (Pritchard et al., 2015: 40).

A similar technique could be applied in Burundi, where success for the Terintambwe programme is assessed by aggregate improvements in over 30 indicators, such as total annual income, dietary diversity, savings, access to health care, involvement in community groups, and so on. These indicators are being monitored, and it is possible to convert a subset of them into an index that will quantify how many households have graduated when the programme ends and how many sustain graduation thereafter. Of course, this 'graduation index' will also be highly sensitive to which indicators are selected, the benchmark set for each, and how many need to be achieved. Even if objectively verifiable indicators are used to assess progress, graduation is in the eye of the beholder.

Conclusion

Graduation-oriented programmes in Africa have failed to graduate large numbers of people as yet. Many people have 'exited' these programmes, and available evidence confirms that they tend to be better off in several respects than they were before they joined the programme, except in cases of premature graduation motivated by political pressure. These indicators of improvement are very encouraging, but to a certain extent they can be characterized as programme effects rather than impacts. Giving cash and assets to poor people makes them better off by definition; it does not necessarily equate to a transformative change in their lives and livelihoods. The true test for the sustainability of these changes comes after programme support is withdrawn, but the evidence base on post-intervention impacts is still being built.

The distinction between 'exit' from a programme and 'graduation' out of poverty or food insecurity is fundamental. Crossing a threshold that makes a participant ineligible for further support does not necessarily mean the household is no longer poor or food insecure, or that they won't become poor or food insecure again if they are struck by an uninsured shock in the future. A 'developmental' approach to graduation would ensure that the safety net is not withdrawn from people next year just because they graduated out of extreme poverty this year.

Given the depth of poverty and food insecurity, and the extreme vulnerability of rural livelihoods in much of Africa, graduation might be an unrealistic or inappropriate objective to strive for. Or rather, graduation should not be prioritized ahead of the primary function of social protection, which is to put a safety net in place that provides effective insurance against livelihood risks. Also important is the recognition that some individuals and households require support indefinitely, and politicians and technocrats need to accept that this welfarist function is entirely valid and appropriate.

The challenge is to find the optimal balance between livelihood protection and livelihood promotion. Integrated social protection or graduation programmes that simultaneously protect and promote the well-being of poor and food-insecure people *can* work for Africa's poorest.

References

Arora, S., Hansford, F., Attah, R. and Williams, R. (2011) *Assessment of the Ubudehe Credit Scheme, Rwanda: Key Findings and Recommendations.* Oxford Policy Management, Oxford.

Asselin, L.-M. (2010) *VUP Targeting and Poverty Surveys 2009.* VUP Monitoring and Evaluation Team, Government of Rwanda, Kigali.

Béné, C., Devereux, S. and Sabates-Wheeler, R. (2012) 'Shocks and social protection in the Horn of Africa: Analysis from the Productive Safety Net Programme in Ethiopia', *IDS Working Paper* 395; *CSP Working Paper* 005. Institute of Development Studies & Centre for Social Protection, Brighton <http://dx.doi.org/10.1111/j.2040-0209.2012.00395.x>.

Berhane, G., Hoddinott, J., Kumar, N., Seyoum Taffesse, A., Tedia Diressie, M., Yohannes Y., Sabates-Wheeler, R., Handino, M., Lind, J., Tefera, M. and Sima, F. (2011) *Evaluation of Ethiopia's Food Security Program: Documenting Progress in the Implementation of the Productive Safety Nets Programme and the Household Asset Building Programme.* International Food Policy Research Institute, Washington, DC.

BRAC (2013) 'An end in sight for ultra-poverty: Scaling up BRAC's graduation model for the poorest', *Briefing Note #1: Ending extreme poverty.* BRAC, Dhaka.

de Montesquiou, A. and Sheldon, T. (2014) *From Extreme Poverty to Sustainable Livelihoods: A Technical Guide to the Graduation Approach.* Consultative Group to Assist the Poor (CGAP) and Ford Foundation, Washington, DC and New York, NY.

Devereux, S. (2010) 'Dependency and graduation', *Frontiers of Social Protection Brief Number 5.* Regional Hunger and Vulnerability Programme, Johannesburg.

Devereux, S. (2012) *3rd Annual Review of DFID Support to the Vision 2020 Umurenge Programme (VUP). Report Commissioned by the UK Department for International Development.* Institute of Development Studies, Brighton.

Devereux, S. (2014) 'Unleashing the capacities of vulnerable households: Concern Worldwide's Graduation Programme in Rwanda', *Briefing Paper*. Concern Worldwide Rwanda, Kigali.

Devereux, S., Roelen, K., Sabates, R., Ssenkubuge, I. and Stoelinga, D. (2014) *Concern Burundi Graduation Model Programme: Midline Report*. Centre for Social Protection, Institute of Development Studies, Brighton.

Freeland, N. (2013) 'Graduation and social protection', *Development Pathways Blog* [online]. Development Pathways Limited, Orpington. Available from: www.developmentpathways.co.uk/resources/graduation-social-protection [accessed 4 April 2015].

Gahamanyi, V. and Kettlewell, A. (2015) 'Evaluating graduation: Insights from the Vision 2020 Umurenge Programme in Rwanda', *IDS Bulletin* 46(2): 48–63 <http://dx.doi.org/10.1111/1759-5436.12128>.

GFDRE (2007) *Graduation Guidance Note*. Food Security Coordination Bureau, Ministry of Agriculture and Rural Development, Addis Ababa.

Government of Rwanda (2012a) *2nd Economic Development and Poverty Reduction Strategy 2013–2018*. Government of Rwanda, Kigali.

Government of Rwanda (2012b) *Vision 2020 Umurenge Programme: Targeting, Exit and Graduation Guidelines*. Ministry of Local Government, Kigali.

Hanlon, J., Barrientos, A. and Hulme, D. (2010) *Just Give Money to the Poor: The Development Revolution from the Global South*. Kumarian Press, Sterling, VA.

Hashemi, S. and Umaira, W. (2011) 'New pathways for the poorest: The graduation model from BRAC', *CSP Research Report* 10. Centre for Social Protection, Institute of Development Studies, Brighton.

Hulme, D. and Moore, K. (2010) 'Assisting the poor in Bangladesh: Learning from BRAC's 'Targeting the Ultra Poor Programme', in D. Lawson, D. Hulme, I. Matin, and K. Moore (eds), *What Works for the Poorest? Poverty Reduction Programmes for the World's Extreme Poor*, pp. 149–68. Practical Action Publishing, Rugby <http://dx.doi.org/10.3362/9781780440439.009>.

Lavers, T. (2013) 'Food security and social protection in highland Ethiopia: Linking the Productive Safety Net to the land question', *Journal of Modern African Studies* 51(3): 459–85 <http://dx.doi.org/10.1017/S0022278X13000402>.

Matin, I., Sulaiman, M. and Rabbani, M. (2008) 'Crafting a graduation pathway for the ultra poor: Lessons and evidence from a BRAC programme', *CPRC Working Paper* 109. Chronic Poverty Research Centre, Manchester.

MINALOC (2010) *Joint Sector Review: Vision 2020 Umurenge Programme*. Ministry of Local Government, Republic of Rwanda, Kigali.

MoARD (2009) *Food Security Programme, 2010–2014*. Ministry of Agriculture and Rural Development, Government of Ethiopia, Addis Ababa.

Office of the Auditor General of State Finances (2011) *Common Development Fund (CDF): Audit Report for the Year Ended 30 June 2010*. Republic of Rwanda, Kigali.

Pritchard, M., Kenward, S. and Hannan, M. (2015) 'The Chars Livelihoods Programme in Bangladesh: Factors that enable, constrain and sustain graduation', *IDS Bulletin* 46(2): 35–47.

Roelen, K. (2015) 'The "twofold investment trap": Children and their role in sustainable graduation', *IDS Bulletin* 46(2): 25–34 <http://dx.doi.org/10.1111/1759-5436.12126>.

Sabates, R., Devereux, S. and Sabates-Wheeler, R. (2015) 'Consolidated analysis cohort 1: Follow-up 1 (18 months after end of last cash transfer)', *Enhancing the Productive Capacity of Extremely Poor People in Rwanda (36 months Programme Survey)*. Concern Worldwide Rwanda, Kigali.

Sabates-Wheeler, R. and Devereux, S. (2010) 'Cash transfers and high food prices: Explaining outcomes on Ethiopia's Productive Safety Net Programme', *Food Policy* 35(4): 274–85 <http://dx.doi.org/10.1016/j.foodpol.2010.01.001>.

Sabates-Wheeler, R. and Devereux, S. (2013) 'Sustainable graduation from social protection programmes', *Development and Change* 44(4): 911–38 <http://dx.doi.org/10.1111/dech.12047>.

Sabates-Wheeler, R., Lind, J. and Hoddinott, J. (2013) 'Implementing social protection in agro-pastoralist and pastoralist areas: How local distribution structures moderate PSNP outcomes in Ethiopia', *World Development* 50(1): 1–12 <http://dx.doi.org/10.1016/j.worlddev.2013.04.005>.

Samson, M. (2015) 'Exit or developmental impact? The role of "graduation" in social protection programmes', *IDS Bulletin* 46(2): 13–24 <http://dx.doi.org/10.1111/1759-5436.12125>.

White, P. and Ellis, F. (2012) *Ethiopia's Productive Safety Net Programme, 2010–2014: A Value for Money Assessment*. Department for International Development, London.

About the author

Stephen Devereux is a research fellow at the Institute of Development Studies, and Director of the Centre for Social Protection. He was a member of DFID's advisory team for the design of the PSNP in Ethiopia in 2004 and team leader for small-scale evaluations of the same in 2006 and 2008. He conducted annual assessments of DFID support to the VUP in Rwanda in 2009, 2010, and 2011. He is team leader for longitudinal evaluations (2012–15) of Concern Worldwide's Graduation Model Programmes in Burundi and Rwanda. In 2015, he was director of an international conference on 'Graduation and Social Protection' in Rwanda.

Poverty reduction for Africa's poorest – implementation and policy thoughts

Institutional and policy challenges in the implementation of social protection: The case of Nigeria[1]

Rebecca Holmes

Over 60 per cent of the population – 110 million people – live in poverty in Nigeria. Recent policy responses to the high rates of poverty have included social protection initiatives, including cash transfers and health financing mechanisms. However, the development of a coordinated and strategic social protection system has stalled, resulting in fragmented programming and extremely low coverage of the poor. This chapter discusses three specific sets of institutional and policy challenges to implementing social protection at scale: fiscal decentralization, which impedes the equitable provision of funds to states; limited capacity to design appropriate programmes at the local level, and to deliver them at scale; and a weak governance context, which curtails transparency and accountability at all levels. Looking at the lessons learnt from the experiences of social protection policy and practice thus far, the chapter concludes by identifying a number of opportunities to develop and strengthen the emerging social protection sector in the future.

Keywords: social protection, Millennium Development Goals (MDGs), decentralization, cash transfers, Nigeria

Introduction

Social protection is one of the recent success stories in development. Evidence from middle- and low-income countries has clearly demonstrated that social protection programmes support the poorest households in numerous ways, including smoothing consumption, increasing household investments in health and education, and supporting income-generating activities (IGAs) (Barrientos, 2012; Fiszbein and Schady, 2009; Holmes and Jones, 2013). In recent years, growing attention has been drawn to the importance of developing social protection *systems*, and the *operationalization* of social protection programmes to reduce poverty, at the same time that the need to focus on the diversity of country context has also been increasing. Ways to overcome persistent poverty in low-income countries affected by fragility and conflict, for example, are important development policy debates, and social protection is

http://dx.doi.org/10.3362/9781780448435.012

Box 12.1 Institutional and governance characteristics of Nigeria

After 30 years of military rule, the Federal Republic of Nigeria reinstated a democratic regime in 1999. Institutionally, Nigeria has a decentralized political and fiscal system which consists of a three-tier government: federal, state, and local. There are 36 state governments, the Federal Capital Territory, and 774 local government areas (LGAs). Across the country, with a population of over 170 million, states and LGAs range considerably in size, population, and resources, resulting in huge variation between states. Moreover, financial resources are allocated from the federal account to the state level, but not equitably: only approximately 50 per cent of the allocation is distributed evenly, regardless of the state's size or population. The Federal Government is responsible for designing policy, while the sub-national governments have autonomy over budget regimes and expenditure patterns, and local government is responsible for the provision of services, receiving logistical support from the state government.

---

increasingly seen to have a role in helping to address lagging poverty indicators in these contexts. But, what are the challenges in social protection policy and practice in contexts where institutions and governance are particularly weak or failing?

This chapter discusses some of these key challenges, using Nigeria as a case study. It draws on research conducted in 2011 looking specifically at the experience of the Government of Nigeria and its development partners in developing a social protection system, and examines the way in which the institutional and governance set-up in Nigeria – a federal republic with 36 states and the Federal Capital Territory – affects the design and delivery of social protection (see Box 12.1). There are numerous social protection programmes being implemented across the country, some of which have been specifically designed to support the Millennium Development Goals (MDGs) in health, education, and livelihoods. However, social protection coverage remains limited, and progress in developing a social protection system has stalled; inadequate leadership, fiscal decentralization, limited capacity, and a weak governance context have led to the uneven and inequitable provision of social protection within the country.

Poverty and social protection in Nigeria

Patterns of poverty and inequality

Although Nigeria is a middle-income country, poverty remains widespread, and many of the MDGs would not have been met by 2015. In 2010, approximately 60 per cent of the population – over 110 million people – lived in 'absolute poverty' (National Bureau of Statistics, 2010). Of particular concern is the fact that the proportion of the population living in poverty has been increasing at the same time the country has experienced strong economic growth (ibid.). Economic growth, however, has only benefited a small proportion of the population (approximately 20 per cent of the population own 65 per cent of the national wealth (UNDP, 2009)), and inequality within the country is high, with strong spatial and gender patterns. For instance, poverty is higher and growth is slower in rural areas compared to urban areas (World Bank, 2014). The north of Nigeria experiences higher poverty; the North-West zone, for example, has the highest rate of absolute poverty (at 70 per cent) compared to the South-West which has the lowest (under 50 per cent). Gender inequality is very high, with significant gender gaps across health, education, economic empowerment, and political participation (SIGI, 2014).

Poverty reduction is limited by weak governance, corruption, instability, conflict, and inadequate infrastructure (IFAD, 2009). The lack of sustainable economic opportunities in the agricultural sector, the high proportion of the population working in the informal sector, and the huge unemployment rate are key challenges for reducing poverty across the country (Aigbokhan, 2008; NHIS, 2010; World Bank, 2010).

Health and education outcomes are low across the country, where a number of indicators are above the regional average despite Nigeria being the wealthiest country in West and Central Africa (UNICEF, 2011). For example, Nigeria ranks 18th out of 193 countries in terms of the under-5 mortality rate (ibid.); 41 per cent of children under 5 are stunted, and maternal mortality rates remain high (NPC, 2010). Nigeria also bears nearly 10 per cent of the global burden of HIV (UNAIDS, 2010). Education rates are similarly poor: the North-West and North-East zones have the highest proportion of people with no education (approximately 7 in 10 women, and half of men); whereas the South-South has the lowest percentage of those who have never been to school (15 per cent among females, and 8 per cent among males) (NPC and ICF Macro, 2009: 14).

Although some poverty indicators such as school enrolment and maternal health have shown signs of improvement (AfDB, 2009; NPC, 2010; Ortiz and Cummins, 2011), Nigeria is not on target to meet the majority of the MDGs. The continued high rates of poverty and inequality in the context of weak governance, corruption, and conflict challenges present a huge challenge for the Government of Nigeria and its development partners.

Social protection responses

Looking back at the recent history of social protection in Nigeria, the sector has been developing a policy response to the high rates of poverty in the country since the early 2000s. In 2004, the government, supported by international partners, developed a social protection strategy which took a lifecycle and gendered approach to understanding and tackling the risks and vulnerabilities the poor faced. It identified four main social protection instruments to help address the poverty challenge: social assistance; social insurance; child protection; and the labour market. Although the strategy was broad and encompassing, there was little political traction to turn the strategy into funded and implementable programmes at that time. However, in 2005, the government

---

Box 12.2 Social protection programmes to support the achievement of the MDGs

In Care of the People (COPE) conditional cash transfer, funded initially through the MDGs-Debt Relief Gains (DRG) in 2007, and targeted at extremely poor households (those headed by a female, and those including elderly, physically challenged, and fistula or HIV/AIDS patients) with children of school-going age. Beneficiary households receive a monthly Basic Income Guarantee (BIG) for one year, and then a lump sum Poverty Reduction Accelerator Investment (PRAI). The payments are subject to two conditions: the enrolment and retention (80 per cent) of children in basic education (Primary 1 to junior secondary education); and participation in all free health care programmes. The BIG ranges from US$10 to $33, depending on the number of children in the household; a further $50 per month is withheld as compulsory savings, which is provided as the PRAI (up to $560) to the head of the household. Entrepreneurship and life skills training are provided to beneficiaries to maximize the PRAI. As of 2011, coverage of the programme was extremely limited, reaching approximately 22,000 households or less than 0.001 per cent of the poor. In 2013, reports suggest that coverage reached 113,000 households.[1]

The Maternal and Child Health Care programme (MCH), a health fee waiver for pregnant women and under-5s, is also funded by the MDGs-DRG fund and provided on a universal basis. To accelerate achievement of MDGs 4 and 5, it provides free primary health care for children under 5, and primary and secondary care for pregnant women up to six weeks after childbirth. As of 2011, the programme was being implemented in the country in phases, and was implemented in 12 states with coverage of 851,198 women and girls (less than 0.01 per cent of the poor).

The Community-Based Health Insurance Scheme (CBHIS), part of the national health insurance scheme, aims to support MDGs in health. The CBHIS was re-launched in 2011 after previous design challenges, and aims to protect the informal sector and marginalized groups against high out-of-pocket health expenditures (PATHS2, 2010) by pooling risks within a community. The policy recognizes that the package may differ by geographic area, given the different epidemiologic profiles of the different zones of Nigeria. The core package covers essential cost-effective maternal, neonatal, and child health services, and control of highly prevalent diseases that contribute to the high disease burden in Nigeria (NHIS, 2010).

---

received debt relief from the Paris Club of creditors, and the MDG-Debt Relief Gains (MDG-DRG) fund was set up to finance projects and programmes to achieve the MDGs in the country. Three social protection programmes were identified and funded by the Federal Government: a conditional cash transfer; a maternal and child health care programme; and a health insurance scheme (see Box 12.2).

Despite Nigeria being a key player in the African Union, the aim of developing a social protection strategy for delivering a coordinated set of programmes beyond the MDGs' focus (and at scale) still failed to gain full political support. In 2009, the National Social Insurance Trust Fund drafted a social security strategy, but was unable to generate sufficient political backing to advance it past draft. By 2011, there was a chapter committed to social protection in the implementation plan of Nigeria's national policy document, Vision 20: 2020. This drew on the 2004 draft social protection strategy, and focused on health insurance, labour market programmes, and social transfers. As such, social protection at the policy level remains compartmentalized, and only implicit in the national development strategy.

In practice, however, there is a wealth of social protection programmes being funded and implemented across the country by numerous state-level government MDAs (ministries, departments, and agencies), international donors, NGOs, and faith-based organizations. These include conditional and unconditional cash transfers for girls' education, and to improve children's health and nutrition in various states (including Bauchi, Katsina, and Kano states, and Jigawa and Zamfara), child savings accounts in Bayelsa state, a disability grant in Jigawa state, plus various health waivers, education support (e.g. free uniforms), and nutrition support (see Holmes et al., 2012a for further details). HIV and AIDS programmes at state level also include social protection subcomponents, including nutrition, health, and education support (Samuels et al., 2012). Labour market programmes include federal and state-level public works (PW) programmes, agricultural subsidies/inputs, and youth skills and employment programmes. A certain amount of social equity legislation has also been passed: the Civil and Political Rights Covenant; the Economic, Social, and Cultural Rights Covenant; the Convention on the Elimination of All Forms of Violence Against Women; and the Convention on the Rights of the Child. However, not all states have passed these, and implementation is weak at best. There is a limited, if any, conceptual link between the broader regulatory policies of equality, and rights and social protection policies.

Despite the number of programmes in existence, they are small in scale, where one estimate puts the coverage of social protection in the country at 0.02 per cent of the poor (Trousseau, 2014). At a programme level, the coverage of the federal-led MDG-focused programmes discussed in Box 12.2 reached less than 0.001 per cent of the poor (COPE) and 0.01 per cent of the poor (MCH) in 2011. Moreover, the numerous programmes remain uncoordinated in the absence of an overarching federal-led strategic social protection plan, resulting in fragmented programming and inefficient service delivery.

Performance of existing social protection programmes

How have the existing social protection programmes in the country performed in terms of reducing poverty and vulnerability? While there is very little empirical evidence on the impacts and effectiveness of existing social protection programmes at a national or local level, smaller-scale assessments demonstrate some indicative findings. Research on the cash transfer COPE reports that there has been no discernible impact on poverty at a national level; the effects are small-scale and localized (Dijkstra et al., 2011a; 2011b; Holmes et al., 2012b). This is not surprising given the low coverage of the programme (Holmes et al., 2012b). However, qualitative research conducted in 2011 on COPE in Adamawa, Benue, Edo, and Lagos (Holmes et al., 2012b) does find that income from COPE is important for poor households at an individual and household level, and especially in the context of the recent food, fuel, and financial crisis (Gavrilovic et al., 2011). Holmes et al. (2012b) found that COPE staff and beneficiaries reported that participation in the

COPE programme provided households living in chronic poverty with an alternative positive coping strategy in the absence of other formal support. COPE beneficiaries reported that even a small income transfer helped households to meet immediate consumption needs and, to a lesser extent, to defray school and health costs. One beneficiary noted, 'The money brought about a big change in our lives. We were able to feed, buy school materials for the children. Besides, the money was timely. It came at a time when we needed to pay the school and one of the children also fell ill at the time and we were able to get medication from the money' (COPE beneficiary, widow, Adamawa).

Despite this important contribution, as suggested by the beneficiaries interviewed, the limited value of the transfer given to households, the short-term nature of the programme, and implementation challenges all served to impede the effectiveness of the programme. For instance, beneficiaries particularly noted that the insufficient value of the transfer was a key challenge in making a sustainable difference to household poverty, especially in large families. Moreover, while some households invested in small-scale productive activities, such as petty trading, many households had not received training or guidance for their lump sum payment, meaning 'sustainable graduation' from the programme within one year was unrealistic (see also Akinola, 2014; Holmes et al., 2012b). One programme staff member reported that 'most of the beneficiaries did not invest the lump sum. Some used it for feeding, others for things like fencing of their houses, etc. This makes a mockery of the process, as beneficiaries soon revert to their former state' (key informant, Adamawa).

Data on the impacts of other social protection initiatives are also thin, and there is no systematized database or central point for gathering data and analysis on the various programmes in operation. Outcomes for a health-related conditional cash transfer operating in nine states, however, report that the intervention had a positive effect on health care uptake (Okoli et al., 2014). One USAID evaluation of the Maternal and Child Health Care programme estimated that up to 470 women's lives and 1,070 children's lives may have been saved within the first 15 months of Phase 1 of the programme (USAID, 2010, as cited in Gavrilovic et al., 2011). However, given that in 2009 there were an estimated 4.2 million pregnant women at any given time, with a population of 25.3 million children under 5, this represents only a tiny fraction of the potential beneficiary population (Gavrilovic et al., 2011).

Challenges and opportunities in social protection policy and implementation

In the context of high rates of poverty and inequality in Nigeria, we have seen only localized, and relatively limited effects, of social protection. The social protection sector has yet to be developed sufficiently to address poverty at scale. Three specific policy and implementation challenges are identified, and discussed in more detail below, to explain the limited progress of social protection in the country: fiscal decentralization; state and local government capacity; and the governance context.

Fiscal decentralization

Spending on social protection in Nigeria is low. Taking a broad definition of social protection, government expenditure was estimated at 1.4 per cent in 2009; looking specifically at social assistance (excluding civil service schemes from the definition), this represented 0.4 per cent of GDP (Hagen-Zanker and Tavakoli, 2012). This is much less than many other African countries; for example, Kenya's spending on social protection was 6.2 per cent of government expenditure in 2007/8 (ibid.). This expenditure is also low when compared to other social sector spending in Nigeria. During the period 2005–10, government expenditure on the combined social sectors (health, education, and social protection without civil servant schemes) amounted to 5.8 per cent of GDP. Education had the highest budget share out of all social sectors, taking an average of about 12 per cent of government expenditure, and health expenditure took around 7 per cent on average (Hagen-Zanker and Tavakoli, 2012). Moreover, while in per capita terms expenditure on social sectors has almost doubled since 2005, social spending has been declining as a proportion of government expenditure in recent years (ibid.). Education and health expenditure shares decreased significantly in 2009, falling below 2005 levels (ibid.).

This contraction is especially problematic because of the nature of fiscal decentralization in the country, which has resulted in significant budget and expenditure variations between states within the country. The sub-national governments have autonomy over economic development policy, budget regimes, and expenditure patterns (Norad, 2010), and LGAs are responsible for delivering essential services at the local level. States and LGAs range considerably in size, population, and resources, which leads to variation between states in terms of poverty and vulnerability profiles. The mechanisms for fiscal decentralization mean that resources are not allocated equitably to the states; only around 50 per cent of the allocation from the federal account is distributed evenly, regardless of states' size or population; the rest is allocated according to oil derivation (Freinkman, 2007) and local revenue effort. This means that poorer states that lack the capacity to generate their own income receive less money from the Federal Government. For instance, between 2001 and 2005, the difference in per capita transfers between the poorest and the richest states increased by between 9 and 17 times. Four states (with around 11 per cent of the population) received a quarter of all transfers in 2001; this had risen to a third by 2005 (Freinkman, 2007).

In 2010, a mechanism called the Conditional Grants Scheme (CGS) was initiated as a way to address some of these challenges. The CGS channels funds and technical assistance from the Federal Government to sub-national governments, in order to support state and local government capacity and funding for service delivery in education, health, water, and cash transfers

(OSSAP, 2010). Specifically, the CGS requires states to provide matched funding from the Federal Government for programmes which have been funded under the MDG-DRG, the aim being that the state's funding is scaled up as the MDG-DRG funding is scaled down, thereby ensuring long-term sustainability of financing such programmes. Grants are conditional on states and their programmes meeting certain requirements, and agreeing to sign and abide by written guidelines (Phillips, 2009). For example, criteria for the approval of the conditional cash transfer (CCT) programme includes that there must be an implementing agency, the state must be conversant with CCTs, and they must have a supply-side in place (tied to school enrolment, primary health care, and schools) (Holmes et al., 2012b).

In 2013, 113 LGAs had received funding through the CGS, with the aim to reach all 774 LGAs by 2015 (Center for Sustainable Development, 2013). Both COPE (the CCT) and MCH (the health fee waiver programme) have been funded through the CGS. As of 2011, however, only a third of state governments committed to matching funding for the COPE programme, with coverage of the programme remaining exceedingly low, as discussed above. As such, despite international evidence that well-designed interventions can be cost-effective and instrumental in reducing poverty and vulnerability, social protection as part of a poverty reduction package has not yet attracted increased fiscal commitment to such programmes at the state level.

Capacity to deliver services

The capacity challenge at the local level hinders effective implementation of social protection programmes. The division of roles and responsibilities between the federal and the local levels means that local government – the level with the least resources as well as the least capacity – is responsible for providing essential basic services (Phillips, 2009). Underqualified and under-skilled personnel, and limited technical capacity and administrative capacity to implement and monitor programmes, are identified as key constraints (Holmes et al., 2012b).

While some of these capacity gaps are, in theory, easier to address, such as investing in human resources through training personnel, increasing numbers of staff and resources etc., there is a longer-term challenge in terms of capacity weaknesses in the *systems* that need to be in place to implement social protection effectively. For, not only is the social protection sector dealing with relatively new types of poverty reduction tools such as CCTs and different health financing mechanisms, but because it aims to increase the demand for services, it is dependent on the delivery and supply of other basic services and infrastructure to function effectively. There is a weakness, however, in the capacity of the overall welfare state, with huge gaps in the social worker system, regulation, and coverage at community level (Holmes et al., 2012b). While there is recognition of the importance of an integrated approach which combines strategies to support both the supply and the demand of services at the policy level – particularly in health and education as part of the overall MDG framework, which the MDG-DRG is financing (such as the community-based health insurance scheme, and the maternal and child care health provision) – in practice, service delivery remains poor. Approaches to improving service delivery over recent years have largely taken a top-down approach, by investing in tertiary and secondary facilities at the expense of primary 'front-line' facilities and sub-national level actors (Phillips, 2009).

The problems of limited capacity are also compounded by design problems. Social protection interventions designed at the national level are not always aligned to context-specific poverty challenges at the local level, especially given the vast variation in poverty and vulnerability patterns across the many different states in the country. Moreover, few states have demonstrated that they have the capacity, tools, or resources to design locally appropriate social protection mechanisms, a bottleneck which is exacerbated by limited support and guidance on appropriate social protection tools and approaches from the federal level.

A case in point is the experience of the COPE programme. While the design of COPE at the federal level included some opportunities for variations at the community level (although mainly prescribed programmes to fit into pre-decided categories that map onto the MDGs), only a handful of states made local-level adaptations to tailor programme design based on a specific understanding of local poverty and vulnerability profiles. For example, in 2011, the CCT proposal to the CGS from Jigawa state made some changes by integrating a skills acquisition component for non-literate adults of selected households to provide a sustainable means of livelihood. In Cross River state, conditions were based on needs and demand identified by baseline studies, which showed high rates of children not in school and not accessing health facilities, and high rates of malnourishment.

Experience has shown that it is important to design social protection to reflect patterns of poverty and vulnerability at the state and local levels, rather than to prescribe a specific social protection tool that does not take local context and variations into account. That is to say, while CCTs may be appropriate in some states, different types of cash transfers, like disability assistance, cash for work, or pensions, may be more suitable in others. Food/nutrition or other in-kind transfers may also be more appropriate to support goals in food security, health, or livelihoods, or targeted fee waivers to support access to education and health services.

Consideration of both capacity and design is therefore essential in the development of social protection policy and programming. And institutional, administrative, and financial resources need to be considered alongside appropriate design at the state and local levels.

Governance context

The third key challenge discussed here is the issue of the weak governance context, which presents a serious constraint to delivering social protection equitably in Nigeria. Indeed, corruption and lack of transparency in the administration of social protection programmes are cited as two of the key challenges by the National Planning Commission (NPC, 2011). Corruption and weak governance challenges occur at all levels of government and across sectors (Freinkman, 2007); there is a mistrust of higher government at the state level, and inter-governmental transfers – both from federal to state, and state to local – are cited as the main source of corruption in the country (Norad, 2010).

There is a lack of upward accountability. Even though the Federal Government is responsible for monitoring the actions of sub-national governments – aside from a few pilot schemes, and increased recognition of the importance of monitoring – it lacks the capacity to do so. There is also a lack of downward accountability from sub-national governments to residents, as sub-national governments do not often make publicly available their revenue allocations and budgets, resulting in a lack of information combined with limited citizen engagement with local government.

Concerns about channelling development aid through the government have also led to a preference to disburse aid 'closer to the people' at the state and LGA levels (Holmes et al., 2012a). Thus, donors tend to work with particular pro-poor state governors rather than across states on structural issues. This has meant that pilot programmes and donor interventions often centre on the same few states (Eldon and Gunby, 2009). It is unsurprising that donors choose to work in states that appear the most likely to adopt responsive behaviour in governance and service delivery in order to provide best practice examples. In reality, though, it is problematic, as the underlying challenges in the majority of states are not addressed or resolved appropriately to make it possible to scale up projects systematically to reach a larger proportion of the poor in the country (Holmes et al., 2012a).

The Nigerian Government has attempted to address governance issues through reforms and the establishment of anti-corruption bodies, with relevance to the nascent social protection sector. Again, the CGS is an important initiative here. This scheme not only attempts to improve fiscal sustainability and build capacity, but also aims to improve efficiency, increase accountability, and improve governance dimensions of service delivery by building on the resources, knowledge, and capacity existing at sub-national level, as well as increasing accountability and communication between federal and state levels. These mechanisms include, for example, electronic disbursements of funds and the establishment of a Virtual Poverty Fund monitoring system, which includes a budget tracking system and a decentralized monitoring and evaluation (M&E) framework involving the private sector and civil society.

While there has been some success through the CGS in improving monitoring and accountability (Dijkstra et al., 2011a), there remain significant capacity and resource gaps in the implementation of the scheme, especially as the scheme expands (Phillips, 2009). In 2007, there were 4,000 projects, which increased to 10,000 in 2008. This rapid expansion placed a large burden on the federal level, responsible for monitoring and evaluating programmes, which compromised M&E and also weakened the stringency with which conditionality was enforced (ibid.).

Concluding remarks

This chapter has discussed the institutional and policy challenges in the implementation of social protection in Nigeria. It has specifically focused on social protection programmes initiated by the government's Debt-Relief Fund to contribute to achieving the MDGs. The chapter has argued that the nascent social protection sector in Nigeria is constrained by challenges in fiscal decentralisation, limited capacity, and a weak governance context. These challenges are exacerbated by tensions and bottlenecks between the federal, state, and local levels of government. However, there are also important lessons and opportunities for strengthening and developing the social protection system in the country to support the delivery of social protection programmes at scale, and which could contribute to Nigeria's efforts to meet the Sustainable Development Goals. The policy implications of these lessons include focusing on mechanisms which work to increase political commitment and fiscal sustainability to fund social protection programmes, build capacity for the design and implementation of locally appropriate programmes, and support accountability and trust between the federal and sub-national levels.

Political commitment and fiscal sustainability: Scaling up social protection programmes and supporting a social protection system to tackle the depth, incidence, and range of poverty and vulnerability in the country will require increased financial commitment at the federal, state, and local levels. At the same time, increasing political commitment to social protection will be vital, especially to ensure sustainability of programmes through the CGS, as federal funding for the schemes declines from the MDG-DRG fund. As such, at the federal level, there is an important role for the government to play in terms of providing support, guidance, and coordination through a strategic social protection plan. Importantly, this also needs to allow for the development of state-led and state-specific social protection interventions.

Initiatives under way which help to support this goal include the Ministry of Finance taking a lead on developing a comprehensive social protection initiative, and the establishment of a social protection task group (Trousseau, 2014). Moving forward, to increase political commitment to social protection will also require an approach to advocate for social protection to a wide range of influential actors in the government as well as development partners, and the establishment of an 'institutional home' in which to drive this agenda forward.

Securing political support is a first step to increasing budget allocations to a scaled-up social protection system. Hagen-Zanker and Tavakoli (2012) also suggest that the options for increasing fiscal space for social protection in the country include the mobilization of domestic resources, possible increases in donor funding specifically targeted at social protection, and improving the public financial management of public expenditure.

Capacity for appropriate design and improved implementation at the local level: Despite the proposed variety of safety nets discussed in various policy documents, in practice limited discussion on the different instruments that might be appropriate in Nigeria has resulted in a very narrow approach. Generating sustained interest in developing a social protection system which could continue to contribute to the MDGs, with appropriately designed programmes at the local level, will be a complex process. It will require a coordinated approach from actors and champions in the government at all levels, as well as development partners and civil society. It will also require generating and sharing evidence on the role that a variety of social protection instruments can play in supporting Nigeria's broader development and growth objectives. This should include a focus beyond the MDG agenda.

Attention to specific design and implementation features is needed if social protection programmes are to be scaled up and have an impact on poverty. Social protection programmes, whether with health, education, livelihoods, and/or equity objectives, need to be grounded in the patterns of poverty and vulnerability faced at the individual, household, and community levels; this may vary at the state level. The analysis of the cash transfer programme COPE clearly demonstrates that cash transfer programmes need to have a longer time horizon than one year, the value of the transfer needs to be sufficient to meet the programme objective, and the delivery of transfers must be regular and predictable so that households can plan their income and expenditure.

Moreover, lessons from Nigeria demonstrate that social protection design needs to match implementation capacity (e.g. programmes should not be overly complicated or administratively intensive), given the context of high poverty levels and institutional capacity and resource constraints. Social sector expenditure remains very low, and delivery of services remains a weak link in the potential scale-up and expansion of social protection. Simultaneous investment in the supply side of services, in both the social and economic spheres, will be vital to maximize the effectiveness of social protection programmes.

Governance and accountability: Finally, learning from other sectors, in terms of strengthening governance, will also be important as social protection develops in the country. At the federal level, a main concern will be putting in place mechanisms for accountability and transparency, which could include donor-funded technical support in ministries, departments, and agencies, and strengthening the capacity of federal and state levels to operate systems such as the CGS. At the local level, it will be equally important to incorporate mechanisms to strengthen downward accountability, for example, ensuring that beneficiaries are informed about programme design, can participate in programme governance committees, and can access fair grievance procedures. This entails sensitizing and engaging not only programme beneficiaries, but also the broader community.

Note

1. This chapter is based on research from ODI's portfolio of studies on social protection in Nigeria, commissioned by UNICEF in 2010. Accessible here: <www.odi.org/projects/2311-social-protection-diagnostic-forward-agenda-unicef-nigeria> [accessed July 2015].

References

AfDB (2009) *International Development Association Country Partnership Strategy for the Federal Republic of Nigeria (2010–2013)*. African Development Bank, UK Department for International Development, United States Agency for International Development and World Bank, Washington, DC.

Aigbokhan, B.E. (2008) 'Poverty, inequality and growth in Nigeria: A case study', *ACGS/MPAMS Discussion Paper No. 3*. United Nations Economic Commission for Africa, Addis Ababa.

Akinola, O. (2014) 'Graduation and social protection in Nigeria: A critical analysis of the COPE CCT programme', paper prepared for conference on *Graduation and Social Protection*, Serena Hotel, Kigali, Rwanda, 6–8 May 2014.

Barrientos, A. (2012) 'Social transfers and growth: What do we know? What do we need to find out?' *World Development* 40(1): 11–20 <http://dx.doi.org/10.1016/j.worlddev.2011.05.012>.

Center for Sustainable Development (2013) *Where We Work: Nigeria* [online]. Columbia University, New York, NY. Available from: <http://cgsd.columbia.edu/where-we-work/nigeria/> [accessed July 2015].

Dijkstra, G., Akanji, B., Hiddink, C., Sangarabalan, S. and de Mevius, F.X. (2011a) *Mutual Interests – Mutual Benefits: Evaluation of the 2005 Debt Relief Agreement between the Paris Club and Nigeria. Summary Report.* Ministry of Foreign Affairs of the Kingdom of the Netherlands, The Hague.

Dijkstra, G., Akanji, B., Hiddink, C., Sangarabalan, S. and de Mevius, F.X. (2011b) *Mutual Interests – Mutual Benefits: Evaluation of the 2005 Debt Relief Agreement between the Paris Club and Nigeria. Main Report.* Ministry of Foreign Affairs of the Kingdom of the Netherlands, The Hague.

Eldon, J. and Gunby, D. (2009) *States in Development: State-building and Service Delivery*. HLSP, London.

Fiszbein, A. and Schady, N. (2009) *Conditional Cash Transfers: Reducing Present and Future Poverty. A World Bank Policy Research Report*. World Bank, Washington, DC <http://dx.doi.org/10.1596/978-0-8213-7352-1>.

Freinkman, L. (2007) *Intergovernmental Relations in Nigeria: Improving Service Delivery in Core Areas*. World Bank, Washington, DC.

Gavrilovic, M., Alder, H., Cali, M., Cullen, E., Harper, C., Jones, N., Samuels, F. and Niño-Zarazúa, M. (2011) *The Impact of the Food, Financial and Fuel (3F) Crises on Women and Children in Nigeria*. Overseas Development Institute, London.

Hagen-Zanker, J. and Tavakoli, H. (2012) *An Analysis of Fiscal Space for Social Protection in Nigeria*. Overseas Development Institute, London.

Holmes, R. and Jones, N. (2013) *Gender and Social Protection in the Developing World: Beyond Mothers and Safety Nets*. ZED Books Ltd, London.

Holmes, R. and Akinrimisi, B., with Morgan, J. and Buck, R. (2012a) *Social Protection in Nigeria: Mapping Programmes and their Effectiveness*. Overseas Development Institute, London.

Holmes, R., Samson, M., Magoronga, W. and Akinrimisi, B., with Morgan, J. (2012b) *The Potential for Cash Transfers in Nigeria*. Overseas Development Institute, London.

IFAD (2009) *IFAD Rural Poverty Portal* [website]. International Fund for Agricultural Development, Rome <www.ruralpovertyportal.org/>.

National Bureau of Statistics (2010) *Nigeria Poverty Profile 2010*. Government of Nigeria, Abuja.

NHIS (2010) *NHIS-MDG/Maternal and Child Health (MCH) Project*. National Health Insurance Scheme, Abuja.

Norad (2010) 'Good governance in Nigeria: A study in political economy and donor support'. *Norad Report 17/2010 Discussion*. Norwegian Agency for Development Cooperation, Oslo.

NPC (2010) *Nigeria: Millennium Development Goals (MDG), Countdown Strategy: 2010–2015*. National Planning Commission, Abuja.

NPC (2011) *Nigeria Vision 20: 2020: First National Implementation Plan 2010–2013*. National Planning Commission, Abuja.

NPC and ICF Macro (2009) *Nigeria Demographic and Health Survey 2008: Key Findings*. National Population Commission and ICF Macro, Calverton, MD.

Okoli, U., Morris, L., Oshin, A., Pate, M.A., Aigbe, C. and Muhammad, A. (2014) 'Conditional cash transfer schemes in Nigeria: Potential gains for maternal and child health service uptake in a national pilot programme', *BMC Pregnancy and Childbirth* 14:408 <http://dx.doi.org/ 10.1186/s12884-014-0408-9>.

Ortiz, I. and Cummins, M. (2011) 'Global inequality: Beyond the bottom billion. A rapid review of income distribution in 141 countries', *Social and Economic Policy Working Paper*. UNICEF, New York, NY.

OSSAP (2010) *Partnering to Achieve the MDGs: The Story of Nigeria's Conditional Grants Scheme 2007–2010*. The Presidency, Government of Nigeria, Abuja.

PATHS2 (2010) *Quarter Ten Report PATHS2/2/QTR/02 October–December 2010*. PATHS2, Abuja.

Phillips, J. (2009) 'Restoring confidence and increasing responsiveness in state and local government through conditional grants: Nigeria', paper prepared for *Conference on Sub-National Jurisdictions in Efforts to Achieve the MDGs*, Abuja, 7–9 May 2014.

Samuels, F., Blake, C. and Akinrimisi, B. (2012) 'HIV vulnerabilities and the potential for strengthening social protection responses in the context of HIV in Nigeria'. Overseas Development Institute/UNICEF-Nigeria, Abuja.

SIGI (2014) *Country profile: Nigeria* [online]. Social Institutions and Gender Index. Available from: <http://genderindex.org/country/nigeria> [accessed July 2015].

Trousseau, V. (2014) *Planning for Government Adoption of a Social Protection Programme in an Insecure Environment: The Child Grant Development Programme in Northern Nigeria. CaLP Case Study*. The Cash Learning Partnership, Oxford.

UNAIDS (2010) *Global Report: UNAIDS Report on the Global AIDS Epidemic 2010*. Joint UN Programme on HIV/AIDS (UNAIDS), Geneva.

UNDP (2009) *Human Development Report Nigeria 2008–2009: Achieving Growth with Equity*. United Nations Development Programme, Abuja.

UNICEF (2011) *Programme Guidance on Social Protection for Children. Final Draft for Consultation*. UNICEF, New York, NY.

World Bank (2010) *Economic Overview and Performance. Country Brief: Nigeria*. World Bank, Washington, DC.

World Bank (2014) *Nigeria Economic Report: Nigeria Economic Report No. 2* [online]. World Bank, Washington, DC. Available from: <http://documents. worldbank.org/curated/en/2014/07/19883231/nigeria-economic-report-no-2> [accessed July 2015].

About the author

Rebecca Holmes is a research fellow in the Social Protection Programme at the Overseas Development Institute. Her research and policy work focuses on social protection and social policy, and she has particular expertise in gender and social inclusion analysis. Her recent research, focusing on South Asia and sub-Saharan Africa, has looked at gender and social protection effectiveness, the effects of social protection on social inclusion and cohesion, and the role of social protection in fragile and post-conflict states.

CHAPTER 13

The conditions for conditionality in cash transfers: Does one size fit all?

Luca Pellerano and Valentina Barca

Popularized since the late 1990s in Latin America, conditional cash transfer programmes (CCTs) are now at the forefront of the international policy debate as one of the most effective social interventions for tackling poverty in developing countries. However, if CCTs have been successful in achieving their desired objectives, have the condition-alities themselves played a central role? This chapter argues that cash transfers can condition behaviour through at least four different channels: conditioning on access; implicit conditioning; indirect conditioning; and 'explicit' conditionality. Only the latter characterizes CCTs, while the other three are generally defined as 'unconditional'. This chapter presents key criteria – using a framework built around the concepts of principles, costs, benefits, and practical/political feasibility – to determine the viability and desirability of using 'explicit' conditionalities in social transfers in contexts such as sub-Saharan Africa.

Keywords: conditionality, behavioural conditioning, CCT, UCT, cash transfer, sub-Saharan Africa

Introduction

At the end of the 1990s, Mexico became the first Latin American country to pursue the idea of complementing traditional policies to address intergenerational poverty, and low human capital accumulation on the supply side, with an intervention targeted at the demand side. The pioneer of conditional cash transfer programmes (CCTs) – *Progresa* – gave life to a tradition whose success appears to be unstoppable. CCTs' rationale is to provide poor families with direct transfers in cash, and make this transfer contingent upon the adoption of certain 'desirable' behaviours, like school attendance or growth monitoring of children. Today, CCTs have become a social policy blueprint, boasting an unprecedented pace of expansion in terms of rapidity, scale, and number of countries involved.

A large number of studies assessing the impact of CCTs have shown positive results on several dimensions of socio-economic well-being, including consumption expenditure and dietary diversity, school enrolment and attendance, and health centre visits by children (Saavedra and Garcia, 2012;

http://dx.doi.org/10.3362/9781780448435.013

Fiszbein and Schady, 2009). However, in the wake of the great success of CCTs and their rapid expansion internationally, an interesting debate has arisen about the opportunity to use conditionality to ensure better policy results for social transfers (de Brauw and Hoddinott, 2008; de Janvry and Sadoulet, 2004; Schubert and Slater, 2006; Reimers et al., 2006).

While CCTs belong to a relatively new generation of social protection programmes, unconditional benefits, subsidies, grants, and pensions (which we will be generally defining as unconditional cash transfer programmes, or UCTs) have long occupied the social protection scene, both in developed and developing countries. Often very similar to CCTs in their overall objectives, UCTs differ because they do not require qualifying households to meet specifically spelt-out 'explicit' conditions in order to continue receiving payments.

Evidence supports the hypothesis that UCTs also have a positive impact on fundamental dimensions of human capital accumulation like nutrition, cognitive development, and education.[1] So, if CCTs have been successful in achieving some of their desired objectives, have the conditionalities themselves played the central role in this achievement? And, if CCTs do offer any advantages, can we expect them to work in any context, whatever the structure of local economies and societies and the capacity of local administrations? What pre-conditions are necessary to guarantee effective CCTs, and in which situations should other (unconditional) policy options be pursued?

We address these issues in the next section by analysing the contentious issue of conditionality. We argue that orienting the way beneficiaries use social transfers, according to 'socially desirable' objectives, can be achieved through different conditioning mechanisms, not only via the 'explicit' conditionality used by CCTs. On this basis, we then proceed to review the available evidence on the effectiveness of conditionality, including an analysis of its benefits, costs, and practical and political feasibility. We conclude by setting out a framework to understand under what conditions CCTs can be an optimal policy choice.

Questioning the premises: conditionality vs unconditionality

CCTs are designed so as to incentivize 'desirable' behaviour through a set of 'spelt-out' conditions. If these conditions are not met, the transfers are not given. However, this approach presumes that desirable behaviour can be obtained *only* by 'explicitly' conditioning the transfer. To the contrary, we argue (together, broadly, with others, for example, Schubert and Slater, 2006; Schüring, 2010; and Özler, 2013) that steering the use of social transfers towards 'socially relevant' outcomes can be, and has often been, achieved through several different mechanisms of less explicit behavioural conditioning (often referred to as 'soft conditionalities'). Such distinctions between different mechanisms of conditioning have only been recently addressed by the literature, and have been referred to as an 'undefined (and hard to define) continuum' (Özler, 2013). Nevertheless, in this chapter we hope to add some order to the 'mess'.

Specifically, we distinguish between four means of conditioning the use of social (cash) transfers that are available to policymakers, and that are widely used:

1. First, beneficiaries of cash transfer programmes are explicitly targeted based on a defined set of socio-economic characteristics aimed at filtering out non-poor households. These explicit eligibility criteria tend to target a set of beneficiaries who have particular needs and therefore display similar patterns in the use of their transfers. We define this as **conditioning on access**.[2]

2. Second, intrinsic characteristics of the subsidy design (e.g. the nature of the transfer, its delivery mechanisms, its name, etc.) may also act as a conditioning or 'nudging' mechanism. The decision to deliver transfers via electronic cards, for instance, may increase a household's propensity to save (Schubert and Slater, 2006). Similarly, the decision to pay child benefits to women, as in most of the Latin American transfers, is based on evidence that mothers tend to have preference structures that are better aligned with their children's best interests (Yoong et al., 2012). The decision whether to deliver support in kind or in cash (or intermediate forms, such as vouchers) also has significant behavioural consequences (Currie and Gahvari, 2008). The name and 'labelling' of the transfer scheme itself (e.g. 'Child Support Grant') signals the existence of an implicit contract between provider and recipient as to how the resources are expected to be used (Benhassine et al., 2013). We call these mechanisms **implicit conditioning**.[3]

3. Third, the use of cash transfers can be further conditioned by complementary policy actions that are implemented in conjunction with the transfer. This happens, for example, when beneficiaries are involved in training/education sessions where they are provided with information on the 'best' use of the transfers (see, for example, Duarte Gómez et al., 2004), or when community-based case management systems are put in place to oversee the 'good use' of the transfer. We define this mechanism as **indirect conditioning**.

4. Finally, the novelty of CCTs, in comparison with previous social transfer programmes, is that they are based on an additional **explicit conditionality**. In this case, the payment of the cash subsidy is contingent upon the adoption of certain 'desirable' behaviours (e.g. school attendance), and these behaviours are explicitly monitored. This establishes a formal or an explicit contract between the provider and the recipient, and beneficiaries are penalized in various ways – the most drastic of which is being expelled from the programme – if they do not abide by the terms of the contract. Policymakers also tend to refer to this set of incentives as 'hard conditionality'.

Two points are worth noting. First, existing cash transfer programmes currently work through schemes of 'mixed' conditionality, where conditions on access are integrated with mechanisms of implicit and indirect conditions. The Colombian CCT *Familias en Acción*, for example, is paid to families who live below the poverty line, and who have children under the age of 17 (*conditioning on access*), money is regularly transferred to mothers using an electronic card (*implicit conditioning*), and mothers are involved in training sessions to share information about adequate child care, health, and nutrition (*indirect conditioning*).

The first three forms of conditioning are common to other UCT transfers around the world. In South Africa, for example, the unconditional Child Support Grant is also targeted to poor households, paid in the vast majority of cases in ad-hoc-created bank accounts, and is accompanied by information on expected use and mechanisms for case management. The distinct element of CCTs is that they impose a further *explicit conditionality*, designed depending on the programme's objectives.

Second, there is a continuum between informal (soft) and formal (hard) conditionality in terms of the rules, and the differences between the two are sometimes blurred in practice. In most CCTs, penalties are de facto not strictly implemented, which sometimes defeats the point of the conditionality itself. Nevertheless, a 'credible threat' can be a sufficient incentive to trigger behavioural change, with the explicit contractual framework between the provider and the recipient acting as a signalling mechanism. On the other hand, in some UCTs there is no explicit contract, but the mechanisms for monitoring abuse and moral suasion can be extremely thorough, leading to behavioural change without the use of any explicit conditionality.

On this basis, we argue that the distinction between CCTs and UCTs is largely linked to how the contract between provider and recipient is framed. In most cases the difference between the two boils down to the fact that in CCTs there is a clear and evident set of 'desired behaviours', while in UCTs recipients are generally left with more freedom to spend their transfers, so long as they do not abuse them.

A new arena for debate: the effectiveness of explicit conditionality

While many arguments have been put forward in favour of or against CCTs in comparison to UCTs, we consider that the debate has failed to stress that both approaches share the first three types of conditioning. Instead, the debate on the relative effectiveness of the two policy options should stem from analysis of the effectiveness of *explicit conditionality* mechanisms.

We propose a framework for the analysis of this trade-off around four main concepts: principles; benefits; costs (private and social efficiency); and practical/political feasibility. Framing the debate in this way may help to untangle the complex question of whether and how CCTs are applicable in other contexts outside Latin America.

Principles

On a first level, the debate between CCTs and UCTs is grounded in the realm of political ethics. Indeed, the discussion of the need to condition, and the degree of conditionality to apply, in social policy interventions has deep philosophical roots (Musgrave, 1959). On the one hand, the traditional anti-paternalistic argument claims that policymakers have an 'ethical' duty to respect households' autonomy of decision: any restriction over the use of resources delivered via social interventions would be an improper intrusion into their freedom of choice. Some researchers take this stance one step further, defending the use of UCTs from a rights-based perspective. According to this view, it is unacceptable to deny a person the fundamental human right of guaranteeing minimum consumption (Künnemann and Leonhard, 2008).

On the opposite side of the spectrum, supporters of CCTs appeal to a principle of 'co-responsibility' that should orient social policy interventions. According to this view, any concession on the state's side should always be accompanied by some sort of commitment on the beneficiaries' side, so that policies do not become acts of mere 'assistentialism', and do not promote dependency in the long run (Coady, 2003). In this respect, CCTs can be seen as a response to the Samaritan's dilemma (Britto, 2005), as they indicate a way to reconcile the objectives of redistribution of resources in the short run, and long-term poverty reduction.

In other words, while opponents of explicit conditionalities attack the concept of the 'deserving poor' (Hindle, 2004) and deride the 'nanny state', supporters defend the idea of the 'state as a partner'; two positions that are often difficult to reconcile, but have important linkages with the political and cultural acceptability of different measures.

Benefits

Moving towards economic considerations, the anti-paternalistic argument finds an interesting match in neo-classical efficiency terms, that is, respecting families' autonomy coincides with the intention not to interfere with the structure of preferences of economic agents, who are in this view held to know much better than any government what they need. If restrictions that prevent poor families from investing in human capital are almost exclusively monetary (direct cost, indirect cost, and opportunity costs), income redistribution will by itself lift budget or credit constraints, and economic agents will use or invest their resources in the most efficient way. In fact, any further restriction imposed on the use of transfers limits the fungibility of cash, creating a harmful distortion of market efficiency.

However, in response, supporters of the need for explicit conditionalities would claim that monetary or credit constraints are not the only ones that matter. For many reasons – some relating to market failures (e.g. imperfect information, asymmetric bargaining power structures, externalities, etc.) and others to bounded rationality (myopia) or preference structures (e.g. impatience, risk-aversion, cultural barriers) – individual investment and resource allocation decisions may lead to sub-optimal individual and social outcomes if they are left to the free will of economic agents. As a result, a further push is required to achieve optimal allocations. In technical terms, while pure cash handouts only operate by lifting households' budget constraints, that is, an income effect, mechanisms of behavioural conditioning also modify – in the case of CCTs via the explicit condition – the structure of relative prices in favour of the individually or socially 'desirable' goods or services, that is, through an income effect and price effect (de Janvry et al., 2006).

The relative importance of income/credit constraints versus preference/institutional constraints for optimal investment in 'desirable' outcomes – like health or education – is unclear (Thaler and Sunstein, 2009). And, even more fragmented, is the understanding of whether less stringent types of behavioural conditioning, on access, means, and informal rules, could lead to optimal results as efficiently as explicit conditionalities. Ideally, the trade-off between CCTs and UCTs could be better analysed if one were able to empirically estimate the marginal impact of the sole explicit conditionality on the level of investments in education or health. However, attempts at quantitatively isolating the net effect of explicit conditionalities, as opposed to the other forms of behavioural conditioning, are still few and far between, although this is partly because this distinction is rarely acknowledged. Nevertheless, a few recent studies provide preliminary indications on the issue.

de Janvry et al. (2006), analysing *Progresa* in Mexico, compare the effect of the explicit conditionality and a pure income effect, which, in their analysis, simulates the potential impact of a UCT on education. Their results indicate that a dollar spent on CCTs would confer an effect on school enrolment eight times higher with respect to a dollar spent on increasing households' income. Bourguignon et al. (2003) find even stronger theoretical predictions in favour of CCTs in Brazil, while Kakwani et al. (2005) conclude, from a micro-simulation on data from 15 sub-Saharan African countries, that 'an increase in income, by itself, would not be sufficient to significantly increase school attendance'.[4] Unfortunately, this strand of literature fails to address the point that UCTs are not fully equivalent to an income effect, as they generally operate through other forms of behavioural conditioning.

Schady and Araujo (2006), using the lack of clarity over the functioning of a UCT in Ecuador as the starting point for their research, shed further light on this issue. They find that, although the programme concerned had a positive influence on school attendance, the most significant impact on enrolment rates was for those families who (mistakenly) thought that the programme was explicitly conditioned on educational attendance. Similarly, research by de Brauw and Hoddinott (2008) took advantage of the fact that some beneficiaries of the Mexican CCT *Progresa/Opportunidades* did not receive monitoring and compliance forms for a substantial period of time after the programme was launched, and were therefore unaware that the transfer was conditional. They found that receiving the forms and understanding the conditions being imposed exerted a stronger effect on school enrolment.

All of this evidence, mostly based on 'accidental glitches in programme implementation or structural models of household behaviour' (Baird et al., 2010: 4), appears to point to the success of explicit conditionality in achieving its goals over the 'soft' approach of UCTs. Indeed, this was confirmed by a controversial World Bank randomized control trial that was explicitly designed to contrast the differential impact of CCTs and UCTs on the school attendance rates of teenage girls in Malawi (Baird et al., 2013).[5] Similar randomized comparative studies have been completed in Zimbabwe (Robertson et al., 2013) and Burkina Faso, where CCTs were 'significantly more effective than [UCTs] in improving the enrolment of "marginal children" who are initially less likely to go to school, such as girls, younger children, and lower ability children' (Akresh et al., 2013: abstract).

It is difficult to make a final judgement, however, as the effectiveness of other types of behavioural conditioning has been under-investigated. The only real attempt to do so was a recent experiment conducted on the *Tayssir* programme in Morocco, where the UCT branch of the transfer actively encouraged enrolment in schools through 'labelling' effects, documenting large gains in school participation, and presenting almost no difference compared to the CCT branch (Benhassine et al., 2013). This is in line with evidence that income acquired through some government assistance programmes is allocated differently to other sources of income, as beneficiaries perceive an informal contract with the government (Kooreman, 2000; Thaler, 1990).

Finally, it is also unclear whether 'explicit' schemes of conditionality can produce a more sustainable change of preferences and thus behaviour in the long run, so as to protect investments in 'desirable' goods from possible shocks and income fluctuations.

Costs

Despite the lack of evidence, on theoretical grounds one can reasonably assume that imposing explicit conditions should, if anything, increase the adoption of 'desired' behaviours. However, the critical point is that using explicit conditions also comes at an extra cost, both at the private and social levels. From a perspective of global efficiency, it becomes clear that only from the comparison of marginal benefits and costs is it possible to assess whether CCTs or UCTs should be used in different contexts.

Private efficiency (and equity): On the private efficiency side, the cost of fulfilling explicit conditions – i.e. the direct, indirect, and opportunity costs of adopting 'desirable' behaviours such as sending children to school – can be extremely high for beneficiaries. This reduces the net benefit of the transfer, and can also have negative impacts in terms of equity and inclusiveness. In fact, meeting the cost of explicit conditions is likely to be most difficult for families in the worst socio-economic conditions, triggering unexpected redistributive effects (Barrientos and de Jong, 2006).

Worryingly, this perverse 'excluding' effect of CCTs can involve other dimensions of the targeting process. In Colombia, for example, the need to condition the transfer to key services led to the geographical selection of municipalities where health and educational facilities were actually available, excluding some of the poorest and most under-served areas in the country (Attanasio et al., 2005). While this does not affect outcomes on education (a UCT would not have had any effects either in communities lacking adequate service supply), it does mean excluding needy households who would have benefited from additional income transfers.

CCTs also impose additional costs on beneficiaries, which are not related to the promoted behaviours, but derive from the operational model itself. The procedure of monitoring and verifying compliance with explicit conditions often implies the direct involvement of beneficiaries, and this may translate into costs when the administrative procedures require time and financial commitment from the beneficiaries. Recent estimates for the Colombian CCT (*Familias en Acción* for internally displaced households) indicate that beneficiaries spent an amount equivalent to 45 per cent of the value of their subsidy to bear the costs of monitoring regular attendance at school, as parents have to obtain and collect attendance certificates from the schools themselves (CNC, 2008). Bradshaw and Quirós Víquez also emphasize the high opportunity cost of time spent by women in monitoring and sensitization activities as part of the conditionality scheme in the Nicaraguan *Red de Protección Social* (RPS), as these happen 'at the expense of other activities' (2009: 6). The private costs of verifying explicit conditions therefore strongly affect the efficiency balance between CCTs and UCTs (Coady et al., 2005; Kakwani et al., 2005).

Social efficiency: On the social efficiency side, the familiar argument against CCTs is that their management is more complex and expensive than that of non-conditional interventions. This increases the administrative burden of transfers, and results in less money being available for the transfers themselves. Specifically, the social cost of monitoring explicit conditions is the principal argument against, or in favour of, UCTs from the perspective of public efficiency (Ayala Consulting, 2003; Barrientos and de Jong, 2006).

In the case of education, for example, the system of monitoring the conditionality compliance of a CCT implies burdens both for schools, such as reporting on the regular attendance of students, and the institution managing the CCT itself, such as in the verification of compliance, and defining administrative procedures for warning or suspending non-compliers from the payment of the transfer. Approximate figures are provided by Grosh et al. (2008), who assume that monitoring compliance takes about the same share of administrative costs as payments and targeting, and that the costs for conditionality amount to 1–3 per cent of total programme resources. Coady et al. (2005)

estimate that the conditionality component in 2002 was the second largest cost item of *Progresa*. They calculated the costs for monitoring conditionality to be as high as 24 per cent of programme costs, after deducting the actual transfers. Caldés et al. (2006) extend the cost analysis to two more countries, Nicaragua (RPS) and Honduras (*Programa de Asignación Familiar*), and show that all three countries spend considerable resources on conditionality, ranging from 16 to 27 per cent of programme costs, if fixed costs, such as an external evaluation and programme design, are excluded. Somewhat lower costs were calculated for the case of *Familias en Acción* in Colombia.[6]

The public cost of monitoring explicit conditions depends on a set of factors that can be controlled at the design level; these include precision, frequency, and complexity of conditions to be monitored, logistics, etc., and the development of verification systems is presumably affected by economies of scale. To reduce associated costs, most CCTs have relied on pre-existing public social service delivery structures (schools, health centres) to develop compliance monitoring systems. But the logistic and financial, and indeed ethical, limitations affecting the state's capacity to effectively monitor individual behaviour are almost insurmountable when 'desired behaviour' and hence conditions are not directly linked to public service utilization, for example, nutrition, contraceptive practices, etc.

Feasibility

Despite often being grounded in an ex-ante analysis of costs and benefits, the tension between UCTs and CCTs is heavily marked by other dimensions. For example, in sub-Saharan Africa implementation feasibility can play a fundamental role, while in Latin America the political economy of CCTs should not be underestimated. We discuss these two aspects in turn.

Implementation feasibility: 'Implementation feasibility' refers to the ease with which implementing agencies – whether national governments or other agencies acting for them – can implement a cash transfer programme. Two considerations are important in this context.

First, the administration of complex conditional programmes may turn out to be extremely difficult for public administrations, particularly when institutions are weak and there is a lack of management capacity (Schubert and Slater, 2006). It is worth remembering here that the trade-off between CCTs and UCTs relates to the marginal capacity required to monitor explicit conditions and enforce penalties specifically, rather than to the general administration of transfer schemes.

Second, one should be aware of the potential added 'pressure' on public services, for example, on education, that transfers can create when they are explicitly conditioned on the use of these public services. The risk is that systems may not have enough capacity to absorb growing demand. The original rationale for CCTs in Latin America drew on the hypothesis that not only is access to social services desirable, but also that there is an unmet supply of services in the sector; a problematic assumption in sub-Saharan Africa.[7]

Because of the above, explicit conditions are often conceived, in the sub-Saharan context, at the design stage but not fully operationalized on the ground because of implementation constraint. Programmes which are conditional on paper and unconditional in practice may lead to a loss of credibility of the Ministry or agency in charge (Regalia, 2006).

Political feasibility/the political economy of CCTs: CCTs were initially introduced as an emergency social protection measure to tackle the effects of the economic crises affecting Latin American economies, including Mexico, Brazil, and Colombia (Ayala Consulting, 2003; Britto, 2005). Although generally starting as pilot projects, they have often been scaled up far beyond the original target population and expanded long after the end of the crisis periods that triggered their introduction. This trend is not surprising, and while this is undoubtedly due to their proven success in some areas, it has, nonetheless, been argued that it is also due to their political attractiveness.

First of all, cash transfers – whether conditional or not – are one of the few policies with longer-term impacts that are politically 'feasible' in the short term. Politicians can have low incentives to promote a programme that they will not benefit from within their electoral cycle. CCTs specifically avoid this disincentive problem by guaranteeing immediate political popularity while simultaneously maintaining a certain coherence with longer-term policy objectives, thanks to their explicit two-pronged objective of increasing wealth today and productivity tomorrow (De La O, 2010, and 2012).[8] Worryingly, by closing the demand gap, CCTs also show results quickly without necessarily pushing governments to make any structural progress associated with the reform of supply-side systems (Reimers et al., 2006).

The explicit conditionality of CCTs, which ultimately establishes a contract between tax-payers and beneficiaries, is also a useful means to buy the support of the middle classes and elites, often worried about benefit 'dependency' and the 'undeserving poor'. Conditioning the transfers on the adoption of positive behaviours is more politically feasible, as it creates a sense of 'co-responsibility' (Fiszbein and Schady, 2009), thus '[making] better citizens of the poor' (Hickey, 2006: 4). Few would dare to argue against conditioning a transfer to guarantee a better future for children.

The political feasibility of CCTs and, to a lesser extent, UCTs should be considered a central aspect of their success. This has been so much the case that few programmes have managed to phase out successfully (or develop an effective graduation policy), raising concerns over the financial and fiscal sustainability of existing cash transfers. Nevertheless, such a success has paved the way for establishing national-level social protection systems for the poor, an important achievement in a context of increasing vulnerability to global economic and climatic shocks.

The conditions for conditionality: a framework for feasibility assessment

The next few paragraphs will attempt to explain why, and under which conditions, CCTs and explicit conditionalities can be implemented successfully. This will be done by using some of the concepts elaborated in this article, analysing the issue from a policy design perspective first, and then from a country context perspective. Table 13.1 summarizes this framework schematically.

Policy Design

Regarding policy design, the lessons from the Latin American experience are relatively clear. In Latin America, the rationale that led to the adoption of CCTs (rather than UCTs) was linked to the solution of a specific local problem of under-accumulation of human capital among the poor, despite soaring growth rates in the aftermath of the 'lost decade' in the 1980s. At the same time, it was informed by a careful understanding of local supply and demand conditions, followed by the intention to tackle demand-side (preference-based and institution-based) barriers to access.

With the rapid expansion of cash transfers in sub-Saharan Africa (Garcia and Moore, 2012) and throughout the developing world (Gentilini et al., 2014), it is reasonable to wonder whether CCTs are the most appropriate policy option in these very different contexts.

First of all, *CCTs should rely on a clear policy objective*, as well as a set of 'desirable' and easily targetable behaviours associated with this objective. In cases where the policy objective is to relieve income poverty in a broader sense – or where the emphasis on short-term poverty reduction is stronger than that on long-term poverty reduction (e.g. an emergency context) – CCTs may not be an optimal strategy. Similarly, in situations where most households live below subsistence levels, and are incapable of satisfying basic needs, spending money on desirable behaviours becomes an additional burden on the most vulnerable households, and can effectively exclude them. As an example, these issues were considered when designing the Hunger Safety Net Programme in Kenya, where, ultimately, the choice was made to adopt a UCT targeted at the poorest households in the arid north of the country (OPM/IDS, 2011).

Second, while the 'desirable' behaviours encouraged can be very broad, *'explicit' conditions should be easy to monitor and strongly linked to final objectives (e.g. accessing a publicly provided service)*. For example, in the case of obligatory school attendance and educational outcomes, the public service and the 'desirable' behaviour tend to coincide. However, in the case of nutrition, the link between regular health checks and adequate child nutrition is less straightforward; the latter involves a broad set of changes, for instance in consumption, that cannot be effectively monitored by the provider.

Table 13.1 The conditions for conditionality: A summary

	Dimension	When are CCTs useful?	When are UCTs and other policies more suitable?
Policy Design	Clarity of policy	Clear policy objectives, set of 'desirable' and easily targetable behaviours associated with this objective	Unclear policy objectives, focus (broadly) on relieving poverty
	Linkage between 'desirable' behaviours, publicly provided service, and objectives	Clear and strong linkage between final objective (e.g. human capital accumulation) and desirable behaviour encouraged (e.g. school attendance) and service provision system (public school system)	Unclear linkage between final objective (e.g. poverty reduction) and desirable behaviour encouraged (e.g. productive investment). Unclear link between behaviour and service provision system
	Consideration of other 'mild' forms of conditionality	Analysis of relative effectiveness of the three 'mild' forms of conditioning as opposed to explicit conditionalities and realization they are ineffective for the policy objectives	Analysis of the three forms of 'mild' conditioning and realization that policy objectives can be reached through those alone
	Analysis of demand and supply of services	Detailed analysis of barriers to demand of 'desirable' goods and services, and of quality and effectiveness of supply. Existence of demand-side barriers to 'desirable' goods and services rooted in information, preferences, and power structures	Lack of analysis or thorough understanding of country-level demand and supply of public services. Most demand-side barriers to 'desirable' goods and services do not depend on information, preferences, and power structures
	Ability to fine-tune policy	Effective usage of monitoring and evaluation to fine-tune cash transfer's design to specific individual sets of constraints to maximize results	No ability or political scope for fine-tuning of the programme to maximize results
Country Context	Supply of services	Developed supply of public services, equitable distribution of services, and high quality and effectiveness of services	Undeveloped supply of services, inequitable distribution of services, and low quality and effectiveness of services
	Capacity for scaling-up of public services provision	Existing capacity for scaling-up of public services provision (due to increased demand for services)	No capacity for scaling-up of public services provision
	Poverty levels	Households live at a subsistence level and generally capable of satisfying basic needs. Spending additional money on desirable behaviours therefore less of a burden	Households live below subsistence level and incapable of satisfying basic needs. Spending money on desirable behaviours therefore an additional burden that detracts from value of benefit (effective exclusion of most vulnerable households)

	Dimension	When are CCTs useful?	When are UCTs and other policies more suitable?
Country Context	Implementation infrastructure and monitoring costs constraint	Reasonable costs involved in monitoring explicit conditions. Presence of pre-existing infrastructure that can be used to decrease costs of monitoring compliance	Budget constraints. No pre-existing infrastructure that can be used to decrease the costs of monitoring compliance
	Beneficiaries' compliance burden	Low burden on beneficiaries in monitoring their compliance (e.g. streamlined system for verifying attendance through schools, etc.). No severe budget constraints (CCTs more expensive to implement)	High burden on beneficiaries in monitoring their compliance (e.g. families having to provide certificates and incur travel costs to prove compliance)
	Political feasibility	Middle class opposed to cash transfers to poor households unless some form of co-responsibility is ensured	Weak middle class and strong focus on creating a safety net for the poorest households

Third, *the distinction between hard and soft conditionality is blurred in practice.* If some conditioning is needed, behavioural change can be achieved by combining conditions on access, on the means (implicit conditioning), and some sort of contract between recipient and provider on the use of resources (indirect conditioning or explicit conditionality). The level of formality of such a contract, for example, whether to introduce and enforce explicit penalties, depends on the local institutional context.

Fourth, the *rationale for implementing CCTs should be based on a detailed analysis of the barriers to demand for 'desirable' goods and services, as well as the traditional analysis of the quality and effectiveness of supply.* Barriers to investment in 'desirable' goods or services can be very heterogeneous. CCTs can be an option to raise sub-optimal levels of consumption/investment in 'desirable' goods and services when demand-side barriers are rooted in information, preferences, and power structures.

Fifth, *CCTs should be encouraged if there is the political will and capacity to fine-tune the programme to the specific conditions of, or barriers faced by, different beneficiaries.* CCTs work on preferences and institutions. These are, by definition, difficult to gauge, and can only be fully effective if the conditions are calibrated properly. In order to do this, the programme needs to be willing to engage in constant monitoring and evaluation that can direct policy towards best practices. For instance, once again in the field of education, incremental subsidy schemes in Colombia and Mexico that increase the value of the transfer for every additional grade attended have proven effective in ensuring continued school attendance.

Country context

A second set of considerations relates to the institutional context of a country or region that chooses to undertake a poverty-reduction strategy involving CCTs. The Latin American region stands out as one where many pre-conditions are satisfied, but this should be carefully assessed in other contexts, especially sub-Saharan Africa.

First of all, an essential prerequisite for the effective implementation of CCTs is the *presence of an adequate supply of public services*. Policy interventions aimed at stimulating the demand for services are based on the assumption that these services are of a satisfactory quality, and hence are 'desirable' from the beneficiaries' standpoint. However, this is often not the case (Schubert and Slater, 2006). At a micro level, conditioning a programme on non-existent, or low-quality, services can be extremely counterproductive. It not only excludes those most marginalized from the transfer, but can also create a perverse incentive that forces households to embark on an investment that is 'unprofitable' compared to other market alternatives. From a macro point of view, then, spending public money on CCTs may not be the most effective use of resources when basic services still need to be developed (Reimers et al., 2006).

Second, it should be pointed out that the *capacity for scaling up these public services, and maintaining quality*, is also an important prerequisite because, even if there is an adequate supply of public services at present, CCTs may, in themselves, put additional pressure on existing services.

Third, in contexts of *generalized poverty*, where households live below subsistence levels, spending money on 'desirable' behaviours is an additional burden that detracts from the value of the benefit, leading to an effective exclusion of the most vulnerable households.

Fourth, the cost-effectiveness of explicit conditionalities, compared to other types of conditioning, depends on the *public and private costs of monitoring and enforcing compliance with explicit conditionalities in CCTs*, a cost that is not faced with UCTs. The additional public cost can either be sustained in the absence of any severe budget constraints, or in the presence of pre-existing infrastructure/human capital that can be used to take on this role, for example, a network of social assistants or well-administered health centres. The private cost – the burden on beneficiaries of proving their compliance – can be lowered by streamlining the certification process, or shifting the burden to institutions (e.g. schools) rather than households. Only countries with the physical and institutional capacity to meet these two objectives can pursue CCTs without the concern of incurring problems at a later stage of implementation (Schubert and Slater, 2006).

Finally, linked to the point above, the *political feasibility* of imposing explicit conditionalities *will depend on the relative power of the middle class within a given country, and the overall political orientation of governments* (and the donor community). In countries where providing a safety net for the poorest and most vulnerable households is viewed as a 'right' to be guaranteed, and the middle classes do not have too much political clout, it is unlikely that imposing explicit conditionalities will be deemed as acceptable, necessary, or feasible, and vice versa.

Conclusions

The success of CCTs is demonstrated by their rapid spread worldwide. Initially focused in the Latin American region, many other developing countries – including within sub-Saharan Africa – have developed flagship programmes. The basic model, moreover, has been gradually extended to include an increasing number of 'desirable' behaviours by conditioning the delivery of cash on the use of other social services. In India, for example, cash transfers are paid to mothers who deliver in hospitals, while in Tanzania and Lesotho a CCT scheme has been designed to tackle the HIV/AIDS pandemic. But does one size fit all? And if not, what are the conditions under which CCTs can be successful?

As shown in this chapter, cash transfers (including UCTs) and many other public interventions share three forms of behavioural conditioning that can also be used to achieve desirable outcomes: conditioning on access; implicit conditioning; and indirect conditioning. What defines the nature of CCTs is the presence of additional, explicit conditionalities within the 'contract' between provider and recipient. When trying to understand under what conditions CCTs are effective, it is therefore the value this additional form of conditionality adds that should be examined.

It is important to recognize that conditionality is a multidimensional concept that can be implemented to many different degrees. While UCTs and CCTs often share various forms of behavioural conditioning, they mainly differ in the way the contract between provider and recipient is framed: for CCTs, the payment of the cash is contingent upon the adoption of a set of 'desired' behaviours which are explicitly monitored, while for UCTs, recipients are generally left with more formal freedom to spend their transfers.

There are two main implications stemming from this distinction. First, a comparative assessment of CCTs and UCTs should be based on the relative benefits as well as costs of introducing, monitoring, and enforcing this 'explicit' contract. Second, countries wishing to adopt CCTs should carefully consider their feasibility based on overall priorities for policy design and also institutional context. The success of CCTs in Latin America was precisely linked to an assessment of this type, that is, a clear policy objective to address problems of low human capital and a thorough understanding of supply and demand for key services such as education. But it was also grounded in a specific political economy environment in which the argument of co-responsibility had a receptive audience. If sub-Saharan Africa countries and elsewhere want to reap the benefits of CCTs, they should first understand whether similar conditions apply to them, and decide accordingly.

Notes

1. See, for example, Case and Deaton (1998), Duflo (2003), Case et al. (2005), Agüero et al. (2006), Edmonds (2006), Schady and Araujo (2006), Paxson and Schady (2007), Schady and Rosero (2008), and Edmonds and Schady (2012).
2. Schüring, who explores similar issues in a different framework, calls this 'ex ante conditionality' (Schüring, 2010).
3. Schüring (2010) and Schubert and Slater (2006) refer to this as 'indirect conditionality' – influencing household behaviour through the choice of implementation modalities.
4. This supports the robust empirical finding that the income elasticity of education for poor households is generally low (Behrman and Knowles, 1999).
5. It should be noted that the 2010 version of the same paper, based on self-reported data rather than school-level data, corroborated exactly the opposite result. This shift in results, due to a radical change in methodology, was extensively criticized in a working paper by Kidd and Calder (2012).
6. Based on estimates provided by the management of *Familias en Acción* in Colombia, in 2008, the programme devotes roughly 0.5 per cent of its total budget (including transfer costs) to the monitoring of 'explicit conditions', while it spends on average between 2.5 per cent and 5 per cent of the budget on administration and operation costs, and about 2 per cent on transfer 'delivery' costs and bank commissions.
7. In situations where service provision systems are structurally weak (sub-investment, saturation, insufficiency of infrastructure, etc.), explicit conditions on cash transfers may simply not be feasible, at least not until investments to expand supply capacity have been undertaken. Not only would CCTs put more pressure than UCTs on already fragile service delivery systems, but they would have very perverse incentives in regard to equity – that is, the exclusion of those who cannot access services or would not constitute a 'credible threat', because the explicit conditions would be, in practice, impossible to meet for many.
8. Evidence from Mexico's *Progresa* shows that long-term enrolment in the programme led to an increase in turnout of 7 per cent, and an increase in incumbent vote share of 16 per cent in the 2000 presidential election.

References

Agüero, J.M., Carter, M.R. and Woolard, I. (2006) 'The impact of unconditional cash transfers on nutrition: The South African child support grant', *SALDRU Working Paper Series Number 06/08*. Southern Africa Labour and Development Research Unit, University of Cape Town, Cape Town.

Akresh, R., de Walque, D. and Kazianga, H. (2013) 'Cash transfers and child schooling: Evidence from a randomized evaluation of the role of conditionality', *Policy Research Working Paper 6340*. World Bank, Washington, DC <http://dx.doi.org/10.1596/1813-9450-6340>.

Attanasio, O., Battistin, E., Fitzsimons, E., Mesnard, A. and Vera-Hernandez, M. (2005) 'How effective are conditional cash transfers? Evidence from Colombia', *IFS Briefing Note No. 54*. Institute for Fiscal Studies, London <http://dx.medra.org/10.1920/bn.ifs.2005.0054>.

Ayala Consulting (2003) *Conditional Cash Transfer Programs (CCTs): Operational Experiences. Final Report Prepared for the World Bank*. Ayala Consulting, Quito.

Baird, S., McIntosh, C. and Özler, B. (2010) 'Cash or condition? Evidence from a randomized cash transfer program', *Policy Research Working Paper 5259*. World Bank, Washington, DC <http://dx.doi.org/10.1596/1813-9450-5259>.

Baird, S., Ferreira, F.H.G., Özler, B. and Woolcock, M. (2013) 'Relative effectiveness of conditional and unconditional cash transfers for schooling outcomes in developing countries: A systematic review', *Campbell Systematic Reviews, 2013:8*. The Campbell Collaboration, Oslo.

Barrientos, A. and de Jong, J. (2006) 'Reducing child poverty with cash transfers: A sure thing?' *Development Policy Review* 24(5): 537–52 <http://dx.doi.org/10.1111/j.1467-7679.2006.00346.x>.

Benhassine, N., Devoto, F., Duflo, E., Dupas, P. and Pouliquen, V. (2013) 'Turning a shove into a nudge? A "labeled cash transfer" for education', *NBER Working Paper No. 19227*. National Bureau of Economic Research, Cambridge, MA <http://dx.doi.org/10.3386/w19227>.

Behrman, J. and Knowles, J. (1999) 'Household income and child schooling in Vietnam', *World Bank Economic Review* 13(2): 211–56 <http://dx.doi.org/10.1093/wber/13.2.211>.

Bourguignon, F., Ferreira, F.H.G. and Leite, P. (2003) 'Conditional cash transfer, schooling, and child labor: Micro-simulating Brazil's Bolsa Escola program', *The World Bank Economic Review* 17(2): 229–54 <http://dx.doi.org/10.1093/wber/lhg018>.

Bradshaw, S. and Quirós Víquez, A. (2009) 'Even if conditionalities work, do women pay the price?' *Poverty Insights issue 80*, IDS Knowledge Services, University of Sussex, Brighton.

Britto, T. (2005) *Recent Trends in the Development Agenda of Latin America: An Analysis of Conditional Cash Transfers*. Institute for Development Policy and Management, Manchester.

Caldés, N., Coady, D. and Maluccio, J.A. (2006) 'The cost of poverty alleviation transfer programs: A comparative analysis of three programs in Latin America', *World Development* 34(5): 818–37 <http://dx.doi.org/10.1016/j.worlddev.2005.10.003>.

Case, A. and Deaton, A. (1998) 'Large cash transfers to the elderly in South Africa', *The Economic Journal* 108(450): 1330–61 <http://dx.doi.org/10.1111/1468-0297.00345>.

Case, A., Hosegood, V. and Lund, F. (2005) 'The reach and impact of Child Support Grants: Evidence from KwaZulu-Natal', *Development Southern Africa* 22(4): 467–82 <http://dx.doi.org/10.1080/03768350500322925>.

CNC (2008) *Evaluación del Programa Familias en Acción Para Población Desplazada: Informe Final*. Centro Nacional de Consultoria, Bogotá.

Coady, D. (2003) 'Alleviating structural poverty in developing countries: The approach of *Progresa* in Mexico', background paper prepared for the *World Development Report 2004*. World Bank, Washington, DC.

Coady, D., Perez, R. and Vera-Ilamas, H. (2005) 'Evaluating the cost of poverty alleviation transfer programs: An illustration based on PROGRESA in Mexico', *FCND Discussion Paper No 199*. International Food Policy Research Institute, Washington, DC.

Currie, J. and Gahvari, F. (2008) 'Transfers in cash and in-kind: Theory meets the data', *Journal of Economic Literature* 46(2): 333–83 <http://dx.doi.org/10.1257/jel.46.2.333>.

de Brauw, A. and Hoddinott, J. (2008) 'Must conditional cash transfer programs be conditioned to be effective? The impact of conditioning transfers on school enrolment in Mexico', *IFPRI Discussion Paper 00757*. International Food Policy Research Institute, Washington, DC.

de Janvry, A. and Sadoulet, E. (2004) 'Conditional cash transfer programs: Are they really magic bullets?', *ARE Update* 7(6): 9–11.

de Janvry, A., Sadoulet, E., Solomon, P. and Vakis, R. (2006) 'Uninsured risk and asset protection: Can conditional cash transfer programs serve as safety nets?', *Social Protection Discussion Paper 0604*. World Bank, Washington, DC.

De La O, A.L. (2010) 'Chapter 1: Introduction', in *The Politics of Conditional Cash Transfers*. Draft manuscript.

De La O, A.L. (2012) 'Do conditional cash transfers affect electoral behavior? Evidence from a randomized experiment in Mexico', *American Journal of Political Science* 57(1): 1–14 <http://dx.doi.org/10.1111/j.1540-5907.2012.00617.x>.

Duarte Gómez, M.B., Morales Miranda, S., Idrovo Velandia, A.J., Ochoa Marín, S.C., Bult van der Wal, S., Caballero García, M. and Hernández Ávila, M. (2004) 'Impact of *Oportunidades* on knowledge and practices of beneficiary mothers and young scholarship recipients: An evaluation of the educational health sessions', in B. Hernández-Prado and M. Hernández-Ávila (eds), *External Evaluation of the Impact of the Human Development Program Oportunidades*. National Institute of Public Health, Cuernavaca.

Duflo, E. (2003) 'Grandmothers and granddaughters: Old-age pensions and intrahousehold allocation in South Africa', *The World Bank Economic Review* 17(1): 1–25 <http://dx.doi.org/10.1093/wber/lhg013>.

Edmonds, E.V. (2006) 'Child labor and schooling responses to anticipated income in South Africa', *Journal of Development Economics* 81(2): 386–414 <http://dx.doi.org/10.1016/j.jdeveco.2005.05.001>.

Edmonds, E.V. and Schady, N. (2012) 'Poverty alleviation and child labor', *American Economic Journal: Economic Policy* 4(4): 100–24 <http://dx.doi.org/10.1257/pol.4.4.100>.

Fiszbein, A. and Schady, N. (2009) *Conditional Cash Transfers: Reducing Present and Future Poverty. A World Bank Policy Research Report*. World Bank, Washington, DC.

Garcia, M. and Moore, C.M.T. (2012) *The Cash Dividend: The Rise of Cash Transfer Programmes in Sub-Saharan Africa*. World Bank, Washington, DC <http://dx.doi.org/10.1596/978-0-8213-8897-6>.

Gentilini, U., Honorati, M. and Yemtsov, R. (2014) *The State of Social Safety Nets 2014*. World Bank, Washington, DC.

Grosh, M.E., del Ninno, C., Tesliuc, E., Oeughi, A., Milazzo, A. and Weigand, C. (2008) *For Protection and Promotion: The Design and Implementation of Effective Safety Nets*. World Bank, Washington, DC.

Hickey, S. (2006) 'The politics of what works in reducing chronic poverty. A synthesis report for the Ministry of Foreign Affairs, The Netherlands', *CPRC Working Paper 91*. Chronic Poverty Research Centre, University of Manchester, Manchester.

Hindle, S. (2004) *'Dependency, shame and belonging: Badging the deserving poor, c.1550–1750'*, Cultural & Social History 1(1): 6–35 <10.1191/1478003804 cs0003oa>.

Kakwani, N. Soares, F. and Son, H.H. (2005) 'Conditional cash transfers in African countries', *Working Paper No. 9*. United Nations Development Programme and International Poverty Centre, Brasilia.

Kidd, S. and Calder, R. (2012) 'The Zomba Conditional Cash Transfer Experiment: An assessment of its methodology', *Pathway's Perspectives, Issue No 6, September 2012*. Development Pathways, London.

Kooreman, P. (2000) 'The labeling effect of a child benefit system', *The American Economic Review* 90(3): 571–83.

Künnemann, R. and Leonhard, R. (2008) *A Human Rights View on the Potential of Social Cash Transfers for Achieving the Millennium Development Goals*. Brot für die Welt and Evangelischer Entwicklungsdienst, Stuttgart.

Musgrave, R.A. (1959) *The Theory of Public Finance: A Study of Public Economy*. McGraw-Hill, New York, NY.

OPM/IDS (2011) *Hunger Safety Net Programme: M&E Targeting Report*. Oxford Policy Management and Institute of Development Studies, Oxford and Brighton.

Özler, B. (2013) 'Defining conditional cash transfer programs: An unconditional mess', in Development Impact [blog] <http://blogs.worldbank. org/impactevaluations/defining-conditional-cash-transfer-programs-unconditional-mess> [posted 13 May 2013].

Paxson, C. and Schady, N. (2007) 'Does money matter? The effects of cash transfers on child health and development in rural Ecuador', *Policy Research Working Paper 4226*. World Bank, Washington, DC.

Regalia, F. (2006) 'Some thoughts about "conditionalities" in cash transfer programs. Lessons from Latin America and the Caribbean', paper prepared for *Learning Workshop on Orphans and Vulnerable Children and Conditional Cash Transfers*, Kenya School of Monetary Studies, Nairobi, Kenya, 20–21 February 2006.

Reimers, F., da Silva, C.D. and Trevino, E. (2006) 'Where is the "education" in conditional cash transfers in education?', *UIS Working Paper No. 4*. UNESCO Institute for Statistics, Montreal.

Robertson, L., Mushati, P., Eaton, J.W., Dumba, L., Mavise, G., Makoni, J., Schumacher, C., Crea, T., Monasch, R., Sherr, L., Garnett, J.P., Nyamukapa, C. and Gregson, S. (2013) 'Effects of unconditional and conditional cash transfers on child health and development in Zimbabwe: A cluster-randomised trial', *The Lancet* 381(9874): 1283–92 <http://dx.doi.org/ 10.1016/S0140-6736(12)62168-0>.

Saavedra, J.E. and Garcia, S. (2012) 'Impacts of conditional cash transfers on educational outcomes in developing countries: A meta-analysis', *Working Paper Series, WR-921-1*. RAND Corporation, Santa Monica, CA.

Schady, N. and Araujo, M.C. (2006) 'Cash transfers, conditions, school enrolment, and child work: Evidence from a randomized experiment in

Ecuador', *Policy Research Working Paper 3930*. World Bank, Washington, DC <http://dx.doi.org/10.1596/1813-9450-3930>.

Schady, N. and Rosero, J. (2008) 'Are cash transfers made to women spent like other sources of income?', *Economics Letters* 101(3): 246–8 <http://dx.doi.org/10.1016/j.econlet.2008.08.015>.

Schubert, R. and Slater, R. (2006) 'Social cash transfers in low-income African countries: Conditional or unconditional?', *Development Policy Review* 24(5): 571–8 <http://dx.doi.org/10.1111/j.1467-7679.2006.00348.x>.

Schüring, E. (2010) 'Conditions, conditionality, conditionalities, responsibilities – finding common ground', *Working Paper 2010WP014*. Maastricht Graduate School of Governance, Maastricht.

Thaler, E. (1990) 'Anomalies: Savings, fungibility, and mental accounts', *The Journal of Economic Perspectives* 4(1): 183–205.

Thaler, E. and Sunstein, C.R. (2009) *Nudge: Improving Decisions About Health, Wealth and Happiness*. Yale University Press, New Haven, CT.

Yoong, J., Rabinovich L. and Diepeveen S. (2012) *The Impact of Economic Resource Transfers to Women Versus Men. A Systematic Review*. EPPI-Centre, Social Science Research Unit, Institute of Education, University of London, London.

About the authors

Luca Pellerano is a development economist with experience in social protection policy design, programme implementation, and evaluation. He is a technical advisor on social security for the International Labour Organization in Southern Africa. Prior to joining the ILO Luca led the Poverty and Social Protection team at Oxford Policy Management. He has participated in the social protection reform debate in Eastern Europe, Central Asia, and sub-Saharan Africa.

Valentina Barca is a consultant in Oxford Policy Management's Poverty and Social Protection portfolio, with a research focus on how delivery systems can facilitate responsiveness and effectiveness of social protection systems. Recent areas of interest include voice and accountability mechanisms, M&E systems, integrated data and information management, and social protection in Indonesia, Moldova, Mozambique, and Zambia, as well as mixed method evaluations of different sub-Saharan African cash transfer programmes.

CHAPTER 14

Effective cash transfers for the poorest in Africa: A focus on supply capacity

Francisco Ayala

This chapter introduces the relevance of supply capacity to social safety nets, with a particular emphasis on cash transfers. This is seen as a vital step prior to implementation so as to foresee constraints and problems related to supply and demand sides that may hinder programme success and undermine such impacts as human capital formation. Also covered are the requirements for a proper supply capacity assessment, both at macro and micro levels, as complementary methodologies that allow a broad overview of geographic areas, able to cater for beneficiaries during programme implementation, and to also have an understanding of which facilities and catchment areas can be selected due to their potential available capacity. On the basis of international evidence and lessons learnt, options are provided for authorities to employ based on local conditions and programme objectives, such as mitigation interventions, in order to address supply-side issues and limitations that prevent the underuse of services by beneficiaries. Likewise, the chapter explains how supply capacity assessments, on a large scale, can benefit from operational and IT instruments assistance, and how they play a crucial role in social safety net planning.

Keywords: cash transfers, social safety nets, supply capacity, micro and macro assessment, programme constraints

Introduction

Programme effectiveness is greater in contexts where social safety nets (SSNs) are complemented by supply-side policies that support infrastructure and service quality. Especially in low-income countries supply constraints can be a significant limitation, and represent one of the main challenges for anti-poverty policy (Barrientos and Niño-Zarazúa, 2011). Supply capacity (SC) is of special relevance for conditional cash transfer (CCT) programmes, in that, as transfers of benefits are linked to compliance of co-responsibilities, beneficiaries usually need to attend compliance institutions such as schools, health centres, and so forth. These, in turn, have to now cope with increased demand generated by the SSN programme. In this sense, the analysis of SC aims to verify whether such service units will be able to cater for the number of beneficiaries expected. Without this previous analysis,

http://dx.doi.org/10.3362/9781780448435.014

the programme cannot ensure that beneficiaries will satisfactorily comply with co-responsibilities.

CCT programmes are often a response to the perceived failure of traditional supply-side interventions to effectively reach the poor. Although CCT programmes can provide incentives for using services, they are not a substitute for the provision of quality supply-side investments, nor are they designed to address supply-side issues (Rawlings, 2004). SC assessments (SCAs), prior to programme design and implementation, have been recognized as a vital aspect to consider before selection of eligible communities.

The objectives of this chapter are: (1) to enable practitioners to have an understanding of SC, SCA methods, and how to implement them; and (2) to demonstrate through evidence-based readings, case studies, and lessons learnt in the field that SCAs shall become an indispensable aspect to consider in SSN design, and that they should constitute an integral part of its project cycle.

The remainder of this chapter is arranged as follows: a definition of SC is presented, which is then situated in the context of SSNs; the subsequent section deals with the objective, and importance, of SCAs, and which methodologies can be used to carry them out, including how design and implementation should be planned; this is followed by illustrating strategies for coping with SC constraints; case studies and best practices of SCAs in selected countries of Africa are then presented, including limitations faced, and solutions found to cope with SC challenges; the conclusion draws lessons from SCAs, and how supply and demand sides should be seen as complementary.

Supply capacity defined

SC refers to the ability of facilities needed to successfully implement an SSN programme. Facilities encompass social services establishments (generally health and education) that are linked to the programme by acting as compliance institutions, but also other key entities such as transfer agencies (post offices, banks, district councils, etc.) and non-governmental organizations/training centres that function either as monitoring/supervision and/or as capacity-building units.

SC is adequate when facilities meet the following requirements:

1. **Availability** refers to the presence of relevant facilities in a certain geographic area that will provide the service to beneficiaries of the SSN intervention.
2. **Capacity** represents the ability of individual service providers to absorb potential (increased) demand resulting from the implementation of the SSN. The available capacity is measured through a simple formula comparing maximum capacity (based on current number of personnel) with expected levels of enrolment.
3. **Accessibility** refers to the physical access, or reachability, of services that meet a minimum standard. Comprehensive measurement of access requires a systematic assessment of physical, financial, and

socio-psychological access to services. Estimates of physical access use travel time (and costs), rather than distance.

4. **Quality** refers to whether the available facilities meet a minimum quality standard, are safe, and possess the basic equipment and materials needed to provide their services efficiently and effectively. For instance, when referring to health centres, this includes drugs and commodities, beds, utensils, and guidelines for treatment, among others (WHO, 2008).

This chapter places its emphasis on supply capacity in terms of health and education facilities. The following section contextualizes SC as a fundamental aspect of SSNs.

Supply capacity in the context of social safety nets

The concept of SC is of crucial relevance in the context of SSNs. While social transfers can promote access to basic services by increasing household income and therefore, overcome the direct and indirect costs of services, problems associated with the supply of services can be a significant constraint to households' utilization of these same services.

Furthermore, SSNs not only affect the demand for services, but their implementation also contributes, directly and indirectly, to improvements on the supply side. Successful SSN programmes need to possess a clear role within a broader social policy agenda in order to ensure quality service provision. In this context, an effective coordination between both demand and supply sides is required (Grosh et al., 2008).

Whatever financing is available, and whatever systems and procedures are in place, there has to be the absorptive capacity within all types of facilities involved in the SSN programme implementation for the programme to be successful. SC is of particular importance in the context of CCT programmes, i.e. cash programmes that are linked to the compliance of conditions. CCT programmes alone will not be capable of interrupting the intergenerational cycle of poverty if the quality of health clinics and schools is inadequate, or no jobs or adequate livelihoods are available when assisted children become earners in their own right (Grosh et al., 2008).

Supply capacity assessment

The concept of a SCA is relatively novel, but has proven extremely important for successful programme design by allowing better planning (Ayala Consulting Group, 2014). Although SCA has been recognized as a particularly important step for the successful implementation of CCTs, agencies, consultants, and programme managers have failed to make that step and/ or to apply the correct methodology. SCAs must be undertaken at the macro and micro levels; however, authorities and donors have been content with assessments at the macro level only. This type of assessment is insufficient in that engaging a micro-level assessment is also required, especially in areas or countries where the service is very uneven in terms of coverage (urban versus remote areas) and also quality. Whatever criteria are used to select programme implementation areas – census, poverty maps, or other means – they must also pass through the SCA filter.

From a macro perspective, government agencies and consultants tend to execute a macro analysis of SC as part of feasibility studies. This is an assessment at the national or regional level, and its main objective is to identify large geographic areas, typically divided into political units (states, departments, districts, municipalities, and the like), that have a general ability to sustain SSN interventions. Specifically, the aim is to estimate the areas of a country with better conditions for the implementation of a transfer programme by drawing upon national- and/or regional-level statistics and other information for calculating the expected demand of services and the SC needed to satisfy the expected demand.

International evidence over the years has demonstrated that macro SCAs are insufficient in determining SSN programme feasibility and effectiveness within a given area, particularly in low-income countries. Macro analysis is advantageous when looking to provide some preliminary information in terms of possible size and coverage of the programme. If macro assessment results are positive (favourable for the specific purpose of the programme), the programme may be implemented in a given geographic area, but not necessarily in all parts of that geographic area. Therefore, in order to decide in which specific sub-areas the SSN can be implemented, it is also necessary to apply a more precise micro assessment.

Results obtained from the micro-level SCA provide SSN programmes with information on the availability (coverage), accessibility (catchment areas), capacity (resources, personnel, etc.), and quality of services (infrastructure, etc.). This information is essential in determining individual institutions' capacity to treat and service programme beneficiaries, and, thus, which institutions are eligible for inclusion in the programme. SCA outcomes are also decisive in defining which communities should be included in the targeting process, and, to a broader extent, this process defines the catchment areas where it is feasible for the programme to be implemented.

Despite the recognized necessity of undertaking SCAs before selecting programme beneficiaries, evidence has shown that most of the SSN programmes are routinely designed and implemented without assessing coverage, accessibility, and infrastructure of transfer agencies and/or centres where co-responsibilities will be monitored (Ayala Consulting Group, 2014). The result is that the micro SCA is usually not executed. Micro analysis gained prominence as a tool to assess available supply within smaller areas. This approach consists of asking each social service institution to provide specific information, which is utilized in calculating its current available capacity, and its future capacity after the SSN is implemented. Those service units mainly responsible know best the reality of working conditions, permitting the possibility of obtaining more precise, accurate, and updated information. Nonetheless, high costs of

Table 14.1 Micro vs macro analysis

	Advantages	Disadvantages and risks
Micro analysis	• Real-time information • Information on restricted geographic areas • Can be tailored to SSN needs • Identification of previously unknown providers or closed providers	• Labour-intensive • Time-consuming • Cooperation of service providers needed to obtain data
Macro analysis	• Supply of first overview during planning stage • Identification of geographic areas with general ability to sustain effective implementation • Projection of expected results vs resources available/required	• Incomplete information • Outdated data • No information about service providers with no available capacity

reviewing the conditions of all service providers within a given overall service provider (e.g. health service providers including public and private posts, health centres, health clinics, health hospitals, etc.), make it difficult to carry out a comprehensive micro SCA.

Table 14.1 summarizes the advantages and disadvantages of micro and macro analysis.

Ideally, if resources are available, both methodologies should be combined. The macro analysis will provide a first overview of the broader geographic areas with a general ability to sustain programme implementation. The results can then guide a micro analysis that enables the selection of facilities and catchment areas where a programme can be effectively implemented, thus providing detailed, updated, and tailored information needed for the specific purposes of the SSN programme.

We now briefly focus on how an SCA is designed and carried out for both macro and micro analysis, before providing a country case study review.

Micro analysis and application to the health and education sectors

For implementation to be successful, the programme must be clear about the available budget, and organize logistics, staff, and fieldwork accordingly. Then, a logistic plan has to be formulated that includes transport, materials needed, mapping of service units to be visited, and so forth. Personnel involved in both fieldwork and data analysis must be trained and allocated to the different geographic areas where service units are to be assessed, before establishing the available capacity of possible facilities (Ayala, 2010).

Moreover, using an automated IT system allows for easier mapping, clustering, and organization of data, and, consequently, better analysis. In this context, social protection terminology introduced the term 'catchment area', which corresponds to the geographic areas that can be served by the

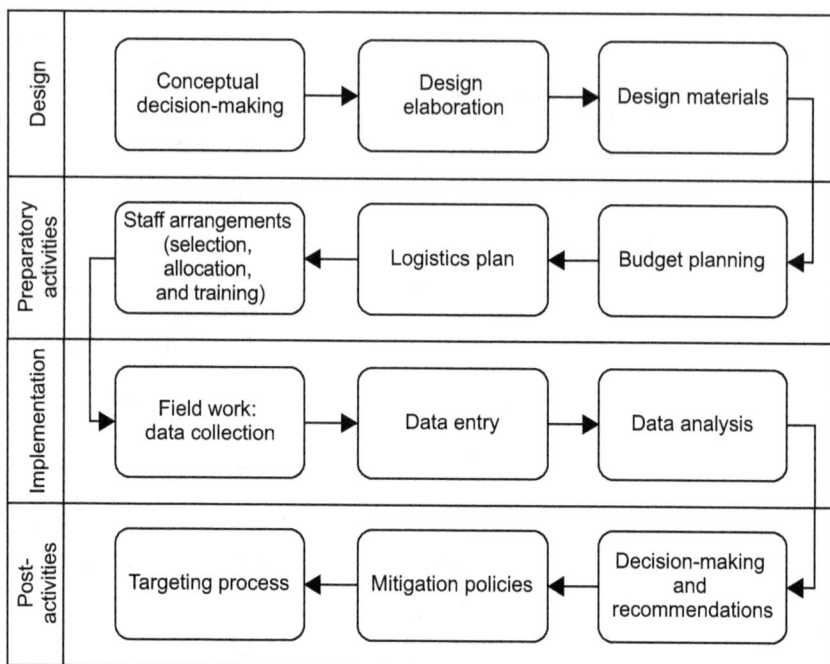

Figure 14.1 Supply capacity assessment: Design and implementation

respective service provider, taking the following into account: (1) maximum radius considering reasonable distance/time/costs that beneficiaries can afford to cover; and (2) capacity and quality of service facility. Catchment area maps help to better visualize which institutions are eligible, and which geographic areas can be served by facilities and, therefore, by the programme. Figure 14.1 illustrates the overall design and implementation process, including preparatory and post activities.

Undertaking a micro assessment of both health and education facilities first requires identification of those health/education facilities that could become potential service providers of the SSN programme. Following this, the scope of assessment is delimited, i.e. defining which characteristics are to be measured within the SCA, in addition to availability: capacity; accessibility; and/or quality. SSN programmes with co-responsibilities must necessarily include capacity and accessibility in order to identify eligible catchment areas.

In terms of capacity, health/education workforce (number of working hours, duty days, and maximum patients/students to assist) and real demand, at least in the last three months, need to be taken into consideration for calculating: current available capacity; the difference between the full capacity of the service provider given the current workforce; and the current real demand. Then, the additional demand is calculated, which is the extra demand expected due to the incentives/penalties established in the CCT programme. As a result, the potential available capacity is calculated as follows:

potential available capacity = full current capacity – real current demand – extra demand due to the cash incentives/penalties of the CCT programme

If the potential available capacity is positive, the service provider and its catchment area are qualified. On the contrary, if the potential available capacity is negative, the service provider is not ready for the new programme. Government authorities are unable to produce quick solutions; they tend to promise solutions for the next fiscal period when financial resources are available. The same happens if donors are funding the improvements, whereas solutions, in the form of adding personnel or infrastructure, take some time. Because of these realities, programme authorities have two options: (1) not to include these catchment areas at all in the programme until improvements are made; or (2) start with unconditional transfers in the meantime. Decisions are made upon the local conditions and overall objectives of the programme.

In terms of quality of service, health facility SCAs include information on infrastructure and equipment availability, as well as condition of the facility (e.g. quality and condition of building; walls, floor, roof, and materials used). In addition, it is important to understand the status of service delivery (drug supply, equipment, and commodities/quality of teaching, etc.). With this information, indexes are developed to qualify the quality level of the service. For the SCA, service providers are qualified as long as they pass a score considered adequate by health/education authorities. The poorer the country is, the lower the quality requirements needed to qualify as service providers.

For large programmes in which hundreds or thousands of service providers need to be assessed, operational and IT instruments are prepared and developed. If a large number of facilities is going to be assessed, it is strongly recommended to develop a management information system (MIS) module, which should be part of the MIS solution for the entire programme. Data must be collected directly from health and education providers using paper, or electronic means such as tablets or smartphones.

The key output of a health/education facility assessment is to qualify the health/education facilities as eligible, and establish the catchment area map. Upon the results of this exercise, it is possible to identify micro areas where the programme should be implemented, and areas where the programme cannot be implemented immediately. This information is shared with central and local government authorities with the aim of including these micro areas in annual development plans to expand/improve the service.

Demand and supply-side issues

SSNs will only be effective if demand-side (SSNs) and supply-side (health and education) demands are balanced and suitable for human capital formation (Grosh et al., 2008). If the results of the SCA demonstrate shortcomings when compared to the minimum characteristics established for the SSN programme at stake, mitigation interventions must be planned and designed in coordination with stakeholders, especially the government.

In order to deal with SC constraints, one strategy is to work to improve service delivery infrastructure through the SSN programme itself by including supply-side support in addition to demand-side aid (Garcia and Moore, 2012). For example, one option consists of providing fee waivers as transfer benefits, since they provide resources for institutions and access to services for poor people, and they include performance bonuses that are paid to service provider officials provided that they meet pre-established targets. Alternatively, the programme can simply establish add-on responsibilities for health and education personnel without providing any incentive (Soares and Britto, 2007).

Other strategies involve supporting communities instead of service providers to enhance supply-side, for example, when services are available but underused due to other limitations that the SSN can address.

However, clearly the decision to provide supply-side support through the funds dedicated to the SSN programme itself must be carefully weighted, considering that the aim of SSN fund allocation is to maximize funds transferred to beneficiaries, reducing administration and other costs as much as possible. Therefore, it is recommended that other alternatives be considered before deciding on supporting supply-side through the SSN programme.

Of particular concern to CCT programmes is the related lack of provision of quality services, without which CCT programme co-responsibilities run the risk of mandating the poor's use of low-quality services, binding them to ineffective service providers, and undermining the potential impact of CCT programmes on long-term welfare impacts (Rawlings, 2004). If some targeted communities fall outside the pre-calculated catchment areas, it might be a good option to apply conditions only in locations with adequate supply-side infrastructure, or in areas that receive additional supply-side investments (Garcia and Moore, 2012). As a result, conditions are not enforced when education and health centres are far from programme communities, or where close facilities do not meet the minimum requirements. Even though communities are exempted from co-responsibility compliance, it is crucial to encourage households, through community awareness campaigns, to invest in their children's education and health care whenever possible.

Case studies and best practices adopted in Africa

SSNs in Africa are less consolidated than in Europe, Asia, or Latin America due to the fact that they were introduced some decades later within this geographic region. Currently, it remains the region least covered by SSN (only 20 per cent of the poorest quintile is covered, compared to more than 50 per cent in Latin America). Furthermore, it is African countries that depend most on external financing and consultancy services in the implementation of SSNs (World Bank, 2014). Nevertheless, some African countries have identified the need to assess SC in order to cope with such shortcomings. In this context, the case of Nigeria is illustrative.

Nigeria

CCT programmes have been implemented in Nigeria through the state education sector in three northern states: Kano, Bauchi, and Katsina. While Bauchi and Katsina states were assisted by DFID and UNICEF, the Kano state was financed through the World Bank and DFID (Salman, 2013). These three cases offer significant insights into how the SCAs were implemented.

Nigeria faces several supply-side constraints. The main challenge identified in relation to cash transfers (CTs) in Nigeria was the inadequate supply of basic services (health and education). Service delivery challenges are compounded by the fact that education and health budgets are significantly lower than international best practice standards, resulting in under-qualified and under-motivated personnel combined with insufficient numbers to meet current demand.

In this context, a key question for Nigeria is whether it makes sense, given supply-side constraints beyond the cost of services, to make CTs conditional on using services. Inadequate health facilities and schools – in terms of quality of service provision and distance – are real constraints to the effectiveness of CCTs in the country. Given these challenges, service availability has often determined where CTs are implemented. CCTs for girls' education, for instance, were implemented only where beneficiaries can access donor-supported education facilities.

Nigeria's Kano pilot CCT for Girls' Education programme focuses on girls' completion of primary school or transition to junior secondary school. It was designed to test the effectiveness of the CCT programme to improve education levels, and covered approximately 300 schools and approximately 6,000 beneficiary girls. The ultimate aim was to extend the programme to cover all girls living in eligible (rural and urban) catchment areas (Holmes et al., 2012). Compliance of co-responsibilities depends on the local availability of schools (Bouchet, 2009). An SCA was undertaken as part of the project cycle, being the first process prior to targeting/registration (Ayala Consulting Group, 2011). The targeting process that followed the SCA was closely linked to the areas where schools were supported by the Education Sector Support Programme in Nigeria, so that supply-side is guaranteed (Holmes et al., 2012).

The SCA analysed capacity and accessibility using the following specific criteria (Ayala Consulting Group, 2011):

- Location within one of the 12 government-supported local government areas (LGAs).
- Existence of a school-based management committee.
- Grade 4, grade 5, and grade 6 are taught at the school.
- Number of pupils per classroom:
    - Rural location: current pupil-to-classroom ratio is ≤ 60 pupils;
    - Urban location: current pupil-to-classroom ratio is ≤ 90 pupils.[1]

In addition, schools with higher dropout rates had a higher chance of being selected. The information gathered was then put into an MIS, and 300 schools were chosen in accordance with the eligibility criteria. In terms of design, the programme unit included, as beneficiaries, girls who were already attending those schools and girls who had previously dropped out. It was assumed that schools that underwent Education Sector Support Programme intervention were going to pass the SCA very easily; nonetheless, the results indicated that a third of them failed to meet the above criteria.

Similar exercises were undertaken in Katsina and Bauchi. The SCA was carried out in nearly 600 schools, with 160 included in the programme. The criteria utilized to assess 'school readiness' were mostly similar to Kano's procedures. Schools excluded during the first SCA then had the opportunity to improve their situation through work by stakeholders. A second SCA was then undertaken to determine if some of the previously excluded schools could then be included.

In Nigeria, SCAs have increasingly held a key role in SSN planning. As social protection has developed in Nigeria, so has the focus on improving service delivery, in part because of the focus on the Millennium Development Goal (MDG) that links the two. In spite of this, there has been a more recent recognition that focusing on the supply of services has been inadequate in reaching the poor, and that there also needs to be a simultaneous focus on addressing the barriers that the poorest face in accessing services (Holmes et al., 2012).

An additional constraint is that Nigeria's social-sector expenditure remains very low, which again impedes potential scale-up and expansion of social protection. Consequently, synchronized investment in the supply side of social (health, education, etc.) and economic (financial infrastructure) services will be essential to maximize the effectiveness of SSN programmes (Holmes et al., 2012).

In short, the three pilot programmes implemented in the northern states were significantly scaled back due to SCAs. About half of the original schools estimated for the programme passed the SCA. Even in places where a specific programme was seeking to improve the conditions of schools, a third of those schools could not pass the test. This uneven situation in countries such as Nigeria shows how the SCA at micro level is essential in identifying areas where a programme can be executed, while a macro-level assessment is not relevant under these conditions.

Conclusions and outlook

Evidence-based knowledge has underlined the importance of undertaking SCAs, first to determine whether institutions are able to cope with a demand increase resulting from programme implementation, and, therefore, if a programme is feasible in a given geographic area. In the case of CCT programmes, SCA assists in determining whether conditions can be applied, and to what extent.

When undertaken, the SC level ideally must be examined with respect to availability, accessibility, quality, and capacity. Local governments and respective institutions must be involved from the beginning of the programme in activities ranging from evaluating the capacity of local schools and health facilities, to meeting increased demands for social services (International Initiative for Impact Evaluation, n.d.). Sharing the results of the analysis with local governments is therefore of crucial importance. Likewise, potential beneficiary communities should be informed of the results to ensure transparency and given justification regarding why some communities can participate in the programme and others not, as well as why some beneficiaries must comply with co-responsibilities while others will be exempted from compliance.

SCAs also help to decide if an SSN is feasible, and whether an unconditional cash transfer (UCT) or a CCT programme better fits in the area where the programme is meant to be implemented. The addition of a conditionality does not necessarily stimulate better programme performance. Whether or not the provision of quality health and education services should be a pre-requisite in the implementation of a CCT programme is inconclusive, as this can deprive poor populations living in remote areas from social assistance. On the other hand, conditioning transfers where services are of poor quality and ineffective brings little hope for anticipated welfare impacts. In these cases, alternative coping strategies should be envisaged. This is more critical in low-income countries where government institutions are weak, and where supply-side challenges in both education and health are common.

Skipping SCAs can engender high non-compliance of co-responsibilities because beneficiaries live too far from facilities and, therefore, may not receive benefits. The case of Nigeria shows that less than 50 per cent of the schools were qualified to participate in the programme. In fact, only about 30 per cent of the communities were included in the CCT programme. The remaining 70 per cent of communities neither had a service provider at hand (or the available capacity was null) nor was the quality of the service efficient. Nevertheless, the three states above undertook CCT programmes. After the SCA, authorities had a better idea of those places and areas where they needed to invest to improve and/or expand services.

However, solutions to cope with SC limitation should not be restricted to mere short-term improvisations to reach the immediate objective of ensuring that beneficiaries can comply with a programme's co-responsibilities and collect their transfers. Even though the target population is critically dependent upon access to high-quality health and education services, issues of access and quality cannot be addressed permanently by UCT and CCT programmes (Rawlings, 2004). Therefore, the broader goal should be to offer, not only beneficiary communities, but also non-beneficiary communities and future generations sustainable access to quality public education and health services.

Note

1. A school is tagged as rural if its location is neither in the Kano metropolitan area nor in an LGA headquarters.

References

Ayala Consulting Group (2011) *Republic of Nigeria: Kano State Pilot CCT for Girls' Education: CCT GE Report*. Ayala Consulting Group, Quito.

Ayala Consulting Group (2014) *Gaps and Challenges in Social Protection: From Knowledge for Design to Tools for Implementation*. Ayala Consulting Group, Quito.

Ayala, F. (2010) *For Protection and Promotion: The Design and Implementation of Effective Social Safety Nets – Livelihood Empowerment Against Poverty Program (LEAP)* [online]. Available from: http://siteresources.worldbank.org/ SAFETYNETSANDTRANSFERS/Resources/281945-1131468287118/1876750-1282583453267/Ayala_Ghana_case_2nd-Session_12-9-2010.pdf

Barrientos, A. and Niño-Zarazúa, M. (2011) *Social Transfers and Chronic Poverty: Objectives, Design, Reach and Impact.* Chronic Poverty Research Centre, Manchester.

Bouchet, B. (2009) *Kano State Pilot CCT for Girls' Education: Operations Manual, Version 1.0.* Nairobi: Federal Republic of Nigeria.

Garcia, M. and Moore, C. (2012) *The Cash Dividend: The Rise of Cash Transfer Programs in Sub-Saharan Africa.* World Bank, Washington, DC.

Grosh, M., del Ninno, C., Tesliuc, E. and Ouerghi, A. (2008) *For Protection and Promotion: The Design and Implementation of Effective Safety Nets.* World Bank, Washington, DC.

Holmes, R., Akinrimisi, B., Morgan, J. and Buck, R. (2012) *Social Protection in Nigeria: Mapping Programmes and Their Effectiveness.* Overseas Development Institute, London.

International Initiative for Impact Evaluation (n.d.) *Evaluating the Effectiveness of a Community-Based Conditional Cash Transfer Program in Tanzania: Policy Influence Plan.* International Initiative for Impact Evaluation, Washington, DC.

Rawlings, L.B. (2004) *A New Approach to Social Assistance: Latin America's Experience with Conditional Cash Transfer Programs.* World Bank, Washington, DC.

Salman, K.K. (2013) *Impact Evaluation of Conditional Cash Transfer (CCT) Programme on Girl-Child School Enrolment, Attendance and Completion in Kano State, Nigeria* [online]. Available from: www.agrodep.org/sites/default/files/ annualmeeting/Seed_Salman_KK_final.pdf

Soares, F.V. and Britto, T. (2007) 'Confronting capacity constraints on conditional cash transfers in Latin America: The cases of El Salvador and Paraguay', *International Poverty Centre Working Paper No. 38.* International Poverty Centre and United Nations Development Programme, Brasilia.

WHO (2008) *Service Delivery: Toolkit on Monitoring Health Systems Strengthening.* World Health Organization, Geneva.

World Bank (2014) *The State of Social Safety Nets 2014.* World Bank, Washington, DC.

About the author

Francisco Ayala developed this chapter in collaboration with Ayala Consulting Corporation staff, based in the USA and Ecuador. He has worked on the design, implementation, coordination, and assessment of SSNs, including UCTs and CCTs in more than 35 countries worldwide over the last 18 years. The firm has provided technical assistance in such areas as the design of methodologies for the formulation, appraisal, and supervision of projects, including SCAs.

CHAPTER 15

Access to justice for the very poorest and marginalized in Uganda

Adam Dubin and David Lawson

As we have seen throughout this volume, some policies and programmes in sub-Saharan Africa (SSA) have positively contributed in various forms to reductions in chronic poverty and marginalization. While in no way seeking to take away from these policies' substantial role in combating poverty, this chapter suggests that of equal importance, and often overlooked by social scientists without a juridical background, is the critical role of promoting rule of law through the expansion of access to justice policies in order to reduce chronic poverty and marginalization, and increase empowerment. Uganda, perhaps more than any other SSA country, provides a unique country case study due to having had significant poverty analysis undertaken and having achieved remarkable success in reducing poverty over the last two or three decades. However, and despite such success, there remains relatively little understanding of how access to justice can impact on the poorest in Uganda. We therefore provide a unique case study to highlight the intersection between poverty, empowerment, and justice, and demonstrate the need for greater integration of justice policies into broader pro-poor programming.

Keywords: access to justice, empowerment, marginalized, extreme poverty, Uganda

Introduction: justice, poverty, and empowerment: inter-related, inter-dependent

Access to justice is a key policy component associated with escaping poverty, and is a broad term that 'cuts a large swath' concerning what exactly it refers to (Mosher, 2008: 808). It is defined by the World Bank as 'access by the people, particularly the poorest and most disadvantaged, to fair, effective and accountable mechanisms for the protection of rights, control of abuse of power and resolution of conflicts' (World Bank, 2007: 1).[1] While there is no estimate as to how many people fall into the broad category of those lacking access to justice, it is reasonable to argue that most of the poor in some way lack some form of access to justice mechanisms.

Legal practitioners and academics often conceptualize access to justice as ranging from access to formal justice mechanisms for dispute resolution, such

http://dx.doi.org/10.3362/9781780448435.015

as the courts, to substantive conceptions of social justice to broader secondary categories of justice, including the ability to access health care, education, and social services. It can also refer to informal justice, which is often the most common route of justice-seeking since it is affordable and most accessible to the poor and marginalized, though it does raise questions concerning its effectiveness and fairness, particularly for females.

Access to justice is guaranteed as a right under such treaties as the Universal Declaration of Human Rights.[2] It is also guaranteed under many domestic legislative documents, such as those found in most African countries.[3] Despite its guarantee as a fundamental right, the chronically poor and marginalized often find it difficult to achieve justice. In many countries, access to justice is a 'commodity' that is more easily obtained by the economically advantaged than the poor and marginalized, who often lack the financial capacity, know-how, and ability to access basic legal services (Dias and Welch, 2011).

However, this lack of access to justice implies more than just the violation of human rights; it also has consequences for development and poverty alleviation, and is closely aligned with questions of individual and community empowerment, and the ability, as Amartya Sen (1999) points out, to exercise freedoms. To highlight this interconnection, take the example of access to justice and maternal mortality. As we have seen in Chapter 4, statistics clearly demonstrate that maternal deaths are more concentrated in sub-Saharan African (SSA) countries than other developing countries; for example, we saw that an African woman's lifetime risk of dying from pregnancy-related causes, in 2010, is 100 times higher than a woman in a developed country (Ado-Kofie and Lawson, this volume). Commonly, there is no domestic legal remedy for someone who has been denied maternal health care to enforce this right through the country's court system, unless the court is willing to accept international law. This is particularly problematic for the poor and marginalized, who are not only most at risk of falling ill, but who also have the least access to health care services.

This chapter commences by discussing the interconnection between access to justice, poverty, and pro-poor policy, before providing a case study of Uganda, and in particular how Justice Centres have created access for the poorest. We find that Justice Centres Uganda (JCU) have been an important breakthrough in providing many of the necessary resources, both human and financial, in widening access to justice for the poor. However, access to justice programmes needs to develop further and 'cut across' government and civil society agencies to ensure coordinated and multifaceted approaches to access to justice provision, whilst simultaneously ensuring geographic availability to remote areas.

Background: interconnecting justice, poverty, and pro-poor policy

Interconnecting justice and poverty

A country's judicial system plays a central role in helping to ensure that an individual's fundamental right to maternal health is not only recognized, but also enforced. Too often, however, countries lack adequate constitutional guarantees, political willpower, or resources to uphold this right and, in many cases, even where this right exists, the poor are unable to have this right enforced due to the financial, geographical, and other constraints associated with commencing litigation and going to court (Twinomugisha, 2007).

This interconnectedness between poverty and access to justice has increasingly been recognized as a central and essential aspect of development policy. In his speech to the United Nations General Assembly, James Goldston, Executive Director of the Open Society, asserted that justice policies are equally as important to development as other, more commonly pursued policy initiatives such as education.

> In short, we now know that justice and governance are no less important to equitable and sustainable development than good schools, functioning health clinics and passable roads. (Goldston, 2014: 2)

Much to the disappointment of many working in development, however, access to justice was not included as one of the Millennium Development Goals. Notwithstanding, the United Nations has increasingly recognized access to justice as an essential component of the Goals. A report by the UN Special Rapporteur for Extreme Poverty and Human Rights noted that 'access to justice is crucial for tackling the root causes of poverty, exclusion and vulnerability' (United Nations, 2012: 3). This report highlights a number of ways in which poverty and access to justice are linked. First, it points out that the poor are inherently vulnerable and are more likely to fall victim to illegal acts and exploitation, which perpetuate their poverty and marginalization.

Second, by achieving easier access to justice, the poor have a greater opportunity to develop jurisprudence on social and economic rights whose absence or lack of enforcement oftentimes disproportionately affects the poor. Twinomugisha (2007) argues, for example, that emergency obstetric care should be considered a human right, even though it is not formally recognized in legislation. To make this a recognized right within a country, however, would require an individual or non-governmental organization (NGO) with standing to bring a case in court in front of a judge who was willing to expand currently recognized notions of socio-economic rights to include emergency obstetric care.

Third, the poor are often forced to take justice into their own hands due to exclusion from the formal justice system. This can lead to civil unrest and the unfair and unequal application of justice by informal justice mechanisms, which often are gender biased and closed off to certain groups. This has been particularly true in the case of land tenure and property rights, which can impact, positively or negatively, the ability of the poor to mitigate the effects of economic shocks by providing certain forms of sustainable livelihoods (Odeney, 2013). Land tenure and property disputes are amongst the most common problems faced by the poor, who are often powerless to defend against those with more economic power or due to gender biases in informal and formal court systems.

For example, Hallward-Driemeier and Hasan (2013) point to an example in rural Malawi, where a local village chief adjudicating a land loss claim of a female by her husband was attempting to pressure the woman into giving him the little land she had retained. Reliance on local courts, chiefs, and particularly customary law can leave females vulnerable due to a 'lack of networks, to counter unlawful land-grabbing and other breaches of their rights by local leaders' (Hallward-Driemeier and Hasan, 2013: 129).

Justice, law, and order sector: integrating justice as a pro-poor policy in Uganda

Having discussed the close intersection between access to justice and poverty, this chapter now explores Uganda's integration of access to justice policies within its anti-poverty agenda. Uganda's experience with the inclusion of JCU within a broader framework of the three-part Justice, Law, and Order Sector (JLOS) reform policy presents an important case study on an access to justice policy that has integrated a pro-poor approach to access to justice.

Uganda, located in East Africa, is classified by the World Bank as a low-income country. It has a population of approximately 37.5 million people, with an income per capita of US$788. The past two or three decades have seen relatively consistent economic growth, which has helped to reduce poverty levels and increase social indicators. Headcount poverty has fallen from 34 per cent in 2000 to 19.5 per cent in 2012 (World Bank, 2016), primary school enrolment is at nearly 100 per cent, and life expectancy since 1995 has increased by nearly 13 years, from 46 to 59.

In Uganda, the distribution of health care closely corresponds to economic well-being, in which the poor, marginalized, and geographically isolated tend to have less and poorer quality care, while the middle and upper classes, who can afford private clinics or medical care in foreign countries, have access to substantially better health care (Lawson, 2004). According to the 2011/12 Ugandan National Panel Survey (UNPS) in Uganda, 23 per cent of respondents complained of a limited range of care in public hospitals, while 22 per cent of respondents complained of long geographic distances to the closest health care clinic (UBOS, 2013: 34). Without a clear codified right within the law, or the ability to access the court system due to financial or other restraints, there is little possibility for the poor or marginalized to realize this right to maternal health and ensure the government's compliance, perpetuating a system that reinforces this interconnectedness between poverty and maternal health.

Despite some of the positive gains Uganda has made in reducing poverty and social inequality, one of the challenges it faces has been to provide access to justice for the hard-to-reach poor and marginalized communities, with extreme and persistent poverty still prevalent. In 2000, to deal with the difficulties in accessing justice, the Ugandan Government launched, under a mandate given to the Ministry of Justice and Constitutional Affairs (MOJCA) and through state and donor funding, the JLOS reform to improve rule of law and access to justice across Uganda. The concept for a sector-wide approach developed as a result of the government's Poverty Eradication Action Plan (PEAP), which was launched in 1997 with the purpose of turning Uganda into a middle-income country (MoFPED, 1997). Government and donors argued that in order to achieve this transformation, economic investment alone was not sufficient; instead, sustainable and inclusive development needed to be a priority.

There were, and continue to be, a number of problems that limit access to justice in Uganda. The Ugandan judicial sector has suffered from what are referred to as supply and demand problems. On the demand side, resulting from a lack of confidence caused by perceived corruption and ineffectiveness, Ugandans express negative sentiment towards their justice, which in turn leads to non-usage, among other problems. On the supply side, the justice system has suffered from severe backlogs of pending cases, poor enforcement mechanisms of domestic and international rights, and inadequate budget and planning for justice resources and infrastructure, all of which make it less used and less accessible (Rukare, 2008: 112).

The first part of the JLOS reform was the launch of the Strategic Investment Plan I (SIP I) in August 2000 with the goal of achieving 'the improved safety of the person, security of property and access to justice that ensures a strong economic environment to encourage economic development and benefit poor and vulnerable people' (JLOS, 2004: 6). SIP I's core objectives were to undertake criminal justice and commercial justice reform through programmes aimed at reducing court backlog, expanding trained staff, and reforming penal and commercial laws.

To align the work of the different institutions that were involved in implementing the policy, committees were created and composed of representatives from the different government institutions in order to monitor and better coordinate the improvement of rule of law in these two areas. This proved to be challenging, if not in some cases a failure, because the indicators developed to track progress were poorly designed, lacked baselines, or, in some cases, were not specific enough to determine whether real progress had been made. It did, however, help to develop some collection of data regarding case processing times and other rule of law deficiencies in the system. One evaluation of the programme points out that JLOS and SIP I were 'more a convening of institutions to share and access resources than what was intended, that is a joint working arrangement which would help address common problems' (Flew and Rynn, 2009: 8). A World Bank Report on the Ugandan legal sector points out that problems that persisted after the conclusion of SIP I included a relative lack of understanding of human rights standards, lack of efficient mechanisms to enforce judgements, lack of effective monitoring and evaluation of sector institutions, and corruption (World Bank, 2009: 19). However, despite the failing of the government institutions to achieve all their objectives, some gains were made (World Bank, 2009: 14):

- There was a reduction in the number of people held in prison in violation of their constitutional rights from 39 per cent to 1 per cent for felony crimes, and 29 per cent to 10 per cent for serious and petty offences.

- There was an increased use of alternative dispute resolution and the establishment of a tax appeals court.
- More legal professionals were available to deal with commercial disputes.
- Commercial laws were reformed.

While some gains were made by the JLOS in the first few years of this programme, the government increasingly recognized that the poor were isolated from formal justice mechanisms, and this was perpetuating a cycle of poverty and marginalization that needed to be dealt with more directly. A *Participatory Poverty Assessment on Safety, Security and Access to Justice*, conducted by JLOS in 2002, underscored the close connection between access to justice and poverty. This report, which has been one of the driving forces behind the government's attempt to expand access to justice, points out that 'the poor have not adequately utilized the formal justice dispensing systems due to expensive, cumbersome and complex procedures within the judicial processes' (Government of Uganda, 2002: 29). It goes on to note that '[t]he vast majority of study participants reiterated helplessness before justice dispensing institutions. Throughout the study it was revealed that court fees, bribes, [and] transport costs, limit the poor from accessing legal services' (Government of Uganda, 2002: 29).

In 2006 the Government of Uganda and JLOS launched a second Strategic Investment Plan (SIP II), which sought to include a stronger approach aimed at service provision for the poor. Under SIP II, there were five primary objectives aligned to the broader goal of poverty reduction and economic development: 1) to promote rule of law and due process; 2) to foster human rights culture across JLOS institutions; 3) to enhance access to justice, particularly for the poor and marginalized; 4) to reduce the incidence of crime and promote safety of the person and property; and 5) to enhance JLOS contribution to economic development (Rukare, 2008: 5). These objectives fit within the expanded scope of JLOS reform to include, in addition to the reform areas of SIP I, land and family justice. This new programme, unlike SIP I, acknowledges in more explicit terms the limitations facing the poor in accessing justice:

> Not all people in Uganda have equal access (includes availability and accessibility) to the justice system. The poor and marginalised groups still bear unreasonable burdens taking the form of physical distance to JLOS institutions, cost of access, language and attitudinal barriers and existence of conflict situations. (JLOS, 2006: 39)

Justice centres Uganda: bringing legal aid to the poor

In 2009 the government, under JLOS SIP II, launched a new programme to expand access to justice to the poor and other hard-to-reach groups. The government launched JCU, a 'one-stop shop' model to provide legal and other support services throughout Uganda. It is funded in part by the Legal

Aid Basket Fund, which provides funding through donors and supports legal aid projects. The centres are also funded through the Democratic Governance Facility, which is a multi-donor mechanism to provide funding and technical support on matters such as access to justice.

The primary work of the centres has been on issues of land disputes and human rights, including issues of gender-based violence (JCU, 2011). The centres serve not only to provide legal aid through the formal court system, but also to mediate disputes amongst parties and conduct outreach and education campaigns, including going door-to-door to educate people about their rights.

In the early period of the JCU launch, the indicators suggested that, while successful, only a handful of individuals were taking advantage of the services, which was to be expected considering the novelty of this institution. However, early on, JCUs served as an important focal point for reporting human rights abuses by the government against marginal and poor individuals. Within approximately nine months of JCUs opening, as a result of heavy outreach to communities around Uganda, the number of human rights cases reported increased from 100 near the beginning to over 300. Similarly, in the Tororo region of Uganda, from August 2010 to May 2011, JCU cases increased in the areas of land, criminal, family, civil, and commercial disputes by over 1,000 per cent in all categories (JLOS, 2012).

In recent years, the impact of JCUs has been more significant and they have reached a much wider demographic of people. According to the JLOS Annual Performance Report 2013–14 (JLOS, 2014), JCUs conducted outreach to over 160,000 individuals through visits to women's groups, schools, groups of persons with disabilities, prisons, and churches. This is more than 300 per cent over the previous year, and in addition JCUs served 8,823 walk-in clients requesting various legal and other support services (3,794 females and 5,029 males). Nearly 4,500 additional clients were served through toll-free phone lines who sought advice on legal problems, primarily dealing with land disputes. JCU has also increasingly focused on providing mediation services – a more cost-effective form of dispute resolution – to poor communities. In 2013/14, 734 disputes were resolved through mediation. JCU also provided direct legal aid to the poor through the appointment of a lawyer, with 1,322 clients using JCU advocates. The evaluation also mentioned that 'some clerks who had been ripping off unsuspecting litigants by charging them exorbitant amounts for free services have since had no business' (JLOS, 2014: 96; emphasis removed). In addition, 'the quality of legal documents filed in court has also improved with the help of professional lawyers ... This has reduced the need for numerous applications for amendment of pleadings that lengthen the already long litigation process' (JLOS, 2014: 96). Although it is difficult to quantify the impact that access to justice policies alone has on economic well-being and headcount poverty, this type of qualitative evidence suggests that many of the practices that contribute to keeping the poor in a perpetual state of poverty are, through access to justice programmes, slowly being eliminated.

In 2012/13, the JLOS launched the third phase of the SIP project (SIP III), which is set to terminate in 2017. This policy project builds on the previous two SIP projects, but includes greater targeting of vulnerable populations based on, for example, age and gender. This policy comes in recognition of continued empowerment limitations amongst certain segments of the population, particularly women, and the need to develop more specific programming to expand access to justice. JLOS is experimenting with fast-tracking adjudication processes for vulnerable populations, increased empowerment outreach to females, and increased profiling of vulnerable populations.

Conclusion: making justice local for the poorest

As through much of sub-Saharan Africa, improving access to justice in Uganda has been a slow process, and continues to face a number of obstacles such as the shortage of financial and human capital and political willpower. Nonetheless, Uganda has demonstrated recognition of the role access to justice must play in reducing headcount poverty and increasing empowerment amongst vulnerable and hard-to-reach groups. The government has integrated access to justice and judicial sector reform as centrepieces of broader programming aimed at improving economic development, and increasing empowerment amongst poor and marginal populations.

Moving forward, access to justice programmes needs to cut across government and civil society agencies to ensure coordinated and multifaceted approaches to access to justice provision, and adequate geographic availability of one-stop shops. Governments and civil society actors need to pay more attention to ways in which justice mechanisms can be extended outside of capital cities and regional hubs, particularly in regions that are geographically isolated and where strong cultural norms perpetuate disempowerment amongst certain populations. Through mobile clinics and by engaging new forms of technology, access to justice has the potential to reach across socio-economic and geographic divides, and arrive to all segments of the population. Africa has the second highest rate of mobile phone usage in the world. Increasingly, the Ugandan government and other actors should seek new ways to interconnect access to justice and technology to provide greater outreach and support for communities not yet readily served by JLOS institutions.

Another way that access to justice can move forward is through greater partnerships with law schools. Law schools have the potential to offer low-cost methods of providing access to justice to poor communities through the development of legal clinics, which allow students to provide basic justice support services to poor and marginalized communities, such as outreach and assistance with self-representation. Currently in Uganda, the only university to offer a clinic is Makerere University, through its Public Interest Law Clinic.

Furthermore, universities also have the ability to provide access to justice organizations with more multi-disciplinary personnel and students, including medical and nursing students, as well as psychology and social work students, to more directly and broadly deal with the multi-dimensionality of problems the poor and marginalized face. Also, since many of the students attending universities come from outside the capital, particularly from more rural provinces, these students could also be trained to assist locals in their home villages to help provide better access to justice mechanisms, such as village paralegals and local dispute resolution assistants.

The progress Uganda has made through its three phases of access to justice programming is laudable. While much work remains to be done and many parts of the population still suffer from an inability to adequately access the justice system, the targeted focus of Uganda's access to justice programme, through multiphase projects, has been an important step in bringing justice to historically excluded populations. Each of these phases of the JLOS has been handled under the broader remit of combating poverty and marginalization, and Uganda's JCUs have been an important breakthrough in providing many of the necessary resources, both human and financial, in widening access to justice for the poor.

Ultimately, pro-poor policies across the world need to recognize that law and economic and social development are not exclusive of each other. Rather, there is a close dependency between social and economic development and an adequately functioning legal system. Practitioners and academics implementing economic and social policies should consider the extent to which such policies could be supported by improvements to the justice system, and policy initiatives that spin off of such recognition can therefore better target the chronically poor and marginalized.

Notes

1. As stated previously, access to justice is a broad and amorphous concept, and no single definition fully captures all conceptualizations of the term. However, the World Bank access to justice definition presents a comprehensive starting point for understanding the baseline objective and significance of the term (World Bank, 2007).
2. Articles 7, 8, 9, 10, and 11, Universal Declaration of Human Rights; Article 14, International Covenant on Civil and Political Rights; Articles 2 and 3, International Covenant on Economic, Social, and Cultural Rights; Convention on the Elimination of Discrimination Against Women; Articles 3 and 18, International Convention on the Protection of the Rights of All Migrant Workers and Members of their Families; Articles 9, 12, 13, and 14, Convention Against Torture and other Cruel, Inhuman, or Degrading Treatment or Punishment; Articles 9 and 27, Convention on the Rights of the Child; Article 9, Aarhus Convention; Principles 1, 2, 3, 4, 5, 6, 7, and 10, Basic Principles on the Independence of the Judiciary; Principles 2, 3, 4, 5, 6, 7, 8, 13, 14, 19, and 21, Basic Principles on the Role of Lawyers; Guidelines 2, 10, 12, 16, 18, and 20, Guidelines on the Role of Prosecutors; Principles 4 and 8, Declaration

of Basic Principles of Justice for Victims of Crime and Abuse of Power; Article 8, Universal Declaration of Human Rights, 1948.
3. See, for example, Articles 10–12, Constitution of the Republic of Namibia, 1990 (Republic of Namibia, 2010).

References

Ado-Kofie, L. and D. Lawson (2016) 'Africa's extreme poor: Surviving early childhood', in D. Lawson, L.K. Ado-Kofie, and D. Hulme (eds), *What Works for Africa's Poorest: Poverty Reduction Strategies for Extremely Poor People*. Practical Action Publishing, Rugby.

Dias, A. and Welch, G. (eds) (2011) *Justice for the Poor: Perspectives on Accelerating Justice*. Oxford University Press India, New Delhi.

Flew, C. and Rynn, S. (2009) *Monitoring and Evaluation Arrangements for the Justice Law and Order Sector in Uganda: A Case Study*. Saferworld Research, London.

Goldston, J.A. (2014) 'Justice for development: Integrating justice and human rights into the post-2015 development framework. Remarks to the President of the General Assembly High Level Event', remarks prepared for the *Contributions of Human Rights and the Rule of Law in the Post-2015 Development Agenda*, United Nations Headquarters, New York, 10 June 2014. Available from: www.opensocietyfoundations.org/sites/default/files/goldston-unga-2015-06102014.pdf [accessed 18 January 2015].

Government of Uganda (2002) *Participatory Poverty Assessment on Safety, Security, and Access to Justice: Voices of the Poor in Uganda*. Ministry of Justice and Constitutional Affairs, Justice, Law, and Order Sector, Republic of Uganda, Kampala.

Hallward-Driemeier, M. and Hasan, T. (2013) *Empowering Women: Legal Rights and Economic Opportunities in Africa. Africa Development Forum Series*. World Bank, Washington, DC.

JCU (2011) *Mapping Trends Analysis of Key Issues in the Justice Centers Uganda Casework*. Justice Centres Uganda, Kampala.

JLOS (2004) *Strategic Investment Plan for the Medium Term, 2001–2006 (SIP I), Part II*. Justice Law and Order Sector, Republic of Uganda, Kampala.

JLOS (2006) *Strategic Investment Plan II, 2006/7–2010/11*. Justice Law and Order Sector, Republic of Uganda, Kampala.

JLOS (2012) *Monitoring and Evaluation 2011–12*. Justice Law and Order Sector, Republic of Uganda, Kampala.

JLOS (2014) *Annual Performance Report 2013/2014*. Justice Law and Order Sector, Republic of Uganda, Kampala.

Lawson, D. (2004) 'Health, poverty and poverty dynamics in Africa', paper prepared for the *IV Mediterranean Seminar on International Development*, Universitat de les Illes Balears, Palma de Mallorca, September 2004.

MoFPED (1997) *Poverty Eradication Action Plan*. Ministry of Finance, Planning, and Economic Development, Republic of Uganda, Kampala.

Mosher, J.E. (2008) 'Lessons in access to justice: Racialized youths and Ontario's safe schools', *Osgoode Hall Law Journal* 46(4): 807–51.

Odeney, M. (2013) *Improving Access to Land and Strengthening Women's Land Rights in Africa*, Annual World Bank Conference on Land and Poverty, World Bank, Washington, DC, 8–11 April.

Republic of Namibia (2010) *The Constitution of The Republic of Namibia, 1990 (as amended up to 2010)*. Government of Namibia, Windhoek.

Rukare, D. (2008) 'The access to justice challenge in Uganda', in D. Banik (ed.) *Rights and Legal Empowerment in Eradicating Poverty*. Ashgate Publishing Group, Farnham.

Sen, A. (1999) *Development as Freedom*. Oxford University Press, Oxford.

Twinomugisha, B. (2007) 'Exploring judicial strategies to protect the right of access to emergency obstetric care in Uganda', *African Human Rights Law Journal* 7(2): 283–306.

UBOS (2013) *Uganda National Panel Survey 2011/12*. Uganda Bureau of Statistics, Republic of Uganda, Kampala.

United Nations (2012) *Report of the Special Rapporteur on Extreme Poverty and Human Rights, A/67/278*. United Nations, New York, NY.

World Bank (2007) *A Framework for Strengthening Access to Justice in Indonesia*. World Bank, Washington, DC.

World Bank (2009) *Uganda: Legal and Judicial Sector Study Report*. World Bank, Washington, DC.

World Bank (2016) *World Bank Online Data: Uganda* [online]. World Bank, Washington, DC. Available from: http://data.worldbank.org/country/uganda [accessed 16 May 2016].

About the authors

Adam Dubin is an Assistant Professor of Law in the International Public Law Department of Universidad Pontificia Comillas in Madrid, Spain, and Adjunct Professor of Politics at New York University's Madrid Campus. He has published and taught extensively on topics related to access to justice and human rights in developing countries, particularly in the SSA region.

David Lawson is a Senior Lecturer in Development Economics and Public Policy at the Global Development Institute, University of Manchester. He has worked extensively on SSA and specializes in poverty dynamics in African countries.

CHAPTER 16
Conclusion

David Hulme, David Lawson,
and Lawrence Ado-Kofie

The early twenty-first century has been kinder to poor people in Africa than the late twentieth century when the 'lost decades' of the 1980s and 1990s trapped almost an entire generation in poverty. But the continent's recent prosperity has only very partially trickled down to the poor and the poorest, with the wealth created by 'Africa rising' largely captured by urban elites and offshore international businesses. The opportunities for poverty reduction that economic growth in Africa created has been only weakly realized and extreme poverty sits shoulder-to-shoulder with extreme and increasing wealth (Oxfam, 2016).

While both economic growth and poverty reduction are evident, the poor quality of data on these and many other crucial indicators make it difficult to draw precise conclusions on what has happened and why (Jerven, 2014). The incidence of extreme income poverty (measured at US\$1.90/day in 2011 PPP terms) appears to have declined from 57 per cent in 1990 to 43 per cent in 2012 (Beegle et al., 2016: xi). But, with an underlying population growth of 2.7 per cent per annum, the absolute number of extremely poor people in sub-Saharan Africa (SSA) rose from around 205 million to 400 million (Olinto and Uematsu, 2013). With an increase of almost 200 million Africans in deep/extreme poverty it is difficult to celebrate the ways in which contemporary globalization is incorporating the continent into the world economy. At the grassroots level African villagers, slum dwellers, and small entrepreneurs are strategizing about how to prosper; but with \$10 of illicit and illegal outflows from SSA for every \$1 of foreign aid received, the tide of international finance moves powerfully against them (Hulme, 2016).

An additional set of structural problems looms, set to undermine the agency and efforts of poor Africans in coming years. First, the commodity 'super cycle' that helped fuel recent growth is, to some extent, over and in some countries, such as Ghana, it leaves a legacy of increased national indebtedness, rather than strengthened human capital and physical infrastructure. Second, the wave of democratization that greatly reduced the number of African countries ruled by despots has broken but only a small number of countries have achieved the 'good enough governance' (Grindle, 2004) that can underpin structural transformation of the economy (workers moving from lower productivity to higher productivity forms of employment) and human development. Many African states remain 'fragile' and poverty reduction in such contexts occurs at much

http://dx.doi.org/10.3362/9781780448435.016

slower rates than in more stable contexts (Beegle et al., 2016: 10). Finally, climate change is now clearly under way. This is damaging, and will continue to damage, the economic and social prospects of Africa's poorest people, many of whom live in difficult agro-ecological environments (arid and semi-arid) where climate variability hits hardest. The Paris Agreement of 2015 has, to date, only attained promises sufficient to cap global warming at 2.7 degrees. That level of global warming would be disastrous for SSA's rural poor.

The evidence presented so far in this conclusion might appear to counsel for a new era of Afro-pessimism. Fortunately, the materials in earlier chapters demonstrate that pessimism would be inappropriate. The emotions that need to be fostered are *outrage* about the lack of political and economic structural change in many African states and in the international relations of twenty-first-century globalization, and *tempered optimism* that the forms of innovation and learning presented in earlier chapters can incrementally contribute to improved prospects for economic and social advancement for Africa's poorest people. Social protection programmes (see Chapters 10, 11, 12, 13, and 14 for broader social welfare aspects) have spread across the continent, from 25 programmes in 9 countries in 2000 to 254 programmes in 41 countries in 2012 (see Chapter 10). They face many challenges, but are a far more effective way of reducing poverty than the microfinance programmes of the 1990s. 'Graduation' programmes that seek to combine elements of social protection (cash transfers and enhanced resilience) with elements of economic promotion (asset transfers and business training) are improving increasing numbers of lives and livelihoods, and creating the knowledge-base for more effective programmes in the future (see Chapters 10 and 11).

The concept of designing national social protection strategies that seek to ensure welfare over the lifecycle is helping to weave life-stage specific programmes into more integrated frameworks. Initiatives that ensure infant survival (Chapter 4) and childcare (Chapter 5) could in the future connect to youth programmes (Chapter 6) and increased participation in higher-income-earning activities (Chapter 7). While programmes often strive to standardize their activities, to facilitate effective delivery and reduce unit costs the needs of different groups have to be appreciated. In many countries this means that programmes have to think carefully about gender relations and gender inequality, and that programmes focused on girls and women (Chapters 6 and 7) may be essential if the social vulnerability of adolescent girls and the economic exclusion of working women are to be tackled.

While some policy prescriptions may be feasible at a pan-African level, the evidence in this volume points to the need for poverty reduction programmes to be context specific – although there are lessons be learnt from Latin America (Chapter 13). Africa has to be understood as a mosaic and programmes, whether cash transfers (Chapters 13 and 14), employment/work (Chapters 6, 7, 8, and 9), graduation (Chapters 10 and 11), or whatever, must be carefully adapted at national level and sometimes at sub-national level.

In many of the programmes examined in this volume there is substantial evidence of improved and improving policy analysis and policymaking, but also of deep problems with policy implementation. To some extent, policies in Africa are improving, although, as we learn more about the unique facets associated with extreme poverty, policymakers need to ensure the fuller understanding of further issues such as providing access to legal frameworks and justice (Chapter 15). Furthermore, policy implementation is lagging for a complex set of political and institutional reasons (see www.effective-states.org for detailed examinations of implementation in Ghana, Rwanda, South Africa, and Uganda). These challenges have led to calls for programme managers and designers to 'think and work politically' (Disandi et al., 2016), to 'do development differently' (DDD Manifesto, n.d.), or to pursue 'problem-driven, iterative adaptation' approaches (Andrews et al., 2013). Often, not aware of these academic and professional documents, the managers of the programmes examined in this book have been pursuing such approaches: focusing on specific problems and gathering data; experimenting with, learning from, and adapting their programmes; ensuring local leadership and local 'ownership'; and making sure that programmes are customized for context. While comprehensive reforms of implementation agencies (national ministries, parastatal agencies, and local governments) are highly desirable, the historical record, with the notable exception of Rwanda, shows that they are unlikely. To improve implementation, then, more modest approaches, building 'pockets of effectiveness' (Hickey et al., 2015; Roll, 2013), may provide a better model. Such 'pockets' can achieve great progress in contexts where it is not anticipated (Chapter 4 case study on DR Congo Maternal Health). A remarkable recent case has emerged in the Upper East District in Ghana (ESID, 2016). This is a disadvantaged and remote area, but child and maternal health services and primary education have rapidly been improved by an informal coalition of professional staff, elected councillors, and traditional authorities (especially local 'queen mothers' who have great legitimacy and authority).

In conclusion, the recent era of 'Africa rising' has seen some progress for poor and very poor people, but the opportunity that this has created has not been seized. Over-arching economic and political structural constraints (poor and bad national governance, an international financial system working against the interests of most Africans, trade regimes … and now climate change) limit progress. But, as the chapters in this book show, these constraints do not stymie all human agency. Poor African men and women, bureaucrats who want to do their job, committed professionals, resilient aid-programme managers, NGO field staff, and other like-minded local politicians are making practical progress and are deepening the understanding of 'what works' for Africa's poorest people. It may be incremental … it may only be part of a patchwork … but it also contributes to the evolution of the political and economic forces that will eventually tackle the over-arching structural constraints.

References

Andrews, M., Pritchett, L. and Woolcock, M. (2013) 'Escaping capability traps through problem driven iterative adaptation (PDIA)', in *World Development* 51: 234–44 <http://dx.doi.org/10.1016/j.worlddev.2013.05.011>.

Beegle, K., Christiaensen, L., Dabelen, A. and Gaddis, I. (2016) *Poverty in a Rising Africa*. World Bank, Washington, DC.

DDD Manifesto (n.d.) Statement from the October 2014 'Doing development differently' workshop. Available from https://buildingstatecapability.com/the-ddd-manifesto/ [accessed 25 May 2016].

Disandi, N., Marguette, H. and Robinson, M. (2016) 'Thinking and working politically: From theory building to building an evidence base', *DLP Research Paper 37*. The Developmental Leadership Programme, International Development Department, University of Birmingham, Birmingham.

ESID (2016) 'Politics and health service delivery: Insights from Ghana', *ESID Briefing No. 16*. Effective States and Inclusive Development Research Centre, Global Development Institute, University of Manchester, Manchester. Available from: www.effective-states.org/wp-content/uploads/briefing_papers/final-pdfs/esid_bp_16_Ghana_health.pdf [accessed 25 May 2016].

Grindle, M.S. (2004) 'Good enough governance: Poverty reduction and reform in developing countries', *Governance* 17(4): 525–48 <http://dx.doi.org/10.1111/j.0952-1895.2004.00256.x>.

Hickey, S., Abdulai, A.-G., Izama, A. and Mohan, G. (2015) 'The politics of governing oil effectively: A comparative study of two new oil-rich states in Africa', *ESID Working Paper No. 54*. Effective States and Inclusive Development Research Centre, University of Manchester, Manchester.

Hulme, D. (2016) Should rich nations help the poor? Cambridge University Press, UK.

Jerven, M. (2014) 'African growth miracle or statistical tragedy? Interpreting trends in the data over the past two decades', *UNU-WIDER Working Paper* 2014/114. United Nations University: World Institute for Development Economics Research, Helsinki.

Olinto, P. and Uematsu, H. (2013) 'The state of the poor: Where are the poor and where are they poorest?' *PREM, Draft Background Note*. World Bank, Washington, DC.

Oxfam (2016) 'An economy for the 1%: How privilege and power in the economy drive extreme inequality and how this can be stopped', *Oxfam Briefing Paper 210*, Oxfam, Oxford.

Roll, M. (2013) *The Politics of Public Sector Performance: Pockets of Effectiveness in Developing Countries* (Routledge Research in Comparative Politics). Routledge, Abingdon.

About the authors

David Hulme is Professor of Development Studies and Founder–Director of the Chronic Poverty Research Centre and the Brooks World Poverty Institute, University of Manchester. He is now Executive Director of the recently established Global Development Institute at Manchester.

David Lawson is a Senior Lecturer in Development Economics and Public Policy at the Global Development Institute, University of Manchester. He has worked extensively on SSA and specializes in poverty dynamics in African countries.

Lawrence Ado-Kofie is a Research Associate at the Global Development Institute, University of Manchester.

Index

Page numbers in *italics* refer to figures and tables.

www.ingramcontent.com/pod-product-compliance
Lightning Source LLC
Chambersburg PA
CBHW060030030426
42334CB00019B/2252